2nd Workshop on Noisy User-generated Text (WNUT 2016)

Osaka, Japan
11 December 2016

ISBN: 978-1-5108-3319-7

Preface

This volume contains papers from the 2nd Workshop on on Noisy User-generated Text (W-NUT)

Organisers

Bo Han (Hugo AI)

Alan Ritter (The Ohio State University)

Leon Derczynski (The University of Sheffield)

Wei Xu (The Ohio State University)

Tim Baldwin (The University of Melbourne)

Programme Committee

David Bamman (University of California, Berkeley)

Kalina Bontcheva (University of Sheffield)

Claire Cardie (Cornell University)

Colin Cherry (National Research Council Canada)

Grzegorz Chrupała (Tilburg University)

Marina Danilevsky (IBM Research)

Seza Doğruöz (Tilburg University)

Heba Elfardy (Columbia University)

Noura Farra (Columbia University)

Eric Fosler-Lussier (The Ohio State University)

Dan Garrette (University of Washington)

Kevin Gimpel (Toyota Technological Institute at Chicago)

Weiwei Guo (Yahoo! Research)

Ben Hachey (Hugo AI)

Masato Hagiwara (Duolingo)

Hua He (University of Maryland)

Ed Hovy (Carnegie Mellon University)

Jing Jiang (Singapore Management University)

Anna Jørgensen (University of Amsterdam)

Nobuhiro Kaji (Yahoo! Research)

Emre Kiciman (Microsoft Research)

Chen Li (University of Texas at Dallas)

Junyi Jessy Li (University of Pennsylvania)

Wang Ling (Google DeepMind)

Fei Liu (University of Central Florida)

Huan Liu (Arizona State University)

Héctor Martínez Alonso (INRIA/University Paris Diderot)

Rada Mihalcea (University of Michigan)

Smaranda Muresan (Columbia University)

Preslav Nakov (Qatar Computing Research Institute)

Naoaki Okazaki (Tohoku University)

Miles Osborne (Bloomberg)

Ellie Pavlick (University of Pennsylvania)

Daniel Preoţiuc-Pietro (University of Pennsylvania)

Will Radford (Hugo AI)

Afshin Rahimi (The University of Melbourne)

Shourya Roy (Xerox Research)

Alla Rozovskaya (City University of New York)

Derek Ruths (McGill University)

Andrew Schwartz (Stony Brook University)

Djamé Seddah (University Paris-Sorbonne)

Richard Sproat (Google Research)

Anders Søgaard (University of Copenhagen)

Benjamin Strauss (The Ohio State University)

Jeniya Tabassum (The Ohio State University)

Joel Tetreault (Yahoo! Research)

Marlies van der Wees (University of Amsterdam)

Svitlana Volkova (Pacific Northwest National Laboratory)

Byron C. Wallace (University of Texas at Austin)

Xiaojun Wan (Peking University)

Jun-Ming Xu (University of Wisconsin-Madison)

Diyi Yang (Carnegie Mellon University)

Yi Yang (Georgia Tech)

Guido Zarrella (MITRE)

Ming Zhou (Microsoft Research)

Table of Contents

Workshop Program

December 11, 2016

9.00   **Opening**

            Invited talk

9.10   *DISAANA and D-SUMM: Large-scale Real Time NLP Systems for Analyzing Disaster Related Reports in Tweets*
            Kentaro Torisawa

            Research talks

9.55   *Private or Corporate? Predicting User Types on Twitter*
            Nikola Ljubešić and Darja Fišer

10.05   *From Noisy Questions to Minecraft Texts: Annotation Challenges in Extreme Syntax Scenario*
            Héctor Martínez Alonso, Djamé Seddah and Benoît Sagot

10.15   *Disaster Analysis using User-Generated Weather Report*
            Yasunobu Asakura, Masatsugu Hangyo and Mamoru Komachi

10.25   *Veracity Computing from Lexical Cues and Perceived Certainty Trends*
            Uwe Reichel and Piroska Lendvai

10.35   *Exploring Word Embeddings for Unsupervised Textual User-Generated Content Normalization*
            Thales Felipe Costa Bertaglia and Maria das Graças Volpe Nunes

10.45   *Name Variation in Community Question Answering Systems*
            Anietie Andy, Satoshi Sekine, Mugizi Rwebangira and Mark Dredze

Invited talk

14.00   *From Entity Linking to Question Answering – Recent Progress on Semantic Ground-*
         ing Tasks
         Ming-Wei Chang

14.45   **Shared task papers**

         Results of the WNUT16 Named Entity Recognition Shared Task
         Benjamin Strauss, Bethany Toma, Alan Ritter, Marie-Catherine de Marneffe and
         Wei Xu

         Bidirectional LSTM for Named Entity Recognition in Twitter Messages
         Nut Limsopatham and Nigel Collier

         Learning to recognise named entities in tweets by exploiting weakly labelled data
         Kurt Junshean Espinosa, Riza Theresa Batista-Navarro and Sophia Ananiadou

         Feature-Rich Twitter Named Entity Recognition and Classification
         Utpal Kumar Sikdar and Björn Gambäck

         Learning to Search for Recognizing Named Entities in Twitter
         Ioannis Partalas, Cédric Lopez, Nadia Derbas and Ruslan Kalitvianski

         DeepNNNER: Applying BLSTM-CNNs and Extended Lexicons to Named Entity
         Recognition in Tweets
         Fabrice Dugas and Eric Nichols

         ASU: An Experimental Study on Applying Deep Learning in Twitter Named Entity
         Recognition.
         Michel Naim Gerguis, Cherif Salama and M. Watheq El-Kharashi

         UQAM-NTL: Named entity recognition in Twitter messages
         Ngoc Tan LE, Fatma Mallek and Fatiha Sadat

         Semi-supervised Named Entity Recognition in noisy-text
         Shubhanshu Mishra and Jana Diesner

         Twitter Geolocation Prediction Shared Task of the 2016 Workshop on Noisy User-
         generated Text
         Bo Han, Afshin Rahimi, Leon Derczynski and Timothy Baldwin

         CSIRO Data61 at the WNUT Geo Shared Task
         Gaya Jayasinghe, Brian Jin, James Mchugh, Bella Robinson and Stephen Wan

Processing non-canonical or noisy text: fortuitous data to the rescue

Barbara Plank
CLCG, University of Groningen
Netherlands
`b.plank@rug.nl`

Abstract

Real world data differs radically from the benchmark corpora we use in NLP, resulting in large performance drops. The reason for this problem is obvious: NLP models are trained on limited samples from canonical varieties considered standard. However, there are many dimensions, e.g., sociodemographic, language, genre, sentence type, etc. on which texts can differ from the standard. The solution is not obvious: we cannot control for all factors, and it is not clear how to best go beyond the current practice of training on homogeneous data from a single domain and language.

In this talk, I review the notion of canonicity, and how it shapes our community's approach to language. I argue for the use of fortuitous data. Fortuitous data is data out there that just waits to be harvested. It includes data which is in plain sight, but is often neglected, and more distant sources like behavioral data, which first need to be refined. They provide additional contexts and a myriad of opportunities to build more adaptive language technology, some of which I will explore in this talk.

Proceedings of the 2nd Workshop on Noisy User-generated Text,
page 1, Osaka, Japan, December 11 2016.

From Entity Linking to Question Answering Recent Progress on Semantic Grounding Tasks

Ming-Wei Chang
Microsoft Research
Redmond, USA
`minchang@microsoft.com`

Abstract

Entity linking and semantic parsing have been shown to be crucial to important applications such as question answering and document understanding. These tasks often require structured learning models, which make predictions on multiple interdependent variables. In this talk, I argue that carefully designed structured learning algorithms play a central role in entity linking and semantic parsing tasks. In particular, I will present several new structured learning models for entity linking, which jointly detect mentions and disambiguate entities as well as capture non-textual information. I will then show how to use a staged search procedure to building a state-of-the-art knowledge base question answering system. Finally, if time permits, I will discuss different supervision protocols for training semantic parsers and the value of labeling semantic parses.

Proceedings of the 2nd Workshop on Noisy User-generated Text,
page 2, Osaka, Japan, December 11 2016.

DISAANA and D-SUMM: Large-scale Real Time NLP Systems for Analyzing Disaster Related Reports in Tweets

Kentaro Torisawa

National Institute of Information and Communications Technology, Tokyo
Japan
`torisawa@nict.go.jp`

Abstract

This talk presents two NLP systems that were developed for helping disaster victims and rescue workers in the aftermath of large-scale disasters. DISAANA provides answers to questions such as "What is in short supply in Tokyo?" and displays locations related to each answer on a map. D-SUMM automatically summarizes a large number of disaster related reports concerning a specified area and helps rescue workers to understand disaster situations from a macro perspective. Both systems are publicly available as Web services. In the aftermath of the 2016 Kumamoto Earthquake (M7.0), the Japanese government actually used DISAANA to analyze the situation.

Proceedings of the 2nd Workshop on Noisy User-generated Text,
page 3, Osaka, Japan, December 11 2016.

Private or Corporate? Predicting User Types on Twitter

Nikola Ljubešić
Dept. of Knowledge Technologies
Jožef Stefan Institute
`nikola.ljubesic@ijs.si`

Darja Fišer
Department of Translation
Faculty of Arts, University of Ljubljana
`darja.fiser@ff.uni-lj.si`

Abstract

In this paper we present a series of experiments on discriminating between private and corporate accounts on Twitter. We define features based on Twitter metadata, morphosyntactic tags and surface forms, showing that the simple bag-of-words model achieves single best results that can, however, be improved by building a weighted soft ensemble of classifiers based on each feature type. Investigating the time and language dependence of each feature type delivers quite unexpecting results showing that features based on metadata are neither time- nor language-insensitive as the way the two user groups use the social network varies heavily through time and space.

1 Introduction

Due to popularity of Twitter and its proactive content harvesting policy, automatic identification of latent user attributes has become a hot research topic in the past couple of years. Tasks range from discriminating between different types of users (Mislove et al., 2011), behaviour (Pennacchiotti and Popescu, 2011; Rao et al., 2010), location (Hecht et al., 2011), gender (Burger et al., 2011), age (Nguyen et al., 2013), occupation (Hu et al., 2016), social class (Borges et al., 2014) and personality type (Quercia et al., 2011).

In this paper we present a series of experiments on discriminating between corporate and private accounts on Twitter. We investigate language-independent features, features extracted from morphosyntactic annotations and simple bag-of-words features. We additionally investigate the time and space dependence of specific feature sets by measuring how well specific features handle training on one time span or closely-related language and testing on another time span or other closely-related language.

2 Related work

Automatic classification of different types of users is an active area of research and has been attempted at various degrees of granularity and for diferent communicative goals. Naaman et al. (2010), for example, distinguish two types of users: those who disseminate information (informers) and those who share what they are doing and how they are feeling (meformers). De Choudhury et al. (2012), on the other hand, distinguish between the accounts of individual persons, organizations, news media and other miscellaneous categories. Kim et al. (2010) use the same set, only adding the celebrities category, while (Wu et al., 2011), suggest a two-stage approach where they first classify users into two broad categories of elite and ordinary users, and then further classify the elite users into more fine-grained groups of media, celebrities, organizations and bloggers.

Similarly different both in terms of number and complexity are the features used for classification. Rao et al. (2010) use 2 categories of over 20 features that are easy to obtain from the Twitter timeline: the network structure (follower-following ratio, follower frequency, following frequency) and the communication behavior of individuals (response frequency, retweet frequency, tweet frequency), showing that tweeting behavior information is not useful for most classification tasks. Therefore, in addition to profile features, tweeting behaviour and social network, (Pennacchiotti and Popescu, 2011), show that,

Proceedings of the 2nd Workshop on Noisy User-generated Text,
pages 4–12, Osaka, Japan, December 11 2016.

rich linguistic features (prototypical words and hashtags, generic and domain-specific LDA, sentiment words) yields consistently better results. Kucukyilmaz et al. (2008) employ a more traditional apparoach to author characterization by relying on a set of term-based features in users' messages and a set of stylistic features (character usage, message length, word length, punctuation usage, punctuation marks, stopword usage, stopwords, smiley usage, smileys, vocabulary richness).

While our work has noticeable overlap with existing research that was carried out on English, it extends that research, beyond the language shift, by (1) performing a more detailed analysis of a broader list of features, and inspecting (2) the stability of those features in different time periods and (3) their portability to a closely-related language.

3   Dataset

The dataset used in this paper consists of 7.5 million Slovene tweets collected from June 2013 to January 2016 with the TweetCaT tool (Ljubešić et al., 2014). Each of the 7778 users in the collection was manually annotated as private or corporate. We performed our experiments on 5842 users for whom we had at least 100 tweets at our disposal. Out of these 5842 users, 4382 were annotated as private and 1460 as corporate.

4   Features

We discriminate between two basic types of features: language-independent (LI) and language-dependent (LD) ones. We calculate our language-independent features both from the text of a tweet and its additional metadata. We use two types of language-dependent features: focused (FLD) and bag-of-words (BoW) features. While the bag-of-words features are simply types found in the text of all the training tweets, the focused ones are mostly based on morphosyntactic annotation of the text. It should be stressed here that we do not pressupose the language-independent features to work well across languages for our task, but just that these features can be found in different languages.

All the features are calculated on user level as we perform our predictions on each Twitter user.

4.1   Language independent features

Among the language-independent features we discriminate between the following feature types:

- `avg` – average number of tweets satisfying a condition

- `mean` – mean of a continuous tweet-level variable

- `med` – median of a continuous tweet-level variable

- `var` – variance of a continuous tweet-level variable

- `user` – user-level metadata

In Table 1 we give an overview of all language-independent features, sorted in descending order by the p-value obtained with the two-sided Mann-Whitney U test (Mann and Whitney, 1947) on the variable in question regarding the distribution in private and corporate accounts. The null hypothesis of this test is that the two samples (variable measurements on private and corporate accounts) come from the same distribution. Beside the feature description and its univariate p-value, we report the effect size as the difference in the median between private and corporate accounts. The variables reporting a positive effect size, like the `average_inreply` variable, therefore have a higher median in private tweets while the variables with a negative effect size, like the `average_http` variable, have a higher median among corporate tweets.

Our univariate feature analysis shows, among many other things, that private accounts are most specific for replying to tweets, mentioning other users, favoring other user's tweets, tweeting in various hours of the day, producing tweets of variable length and posting more frequently during weekends. On the other

Variable	Description	p-value	Effect size
`avg_http`	average number of tweets containing URLs	0.0	-0.61704
`avg_inreply`	average number of tweets that are replies	0.0	0.38549
`avg_mention`	average number of tweets containing mentions	10^{-306}	0.45676
`avg_work_hrs`	average number of tweets published in working hours	10^{-235}	-0.15252
`user_favor`	number of tweets the user has favorited	10^{-209}	302
`var_hour`	variance of the posting hour	10^{-208}	5.96132
`var_len_text`	variance of the tweet length	10^{-203}	279.092
`mean_hour`	mean of the posting hour	10^{-188}	1.71806
`median_hour`	median of the posting hour	10^{-185}	2
`mean_len_text`	mean of the tweet length	10^{-113}	-12.8003
`med_len_text`	median of the tweet length	10^{-99}	-17.25
`avg_weekend`	average number of tweets posted on weekends	10^{-97}	0.03847
`mean_day`	mean of the posting weekday	10^{-95}	0.25134
`var_day`	variance of the posting weekday	10^{-78}	0.36336
`user_ff_ratio`	followers / friends ratio of a user	10^{-63}	-0.61667
`var_favor`	variance of number of favorites	10^{-61}	0.28596
`avg_favor`	average number of favorited tweets	10^{-55}	0.10024
`mean_favor`	mean of number of favorites	10^{-55}	0.15367
`med_day`	median of the posting day	10^{-53}	0
`avg_comma`	average number of tweets containing a comma	10^{-49}	0.08569
`avg_quest`	average number of tweets containing a questionmark	10^{-49}	0.04413
`avg_emoji`	average number of tweets containing an emoji	10^{-40}	0.0
`avg_is_quote`	average number of tweets that are quotes	10^{-37}	0.00196
`avg_excl`	average number of tweets with an exclamation mark	10^{-31}	-0.05624
`user_status`	number of statuses the user produced	10^{-26}	518
`avg_client`	average number of tweets sent through the web client	10^{-16}	0.12875
`user_friend`	number of friends the user has	10^{-16}	69
`avg_retweet`	average number of retweeted tweets	10^{-14}	-0.03827
`user_per_day`	number of statuses a users sends per day	10^{-11}	0.18937
`avg_ellipsis`	average number of tweets containing an ellipsis	10^{-8}	0.01381
`avg_hash`	average number of tweets containing a hashtag	10^{-5}	0.03624
`user_follow`	number of followers the user has	10^{-5}	-40.5
`mean_retweet`	mean of number of retweets	10^{-5}	-0.03772
`med_retweet`	median of number of retweets	0.002	0.0
`var_retweet`	variance of number of retweets	0.011	0.01123
`user_listed`	number of lists the user is on	0.041	0.0
`med_favor`	median of number of favorites	0.287	0.0
`avg_trunc`	average number of tweets that are truncated	0.999	0.0

Table 1: An overview of the language-independent features, sorted by their p-value,

Variable	Description	p-value	Effect size
`adjpos`	adjective in positive degree	0.0	-0.02052
`prondemsgdl`	demonstrative pronoun in singular / dual	0.0	0.0059
`verb12sgdl`	verb in first / second person singular / dual	0.0	0.01406
`pronneg`	negative pronoun	10^{-257}	0.00088
`supine`	supine	10^{-251}	0.00146
`verbmainpl`	main verb in plural	10^{-245}	-0.00963
`verbimppl`	verb in imperative plural	10^{-238}	-0.00198
`private_words`	list of auxiliary verb and personal pronoun forms	10^{-212}	0.00641
`num`	number	10^{-204}	-0.00942
`pronind`	indefinitive pronoun	10^{-203}	0.00097
`lower`	lowercased word	10^{-181}	0.0721
`adjpart`	adjectival participle	10^{-153}	-0.00219
`pronperspl`	personal pronoun plural	10^{-151}	-0.00235
`normalised`	word automatically normalised	10^{-137}	-0.05837
`interjection`	interjection	10^{-130}	0.00105
`adjsup`	adjective in superlative degree	10^{-119}	-0.00054
`content`	content word	10^{-108}	-0.04989
`nounprop`	proper noun	10^{-105}	-0.01867
`title`	titlecase word	10^{-92}	-0.02505
`pronpers`	personal pronoun	10^{-79}	0.00453
`double`	token repetition	10^{-62}	0.00014
`foreign`	foreign word	10^{-48}	0.04383
`upper`	uppercase word	10^{-44}	-0.00862
`pronposs1sgdl`	possesive pronoun in singular / dual	10^{-44}	-0.00022
`adjposs`	possesive adjective	10^{-42}	-0.00049
`pronposspl`	possesive pronoun in plural	10^{-37}	-0.00016
`emoticon`	emoticon	10^{-13}	0.00595

Table 2: An overview of the language-dependent focused features, sorted by their p-value

hand, corporate accounts use more URLs, post more during working hours, produce longer tweets and have a higher followers / friends ratio.

All the engineered features, except for the median of number of favorites (because it is most frequently 0) and the average number of truncated tweets (most frequently 0 as well) have shown to be statistically significant with $p < .05$.

4.2 Language-dependent features

In Table 2 we give an overview of the focused language-dependent features, with a statistical analysis identical to the one of the language-independent features. All the variables are user-level probabilities of specific linguistic phenomena. Again, the effect size is the difference in the median between private and corporate accounts, i.e. a positive effect size points at higher values among private users.

This univariate analysis shows, among other things, for private accounts to use more singular / dual demonstrative pronouns, singular / dual verbs, negative pronouns and supines (short verb infinitive forms). On the other hand, corporate accounts use more adjectives, verbs in plural, numbers, superlatives and content words.

In Table 3 we give an overview of the 20 strongest word features identified through the coeffecient value of the linear discriminative classifier that will be described in the Experiments section. As the table shows, private users prefer pronouns and verbs in 1st person singular (I, me, my, I did, I wish, I hope), nouns and verbs depicting thoughts and activities carried out in their spare time (wish, grill, slim), while 3rd and 2nd person plural forms (we, our, we did, we can, you check, we congratulate), nouns describing

sem(did-1st prs sg) i moj(my) cerar http://t.co/h7jwauc0rv me my bravo želim(wish-1st prs sg) zalogi(stock) mesto(city) upam(hope-1st prs sg) zoya #delajvitko(#workslim) ko(when) http://t.co/qcfz6ii342 pod(under) salesforce žaru(grill) @delo tv
zaradi(because) smo(did-3rd prs pl) teden(week) klik(click) čestitamo(congratulations) evrov(euro) tf2 piše(writes) festival preveri(check-2nd prs sg) we people ste(did-2nd prs pl) naš(our) kamala #volitve14(#election14) lahko(can) novo(new) akcija(sale) facebook

Table 3: List of the strongest language-dependent bag-of-word features, for private and for corporate users

Feature type	Corporate	Private	All	FLD	BoW	ENS
Most frequent class (MFC)	0.0000	0.8572	0.6430			
Language independent (LI)	0.7944	0.9335	0.8987	< 0.001	< 0.001	< 0.001
Focused lang. dependent (FLD)	0.8520	0.9510	0.9263		< 0.001	< 0.001
Bag of words (BoW)	0.8742	0.9577	0.9368			< 0.01
Ensemble (ENS)	0.8864	0.9620	**0.9431**			

Table 4: Evaluation results via weighted F1 on the per-feature-type classifiers and the ensemble classifier. Statistical significance of the differences is calculated via approximate randomisation.

public events (festival, sales, election, Euro) and named entities (Kamala, Facebook), as well as verbs lexicalizing professional activities (he writes, you check) are characteristic of the corporate users.

5 Experiments

We run three batches of experiments. In the first batch we experiment with the three types of features presented in the previous section. Additionally, we build an ensemble classifier which uses the output of the three feature-type classifiers. In the second batch we investigate the time sensitivity of the presented feature types by training on data from one time span and testing on a later one. Finally, in the third batch we investigate the portability of two feature types, namely language-independent features and bag-of-words features, to a closely-related language.

As our weak baseline we use the most-frequent-class (MFC) baseline. Our classifier of choice on all feature types are support vector machines (SVM). In case where the number of features is smaller than the number of instances we use the RBF kernel while in the opposite case we use a linear kernel.

In all the experiments we 5-fold with stratification over all our data, optimising in each iteration the classifier via grid search on the development data and evaluating it on the test data via weighted F1.

In case of the RBF kernel we optimise the C ($2^n, n \in \{-5, -3, -1, ...15\}$) and γ ($2^n, n \in \{-15, -13, -11, ...3\}$) hyperparameters while for the linear kernel we optimise the C parameter in the same range as with the RBF kernel.

5.1 Feature type comparison

We present the results of training a classifier on each type of features, the language independent (LI), focused language dependent (FLD) and bag-of-words (BoW), in Table 4. We additionally compare these classifiers to our weak most-frequent-class (MFC) baseline and an weighted soft ensemble of all three classifier outputs. The weighted soft ensemble classifier uses the per-class probability output of each classifier, weights each class distribution with the weighted F1 of that classifier estimated on the development data, averages over all the distributions and picks the class with maximum probability.

We report F1 on each class and an overall weighted F1. We additionally report a p-value obtained through the approximate randomisation test (Yeh, 2000) with $R = 1000$ for each classifier combination. Approximate randomisation estimates the p-value as $p = \frac{r}{R}$ where r is the number of iterations where randomly switching responses of system 1 and system 2 has produced a greater or equal difference in the evaluation metric than the original difference between system 1 and system 2, while R is the number of iterations over the responses.

Feature type	All	Time dependence		Close language	
		$\geq$ 2015	Loss (%)	Croatian	Loss (%)
Most frequent class (MFC)	0.6430	0.6430	-	0.3388	-
Language independent (LI)	0.8987	0.8370	7%	0.6270	30%
Focused language dependent (FLD)	0.9263	0.9149	1%	-	-
Bag of words (BoW)	0.9368	0.9280	1%	0.7304	22%

Table 5: Results on the time and language sensitivity of specific feature types

The results show that each of the feature types improves over the weak MFC baseline by a large margin. While all the three feature types come quite close to each other, the weakest one are the language-independent features, mostly relying on tweet and user metadata. We find it quite surprising that the bag-of-words model improves over the focused language-dependent model which uses a language abstraction in form of morphosyntactic descriptions. [1] Finally, the weighted soft ensemble improves over each of the classifiers.[2] The difference between each classifier combination has proven to be statistically significant.

The performance of each classifier on specific classes did not yield any surprises. The private class, which is more represented, performs regularly better. The best-performing ensemble classifier yields weighted F1 of 0.89 on the corporate and 0.96 on the private class.

Regarding the number of features, the single best performing classifier is also the heaviest one with 3,978,030 features. On the other hand the LI classifier works with 38 features, while the FLD classifier works with 27 features.

5.2 Time sensitivity

In this set of experiments we investigate the impact of training on one time span and evaluating on another one. We again experiment with our three types of features. In each iteration of cross-validation, the development set consists only of tweets published before 2015, removing all users for which after filtering we do not have 100 tweets available. We repeat the same process on the test set by keeping only tweets published 2015 onward.

Along with our new time dependence evaluation results, we repeat the results from the previous batch of experiments which presents the performance of the feature type in the same time span.

The results of this experimental batch are presented in the left hand side of Table 5.

The results are somewhat surprising showing that the LI features are actually the least time insensitive. Probably due to the way the Twitter social network was used before and after 2015 the loss reaches 7% of weighted F1. On the other hand, the FLD and BoW classifiers measure a minor loss of 1%.

5.3 Portability to a similar language

We perform a final set of experiments investigating the portability of the language independent (LI) and the bag-of-words (BoW) features to a closely related language. As our closely related language we chose Croatian as the two countries are strongly interconnected, expecting therefore that Twitter is used in a comparable manner and that a usable overlap in surface forms among the two closely-related languages should occur. This lexical overlap has already been used in previous work on bilingual lexicon extraction (Fišer and Ljubešić, 2011) and identification of false friends (Ljubešić and Fišer, 2013).

We discard the focused language dependent (LFD) features from these experiments as they require the texts of the tweets to be morphosyntactically annotated with the same tagset which would require a tagset mapping.

In these experiments we use the full Slovene data for development and evaluate on a set of 101 Croatian users that were annotated by hand, using the same criteria applied while annotating Slovene data. In the Croatian dataset 50 users were annotated as private and 51 as corporate.

---

[1] We have investigated expanding the BoW model with character and word n-grams, but it did not improve over the simple word unigram model.

[2] Beside the weighted soft ensemble we also experimented with a stacked classifier, but this classifier, being more complex than our ensemble, did not yield any significant improvement.

The results are presented in the right hand side of Table 5. While both classifiers outperform the weak baseline by a wide margin, interestingly, the language independent features prove to be the less stable feature type when a shift in the target domain / language occurs. While, naturally, the BoW feature set experiences a heavy loss of 22% when evaluating on Croatian data, the loss of 30% on the LI features is even greater, in addition to the initial lower results.

5.4 Error analysis

We conclude the experiments with an error analysis of the instances misclassified by the enseble classifier. Among those instances we specifically analyse the cases where the classifier based on language-independent features (LI) and the bag-of-words classifier (BoW) disagree.

We performed a detailed qualitative analysis of the tweeting behaviour and language of 10 random accounts per class misclassified by each system in order to gain more insight into why the misclassification might have occured. In total, 4 scenarios were analysed: (1a) corporate and (1b) private accounts misclassified by LI but correctly classified by BoW, and (2a) corporate and (2b) private accounts misclassified by BoW but correctly classified by LI.

As far as the corporate accounts misclassified by the LI approach but correctly classified by the BoW approach (1a) are concerned, they were smaller / early-stage societies / NGOs / civil initiatives, popular radio stations, records companies, event agencies and bloggers who (probably deliberately) share many tweeting characteristics of private accounts in terms of tweeting amount, time, retweets, mentions, favourites and hashtags. Among the private accounts misclassified by the LI approach (1b), 9 out of 10 examined accounts belong to journalists, politicians and professionals who do not explicitly disclose their professional status or affiliation in their account profiles but nevertheless tweet for professional purposes and demonstrate all the behaviour of the corporate accounts. This suggests that in addition to straightforward binary categories, there is a grey zone of borderline, difficult to define account types which call for more detailed annotation guidelines.

Interestingly, there was only one corporate account that was misclassified by the BoW approach but correctly classified by the LI one (2a), which is a fair-trade store that raises awareness for fair-trade home products, clothes and food in a communicative, conversational, friendly way. The topics covered and vocabulary used is therefore closely related to our every-day lives, not unlike the topics and vocabulary present in the tweets published by private accounts. Similar results were obtain with the qualitative analysis of 10 private accounts erroneously classified by BoW but correctly by LI (2b). They show that 9 of them are borderline because they are accounts of journalists, managers and small business owners whose tweets, published with the typical corporate dynamics, cover topics conveyed by the linguistic features that are tipically associated with people's private lives, such as health and lifestyle, food, cosmetics, hairstyle, sports and charity.

The error analysis clearly shows that the erroneously classified accounts are indeed outliers, either by tweeting behaviour, or by tweeting content and / or language style. This suggests that manual annotation guidelines should be refined to include advice how to treat such potentially difficult cases and / or extend the classification beyond a binary approach.

6 Conclusion

In this paper we have presented a series of experiments on discriminating between private and corporate Twitter accounts among Slovene Twitter users.

In the first part of the paper we have analysed a series of features, casting some light on the way the two groups use our medium of interest.

In our classification experiments we have shown that the simple bag-of-words model outperforms the language-independent and focused language-dependent features. Building a classifier ensemble yielded a statistically significant improvement, showing that these feature sets are at least partially complementary.

We have shown that language-independent features based mostly on Twitter metadata are actually very unreliable, showing bad performance both when different time spans or different languages are used for training and evaluation. A big surprise was that the bag-of-words model was more portable to a closely related language than the feature set based on metadata. These results point at significant differences in the way the social network is used across time and space.

Overall we have achieved very good results when combining all classifiers in a weighted soft ensemble. Given that most researchers are interested in removing corporate accounts from their Twitter collections, we can expect that our classifier will be very useful for Slovene as F1 on the private class is more than 96%.

References

Guilherme R Borges, Jussara M Almeida, Gisele L Pappa, et al. 2014. Inferring user social class in online social networks. In *Proceedings of the 8th Workshop on Social Network Mining and Analysis*, page 10. ACM.

John D. Burger, John Henderson, George Kim, and Guido Zarrella. 2011. Discriminating Gender on Twitter. In *Proceedings of the Conference on Empirical Methods in Natural Language Processing*, EMNLP '11, pages 1301–1309, Stroudsburg, PA, USA. Association for Computational Linguistics.

Munmun De Choudhury, Nicholas Diakopoulos, and Mor Naaman. 2012. Unfolding the event landscape on twitter: classification and exploration of user categories. In *Proceedings of the ACM 2012 conference on Computer Supported Cooperative Work*, pages 241–244. ACM.

Darja Fišer and Nikola Ljubešić. 2011. Bilingual lexicon extraction from comparable corpora for closely related languages. In *Proceedings of the International Conference Recent Advances in Natural Language Processing 2011*, pages 125–131, Hissar, Bulgaria. RANLP 2011 Organising Committee.

Brent Hecht, Lichan Hong, Bongwon Suh, and Ed H. Chi. 2011. Tweets from Justin Bieber's Heart: The Dynamics of the Location Field in User Profiles. In *Proceedings of the SIGCHI Conference on Human Factors in Computing Systems*, CHI '11, pages 237–246, New York, NY, USA. ACM.

Tianran Hu, Haoyuan Xiao, Jiebo Luo, and Thuy vy Thi Nguyen. 2016. What the Language You Tweet Says About Your Occupation.

Dongwoo Kim, Yohan Jo, Il-Chul Moon, and Alice Oh. 2010. Analysis of twitter lists as a potential source for discovering latent characteristics of users. In *ACM CHI workshop on microblogging*. Citeseer.

Tayfun Kucukyilmaz, B Barla Cambazoglu, Cevdet Aykanat, and Fazli Can. 2008. Chat mining: Predicting user and message attributes in computer-mediated communication. *Information Processing & Management*, 44(4):1448–1466.

Nikola Ljubešić, Darja Fišer, and Tomaž Erjavec. 2014. TweetCaT: a Tool for Building Twitter Corpora of Smaller Languages. In Nicoletta Calzolari (Conference Chair), Khalid Choukri, Thierry Declerck, Hrafn Loftsson, Bente Maegaard, Joseph Mariani, Asuncion Moreno, Jan Odijk, and Stelios Piperidis, editors, *Proceedings of the Ninth International Conference on Language Resources and Evaluation (LREC'14)*, Reykjavik, Iceland. European Language Resources Association (ELRA).

Nikola Ljubešić and Darja Fišer. 2013. Identifying false friends between closely related languages. In *Proceedings of the 4th Biennial International Workshop on Balto-Slavic Natural Language Processing*, pages 69–77, Sofia, Bulgaria, August. Association for Computational Linguistics.

H.B. Mann and D.R. Whitney. 1947. On a test of whether one of two random variables is stochastically larger than the other. *Annals of Mathematical Statistics*, 18:50–60.

Alan Mislove, Sune Lehmann Jørgensen, Yong-Yeol Ahn, Jukka-Pekka Onnela, and J. Niels Rosenquist, 2011. *Understanding the Demographics of Twitter Users*, pages 554–557. AAAI Press.

Mor Naaman, Jeffrey Boase, and Chih-Hui Lai. 2010. Is it really about me?: message content in social awareness streams. In *Proceedings of the 2010 ACM conference on Computer supported cooperative work*, pages 189–192. ACM.

Dong-Phuong Nguyen, Rilana Gravel, RB Trieschnigg, and Theo Meder. 2013. "how old do you think i am?" a study of language and age in twitter.

Marco Pennacchiotti and Ana-Maria Popescu. 2011. A machine learning approach to twitter user classification.

Daniele Quercia, Michal Kosinski, David Stillwell, and Jon Crowcroft. 2011. Our twitter profiles, our selves: Predicting personality with twitter. In *Privacy, Security, Risk and Trust (PASSAT) and 2011 IEEE Third Inernational Conference on Social Computing (SocialCom), 2011 IEEE Third International Conference on*, pages 180–185. IEEE.

Delip Rao, David Yarowsky, Abhishek Shreevats, and Manaswi Gupta. 2010. Classifying latent user attributes in twitter. In *Proceedings of the 2Nd International Workshop on Search and Mining User-generated Contents*, SMUC '10, pages 37–44, New York, NY, USA. ACM.

Shaomei Wu, Jake M Hofman, Winter A Mason, and Duncan J Watts. 2011. Who says what to whom on twitter. In *Proceedings of the 20th international conference on World wide web*, pages 705–714. ACM.

Alexander Yeh. 2000. More accurate tests for the statistical significance of result differences. In *Proceedings of the 18th conference on Computational linguistics - Volume 2*, COLING '00, pages 947–953, Stroudsburg, PA, USA. Association for Computational Linguistics.

From Noisy Questions to Minecraft Texts:
Annotation Challenges in *Extreme Syntax* Scenarios

Héctor Martínez Alonso[1]   Djamé Seddah[1,2]   Benoît Sagot[1]

(1) Inria Alpage & Université Paris Diderot   (2) Université Paris Sorbonne

`{firstname.lastname}@inria.fr`

Abstract

User-generated content presents many challenges for its automatic processing. While many of them do come from out-of-vocabulary effects, others spawn from different linguistic phenomena such as unusual syntax. In this work we present a French three-domain data set made up of question headlines from a cooking forum, game chat logs and associated forums from two popular online games (MINECRAFT & LEAGUE OF LEGENDS). We chose these domains because they encompass different degrees of lexical and syntactic compliance with canonical language. We conduct an automatic and manual evaluation of the difficulties of processing these domains for part-of-speech prediction, and introduce a pilot study to determine whether dependency analysis lends itself well to annotate these data. We also discuss the development cost of our data set.

1   Introduction

The continuous growth of the volume of user-generated content (UGC) published on the web stresses the need for efficient way to automatically process this type of data. Yet not only the volume of UGC increases; it also becomes increasingly varied, resulting in the need for domain- and register-adaptation methods and resources for processing UGC in all its diversity.

In this work, we present a feasibility study on dependency syntax annotation for three UGC domains in French, namely a cooking forum, in-game chat logs, and associated gaming forums. While these data sources are very different, they share the characteristic that their content was produced within time or space constraints. Such constraints force the users to resort to a variety of linguistic strategies to efficiently convey their message.

The work described here shows that, on top of the well-known problem of out-of-vocabulary words, automatic annotation and processing of UGC presents a double challenge. First, in order to interpret most of the data , it is crucial to take into account the interplay between **context and domain knowledge** on the one hand and their linguistic impact. This is because most messages can only be fully analysed with a good knowledge of the domain and context at hand. For instance, in-game chat logs can only be understood with a knowledge of the video game being played and of many game-specific terms, a representation of the game situation when a chat message is written and of, as well as a model of the ongoing dialogue, as such data is conversational by nature. Also, time- or space-constrained writing favors **fragmentary writing** that is more prone to ellipses, which makes linguistic analysis, especially parsing, more difficult. In addition to this highly contextual nature, the many idiosyncrasies plaguing UGC and make its analysis more challenging than regular out-of-domain text force most morpho-syntactic processing to be *extremely* robust at all levels of analysis.

In Section 3 we describe the data collection process, and give a first quantiative description of how our datasets are different from standard datasets. Two of our datasets were already annotated, and we manually annotated the third one. In Section 4 we provide a threefold categorisation of lexical variation in UGC. Finally, Section 5 is dedicated to our feasibility study regarding dependency annotation of our data using the Universal Dependencies annotation scheme. It also includes a brief discussion about annotation costs, an issue rarely explicitly discussed.

Our contribution is threefold: (i) an empirical account of the phenomena behind domain-shift performance drops in French UGC data processing, (ii) a syntactic study on the applicability of Universal Dependencies to French UGC, and (iii) the first corpus obtained from MINECRAFT and LEAGUE OF LEGENDS gaming logs. All corpora and annotations are freely available.

Proceedings of the 2nd Workshop on Noisy User-generated Text,
pages 13–23, Osaka, Japan, December 11 2016.

2 Related Work

Before the global availability of social-media feeds, studies on the difficulties of out-of-domain statistical parsing have been focusing mainly on slightly different newspaper texts (Gildea, 2001; McClosky et al., 2006b; McClosky et al., 2006a), biomedical data (Lease and Charniak, 2005; McClosky and Charniak, 2008) or balanced corpora mixing different genres (Foster et al., 2007).

For such data, which is as edited as standard data sources, the problem is "simply" a matter of domain adaptation. It is far from being the case for UGC data, as shown by Foster (2010). Indeed, in her seminal work on parsing web data, different issues preventing reasonably good parsing performance were highlighted; most of them were tied to lexical differences (coming from either genuine unknown words, typographical divergences, bad segmentation, etc.) or syntactic structures absent from training data (imperative usage, direct discourse, slang, etc.). This suboptimal parsing behavior on web data was in turn confirmed in follow-up works on Twitter and IRC chat (Foster et al., 2011a; Gimpel et al., 2010; Elsner and Charniak, 2011). They were again confirmed during the SANCL shared task, organised by Google, aimed at assessing the performances of parsers on various genres of Web texts (Petrov and McDonald, 2012). Foster (2010) and Foster et al. (2011b) noted that simple lexical and tokenisation convention adaptation to the Wall-Street Journal text genre could increase the parsing performance by a large margin. In addition, Seddah et al. (2012) showed that a certain amount of normalisation brought a large improvement in POS tagger performance of French social media texts. These normalisation steps mostly apply at the lexical level, at the very definition of what constitutes a minimal unit. Plank et al. (2014) attempt to quantify how much of the domain-specific variation of POS labeling is a result of different interpretations, and how much is arguably just noise.

Regarding the study of French UGC, our starting point is the part-of-speech and phrase-structure annotation guidelines by Seddah et al. (2012). However, we conduct our syntactic analysis in terms of dependency structures.

3 Data Collection and Part-of-Speech Annotation

Our dataset contains three different sources of user-generated content. Two of them are logs of multi-player video-game chat sessions, MINECRAFT and LEAGUE OF LEGENDS[1], the last one is made of instant cooking-related web questions from MARMITON[2], a widely popular French recipe website. This set of questions was collected during the building of the French QuestionBank (Seddah and Candito, 2016) but was not described nor analysed because of its syntactic peculiarity and was thus considered by the authors as a clear outlier. We chose to include this sample in our study because it offers a sharp contrast with video games chat logs in term of domain variation while retaining a *live* nature: users asks questions related to their immediate needs and expect a quick answer.

The LEAGUE OF LEGENDS data set was collected by Lamy (2015) in early 2015 and consists of two types of recorded user interactions: a first part is the record of discussions occurring during an on-going game session while the second part consists of different players post-game discussion that took place both on official game forums and on unofficial boards.

Table 1 presents the corpus properties. The figures highlight its unbalanced nature and confirm the weight of the medium of appearance, be it a "crude" chat system, tweets or a classic web forum. Both live in-game chat sessions (MINECRAFT and LEAGUE OF LEGENDS *in-game*) display similar properties in term of small average length, while the MARMITON and LEAGUE OF LEGENDS *outside* data exhibit rather different properties: sentences are either smaller with a small standard deviation for the former or on average longer with a strong variation for the latter.

3.1 Measuring the "Non-Canonical-ness" of our Data

In order to quantitatively corroborate our intuitions concerning the level of noise in our corpora, and for measuring their various levels of divergence compared to the French Treebank (Abeillé et al., 2003), we used an *ad hoc* noisiness metric. It is simply defined as a variant of the Kullback–Leibler (KL)

---

[1]Resp. `http://www.minecraft.com` and `http://leagueoflegends.com`
[2]`http://www.marmitton.org`

	# OF SENTENCES	# OF TOKENS	AV. LENGHT	STD DEVIATION	*noisiness* LEVEL (KL)
MARMITON	285	2080	7.30	2.57	3.43
LEAGUE OF LEGENDS	453	5106	11.27	12.55	3.48
in-game	254	961	3.78	2.95	2.98
outside	199	4145	20.82	13.57	3.46
MINECRAFT	236	913	3.87	3.94	3.10
ALL	974	8099	8.32	9.38	3.58

Table 1: Corpus properties.

divergence[3] between the distribution of trigrams of characters in a given corpus compared to a reference. Unlike the raw text properties, the KL divergences we computed (Table 1) range around the same figures (between 2.98 and 3.50). These levels of *noisiness* appear much higher than the ones reported by Seddah et al. (2012) for more classical source of user-generated content. This discrepancy can be caused by two factors: either the texts themselves contain a lot of noise and depart strongly from the writing norm, or their lexical domain is so different from the French Treebank's one that the variation it carries can be considered as noise. If we compare the KL divergence between our 3 data sources (Table 2), we can see that the trigrams distributions are somehow "closer" to each other than they are to edited text.

	A / B	A vs B	B vs A
MARMITON / LEAGUE OF LEGENDS		1.36	0.81
MARMITON / MINECRAFT		1.88	1.38
LEAGUE OF LEGENDS / MINECRAFT		1.30	1.40

Table 2: *noisiness* levels for each of our sub-corpora.

3.2 PoS Annotation of Additional Data

As we mentioned in the introduction, our work takes its source in a will to build robust parsing models regardless of the domain variation. The challenge here is that variation may cover anything from historical to biomedical texts, Twitter's feeds subtitles, chat logs and so on. For some machine learning purists, anything not present in the training data is purely an out-of-domain instance and coping with this variation should be left only to the model. In this point of view, the loss of performance can be circumvented by adding more data, annotated or not, thus enlarging the training set. However, in the case of UGC, the very notion of adding more data can be problematic: UGC covers basically everything that can be produced by someone with an internet access and at least some notion of a writing system. The need for more insights in terms of what to expect is becoming a striking issue.

This is why in order to allow further exploration of the language divergence at stake in our UGC sample data set and because the MARMITON and LEAGUE OF LEGENDS sub corpora were already annotated using the extended FTB tagset used for the French Social Media Bank, we annotated the MINECRAFT data set with the same type of annotations. This was done by one expert annotator. We also checked the consistency of the LEAGUE OF LEGENDS subset and corrected a few obvious errors. Let us add that this work is part of a pilot study investigating the development of a much larger data set, made of video games interaction, the annotations are then likely to evolve.

3.3 Exploring our Data: Automatic PoS Annotation Results

To provide a first glance on the difference between our three domains and the training data from FTB, we provide in Table 3 the PoS tagging accuracy results obtained with the PoS tagger *MElt* (Denis and Sagot, 2012) trained on edited journalistic data. Results are on-par with previously reported results on French

---

[3]It differs from a standard Kullback–Leibler distance because we apply a preliminary pre-processing to the corpora involved: (i) URLs, e-mail addresses and such, are removed, (ii) all characters that do not belong to an extensive list of characters that might be used in French sentences are replaced by a unique "non-standard character,"

	OOV(%)	Baseline (FTB trained)		FTB trained+ Normalisation	
		All	Unseen	All	Unseen
MARMITON	27.29	81.84	70.82	83.15	75.44
LEAGUE OF LEGENDS	29.21	80.02	**52.92**	80.35	**45.77**
in-game chat	61.81	58.79	47.46	55.25	40.40
off-game session	21.64	84.95	56.41	86.13	60.42
MINECRAFT	52.57	53.12	28.13	58.27	36.04
all	31.36	77.44	52.19	78.62	45.42
FRENCH SOCIAL MEDIA BANK (DEV)	23.40	80.64	-	84.72	-
FTB (DEV)	5.20	97.42	-	97.42	-

Table 3: POS tagging results using *MElt* trained on the French Treebank with and without normalisation. The tagger (Denis and Sagot, 2012) was trained on the canonical training section of the French Treebank (Abeillé et al., 2003) instance, FTB-UC, from (Candito and Crabbé, 2009). We used an extended version of the rewriting rules used to pre-annotate the French Social Media Bank (Seddah et al., 2012). They work jointly with the tagger to provide internal cleaned versions of a token, or a sequence of, which are tagged separately. Resulting POS tags are finally merged to the original token(s). (*e.g.wanna* → *want/VB to/TO* → *wanna/VB+TO*).

UGC tagging (Seddah et al., 2012; Nooralahzadeh et al., 2014): normalisation helps to cover some of the most frequent lexical variations and hence improves substantially the tagging accuracy. However in the case of *in-game* LEAGUE OF LEGENDS chat session, the normalisation is detrimental to the overall tagging performance as well as for unseen words. One obvious hypothesis is simply that the rules are applied deterministically and assign wrong PoSs while letting the pure tagging model work alone provide reasonable assumption on what would be the correct label for an out-of-domain word. Let us add that the *MElt* tagger makes a heavy use of features extracted from wide coverage lexicon, this lexicon itself adds a domain bias in case of known words used in a totally different syntactic context (which, according to the FTB guidelines, implies a different category). While MARMITON and LEAGUE OF LEGENDS *off-games* tagging results are in the same range than the FTB ones, MARMITON results exhibit vastly inferior performance but seem to benefit from a normalisation step.[4] To summarise, in-game live session logs are harder to process than "regular" user-generated content.

However, a difference in a single metric such as POS accuracy or Kullback-Lubler divergence offers little information on the causes of such difference. In other words, each domain has its idiosyncrasies, and a domain shift is the result of the Cartesian product of the idiosyncrasies of source and target data.

The particularities of UGC are unbound, each new data source—defined by user demographics, user scenario, technical constraints and communication purpose—can spawn a myriad of idiosyncrasies that are beyond most domain-adaptation techniques that depend on selective sampling, self-training or other semi-supervised learning techniques. Therefore, the purpose of the present work is not only to potentially provide a new dataset to be used as additional training data for domain adaptation. Rather, we provide a close inspection of the main causes behind the expectable performance drops in tagging and parsing.

We therefore conduct a series of automatic and manual inspections to better understand the linguistic phenomena behind UGC linguistic variability. We explore the relation between predicting performance and annotation difficulty, which is seldom explicitly addressed (Plank et al., 2015).

4 A Threefold Categorisation for UGC Idiosyncrasies

Even though user-generated content does not constitute a uniform genre, many works have characterised its idiosyncrasies (Foster, 2010; Gimpel et al., 2011; Seddah et al., 2012; Eisenstein, 2013), which can be characterised on three axes, defined by the intentionality or communication needs of the word variants:
   1. **Encoding simplification:** This axis covers ergographic phenomena, *i.e.,*phenomena aiming at reducing the writing effort, perceived as first glance as genuine misspell errors, and transverse phe-

---

[4] In fact, in the case of LEAGUE OF LEGENDS in-game data, the normalisation step adds a significant amount of noise. A solution to this problem and more generally to the limitations of deterministic rule-based normalisation lies in the development of non-supervised or semi-supervised adaptative approaches.

nomena that include token contraction, "`iwuz`" for "`I was`" and over-splitting, "`c t`" instead of "`c'était`" (*it was*). Word types resulting form these categories pose challenges for their appropriate tokenisation, because they can either be split away by conventional tokenisers or retain conflated tokens, cf. Section 5.1.

2. **Sentiment expression:** This axis corresponds to marks of expressiveness, e.g., graphical stretching, replication of punctuation marks such as `???`, emoticons, sometimes used as a verb such as `Je t'<3` standing for `Je t'aime` (*I love you*). These phenomena aim at emulating sentiments expressed through prosody and gesture in direct interaction. Many of these symbols contain punctuation, that can lead to spurious tokenisation. Game logs have also a lot of platform-dependent particularities in the way they encode emoticons, e.g. the `:smile:` symbol, which is a placeholder to show a smile icon, is split as three different tokens (`: smile :`) by the tokeniser.

3. **Context dependency** This axis corresponds to the amount of context needed to understand a post. The nature of different user platforms will influence the domain knowledge necessary to understand the specific terms, from ingredients in MARMITON to weapon characteristics in LEAGUE OF LEGENDS. As in dialogue-based interaction, speech turns are marked by the thread structure and provide a context rich enough to allow varying level of ellipsis and anaphora. This structure can be superseded by hashtags (which example to add a meta data susceptible to attract attention ("likes")), providing a parallel source of information. Maybe more importantly, additional multimedia content can provides a rich source of context that we no dot have full access to when annotating, such as game state, sounds and images being displayed, etc.

5 Annotating Syntactic Dependencies

Before engaging in an annotation task, we conduct a feasibility study for the three domains at hand. While part-of-speech and syntactic annotation are not mutually independent, in this section we focus on how different typographic, lexical and syntactic phenomena can increase the difficulty of syntactic analysis. The previous work of (Kaljahi et al., 2015) has focused on phrase-structure parsing of forum text, which was made more difficult by the presence of grammatical errors. They report the benefits of correcting grammatical errors before conducting constituency parsing. Nevertheless, our corpora of choice are even more removed from the expectable newswire training data than theirs, and error correction as such is largely impossible.

Analysing noisy data using phrase structure might require postulating empty elements to be able to name non-terminals, or even provide a complete tree altogether. In contrast, dependency analysis reduces this problem by ensuring every token has a head, and that all edges form a tree. This alleged relative ease of annotation of dependency syntax over phrase structure led us to conduct our feasibility study using dependency.

As a dependency formalism, we use UD or Universal Dependencies (Nivre et al., 2016). In this formalism, there are no empty elements, and there is a preference for assigning headedness to content words. For instance, for 'under the table', 'table' is the head of both the article and the preposition. We choose this formalism because we consider it more reliable to annotate our utterances when they are missing function words.

5.1 Tokenisation

UD defines dependency relations between *syntactic* words, and not between orthograpic words. To give account for this principe, orthographic words can be internally broken down in their forming syntactic words. In the general case of French, preposition-article contractions such as 'du' (*of the*, singular masculine) must be treated as two token for syntactic purposes, namely 'de' and 'le'. Beyond these few—but highly frequent—cases, French words do not need internal syntactic token analysis in the general case.

However, user-generated data has plenty of ergographic phenomena that blur the practical equivalence between tokens and syntactic words. For instance, the standard French expression"j'aime" (*I like*) gets split by the apostrophe into two tokens by any regular tokeniser, but dropping apostrophes that would otherwise be obligatory is a common practice in user-generated data. Thus, 'jaime' would not be auto-maticaly analysable without using strategies for apostrophe recovery. While the UD formalism does not oblige us to correct every single typographical or grammatical error, we are obliged to do so when an or-tographic word corresponds to more than one syntactic words. Table 4 provides some detailed examples of these conflated tokens and the syntactic tokens they contain in their UD representation.

Form	Standardised	POS	Translation
ta	tu as	PRON VERB or PRON AUX	*you have*
ya	il y a	PRON PRON VERB	*there is*
jaime	j'aime	PRON VERB	*I like*
o	au (à le)	ADP DET	*in the*

Table 4: Usual non-standard conflated tokens in UGC, along with their standardised form and UD part-of-speech for their syntactic tokens once analysed.

5.2 Effects on Syntax of Time and Space Limits

Many user-generated data sources share the common characteristic that they are written under time and space limits. Twitter and SMS messages present well-known case of spatial contraints, namely 140 and 160 characters respectively. The MARMITON data presents a more lenient spatial restriction, because the sentences we use are discussion forum header questions. In our game log data, we find that text has been written under time constraints. In particular on Minecraft, we observe shorter messages and a higher prevalence of contractions, ergographism and typos.

Besides the obvious effect on spelling, time and space limitations also influence syntactic choices, be-cause they also foster dropping less-relevant elements like articles or punctuations, but more importantly also whole lexical items or spans. Indeed, user-generated data presents plenty of candidates can we can interpret as ellipsis. While the pragmatics of an internet cooking forum can be very idiosyncratic, even newswire has a frequent source of syntactic anomalies, namely headlines (Perfetti et al., 1987). Head-linese is also a result of writing under space constraints, and is a particular use of language that is very prone to ellipses, e.g the 'U.S. Futures Higher Ahead of GDP Data'[5] has no main verb and only one function word. We expect the headline-esque, conversation-starting MARMITON questions to present ellipsis and disfluences resulting from its spatial limitations and its almost oral nature.

Finally, in the scenario of syntax under space and time contraints, we also observe that many relations between clauses are not explicitly marked. We also give account for the cases of parataxis in our data.

5.3 Code-Switching and Direct Speech

The two game-log domains contain plenty of English game terms, and we observe quite a lot of code-switching. When only a token is code-switched, it's potential difficulties of analysis can be resolved during part-of-speech annotation. In this aspect, an atomic code-switch does not differ from using a loanword (Example 1). When the code-switching spans more than one token, difficulties arise, as a certain span can have its own internal syntactic structure in English (Example 2), while being embedded in a French clause. Similarly, we also observe examples of direct speech with an embedded full clause in English (Example 3).

1. LoL: J' adore jouer Elise mais faut la **up** merci .
   I love playing Elise but must up her thanks .
2. Minecraft: qui a **stuff** ? **for me**
   who has stuff ? for me
3. LoL: J' ai donc dit d' un ton désperé en **all "GG guys, you were better , can' t carry this: "**
   I have thus said in a desperate tone in all "GG guys, you were better, can' t carry this: "

For Examples 2 and 3, it is necessary devise strategies that allow a full analysis of the main language, and potentially provide an analysis for the code-switched language in an alternative layer.

---

[5]The Wall Street Journal, online edition, October 28, 2016.

5.4 Quantitative Analysis

We have taken a sample of 100 unique sentences with at least 4 tokens from each of the three domains. One of the authors of this article, experienced in dependency annotation, evaluated the difficulties in annotating them using UD dependencies. Sentences are shorter in Minecraft, and only retrieved 87. Notice that we do not conduct any sentence splitting, and we treat each of the statements entered by the users as complete utterances. While some of these utterances could be split in clauses, other sequences of utterances could be joined to form a single sentence. However, we believe that treating each statement as a complete utterance is the most realistic scenario for later automatic processing.

Table 5 presents the percentage of sentences in each sample that present annotation difficulties in our UD pilot. From the phenomena described in this section, we have determined a series of categories, such as missing main verb (NoVerb), conflicting candidates to main predicate (Pred), parataxis (Parat), code-switching (CoSwi), missing punctuation that harms understanding (Punct), tokenisation problems such as fragments or overzealous tokenisation (Tok), and cases of conflated tokens such as the ones presented in Section 5.1.

Domain	NoVerb	Pred	Parat	CoSwi	Punct	Tok	Conf
LEAGUE OF LEGENDS	3	3	17	39	10	8	0
MARMITON	42	7	2	0	0	2	11
MINECRAFT	16	1	14	17	15	8	31

Table 5: Corpus-wise percentages of annotation difficulties.

As expected, the two gaming corpora are more similar between themselves than to MARMITON, which presents a defining particularity in that 42% of the examples do not have a main verb. In this domain, users rely heavily on domain knownledge, using a language that is often very close to spoken French, such as "Steak , pâtes et ???" (*"Steak, pasta and ???"*), where the last conjunct is ommited in order to formulate a question. While we only find two examples of parataxis in MARMITON, we observe 17 and 14 in LoL and Minecraft. These two domains respond to more real-time data, and the relation between clauses is less often made explicit. In addition, most statements in MARMITON are monoclausal.

Code-switching and heavy loanword and in-game vocabulary are defining traits for the gaming corpora, which LoL being the corpus with more code-switching and more instances of direct speech. The sentences with these phenomena present the difficulty of how to represent both the contribution to the main French sentence, and the internal structure of the cited or code-switched span.

5.5 Annotated Examples

We have conducted some preliminary full dependency annotations for examples we considered illustrative of the different domains and their characteristic syntactic phenomena. Figures 1 and 2 shows three examples of non-trivial analyses, one for each domain. We provide glosses for the examples in the figure, and their translations are: A: "Which wine with a pig roast?", B: "But we have to think: assault tank" and C: "Every time 3VS1 and suddenly -2 P4".

Example A is a MARMITON example, which has no main verb. However, the main term of the question is "wine"(*wine*), and we treat is as the main predicate. Example B presents an ambiguity in main predicate choice. While "penser"(*think*) is the only verb of the sentence and makes a good candidate for main predicate, we can also see the whole span before the colon it as an extrapredicative, with "char"(*tank*) being the head of the predication.

Example C presents a series of idiosyncrasies. First of all, we had to treat the contractions "du" (*of the*, singular) and "des" (*of the*, plural) as two separate tokens, marked in parentheses following UD tokenisation principles, as well as an unusual typo,i.e. "cou^" should be "coup", literally *hit*, a formant of the expression "du coup", which means *literally*. This last multiword, treated with a flat structure with the *mwe* label, is very common in spoken French, but not present in the French UD treebank.

More importantly, C shows an attachment ambiguity caused by part-of-speech ambiguity and verb ellipsis. A natural ellipsis recovery of example C would read as "Every time **there are** 3VS1, and

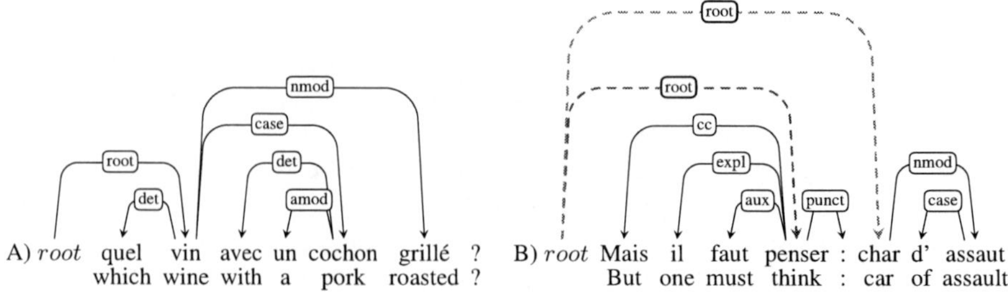

Figure 1: Example A, lacking a main verb, and B, with two contesting candidates for main predicated marked with dashed edges.

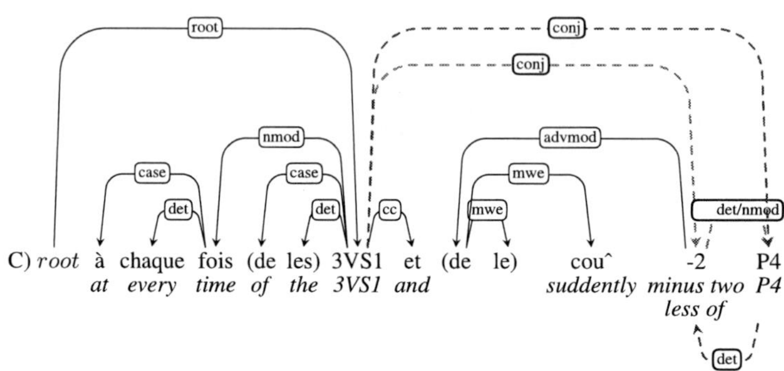

Figure 2: Example C, with two contesting structures from two different readings of the token "'-2".

suddenly **I have** -2 P4". The word "3VS1" stands for "3 versus 1", namely an uneven combat setting, and 'P4" refers to the character's protection armor. The token "-2" admits more than one analysis. The first analysis is the simple reading as number, complementing the noun "P4". A second analysis treats "-2" as a trascription of "moins de" (less than, less of), which would be the preferred analysis in case the verb recovery held. This example shows the interplay between frequent ellipses, ergographic phenomena (Seddah et al., 2012) and the need for domain knowledge in user-generated data.

5.6 Feasibility of Dependency Annotation

As said above, elliptical structures are frequent in our corpora and are a direct consequence of the *live* nature of the medias we choose to study. This is why at the beginning of this work, we decided to annotate these ellipsis, breaking thus the French Treebank guidelines, because we pretentiously thought we could always remain neutral in our interpretation of the missing syntactic context while agreeing on it and that it would be actually useful. Figure 3 shows an example of such annotation, here prototyped in a phrase-based manner, following the FTB guidelines. In this example, the two VNs (Verbal Nucleus in

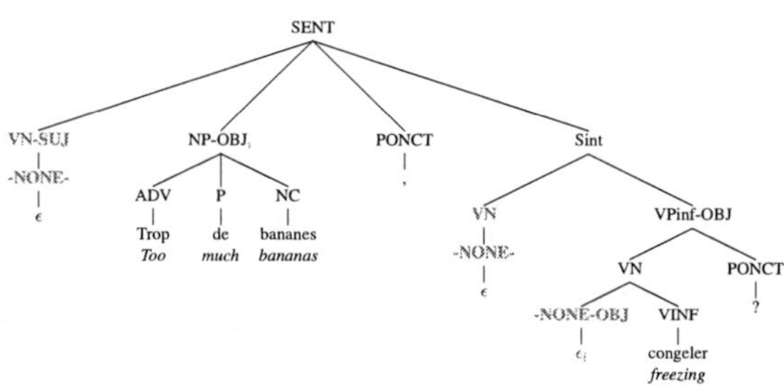

Figure 3: Prototype phrase-based analysis of an extreme elliptic case: *Too much bananas, freezing?*

the FTB terminology) were supposed to respectively stand for "J'ai"/*I have* and "dois-je"/*should I* but they could have stand for anything else (preposition, adverbial phrase) while the strictly transitive verb "congeler"/*to freeze* is expecting a direct-object (showed by a trace in the clitics position pointing to the preceding NP). In short, trying to annotate such missing constructions was akin to numerous, if not pointless, inferences and led us to consider a UD analysis where we only had to make *bananas* the main predicate, and treat *freeze* as a subordinate clause.

Regardless of the difficulty of the domain, it appears that a UD dependency analysis lends itself to dependency annotation in an easier way: Since non-leaf relations appear between lexical words, this representation is more robust to missing determiners, prepositions and punctuations, even phrases. Also, if we used other dependency formalisms that for instance place prepositions as heads of nouns, it would be more difficult to annotate as it is the case using the current French Treebank dependency scheme (Candito et al., 2010). Nevertheless, dependency analyses conflate functional and structural information (Silveira and Manning, 2015), and some of the structural information can be lost in cases such as the Example C, discussed above.

Annotating dependencies lends itself well to noisy user-generated data. In a strict lexicalist analysis such as UD, where there are no tokens for unobserved words (e.g. dropped subjects, missing main verbs), we must build a structure from the existing words, and not from idealised sentence representations. We finally observe that for UGC, shorter sentences are harder to annotate. Indeed, sentences closer to the lower threshold of 4 tokens we have determined, seem to present more ellipsis, while longer sentences in our data have structures closer to more canonical syntax.

5.7 The Unspoken Costs of Treebank Annotation

As we all know, creating annotated data is a rewarding task, extremely useful for evaluation as well as for building feature-rich supervised models. Yet, it is time consuming and as generally said, relatively costly (Schneider, 2015) even though crowd-sourcing solutions through games with a purpose start to emerge (Guillaume et al., 2016). The dataset we presented in that paper are part of process that was initiated 5 years ago when we were confronted to the lack of syntactically-annotated out-of-domain dataset for French. The purely syntactic annotation phase for the LoL and Minecraft data is still ongoing and we expect it to be finished in the first few months of 2017. It is important to consider that such a task was made possible because of the experience we gained along the years and because we relied on a highly trained team of annotators. This training was the most important point in term of costs and had to be extended each time we added a new major annotation layer (from surface syntax to deep syntax for example, see (Candito et al., 2014) for details). Table 6 presents the costs of the treebanking effort (mainly led by Marie Candito and the second author) that was carried out by the INRIA's Alpage team since 2011 and led to the release of many out-of-domain and user-generated content treebanks. The figures do not include the costs of the permanent-position researchers involved in the design of the annotation scheme, in preliminary annotation, in the development of pre-annotation pipelines, post-annotation error detection and correction tools and in the training and supervision of the annotators. Considering that we annotated 4 different layers for about 7k out-of-domain sentences and 2 layers for 3.7k of UGC data, the average cost per sentence is about 3 euros, on par with what is known about the English Web Treebank (Bies et al., 2012) development costs (Mc Donald, PC). Unlike less costly initiatives that focused on gold standard or training data creation, our goal was also to provide a linguistic snapshot of a specific domain at a given time, useful as such for linguists.

	Start	Size	Morph.	Const.	Dep.	Deep Synt.[4]	Cost
		sent.			*man/month*		*euros*
Sequoia[1]	2011	3200	2	9	1	6	59k
FSMB 1[2]	2012	1700	1	2	-	-	13k
FSMB 2[2]	2014	2000	2	4	-	-	20k
FQB[3]	2014	2600	2	4	1	4	36k
LoL	2015	450	3	-	-	-	3k
Minecraft	2016	230	0.5	-	-	-	2k
		10180			41.5		133k

Table 6: Treebanking Cost at the Alpage team. *Morph.: morpho-syntactic annotation, Const: Phrase-based annotation, Dep: dependency conversion, Deep Synt: Deep syntax annotation.*
[1]:(Candito and Seddah, 2012),[2]:(Seddah et al., 2012),[3]:(Seddah and Candito, 2016),[4]:(Candito et al., 2014)

6 Conclusion

We have presented a three-corpus dataset of user-generated French data. We have shown how the deviation from conventional newswire data manifests in different ways, and not only lexical elements. For lexical elements, we have presented a threefold categorisation of UGC idiosyncracies.

We have subsequently conducted a pilot study to evaluate the a priori difficulties of applying a UD analysis on our data. We have determined that for our data set, after POS analysis, the difficulty of annotating depends on the amount of elided material and on the ability of the representation scheme to cope with the discrepancies between raw and syntactic tokens. While dependency syntax is more robust towards missing elements that phrase-structure representations, many the examples of the forum text presented cases of i.a. main-verb ellipsis, which are still difficult to tackle using dependency analysis. While the main problem for analysis of term-rich texts like those of gaming logs lies (LEAGUE OF LEGENDS and MINECRAFT) at the POS level, the *hidden* problem arises with perfectly standard text lacking most of the usual syntactic glue, including verbal predicates, which we find in MARMITON. For games, however, the other main problem lies in the strong contextualization of such production, making them barely understandable by a domain-outsider. Lastly, we believe our data can be used as a very interesting crash-test or a valuable reference material, so we make all data freely available at `http://alpage.inria.fr/Treebanks/ExtremeUGC/` :smile:

Acknowledgments

We thank our anonymous reviewers for their comments. This work was partly funded by the ANR SOSWEET and PARSITI projects, as well as by the Program "Investissements d'avenir" managed by the Agence Nationale de la Recherche ANR-10-LABX-0083 (Labex EFL).

References

Anne Abeillé, Lionel Clément, and François Toussenel, 2003. *Building a Treebank for French*. Kluwer, Dordrecht.

Ann Bies, Justin Mott, Colin Warner, and Seth Kulick. 2012. English web treebank. Technical report, Linguistic Data Consortium,, Philadelphia, PA, USA.

Marie Candito and Benoît Crabbé. 2009. Improving generative statistical parsing with semi-supervised word clustering. In *IWPT*, Paris, France.

Marie Candito and Djamé Seddah. 2012. Le corpus sequoia: annotation syntaxique et exploitation pour l'adaptation d'analyseur par pont lexical. In *TALN 2012-19e conférence sur le Traitement Automatique des Langues Naturelles*.

Marie Candito, Joakim Nivre, Pascal Denis, and Enrique Henestroza Anguiano. 2010. Benchmarking of statistical dependency parsers for french. In *Proceedings of COLING 2010*, Beijing, China.

Marie Candito, Guy Perrier, Bruno Guillaume, Corentin Ribeyre, Karën Fort, Djamé Seddah, and Éric Villemonte de La Clergerie. 2014. Deep syntax annotation of the sequoia french treebank. In *International Conference on Language Resources and Evaluation (LREC)*.

Pascal Denis and Benoît Sagot. 2012. Coupling an annotated corpus and a lexicon for state-of-the-art POS tagging. *Language Resources and Evaluation*, 46(4):721–736.

Jacob Eisenstein. 2013. What to do about bad language on the internet. In *HLT-NAACL*, Atlanta, USA.

M. Elsner and E. Charniak. 2011. Disentangling chat with local coherence models. In *ACL*.

J. Foster, J. Wagner, D. Seddah, and J. Van Genabith. 2007. Adapting wsj-trained parsers to the british national corpus using in-domain self-training. In *IWPT*.

J. Foster, O. Cetinoglu, J. Wagner, J. Le Roux, S. Hogan, J. Nivre, D. Hogan, and J. van Genabith. 2011a. #hardtoparse: Pos tagging and parsing the twitterverse. In *WOAM*.

Jennifer Foster, Ozlem Cetinoglu, Joachim Wagner, Joseph Le Roux, Joakim Nivre, Deirdre Hogan, and Josef van Genabith. 2011b. From news to comment: Resources and benchmarks for parsing the language of web 2.0. In *IJCNLP*, Chiang Mai, Thailand.

Jennifer Foster. 2010. "cba to check the spelling": Investigating parser performance on discussion forum posts. In *NAACL*, Los Angeles, California.

Daniel Gildea. 2001. Corpus variation and parser performance. In *EMNLP*, Pittsburgh, USA.

K. Gimpel, N. Schneider, B. O'Connor, D. Das, D. Mills, J. Eisenstein, M. Heilman, D. Yogatama, J. Flanigan, and N.A. Smith. 2010. Part-of-speech tagging for twitter: Annotation, features, and experiments. Technical report, School of Computer Science, Carnegie Mellon University.

Kevin Gimpel, Nathan Schneider, Brendan O'Connor, Dipanjan Das, Daniel Mills, Jacob Eisenstein, Michael Heilman, Dani Yogatama, Jeffrey Flanigan, and Noah A. Smith. 2011. Part-of-speech tagging for twitter: Annotation, features, and experiments. In *ACL*, Portland, Oregon, USA.

Bruno Guillaume, Karen Fort, and Nicolas Lefebvre. 2016. Crowdsourcing complex language resources: Playing to annotate dependency syntax. In *Proceedings of the International Conference on Computational Linguistics (COLING)*, Osaka (Japon).

Rasoul Kaljahi, Jennifer Foster, Johann Roturier, Corentin Ribeyre, Teresa Lynn, and Joseph Le Roux. 2015. Foreebank: Syntactic analysis of customer support forums. In *Conference on Empirical Methods in Natural Language Processing (EMNLP)*.

Laurine Lamy. 2015. Constitution d'un corpus d'évaluation web 2.0 fortement bruité et analyse syntaxique automatique préliminaire. Master's thesis, Université Paris Sorbonne (Paris IV), Paris, France, Septembre.

M. Lease and E. Charniak. 2005. Parsing biomedical literature. *IJCNLP*.

David McClosky and Eugene Charniak. 2008. Self-training for biomedical parsing. In *ACL*, Columbus, Ohio.

D. McClosky, E. Charniak, and M. Johnson. 2006a. Reranking and self-training for parser adaptation. In *CoLing*.

David McClosky, Eugene Charniak, and Mark Johnson. 2006b. Effective self-training for parsing. In *NAACL*, New York City, USA.

Joakim Nivre, Marie-Catherine de Marneffe, Filip Ginter, Yoav Goldberg, Jan Hajic, Christopher D Manning, Ryan McDonald, Slav Petrov, Sampo Pyysalo, Natalia Silveira, et al. 2016. Universal dependencies v1: A multilingual treebank collection. In *Proceedings of the 10th International Conference on Language Resources and Evaluation (LREC 2016)*.

Farhad Nooralahzadeh, Caroline Brun, and Claude Roux. 2014. Part of speech tagging for french social media data. In *Proceedings of COLING 2014, the 25th International Conference on Computational Linguistics: Technical Papers*, pages 1764–1772, Dublin, Ireland, August. Dublin City University and Association for Computational Linguistics.

Charles A Perfetti, Sylvia Beverly, Laura Bell, Kimberly Rodgers, and Robert Faux. 1987. Comprehending newspaper headlines. *Journal of Memory and Language*, 26(6):692–713.

Slav Petrov and Ryan McDonald. 2012. Overview of the 2012 Shared Task on Parsing the Web. In *SANCL*, Montreal, Canada.

Barbara Plank, Dirk Hovy, and Anders Søgaard. 2014. Linguistically debatable or just plain wrong? In *ACL (2)*, pages 507–511.

Barbara Plank, Héctor Martínez Alonso, and Anders Søgaard. 2015. Non-canonical language is not harder to annotate than canonical language. In *The 9th Linguistic Annotation Workshop held in conjuncion with NAACL 2015*, page 148.

Nathan Schneider. 2015. What I've learned about annotating informal text (and why you shouldn't take my word for it). In *The 9th Linguistic Annotation Workshop held in conjuncion with NAACL 2015*, page 152.

Djamé Seddah and Marie Candito. 2016. Hard time parsing questions: Building a questionbank for french. In *in Proceedings of LREC*.

Djamé Seddah, Benoît Sagot, Marie Candito, Virginie Mouilleron, and Vanessa Combet. 2012. The French Social Media Bank: a Treebank of Noisy User Generated Content. In *CoLing*, Mumbai, India.

Natalia Silveira and Christopher Manning. 2015. Does universal dependencies need a parsing representation? an investigation of english. *Depling 2015*, page 310.

Disaster Analysis using User-Generated Weather Report

Yasunobu Asakura
Tokyo Metropolitan University
`asakura-yasunobu@ed.tmu.ac.jp`

Masatsugu Hangyo
Weathernews Inc.
`hangyo@wni.com`

Mamoru Komachi
Tokyo Metropolitan University
`komachi@tmu.ac.jp`

Abstract

Information extraction from user-generated text has gained much attention with the growth of the Web. Disaster analysis using information from social media provides valuable, real-time, geolocated information for helping people caught up these in disasters. However, it is challenging to analyze texts posted on social media because disaster keywords match any texts that contain words. For collecting posts about a disaster from social media, we need to develop a classifier to filter posts irrelevant to disasters. Moreover, because of the nature of social media, we can take advantage of posts that come with GPS information. However, a post does not always refer to an event occurring at the place where it has been posted.

Therefore, we propose a new task of classifying whether a flood disaster occurred, in addition to predicting the geolocation of events from user-generated text. We report the annotation of the flood disaster corpus and develop a classifier to demonstrate the use of this corpus for disaster analysis.

1 Introduction

With the recent spread of the Web, disaster information is now being posted to the social media in real time. In the case of the 2011 Great East Japan Earthquake, Twitter was used to share information regarding damage states, tsunami warnings, and safety confirmations. As increasing amounts of information have been produced by users, information extraction from social media has attracted attention in the field of natural language processing. Flood disaster analysis using information from social media is heavily awaited because precise information such as time and location of a flood is crucial for supporting (potential) victims of the disaster. However, information extraction from social media faces several problems. Here, we address two important problems.

First, collecting posts including keywords about a disaster is not sufficient to judge whether the disaster actually occurred. The following posts concerning disasters illustrate this problem.

(1) The street in front of my house is <u>flooded</u>.

(2) There are several <u>flood</u> disasters around here.

(3) Last year's <u>flood</u> was terrible.

(4) Please be aware of <u>flood</u> hazards.

We desire to extract posts such as post (1) refer to a disaster but there are posts that do not refer to any specific disaster, (2) refer to a generic event rather than a specific event, (3) refer to a past accident instead of a current situation, and (4) does not refer to any disaster but alerts a reader regarding the possibility of future catastrophe.

Second, another important problem in disaster analysis is temporal and/or geographical uncertainty. Although 0.77% posts on Twitter[1] contain GPS information (Hecht et al., 2011), not all posts include exact geolocation. In addition, a post that contains GPS information need not refer to the location of a disaster event described in the post. The following post concerning a disaster illustrates this problem.

(5) I heard that it was <u>flooded</u> in Okinawa.

In the case of (5), the disaster occurs not in the place that GPS information indicates but in Okinawa prefecture.

Therefore, we propose new tasks (1) that classify whether a disaster occurred and (2) that predict the geolocation of events from social media. The task of geolocation prediction from Twitter has also been recently addressed (Han

---

[1]`https://twitter.com/`

Proceedings of the 2nd Workshop on Noisy User-generated Text,
pages 24–32, Osaka, Japan, December 11 2016.

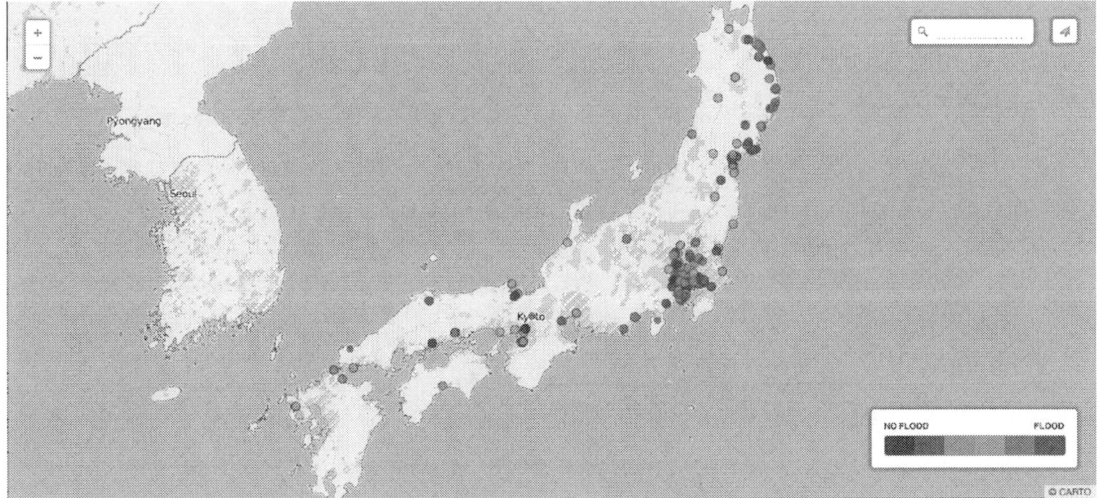

Figure 1: Visualization system of flood disaster for the Typhoon Lionrock crossed northern Japan on August 29, 2016. It caused heavy flood in Iwate prefecture, and its damage is clearly found in this visualization (red circles in the upper right coastline). The flood did not cause severe damage in other parts of northern Japan (shown in blue circles).

et al., 2014). However, in the present study, we attempt to predict the location of an event that a post refers to rather than the location of the post.

Figure 1 is a demonstration of our visualization system[2] of flood disaster. This visualization system uses the disaster classifier we built in this study. We aim to make a visualization system that can capture the exact location of the disaster in real time.

The main contributions of this study are as follows:

- We proposed a new task of flood disaster analysis and created a flood event dataset.

- We developed a supervised classifier to classify whether a disaster occurs to predict time when a disaster occurs and to predict distance between a reporter and disaster.

2   Related Work

With the development of the information society, studies of disaster information analysis from social media have attracted attention in the NLP literature.

In the case of the Great East Japan Earthquake, Neubig et al. (2011) constructed an information extraction system that visualized the security of the people in the disaster-stricken area using Twitter. They made a corpus by annotating safety information to tweets and trained a classifier to categorize the security of the population. We also perform disaster information analysis; however, we focus on event classification rather than classification of personal information. In addition, Varga et al. (2013) extracted distress and support information concerning disaster from tweets. Their distress recognizer used geographical information as a feature; however, they did not estimate the location of the disaster event. Our work differs in that we try to estimate how far the disaster event is from the person posting in terms of time and location.

Similar to our study, Sakaki et al. (2010) constructed a reporting system that classifies whether an earthquake or typhoon occurs when the text was posted. They predicted the location of disaster events using GPS data from the tweets; however, they did not address the problem of tempo-spatial distance between the person posting and the event. They were not able to tackle this problem because there were very few tweets posted with GPS data (Hecht et al., 2011). In this study, we created a flood event corpus from a blog in which almost all users posted their reports with the geolocation. Moreover, we separated the task of location prediction of posts and location prediction of events.

Regarding information extraction concerning a flood, Herfort et al. (2014) used specific geographical features like hydrological data and digital elevation models to prioritize crisis-relevant Twitter messages. In this study,

---

label		value	description
disaster		positive	From the post, we can judge that a flood disaster is occurring when the text is posted.
		negative	From the post, we can judge that a flood disaster is not occurring when the text is posted.
time	future	high probability	From the post, we can judge that a reporter alerts a future flood in advance.
		low probability	From the post, we can judge that a reporter is anxious about a future flood.
		unmentioned	From the post, we can judge that a reporter does not mention about a future flood.
	present	occurring	From the post, we can judge that the flood is occurring.
		probably occurring	From the post, we can presume that the flood is occurring.
		not occurring	From the post, we can judge that a flood is not occurring.
	past	occurred	From the post, we can judge that a flood occurred recently.
		occurred long before	From the post, we can judge that a flood occurred long before.
		unmentioned	From the post, we can judge that a reporter does not mention a post flood in the past.
distance		close	We can judge from the post that a reporter reports flood in front of him/her.
		far	We can judge from the post that a reporter reports flood but he/she is not at the place where he/she experienced flood.
		misc	Except close and far.

Table 1: Labels for the flood disaster events.

we focus on the prediction of an event using linguistic features to discuss potential issues in text-based event classification. Vieweg et al. (2010) analyzed tweets generated during a flood event. They found that 6% of the tweets contained location information. In this study, we focus on annotating the locational relation of a reporter and disaster. Bruns et al. (2012) compiled a dataset of tweets that relates to the crisis event by using hashtags. We made a flood disaster dataset by collecting report containing keywords related to floods because the social media used in this paper does not support hashtags. However, almost all of our data already has the exact GPS information.

3 Annotation of Flood Event

3.1 Data

We collected 567 posts including Japanese keywords for a flood event such as "inundation" and "flood" from a weather report sharing site known as "weathernews[3]." Approximately, 500,000 reports on weather are posted on this site every month by users, and these reports contain posting time and GPS information. Each reports comprises picture and text about weather, and some exclusive label of weather (e.g., onomatopoeia such as ポツポツ, ザーザー etc.) and temperature (e.g., hot or cold) by users' subjective judgment. In this study, we used only the text of weather reports.

We used posts of 17 days that included July, which is during the typhoon season, and February, which is the snowy season in Japan, and 4 days during the 2011 Great East Japan Earthquake. The average number of sentences in one post is 5, while the average number of phrases and words in one sentence are 5 and 17, respectively.

We labeled the posts according to whether a disaster occurred when the text was posted. We call this binary label *disaster label*. In addition, we annotated the time and distance of the disaster event from the post because flood disaster analysis should predict the time and place where a disaster occurred or is still occurring from a post. We call these labels *time label* and *disaster label*. In disaster labels, we annotated only one label for each post including at least one keyword. If there were more than one disaster event, we annotated the event that was closer to the keyword. In time and distance labels, we annotated each keyword in a post.

3.2 Labels

Table 1 summarizes the labels of this task. With regard to the time label, it is necessary to recognize not only whether a flood occurs but also whether a disaster persists. Therefore we divided the time label into following labels: future, present, and past instead of using generic time specification such as TimeML (Pustejovsky et al., 2003). Unlike TimeML, we assigned the time label to only the disaster keyword based on a relationship between the posting time and time of the reported disaster by considering the tense expression in the report. In addition, we assigned values of all three tenses (future, present, past) to the disaster keyword because we supposed to construct applications that estimate the ordering of flood disaster at the posting time, future and past. We prepared three values for each time label. We will describe details of the labels below.

Disaster label. We prepared *positive* and *negative* to estimate the presence of flood disaster at the time of posting.

---

[3]http://weathernews.jp

Future label.   We prepared *high probability*, *low probability* and *unmentioned* because there are three patterns of reports that mentioned alerts, anxiety, and nothing about a flood event. We labeled the report such as an alert future catastrophe like "It seems to be flood!," to *high probability* and labeled the report that mentioned only an anxiety about the occurrence of a flood, e.g., "I am anxious about a disaster," to *low probability*.

Present label.   We prepared *occurring, probably occurring* and *not occurring*. The value of probably occurring is created to reflect the temporal uncertainty of a flood. There is ambiguity in terms of tense in the representation such as "浸水していました (had flooded)," which refers to a disaster that occurred or is occurring. For such a representation, we labeled the posts as "probably occurring." We did not prepare *unmentioned* because we label the post as *not occurring* if a disaster is not mentioned in the case of present.

Past label.   We prepared *occurred, occurred long before* and *unmentioned*. The value of occurred long before is necessary to distinguish a report that refers to a recent accident and an accident that occurred long time before.

Distance label.   We just annotated whether a reporter is in front of the place (*close*) or has already left the place (*far*) because we use the flood event corpus constructed from a social media where almost all users post their reports with location information. We assigned a *misc* label in case where it is difficult to estimate the distance only from the post. For example, we labeled the report that did not mention about disaster that reporter experienced but disaster that reporter heard in the news to *misc*.

Examples of annotated posts are as follows.

(6) Tokyo Station was <u>flooded</u>, but this street is safe.

[disaster]: positive

[time]: future = unmentioned, present = probably occurring, past = occurred

[distance]: far

(7) My balcony is <u>flooded</u>.

[disaster]: negative

[time]: future = unmentioned, present = occurring, past = unmentioned

[distance]: close

(8) Although there are several past <u>flood</u> hazards around here, at present, there has not been any such hazard.

[disaster]: negative

[time]: future = unmentioned, present = not occurring, past = occurred long before

[distance]: misc

In the case of (6), a flood has not occurred near the reporter; however, the flood likely occurred somewhere nearby. In the case of (7), a flood occurs in the balcony of the poster; however, it is not considered to be a disaster. In the case of (8), a flood does not occur when the text is posted.

3.3   Analysis

The annotation was conducted using two annotators. The κ coefficient is 0.870 for the disaster label, 0.796 for the future label, 0.691 for the present label, 0.672 for the past label and 0.637 for the distance label.

Table 2 shows the number of labels. There are some labels in which the number is small like *occurred long before*. However, for disaster reports, it is necessary to distinguish between a past report that mentions an ancient disaster and an up-to-date report that mentions a recent disaster. Moreover, we would like to distinguish between reports that alert future catastrophe and reports that mention only anxiety to help evacuation. Therefore, we define and annotate those labels although their numbers are small. If we focus on developing a practical system, infrequent labels can be merged to alleviate data sparseness. In addition, these fine labels can be used not only in this task that estimates the presence of flood disaster at the time of posting but also in other tasks (e.g., the task of predicting that a disaster occurs in the future).

4   Classification of Flood Event

In this study, we conducted three experiments using disaster corpus that we developed. We formulated the flood information analysis as a classification problem and proposed a supervised approach to classify flood event. Table 3 shows the description of features used in these experiments.

label		number
disaster		positive:329 / negative:238
time	future	high probability:83 / low probability:48 / unmentioned:498
	present	occurring:272 / probably occurring:100 / not occurring:257
	past	occurred:121 / occurred long before:13 / unmentioned:495
distance		close:322 / far:59 /misc:248

Table 2: Number of labels.

example	今日は大雨が降るので <u>浸水</u> する予定。 (Today there is going to be flooding because of heavy rain.)
BoN	Bag of n-grams of word from the sentences including the keywords of flooding. ($n = 1, 2, 3, 4$) We use either the entire sentence or a window around the keywords (window size = 5).
	example：今日_[uni] は_[uni] 大雨_[uni] が_[uni] 降る_[uni] ので_[uni] 浸水_[uni] する_[uni] 予定_[uni] 。_[uni] ($n = 1$)
Dep	Bag of n-grams of words from the chunks of words including a keyword and chunks that depend on or are dependent on chunks that include a keyword.
	example：大雨_[dep] が_[dep] 降る_[dep] ので_[dep] 浸水_[dep] する_[dep] 予定_[dep] 。 _[dep] 大雨_が_[dep] が_降る_[dep] 降る_ので_[dep] ので_浸水_[dep] 浸水_する_[dep] する_予定_[dep] 予定_。 _[dep] (n=1,2)

Table 3: Features used for the experiments.

First, we built a supervised classifier to estimate the presence of a flood disaster at the time of posting using disaster labels of disaster corpus (single model). We used the BoN (bag-of-ngram) and Dep (dependency) features extracted from the sentence including in the keywords.

Second, we built a time analyzer that predicts the occurrence time of a disaster using time labels of disaster corpus and a distance analyzer that predicts the positional relationship between a reporter and the disaster that has occurred using distance labels from the disaster corpus. In the time analyzer and distance analyzer, we used the BoN around keywords and the Dep features.

Finally, we proposed an improved disaster analysis model based on time analysis. In time analysis, the present labels are almost equivalent to the disaster label. A big difference between the present label and the disaster labels is that the present labels are labeled for each disaster keyword whereas the disaster labels are labeled for each report. Therefore, we compared two classifiers. Baseline classifier is a single model. The other classifier aggregates time labels for all the keywords in the report to judge whether a disaster occurred or not (aggregate model). In order to identify a disaster label from present labels, we considered that the disaster label of a report is positive if at least one *occurring* label or one *probably occurring* label is included in the report.

5   Experiment

5.1   Setting

In this task, we used MeCab[4] (ver.0.996) with IPADic (ver.2.7.0) for word segmentation and CaboCha[5] (ver.0.68) for dependency parsing.

We conducted a 5-fold cross-validation and evaluated the performance of the analysis by its accuracy, precision, recall and F1 score.

In this study, we used linear and polynomial kernels for the SVM as the linear and non-linear classifiers in the disaster label classification and linear kernel SVM in the time and distance label classification, respectively. We used libSVM (ver.1.04) to train the model. We tuned the cost parameter C and coefficient of the kernel function during preliminary experiments. We set the degree of the polynomial kernel to 3. When comparing the single model and the aggregate model, both models are trained on linear kernel SVM, while the single model uses the Dep feature and the aggregated model uses the BoN feature.

5.2   Result

Table 4 shows the results of the flood disaster classification using the linear and polynomial kernel SVMs. In this experiment, there are no notable differences between the linear and polynomial kernel SVMs. Therefore, I will discuss only the result of linear SVM in the next section.

---

[4] http://taku910.github.io/mecab/
[5] http://taku910.github.io/cabocha/

Feature	Linear			Polynomial		
	Precision	Recall	F1	Precision	Recall	F1
BoN	75.9	**85.9**	80.4	75.6	85.0	79.8
Dep	**79.2**	84.7	**81.6**	**79.2**	83.7	81.1
BoN+Dep	76.7	**85.9**	80.8	78.0	**85.6**	**81.3**

Table 4: Accuracy of the disaster label classification of SVMs.

Feature	Accuracy			
	Past	Present	Future	Distance
BoN	85.9	**74.7**	85.1	**71.4**
Dep	**87.9**	73.3	84.6	70.0
BoN+Dep	86.0	73.8	**85.7**	70.0

Table 5: Accuracy of time and distance label classification.

label	value	Precision	Recall	F1
future	high probability	71.4	42.2	53.0
	low probability	80.0	16.7	27.6
	unmentioned	86.5	98.8	92.2
present	occurring	75.0	82.7	78.7
	probably occurring	66.1	41.0	50.6
	not occurring	76.4	79.4	77.9
past	occurred	78.7	48.8	60.2
	occurred long before	100.0	13.3	23.5
	unmentioned	86.8	97.2	91.7
distance	close	70.7	83.2	76.4
	far	77.8	11.9	20.6
	misc	72.2	70.2	71.2

Table 6: Precision, Recall and F1-score of time and distance label classification.

classifier	Precision	Recall	F1
aggregated model	**84.3**	**88.4**	**86.4**
single model	79.2	84.7	81.6

Table 7: Accuracy of disaster label classification.

Table 5 shows the accuracy of the time and distance label classification and Table 6 shows the precision, recall and F1-score of time and distance label classification using linear kernel SVM with the BoN feature.

Table 7 shows the result of model comparison of the classifier using the document level disaster label (single model) and the classifier using the keyword level time labels (aggregated model). Aggregated model achieved better performance over single model in all the evaluation measures.

6 Discussion

Table 4 shows that we can obtain the highest precision using the Dep feature. Comparing the Dep feature and the BoN feature, it appears that the Dep feature is strongly related to the flood keywords because it considers only the chunks near a keyword. On the other hand, the BoN feature gave a strong positive bias to the classifier. Therefore, the BoN results in low precision compared with the result of the Dep feature. It is thought that the Dep feature enhances the precision because it filters the noise of the BoN feature by removing phrases that are not related to the keyword. We examined the Dep features from the linear kernel SVM. Table 8 shows features and corresponding weights. There are many negative features related to an advance alert, such as "注意 (attention)" , "心配 (worry)."

Table 9 shows examples of the primary classification errors. There are multiple classification errors, such as the first example, that are caused by complex modality. In this study, we used the polynomial kernel SVM in addition to the linear kernel SVM; however, the polynomial kernel SVM was ineffective because the amount of data used in this study was so small that it made the combinatorial features sparse. The second example demonstrates that

Positive feature	weight	Negative feature	weight
津波 (tsunami)	0.32826	冠水_する (to be flood)	-0.43767
冠水_と (flooding and)	0.31268	dative case marker	-0.37203
、_冠水 (, flood)	0.25815	accusative case marker	-0.34530
冠水_し_て (is flooded)	0.25528	注意 (attention)	-0.34294
の_冠水 (flooding of)	0.23073	心配 (worry)	-0.34058
冠水_状態 (flood state)	0.22084	道路_の (of road)	-0.31980
道 (road)	0.20543	冠水_や (flood or)	-0.30046
し_て_いる (ing)	0.20365	し_そう (be about to)	-0.29838
あちこち (here and there)	0.20088	そう (likely)	-0.28952
bias term	0.41139		

Table 8: Feature and weight of the linear classifier using Dep features.

Error example 1	浸水しているそうなので注意です。	False negative
	(Please be attention because it seems to be flooded.)	
Error example 2	昔ね。我が家も床下浸水した。	False positive
	(It is all history. My house was flooded.)	

Table 9: Examples of classification errors.

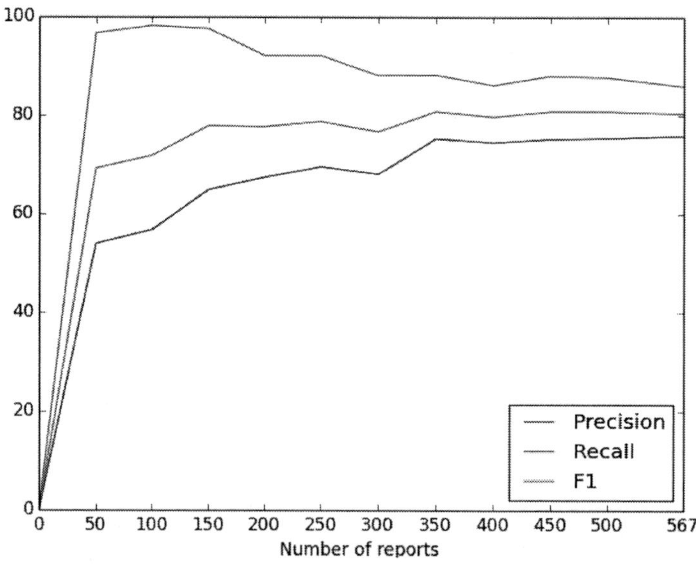

Figure 2: The learning curve of the flood disaster classification.

the classifier cannot classify a post that requires the consideration of inter-sentential context. Features used in this study considered only the words in a sentence, including the flood keyword. We need to employ discourse-level information to appropriately classify these examples.

Figure 2 shows the learning curve for disaster label classification. The classifier converges after the amount of data exceeds 350. It was thought that most surface keywords in posts concerning flood disasters could be learned with a small amount of data because we used only two keywords that directly indicated a flood disaster. However, it will be necessary to learn generic words that do not necessarily refer to flood disasters to boost the recall in flood disaster analysis.

Regarding time and distance classification, Table 6 shows that recall of *low probability*, *occurred long before* and *far* is very low. It is inferred that the number of the label is small. We examined the number of errors of the time analyzer and distance analyzer that use the BoN feature. Table 10 shows the number of errors. In time and distance analysis, there are errors that predict rare labels. As shown in Table 10, minor labels tend to be predicted as major labels. Therefore, it is necessary to search an effective feature for rare labels, especially for present labels

future			
	high probability	low probability	unmentioned
high probability	35	2	46
low probability	8	8	32
unmentioned	6	0	498

present			
	occurring	probably occurring	not occurring
occurring	225	7	40
probably occurring	36	41	23
not occurring	39	14	204

past			
	occurred	occurred long before	unmentioned
occurred	59	0	62
occurred long before	2	2	11
unmentioned	14	0	481

distance			
	close	far	misc
close	268	1	53
far	38	7	14
misc	73	1	174

Table 10: The confusion matrice of time and distance label classification error. Row shows gold label and column shows predicted label.

that contribute to disaster analysis.

Table 7 shows that the classifier using the time label (aggregated model) has better precision, recall, and F1-score than the classifier using the disaster label (single model). It is inferred that fine-grained annotation for each disaster keyword is more effective than coarse-grained annotation for each report in the disaster classification, because there are reports that mention two events in one report such as "It is <u>flooded</u> in Tokyo, but this place is not <u>flooded</u>." The single model did not perform well in complex tasks such as disaster analysis. Moreover, the aggregated model successfully decomposed a disaster analysis into simpler problems and achieved better performance. Modality analysis is shown to improve the accuracy of factuality analysis (Saurí and Pustejovsky, 2012), and can be applied to this task as well.

7   Conclusion

In this study, we collected posts concerning flood disasters from social media about weather and created a flood disaster corpus. We annotated whether a flood disaster occurred. Furthermore, we annotated the time of disaster and distance between the poster and disaster. In addition, we developed a classifier using linear and polynomial kernel SVMs. In the classification of disaster label, the experimental results show that the use of bag of n-grams from the subtree of a dependency parse is effective for classification of disaster label in terms of F1-score. In addition, we proposed an aggregated model using predicted time labels for disaster label classification. Experimental result showed that the aggregated model is better than the single model. Moreover, it is suggested that modality analysis is necessary for enhancing the performance of a disaster analysis.

In this study, we focus on flood disaster, but this data label creation and the classification can be extended to other natural disasters if the keyword of the disaster is found and has a similar nature to the flood disaster, such as landslides and heavy snowfalls.

In the future, we plan to expand our flood disaster corpus by adding new keywords. It is not straightforward to find appropriate keywords that increase recall without losing too much precision. In addition, we would like to improve the visualization system of flood disaster information using user-generated text to assist relief efforts in future large-scale disasters.

Acknowledgments

This research was (partly) supported by Grant-in-Aid for Research on Priority Areas, Tokyo Metropolitan University, "Research on social big data." We thank the anonymous reviewers for their constructive comments on the earlier versions of this document. We also thank Yoshiaki Kitagawa for his careful annotation.

References

Axel Bruns, Jean E Burgess, Kate Crawford, and Frances Shaw. 2012. #qldfloods and @qpsmedia: Crisis communication on Twitter in the 2011 South East Queensland Floods. *Technical report, ARC Centre of Excellence for Creative Industries and Innovation, QUT Z1-515,*.

Bo Han, Paul Cook, and Timothy Baldwin. 2014. Text-based Twitter user geolocation prediction. *Journal of Artificial Inteligence Research*, 49(1):451–500.

Brent Hecht, Lichan Hong, Bongwon Suh, and Ed H. Chi. 2011. Tweets from Justin Bieber's heart: The dynamics of the location field in user profiles. In *Proceedings of the SIGCHI conference on human factors in computing systems*, pages 237–246.

Benjamin Herfort, João Porto de Albuquerque, Svend-Jonas Schelhorn, and Alexander Zipf. 2014. Exploring the geographical relations between social media and flood phenomena to improve situational awareness. In *Proceedings of the 17th AGILE Conference on Geographic Information Science*, pages 55–71.

Graham Neubig, Yuichiroh Matsubayashi, Masato Hagiwara, and Koji Murakami. 2011. Safety information mining — What can NLP do in a disaster—. In *Proceedings of 5th International Joint Conference on Natural Language Processing*, pages 965–973.

James Pustejovsky, Jose M. Castano, Robert Ingria, Roser Sauri, Robert J. Gaizauskas, Andrea Setzer, Graham Katz, and Dragomir R. Radev. 2003. TimeML: Robust specification of event and temporal expressions in text. In *New Directions in Question Answering*, pages 28–34.

Takeshi Sakaki, Makoto Okazaki, and Yutaka Matsuo. 2010. Earthquake shakes Twitter users: Real-time event detection by social sensors. In *Proceedings of the 19th International Conference on World Wide Web*, WWW '10, pages 851–860.

Roser Saurí and James Pustejovsky. 2012. Are you sure that this happened? Assessing the factuality degree of events in text. *Computational Linguistics*, 38(2):261–299.

István Varga, Motoki Sano, Kentaro Torisawa, Chikara Hashimoto, Kiyonori Ohtake, Takao Kawai, Jong-Hoon Oh, and Stijn De Saeger. 2013. Aid is out there: Looking for help from tweets during a large scale disaster. In *Proceedings of the 51st Annual Meeting of the Association for Computational Linguistics*, pages 1619–1629.

Sarah Vieweg, Amanda L Hughes, Kate Starbird, and Leysia Palen. 2010. Microblogging during two natural hazards events: What Twitter may contribute to situational awareness. In *Proceedings of the SIGCHI conference on human factors in computing systems*, pages 1079–1088.

Veracity Computing from Lexical Cues and Perceived Certainty Trends

Uwe D. Reichel[*]
Research Institute for Linguistics
Hungarian Academy of Sciences
Budapest, Hungary
uwe.reichel@nytud.mta.hu

Piroska Lendvai[†]
Computational Linguistics
Saarland University
Saarbrücken, Germany
piroska.r@gmail.com

Abstract

We present a data-driven method for determining the veracity of a set of rumorous claims on social media data. Tweets from different sources pertaining to a rumor are processed on three levels: first, factuality values are assigned to each tweet based on four textual cue categories relevant for our journalism use case; these amalgamate speaker support in terms of polarity and commitment in terms of certainty and speculation. Next, the proportions of these lexical cues are utilized as predictors for tweet certainty in a generalized linear regression model. Subsequently, lexical cue proportions, predicted certainty, as well as their time course characteristics are used to compute veracity for each rumor in terms of the identity of the rumor-resolving tweet and its binary resolution value judgment. The system operates without access to extralinguistic resources. Evaluated on the data portion for which hand-labeled examples were available, it achieves .74 F1-score on identifying rumor resolving tweets and .76 F1-score on predicting if a rumor is resolved as true or false.

1 Background and Task Definition

A growing amount of studies investigate how rumors and memes spread and change on social media platforms (Leskovec et al., 2009; Qazvinian et al., 2011; Procter et al., 2013); given the amount of user-generated content, the need for automatic fact checking and claim verification procedures is obvious. To compute veracity, systems have been created recently for assessing the credibility of sources and claims (Berti-Équille and Borge-Holthoefer, 2015). Upcoming initiatives endorsed veracity detection in social media content as a shared task, calling for targeted applications and releasing benchmark data[1].

To tackle this challenge, we implemented a system that seeks to achieve three goals: (i) to compute a judgment indicating how factual a claim is, based on textual cues and predicted speaker certainty, (ii) to identify which tweet is resolving a rumor, in a set of tweets that discuss this rumor, and (iii) to predict the resolution value for the rumor, i.e., whether the rumor is verified as true or false. Veracity computation is based on information from three information layers related to rumorousness: (1) lexical-level factuality cues, (2) temporal patterns, and (3) speaker certainty. The system is purely data-driven and operates without building claim source profiles for the analyzed content. Below we introduce our motivation in the context of previous and related work.

The means by which factuality is conveyed are largely but not exclusively encoded on linguistic levels and are tightly related to the notion of certainty. Certainty and other extra-propositional aspects of meaning have prominently been investigated in terms of modality, negation and speculative language phenomena (Morante and Blanco, 2012; Morante and Sporleder, 2012). Benchmark corpora with annotations emerged (Saurí and Pustejovsky, 2009; Farkas et al., 2010), and systems have been built (Saurí and Pustejovsky, 2012; de Marneffe et al., 2012; Velldal and Read, 2012) to process texts from the genres of literature, newswire, biomedicine and online encyclopedia, typically drawing on lexical and syntactic cues. (Szarvas et al., 2012) propose a method for porting uncertainty detection across genres and domains. (Kilicoglu et al., 2015) present a full-fledged, compositional approach to factuality

---

[*]UDR is supported by an Alexander von Humboldt Society grant.

[†]PL is supported by the PHEME FP7 project (Grant No. 611233).

[1]http://alt.qcri.org/semeval2017/task8/

Proceedings of the 2nd Workshop on Noisy User-generated Text,
pages 33–42, Osaka, Japan, December 11 2016.

modeling and detection on texts from the domain of biomedicine based on fine-grained typology and dictionary-based classification of extra-propositional phenomena. Several components of the model are motivated by the nature of scientific communication that serves to track hypothesis building processes with tentative results, analogously to journalistic reports about breaking news. (Soni et al., 2014) focus on factuality framing in social media data in quoted claims with a small set of cues, whereas (Finn et al., 2014) implement keyword-based negation detection without providing quantitative evaluation.

Next to linguistically expressed uncertainty, extralinguistic information such as the temporal distribution of claims is shown to be an important aspect of veracity computation. Previous studies that investigated temporal patterns of linguistic cues tied to claims emerging in real-world events focus on keywords related to sentiment, named entities and domain terms (Temnikova et al., 2014), but not factuality-conveying cues. (Wei et al., 2013) report on the first uncertainty corpus based on tweets, as well as on classification results for uncertain tweets. Next to platform-specific metadata, they utilized cue phrases in annotated uncertain tweets and an algorithm to detect peaks in the data. (Kwon and Cha, 2014) and (Ma et al., 2015) show for rumor detection that accuracy can be improved by not only looking at message-related properties but also at how these properties change over time. (Ma et al., 2015) propose a time series structure for features and their deltas as the input for classification.

On the full PHEME dataset, (Lukasik et al., 2016) report on stance detection in the context of temporal dynamics. They utilize textual information via language modeling but do not evaluate the contribution of textual as opposed to other features. On the same dataset, (Zubiaga et al., 2016) analyzed labeled certainty values in dependence of claim resolution, and found that tweeters post messages with statistically similar certainty before and after a claim is resolved, moreover, irrespective of the resolution value.

In (Lendvai et al., 2016) we analyzed and validated a subset of the PHEME data on English and German data that temporal distribution and polarity of lexical markers can be used to represent and quantify changes in factuality framing in a rumor's lifecycle. Our current study furthers this research by incorporating, evaluating, and visualizing temporally anchored features for claim resolution point as well as claim resolution value prediction in English language rumors discussed in potentially noisy, user-generated content.

The paper is structured as follows. In Section 2 we introduce the underlying data and certainty annotations, and describe the automatic extension of lexical cues assigned to four levels of factuality. In Section 3 the relation between certainty and each of the factuality levels is assessed, and regression analysis is used for predicting certainty values by cue-type ratios. In Section 4 we quantify trend discontinuities in time series data of lexical cue ratios and predicted certainty scores to describe rumor resolution points. Cue ratios, certainty, as well as their time course characteristics are exploited in Section 5, where we train classifiers to identify claim-resolving tweets within series of tweets spanning a claim's lifetime, and additionally predict the claim's resolution value. The findings are discussed in Section 6.

2   Data

2.1   Corpus

We worked on a subset of a freely available, annotated social media corpus[2] collected from the Twitter platform[3], containing tweets in English related to three crisis events: the Ottawa shooting[4], the Sydney Siege[5], and the Germanwings crash[6]. Each event is annotated in terms of several rumorous claims[7] – plausible but at the time of emergence unconfirmed statements, e.g. in the Sydney Siege collection two example claims are "There is a hostage situation at a cafe in Sydney" and "Police (authorities) have been in contact with the hostage-taker". For each claim, there are a set of tweets that discuss or mention that claim, and a single one of these tweet has been manually identified and judged to be authoritatively resolving the claim either as true or false. A resolving tweet for the claim "The Germanwings plane experienced

---

[2]https://figshare.com/articles/PHEME_rumour_scheme_dataset_journalism_use_case/2068650
[3]twitter.com
[4]https://en.wikipedia.org/wiki/2014_shootings_at_Parliament_Hill,_Ottawa
[5]https://en.wikipedia.org/wiki/2014_Sydney_hostage_crisis
[6]https://en.wikipedia.org/wiki/Germanwings_Flight_9525
[7]We use *rumor*, *rumorous claim*, and *claim* interchangeably to refer to the same concept.

a rapid descent before crashing" is: *#4U9525 took eight minutes to descend from 38,000 feet to impact, says Germanwings CEO Winkelmann*; this rumor is annotated by a journalist as resolved True. The verification value is inherited by all the tweets that relate to this claim, also in retrospect. To ensure that there is always exactly a single resolving tweet per claim we discarded the unresolved claims in the given corpus so that the data underlying this study amounts 45 claims containing in sum 11,420 tweets. Tweets are organized into threaded conversations and are marked up with respect to seven categories of evidence, among others stance and certainty; for full details on the corpus we refer to (Zubiaga et al., 2015).

2.2 Certainty annotations

Certainty annotations were pre-assigned in the corpus in relation to stance value annotations by (Zubiaga et al., 2015). Stance represents speaker attitude toward a target: in this corpus, the target is a rumorous claim, and each tweet was manually marked as either supporting, denying, questioning, or commenting a claim. Tweets that received either of the stance labels *supporting* or *denying* were additionally assigned a certainty value. This value served to express tweeter confidence with respect to their stance, as perceived by independent, crowdsourced annotators. Each tweet was annotated by 5-7 crowdsourced annotators, in terms of the four labels *uncertain, somewhat certain, certain*, and *underspecified*.

We further processed these annotations as follows. To cope with frequent annotation mismatches, we did not simply pick the majority-voted certainty label for our subsequent analyses, but aggregated the annotated values for each tweet as follows. The original certainty labels were mapped to the numerical values 0, 1, 2, and *NaN*, respectively. We then calculated the mean of all non-*NaN* values and normalized this to the interval between 0 and 1 by dividing it by the maximum score 2. For example, the tweet *"Now hearing 148 passengers + crew on board the #A320 that has crashed in southern French Alps. #GermanWings flight. @BBCWorld"* was labeled as 'certain' by 4 annotators and labeled as 'somewhat-certain' by 1 annotator, so this tweet was assigned by us the certainty score of 0.9.

The intersection of tweets that relate to claims that were not only annotated as relating to a resolved claim, but also annotated with the three utilizable certainty labels *uncertain, somewhat certain, certain* left us with a relatively small amount of tweets (266), while we also had at our disposal a larger set of tweets (946) with claim resolution annotation but no certainty values assigned. We made use of both collections as described below.

2.3 Factuality cues: from seeds to extended lists

The material underlying our study is user-generated content. The data collection method, cf. (Zubiaga et al., 2015) retained only microposts that passed a retweet count threshold, often by media outlets using well-formed language. Since replying tweets are also included in the corpus, a large portion of the data involves noisy texts. Based on the factuality literature, most prominently (Saurí and Pustejovsky, 2009) and (Soni et al., 2014), we devised four factuality groups, each holding up to 40 single-token lexical cues. There is no restriction on which part of speech category a cue may belong to.

- **Knowledge** cues, e.g. clarify, confirm, definitely, discover, evidence, explain, official ...
- **Report** cues, e.g. according, capture, claim, footage, observe, report, say, show, source ...
- **Belief** cues, e.g. apparent, assume, believe, consider, perhaps, potential, presume, suspect ...
- **Doubt** cues, e.g. ?, accuse, allege, contrary, deny, incorrect, misstate, not, unsure, why, wrong ...

Each group represents one complex aspect of factuality that can be intuitively understood by non-linguists, i.e. end users in the journalistic verification scenario. Knowledge and belief cues express affirmative factuality polarity on graded levels of certainty. Report cues express affirmative factuality polarity as well, and additionally delegate speaker commitment, as they typically occur in externally-attributed statements and evidence, indicating a stronger level of speculation than knowledge cues. Doubt cues express negative factuality polarity and were selected to be indicative of contradictory or opposing-stance statements which can be extremely strong signals for rumorous claims. Involving categories that have been suggested in previous work in fully-fledged factuality taxonomies (see Section 1) would

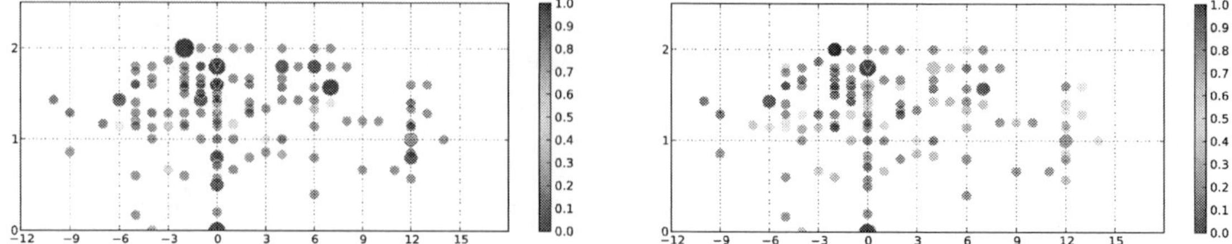

Figure 1: *Color-coded factuality cue ratio (FCR)* derived from matched cues in the two affirmative-polarity and high-commitment featuring factuality cue groups ('knowledge cue ratio' + 'report cue ratio'), using seed cues (left) vs extended cues (right). Factuality ratios are plotted on perceived certainty patterns (cf. Section 2.2) in 163 argumentative Twitter microposts related to 5 rumorous claims resolved as *True* during Sydney Siege. x axis: 10-minute intervals normalized to *claim resolution point at 0* (resolving tweets marked by triangles), y axis: *certainty score* averaged over perceived certainty judgments. Partial time window, size-coded amount of evidence.

require extracting higher-level linguistic information such as dependency parses, which are difficult to obtain from noisy data, and are reserved for the extended version of our system.

Starting from the seed cues, each of the four lists were automatically further populated from available semantic resources: via extracting the top-3 most similar items from the pretrained Google News word embeddings vector[8], as well as lemmas from the top-3 synsets from the English WordNet (Fellbaum, 1998) via NLTK[9] (Bird et al., 2009). Only single-token items were harvested; each cue token was subsequently extended by its derivationally related forms via the corresponding NLTK function. Using the extended trigger lists, we obtained counts for each tweet via matching each cue list to a tweet's content, applying the NLTK Snowball Stemmer[10] prior to lookup. We have also experimented with syntax-based cue disambiguation, but opted to abandon it for no proven impact on our current task setup. To exemplify cue matching, in the tweet *"#BREAKING: @nswpolice say a photo circulating of arrest of man near #MartinPlace is NOT related to the police operation #sydneysiege"* our lookup matches two 'report' cues (*say* and *photo*) and one 'doubt' cue (*not*). The cue extension procedure boosted the seed lists with a few hundred new tokens per cue group, leading to more cue matches in tweets.

Arguably, there are cues that might belong to more than one factuality group, most prominently negation words that, depending on their scope, may express certainty as well. We hypothesized however that utilizing the contextual distribution of a cue will represent its certainty-encoding function in rumor resolution timelines in a robust way. We exemplify such a timeline in Figure 1, differentiated by certainty values plotted to the y axis. The increase in cue recall based on extended lists aimed to benefit the certainty and rumor resolution modeling steps that we introduce in the next sections.

Features derived from matched cues   Based on the extended cue matching counts, for each tweet we calculated the proportion of cues for each factuality group over all cues: each proportion ranges from 0 (no cue of the respective type) to 1 (cues exclusively of the respective type). Each tweet is thus represented by the four ratios *KCR* ('knowledge' cue ratio), *RCR* ('report' cue ratio), *BCR* ('belief' cue ratio), *DCR* ('doubt' cue ratio). The *RCR* for the above example tweet is 2/3, the *DCR* 1/3, while *KCR* and *BCR* are 0.

3   Certainty prediction

Next, we examined the relation of cue ratios to certainty values assigned to tweets via regression analysis.

---

[8]http://code.google.com/p/word2vec/
[9]http://www.nltk.org/_modules/nltk/corpus/reader/wordnet.html
[10]http://www.nltk.org/api/nltk.stem.html

Method   To predict the degree of certainty for each tweet, we fitted generalized linear models (GLM) to the tweets manually annotated for perceived certainty. The four lexical cue ratios were defined as predictors and the certainty score (see Section 2.2) as target. To restrict the output to interval $[0\ 1]$, the distribution of the response was set to binomial, and a logit link function was chosen. A zero inflation problem is given due to the frequent absence of cue words, which we addressed by adding observation weights to the data points as follows: for each of a predictor's values the variance of the associated target values was measured, normalized by the variance sum, and its inverse taken. Zero values of a predictor co-occurring with a high variance of certainty values thus received a low weight when fed into the regression. The weight of each feature vector was then derived by taking the mean of the predictor-related weights.

Results   Spearman's Rho correlations between the single lexical cue ratios and the normalized certainty score are small. Only for *KCR* (.14) and *DCR* ($-.39$) the correlations are significant (Wilcoxon two sided signed rank tests for paired samples, $p < 0.05$). These two correlations point in the expected direction. The 10-fold cross validation of the GLMs on held out data yielded an average root mean square error of 0.22 (maximum: 0.28), which is significantly lower than the error of the baseline model always predicting the observed mean certainty value (two-sided Wilcoxon signed rank test for paired samples, $p < 0.01$). Finally, we fitted a GLM to all available training data for certainty prediction of all tweets used for the subsequent claim resolution prediction and resolving tweet localization tasks.

4   Certainty trend quantification

Method   In our approach we address time course characteristics more explicitly than previous studies (Kwon and Cha, 2014; Ma et al., 2015). That is, instead of bundling feature vectors at different time stamps to a joint vector, we capture time course characteristics by parameters of regression lines fitted through the feature values over time. These regression lines will be used for trend discontinuity analyses as described in detail below. By means of this analysis we augmented the set of variables the following way: for all four cue ratios and the derived certainty score we calculated four discontinuity features yielding five features for each cue ratio and certainty. These variables will be introduced in the following paragraphs and represent:

- tweet-intrinsic properties (lexical cue ratios *KCR, RCR, BCR, DCR*, predicted certainty *CRT*)
- local discontinuities across pairs of subsequent tweets (**_Delta*)
- global discontinuities in linear cue and certainty trends (**_Reset, *_RMSD_p, *_RMSD_f*), where the asterisk stands for the tweet-intrinsic variables, i.e. the cue ratios and certainty.

For measuring discontinuities, tweets were indexed in the order of their time stamps. Local discontinuities are measured in terms of the delta deviations of each tweet i from the preceding tweet, i.e. by subtracting each intrinsic variable's value of tweet $i-1$ from the corresponding value of tweet i (**_Delta*). To quantify the amount of discontinuity a tweet induces in the overall trend of a variable, we fitted three regression lines: line l_p through the intrinsic values of the preceding tweet sequence $1 \ldots i-1$, line l_f through the values of the following tweet sequence $i+1 \ldots n$ (n be the number of tweets in a claim), and line l_a through the entire tweet sequence $1 \ldots n$. The method is illustrated in Figure 2.

In order to measure the amount of discontinuity for each intrinsic variable at each tweet, we calculated the reset, i.e. the difference between the offset of l_p and the onset of l_f (*Reset*), and the deviation of each of these lines l_p and l_f from l_a in terms of root mean squared deviation (*RMSD_p*, and *RMSD_f*, respectively). The method was adopted from intonation research (Reichel and Mády, 2014), where it is used to quantify pitch discontinuities for prosodic boundary strength prediction.

Applying the reasoning of (Reichel and Mády, 2014), *Reset* quantifies the disruption at each tweet, and *RMSD_p,f* quantify the deviation of the tweet preceding and following regression lines from a common trend. Figure 2 gives an example how the regression lines preceding and following a tweet deviate less from a common trend for non-resolving tweets (left half) than for resolving tweets, expressed by lower values for *Reset, RMSD_p*, and *RMSD_f*. This example therefore illustrates a higher impact of the resolving tweet on the claim-level trends.

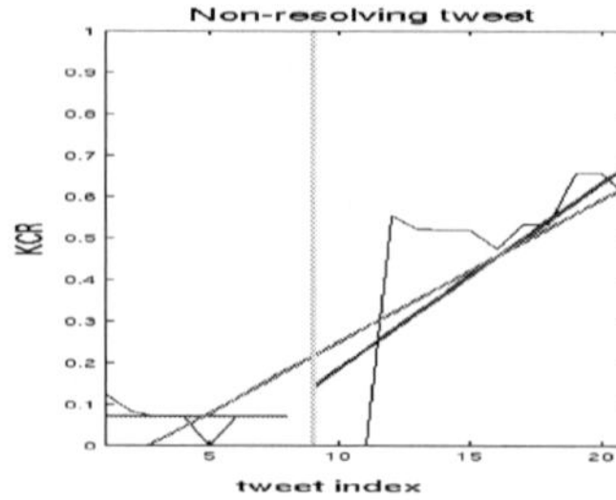
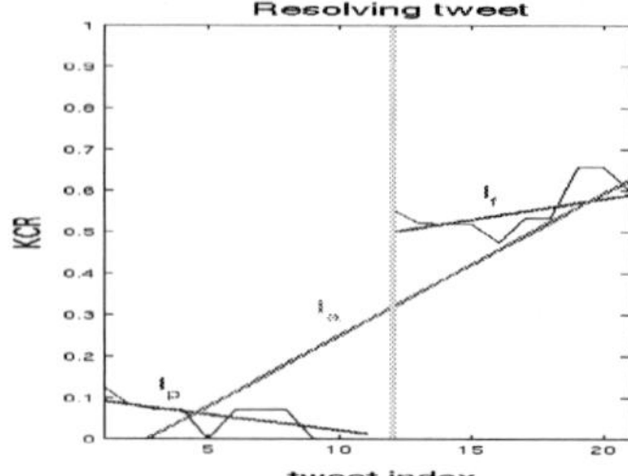

Figure 2: KCR trend analysis. For each tweet (green vertical line) three regression lines are fitted to the *KCR* sequence (black): to the preceding and the following sequence (l_p, l_f; blue), and to the entire rumor (l_a; red), the latter representing the general trend. For resolving tweets (right) l_p and l_f deviate more from a common trend, which is expressed by a larger reset as well as by larger root mean squared deviation values from the overall trend line l_a.

Results For all five tweet-intrinsic measures as well for the related sets of four derived local and global discontinuity measures we tested the difference between resolving and non-resolving tweets by linear mixed-effect models with each of the measures as dependent variable, $+/-$ *resolving tweet* (*RES*) and *Rumor is Resolved as True vs False* (*VAL*) as the fixed effects, and *event* as random effect. Due to the large number of tests p-values were corrected for false discovery rate (Benjamini and Yekutieli, 2001). All significant feature differences (after p-value correction, $p < 0.05$) for *RES* are shown in Figure 3.

The claim resolution value *VAL* turned out to affect the variables related to doubt cue ratio and to predicted certainty which is shown in Figure 4 ($p < 0.01$). Significant interactions between *RES* and *VAL* solely affect the doubt cue and certainty variables and are presented in Figure 5. All reported findings are discussed in Section 6.

5   Predicting the resolving tweet and its resolution value

As illustrated in Section 4 the distinction of tweets in rumor resolving and non-resolving as well as their resolution values have an impact on several of the examined cue ratio, certainty and discontinuity variables. Our next step thus was to use these variables to predict:

- for each tweet whether it resolves a rumor or not (*RES*),
- for each resolving tweet, whether its resolution value is True or False (*VAL*).

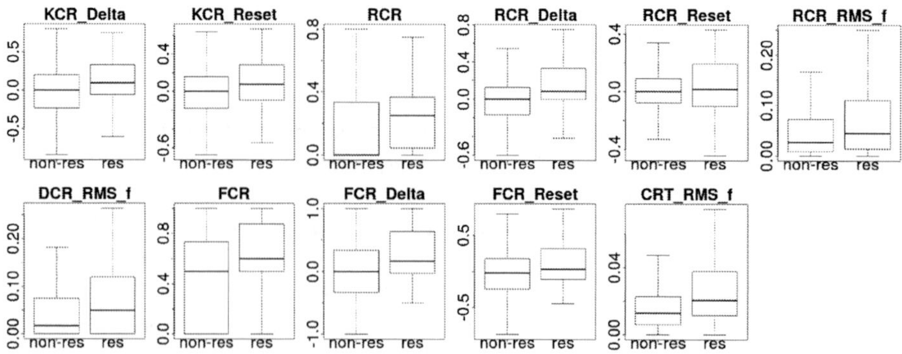

Figure 3: Significant differences between non-resolving (*non-res*) and resolving (*res*) tweets. Resolving tweets show higher values for tweet intrinsic properties (RCR, FCR=KCR+RCR), their local discontinuities (*_Delta), and their global trend discontinuities (*_Reset, *_RMS_f).

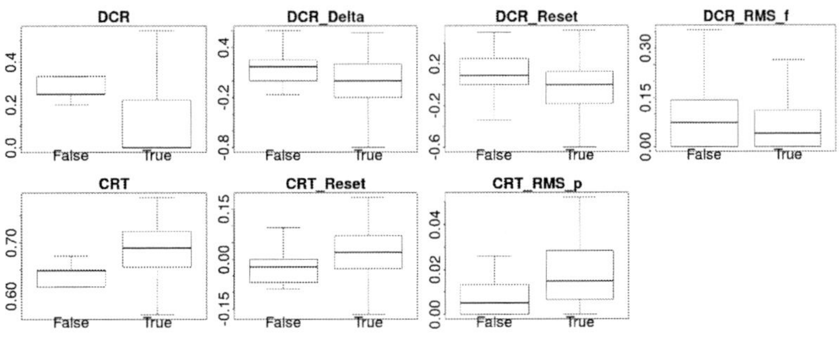

Figure 4: Significant differences for resolving tweets in claims validated as *True* vs *False*. In *verified* claims, resolving tweets show higher certainty cue (CRT) related values than non-resolving tweets. In *falsified* claims, resolving tweets show higher doubt cue (DCR) related values than non-resolving tweets.

Method For both binary classification tasks we enlarged the feature vector for each tweet by *tweet density*, i.e. the mean number of tweets per minute in a 10 minutes time window centered on the respective tweet. As for the features introduced above, also together with tweet density its four discontinuity measures (cf. Section 4) were added. We then subdivided the features into two sets:

- *CueSet:* consisting of all lexical knowledge, report, belief, and doubt cue ratios, their derived discontinuities, as well as tweet density and its discontinuities.
- *CertSet:* consisting of the predicted certainty values (cf. section 3) and their discontinuities instead of the raw cue ratios, and of the tweet density features.

This division serves to test whether raw cue ratio or derived certainty features are better suited for the two classification tasks. Task *RES* is carried out on all tweets in our data, whereas task *VAL* only applies to resolving tweets. Both tasks were carried out and evaluated in isolation to independently assess the respective performance. That is, the training and testing items for *VAL* were not taken over from the preceding *RES* classification output but from the original data set.

Since in both data sets the target value distributions are highly skewed, we applied resampling without replacement to avoid overlaps of training and test items in subsequent 10-fold cross-validation. The maximum sample size was determined as a weighted mean of the given sample sizes to ensure that for *VAL* and for *RES* the more frequent class occurs maximally twice as often as the less frequent one. By this resampling the amounts of claims and tweets (cf. section 2.1) were reduced to 39 (13 falsified, 26 verified claims) and 138 (46 resolving, 92 non-resolving tweets), respectively.

We then applied AdaBoostM1 classifiers (Freund and Schapire, 1999) (Matlab function *fitensemble*, 40 weak learners, minimum 2 items per leaf and 3 items per non-final node) to both data sets and comparatively evaluated the results in a ten-fold cross validation.

Results Table 1 summarizes the mean performance values on the held-out data after cross-validation. *BL Accuracy* represents the baseline performance which is defined as predicting only the most frequent class and is quite high due to the not entirely resolved skewedness. The results are discussed in the next section.

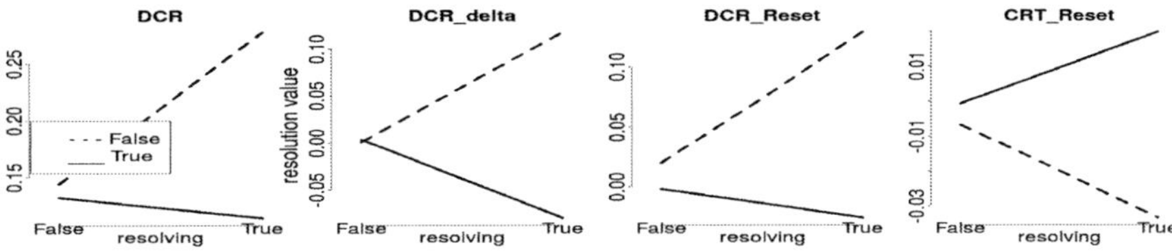

Figure 5: Interactions of the effects *Resolving* and *Resolution value*. For resolving tweets in verified and falsified claims, certainty (CRT) and doubt (DCR) cues behave in an opposite way; see Discussion.

Task	Feature set	wgt F1	wgt Recall	wgt Precision	Accuracy	BL Accuracy
RES	CueSet	0.74	0.73	0.74	0.77	0.67
RES	CertSet	0.69	0.71	0.75	0.70	0.67
VAL	CueSet	0.68	0.63	0.71	0.70	0.67
VAL	CertSet	0.76	0.79	0.96	0.74	0.67

Table 1: Average results after 10-fold cross validation on held-out data for the two tasks: tweet resolution (*RES*) and resolution value (*VAL*) prediction and the two feature sets *CueSet* (lexical cue ratios) and *CertSet* (predicted certainty values).

6 Discussion and conclusion

Relation between lexical cues and certainty   As described in Section 3, we established a link between lexical cue ratios of different certainty levels and the certainty associated to tweets by means of regression analysis. The zero-inflation problem as well as the reported low correlations between each cue ratio and the certainty values indicate that factuality values cannot fully be expressed by cue-type ratios in isolation but require a more complex model. Applying GLMs to bundle and therefore strengthen these weak relations was a first step in this direction. Certainty is a discourse-level phenomenon that lexical means can represent to some extent but not entirely. In future work we are going to address the representation of certainty phenomena related to higher linguistic levels.

Impact of rumor resolution on cue ratios and certainty   As pointed out in Section 4, for several examined cue ratio and certainty variables significant differences were observed with respect to claim resolution and resolution value. Resolving tweets show higher knowledge (*KCR*) and report cue ratios (*RCR*) as well as related discontinuities. Positive resets mark an abrupt increase in knowledge and report cues at the time point of resolution. This is even more pronounced when combining both cue ratio related features to a common one, the factuality cue ratio (*FCR= KCR + RCR*). Claim resolution has a major impact on the distribution of lexical cues associated with a high certainty level, as after resolution their amount increases. Belief cue ratios, on the contrary, have not proven to be of relevance for distinguishing between resolving and non-resolving tweets. Doubt cue and certainty variables are additionally highly dependent on the claim resolution value. Doubt cues occur more often in falsified claims and show a higher increase after claim resolution when compared to verified claims (*DCR_Delta, DCR_Reset, DCR_RMS_f*). Certainty cues behave exactly the opposite way: they are generally more frequent in verified claims (*CRT*) and at the resolution point they show an upward shift in verified but a downward shift in falsified claims (*CRT_Reset*). These interpretations are further supported by the *RES-VAL* interactions for the doubt cue and certainty variables, i.e. the amount and the direction of discontinuity at the resolution point of doubt cues and certainty values depends on whether the claim is verified or falsified.

Prediction of resolution and its value   Table 1 shows that the prediction tasks benefit from the feature sets in different ways. For task *RES*, the lexical cue set *CueSet* turned out to be more appropriate, while for *VAL* the certainty values *CertSet*. The reason might be that for *VAL* only resolving tweets and thus a lower amount of data is available suggesting the utility of shorter vectors containing derived instead of raw features. Importantly for sparse data scenarios, the generation of such an intermediate level of cue-integrating features, in our case the predicted certainty, turns out to be beneficial.

References

Yoav Benjamini and Daniel Yekutieli. 2001. The control of the false discovery rate in multiple testing under dependency. *Annals of Statistics*, 29:1165–1188.

Laure Berti-Équille and Javier Borge-Holthoefer. 2015. Veracity of data: From truth discovery computation algorithms to models of misinformation dynamics. *Synthesis Lectures on Data Management*, 7(3):1–155.

Steven Bird, Ewan Klein, and Edward Loper. 2009. *Natural Language Processing with Python*. O'Reilly Media.

Marie-Catherine de Marneffe, Christopher D Manning, and Christopher Potts. 2012. Did it happen? the pragmatic complexity of veridicality assessment. *Computational Linguistics*, 38(2):301–333.

Richárd Farkas, Veronika Vincze, György Móra, János Csirik, and György Szarvas. 2010. The CoNLL-2010 Shared Task: Learning to detect hedges and their scope in natural language text. In *Proceedings of the 14th Conference on Natural Language Learning*.

Christiane Fellbaum, editor. 1998. *WordNet: An Electronic Lexical Database*. MIT press, Cambridge, MA.

Samantha Finn, Panagiotis Takis Metaxas, and Eni Mustafaraj. 2014. Investigating rumor propagation with TwitterTrails. *arXiv preprint arXiv:1411.3550*.

Yoav Freund and Robert E. Schapire. 1999. A short introduction to boosting. *J. Japanese Society for Artificial Intelligence*, 14(5):771–780.

Halil Kilicoglu, Graciela Rosemblat, Michael J Cairelli, and Thomas C Rindflesch. 2015. A compositional interpretation of biomedical event factuality. *ExProM 2015*, page 22.

Sejeong Kwon and Meeyoung Cha. 2014. Modeling bursty temporal pattern of rumors. In *Proc. ICWSM*, pages 650–651.

Piroska Lendvai, Uwe D Reichel, and Thierry Declerck. 2016. Factuality drift assessment by lexical markers in resolved rumors. In *Joint Proceedings of the Posters and Demos Track of the 12th International Conference on Semantic Systems (SEMANTiCS 2016) and the 1st International Workshop on Semantic Change & Evolving Semantics, Leipzig*.

Jure Leskovec, Lars Backstrom, and Jon Kleinberg. 2009. Meme-tracking and the dynamics of the news cycle. In *Proc. of KDD-09*.

Michal Lukasik, P.K. Srijith, Duy Vu, Kalina Bontcheva, Arkaitz Zubiaga, and Trevor Cohn. 2016. Hawkes Processes for Continuous Time Sequence Classification: An Application to Rumour Stance Classification in Twitter. In *Proceedings of ACL-16*.

Jing Ma, Wei Gao, Zhongyu Wei, Yueming Lu, and Kam-Fai Wong. 2015. Detect rumors using time series of social context information on microblogging websites. In *Proceedings of the 24th ACM International on Conference on Information and Knowledge Management*, pages 1751–1754. ACM.

Roser Morante and Eduardo Blanco. 2012. *SEM 2012 shared task: Resolving the scope and focus of negation. In *Proceedings of the First Joint Conference on Lexical and Computational Semantics*.

Roser Morante and Caroline Sporleder, editors. 2012. *ExProm '12: Proceedings of the ACL-2012 Workshop on Extra-Propositional Aspects of Meaning in Computational Linguistics*. Association for Computational Linguistics.

Rob Procter, Farida Vis, and Alex Voss. 2013. Reading the riots on Twitter: methodological innovation for the analysis of big data. *International Journal of Social Research Methodology*, 16(3):197–214.

Vahed Qazvinian, Emily Rosengren, Dragomir R. Radev, and Qiaozhu Mei. 2011. Rumor has it: Identifying misinformation in microblogs. In *Proceedings of the Conference on Empirical Methods in Natural Language Processing*, EMNLP '11, pages 1589–1599.

Uwe D. Reichel and Katalin Mády. 2014. Comparing parameterizations of pitch register and its discontinuities at prosodic boundaries for Hungarian. In *Proc. Interspeech 2014*, pages 111–115.

Roser Saurí and James Pustejovsky. 2009. Factbank: A corpus annotated with event factuality. *Language Resources and Evaluation*, 43(3).

Roser Saurí and James Pustejovsky. 2012. Are you sure that this happened? Assessing the factuality degree of events in text. *Computational Linguistics*, 38(2):261–299.

Sandeep Soni, Tanushree Mitra, Eric Gilbert, and Jacob Eisenstein. 2014. Modeling factuality judgments in social media text. In *In Proc. of ACL*.

György Szarvas, Veronika Vincze, Richárd Farkas, György Móra, and Iryna Gurevych. 2012. Cross-genre and cross-domain detection of semantic uncertainty. *Computational Linguistics*, 38(2).

Irina P Temnikova, Andrea Varga, and Dogan Biyikli. 2014. Building a crisis management term resource for social media: The case of floods and protests. In *LREC*, pages 740–747.

Erik Velldal and Jonathon Read. 2012. Factuality detection on the cheap: Inferring factuality for increased precision in detecting negated events. In *Proceedings of the ACL-2012 Workshop on Extra-Propositional Aspects of Meaning in Computational Linguistics*.

Zhongyu Wei, Junwen Chen, Wei Gao, Binyang Li, Lanjun Zhou, Yulan He, and Kam-fai Wong. 2013. An Empirical Study on Uncertainty Identification in Social Media Context. In *Proceedings of ACL*.

Arkaitz Zubiaga, Maria Liakata, Rob Procter, Kalina Bontcheva, and Peter Tolmie. 2015. Towards Detecting Rumours in Social Media. *CoRR*, abs/1504.04712.

Arkaitz Zubiaga, Maria Liakata, Rob Procter, Geraldine Wong Sak Hoi, and Peter Tolmie. 2016. Analysing how people orient to and spread rumours in social media by looking at conversational threads. *PLoS ONE*, 11(3).

A Simple but Effective Approach to Improve Arabizi-to-English Statistical Machine Translation

Marlies van der Wees   **Arianna Bisazza**   **Christof Monz**
Informatics Institute, University of Amsterdam
`{m.e.vanderwees,a.bisazza,c.monz}@uva.nl`

Abstract

A major challenge for statistical machine translation (SMT) of Arabic-to-English user-generated text is the prevalence of text written in *Arabizi*, or Romanized Arabic. When facing such texts, a translation system trained on conventional Arabic-English data will suffer from extremely low model coverage. In addition, Arabizi is not regulated by any official standardization and therefore highly ambiguous, which prevents rule-based approaches from achieving good translation results. In this paper, we improve Arabizi-to-English machine translation by presenting a simple but effective Arabizi-to-Arabic transliteration pipeline that does not require knowledge by experts or native Arabic speakers. We incorporate this pipeline into a phrase-based SMT system, and show that translation quality after automatically transliterating Arabizi to Arabic yields results that are comparable to those achieved after human transliteration.

1 Introduction

Almost all current state-of-the-art statistical machine translation (SMT) systems for Arabic-to-English translation are trained on data comprising Modern Standard Arabic (MSA). MSA is widely used by professional publishers, such as news agencies, government agencies, and non-governmental organisations (NGOs). On the other hand, in user-generated content, such as weblogs, Internet forums, and short text messages, MSA is substantially less prevalent. Here one can often encounter dialectal variations resulting in a slightly different vocabulary and morphological constructions.

In addition to dialectal variations, user-generated content often also contains Arabic that is not written in the Arabic script, but in Romanized form, typically referred to as *Arabizi*. This is not to be confused with standardized research transliteration schemes such as the Buckwalter encoding for Arabic, or an official phonetic system such as Pinyin for Chinese. Instead, Arabizi encountered in user-generated text emerged from practical limitations such as the lack of an Arabic keyboard.

While Arabizi is not regulated by any standardization and many-to-many Arabizi-Arabic character mappings are ubiquitous, certain conventions have emerged. These conventions mostly rely on reflecting phonetic approximations by using a combination of numbers and Latin letters. Since Arabizi is mostly guided by pronunciation, it is also very sensitive to dialectal variations, which are more noticeable in spoken than in written Arabic. Note that some Arabizi representations are also based on orthographic similarities, such as '3' for the Arabic letter ع. Table 1 shows an example sentence in Arabizi, along with its MSA transliteration, Buckwalter transliteration and English translation, and illustrates the difference between Arabizi and formal transliteration.

Since Arabizi is highly ambiguous and difficult to transliterate with rule-based approaches, there is an extreme scarcity of gold standard transliterated Arabizi, making it a challenging task to develop data-driven statistical approaches involving Arabizi, such as Arabizi-to-English machine translation. Moreover, the standard data sets used by the MT research community do not contain Arabizi, meaning that any attempt to translate Arabic in Arabizi writing will suffer from extremely high (close to 100%) out-of-vocabulary (OOV) rates.

In this paper, we use a handful of small resources to build a simple but effective Arabizi-to-Arabic

43

Proceedings of the 2nd Workshop on Noisy User-generated Text,
pages 43–50, Osaka, Japan, December 11 2016.

Arabizi (lowercased)	la2 laa m7adsh by7eb el ka7k ela pappi :(w howa mesh henaaa
Arabic (human)	لا لا محدش بيحب ال كحك الا بابا : (و هو مش هنا
Arabic (Buckwalter)	lA lA mHd\$ byHb Al kHk AlA bAbA :(w hw m\$ hnA
English (human)	No, no one likes cookies except my father :(and he's not here

Table 1: Example sentence in Arabizi, along with its human Arabic transliteration, the corresponding Buckwalter transliteration, and its human English translation.

transliteration pipeline, which we incorporate into a state-of-the-art phrase-based SMT system. Concretely, our contributions are as follows:

(i) We present and release an Arabizi-to-Arabic transliteration pipeline that combines character-level mapping with contextual disambiguation of Arabic candidate words. We improve transliteration candidate selection by incorporating common Arabizi-Arabic word pairs. We evaluate our end-to-end Arabizi-English translation system using two test sets, and show that translation quality after automatically transliterating Arabizi to Arabic yields results that are comparable to those achieved after human transliteration.

(ii) We collect and release a web-crawled Arabizi-English parallel corpus of approximately 10,000 sentence pairs. Despite being too small to train a fully data-driven translation system, this corpus is useful for words that cannot be transliterated successfully by our transliteration pipeline.

2 Data sets and resources

For our Arabizi-to-English translation approach we use a number of data sources: First, in order to transliterate Arabizi to Arabic *words*, we start with an Arabizi to Arabic *character* mapping. Several such mappings can be found online, but the most comprehensive one we could find was the one from Wikipedia, see Table 2. We use this resource in Section 3.1 to generate transliteration candidates.

Arabic	Arabizi	Arabic	Arabizi	Arabic	Arabizi
آ , ئ , إ , ؤ , أ , ء	2	ز	z	ك	k , g
ا	a , e	س	s	ل	l
ب	b , p	ش	sh , ch	م	m
ت	t	ص	s , 9	ن	n
ث	s , th	ض	d , 9'	ه	h , a , e , ah , eh
ج	g , j , dj	ط	t , 6	ة	a , e , ah , eh
ح	7	ظ	z , dh , t' , 6'	و	w , o , u , ou , oo
خ	kh , 7' , 5	ع	3	ى , ي	y , i , ee , ei , ai , a
د	d	غ	gh , 3'	پ	p
ذ	z , dh , th	ف	f , v	چ	j , tsh , ch , tch
ر	r	ق	2 , g , q , 8 , 9		

Table 2: Mapping of Arabic letters to Arabizi character sequences. Source: Wikipedia. (http://en.wikipedia.org/wiki/Arabic_chat_alphabet).

Next, we use a large Arabic-English parallel corpus containing text in several genres. Since Arabizi is characteristic to user-generated text, we have included as much informal, user-generated parallel data as available. The resulting bitext contains 1.75M sentence pairs and 52.9M Arabic tokens, and comprises approximately 70% news data, mostly LDC-distributed, and 30% data in various other genres (weblogs, comments, editorials, speech transcripts, and small amounts of chat data), mostly harvested from the web. We use this corpus to (i) generate an Arabic vocabulary that guides transliteration candidate selection (Section 3.2), and (ii) to build our main Arabic-English SMT system in Section 4.

Next, we use a small data set released for the most recent NIST OpenMT evaluation campaign[1], containing approximately 10,000 triplets of manually transliterated and translated Arabizi/Arabic/English sentences belonging to the SMS and chat genres. Despite its small size, this 'tritext' contains information of very high quality that we exploit to improve our Arabizi-to-Arabic transliteration approach in Section 3.4. In addition, we extract from this corpus 1,788 Arabizi-Arabic triplets which we split into two test sets to test our pipeline in Sections 3.3 and 3.4, and to evaluate downstream Arabizi-to-English SMT performance in Section 4.

Finally, we use an Arabizi-English bitext crawled from a variety of web pages, containing user-generated comments to news articles which where originally written in Arabizi and translated into English by professional translators. This corpus contains approximately 10K sentence pairs and 180K Arabizi tokens. We use this bitext in Section 4 as part of our end-to-end SMT pipeline. While being too small to train an end-to-end SMT system, we believe that this corpus is a useful resource for researchers working with Arabizi, and we make the bitext available for download.[2]

3   Arabizi-to-Arabic Transliteration

In this section we describe our efforts to convert Arabizi words to Arabic words, which can then be translated into English using our MSA-to-English phrase-based SMT system. The complete transliteration pipeline, which we make available for download[2], is illustrated in Figure 1. The pipeline's methodological components (white boxes) are described in detail in Sections 3.1–3.4.

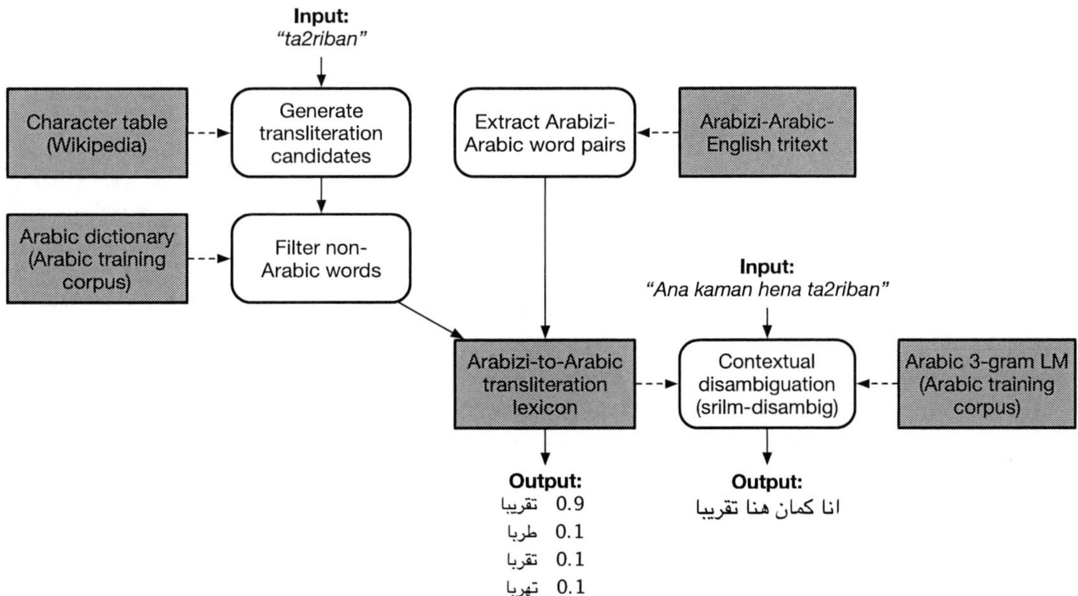

Figure 1: Arabizi-to-Arabic transliteration pipeline. White boxes represent methodological components, and grey boxes represent data components.

---

[1]LDC catalog number: LDC2013E125
[2]http://ilps.science.uva.nl/resources/arabizi/

3.1 Generating transliteration candidates

Table 2 shows that Arabizi-to-Arabic character mappings are often ambiguous, and in many cases Arabic script letters are represented by a sequence of two characters. This in turn introduces segmentation ambiguity as two individual Arabizi characters can be mapped separately to a sequence of two Arabic letters or the two Arabizi characters can be mapped together to a single Arabic script letter. This type of mapping problem is very reminiscent of the phrase-based SMT task assuming that Arabizi characters correspond to source words and sequences of Arabizi characters correspond to source word phrases.

Given this similarity we first cast the Arabizi to Arabic transliteration problem as a machine translation problem. The phrase table, i.e., translation model, consists of all possible character and character sequence mappings. Standard statistical machine translation systems use a word-based language model over target language sequences to estimate the fluency of translation hypotheses. Here, we use an Arabic-character based language model instead. Decoding is carried out in the same manner as the normal translation setting, except that the distortion limit is set to 0, enforcing monotone decoding. Note that while we opt for using a publicly available character table, it would also be possible to learn a character mapping and its corresponding probabilities from an Arabizi-Arabic bitext. This is done for example in related work by May et al. (2014).

An important problem at this point is that vowel mappings result in Arabic words having too many vowels orthographically present. This is particularly problematic for Arabizi words with repetitive vowels, a common phenomenon in user-generated text, such as observed in the word *henaaa* in Table 1. In order to address this problem, we allow for more flexible character mappings of vowels in which Arabizi vowels can be dropped. As a result, transliteration candidates for *henaaa* also include candidates for *hena*, among which the correct Arabic word هنا.

3.2 Filtering non-Arabic words

Using the described character mapping approach, we exhaustively consider all possible mappings, and therefore deliberately over-generate the number of Arabic word candidates. This can result in dozens and sometimes hundreds of Arabic character sequences, the vast majority of which are character sequences that are possible in Arabic, at least according to the 5-gram Arabic character language model, but are not actual words. To filter out these character sequences, all candidates are compared to a large Arabic vocabulary, and all candidates not occurring in the vocabulary are eliminated from further processing. The vocabulary contains 200K unique words, and is constructed from the Arabic side of all parallel corpora that we use for our SMT experiments in Section 4. Note that using this vocabulary can cause potentially correct Arabic words to be removed from the transliteration candidate list, as the vocabulary only covers the bitext. However, for the task of Arabizi-to-English translation this does not affect the final outcome as our SMT system can only predict English translations for Arabic words occurring in the bitext. For other downstream applications, a different or larger Arabic vocabulary can be used.

Restricting Arabic candidates to words occurring in the vocabulary reduces the number of candidates for a given Arabizi word considerably to approximately 5 to 10, and excludes transliteration candidates for Arabizi words with character repetitions, such as *henaaa* in Table 1.

3.3 Contextual disambiguation

The character mapping and filtering process results in an ambiguous Arabizi-to-Arabic transliteration lexicon. We feed this lexicon to srilm-disambig[3], a publicly available tool that searches for the best transliteration of each Arabizi sentence according to a 3-gram Arabic language model trained on the source side of the available parallel Arabic-English corpora.

Evaluated on the two Arabizi-Arabic test sets described in Section 2, our pipeline up to this point achieves a word-level transliteration error rate of about 50%, see top row in Table 3. Note that word-level error rate is much harsher than character-level error rate, but it gives us a better estimate of how

---

[3] http://www.speech.sri.com/projects/srilm/manpages/disambig.1.html

Transliteration method	Test set 1	Test set 2
Char.map.+disambig	46.4%	50.8%
Char.map.+disambig+word pairs	25.7%	27.9%

Table 3: Word-level transliteration error rates for two variants of our transliteration pipeline measured on two held-out test sets.

much noise will be propagated into the SMT system. With half of the words being wrongly transliterated, we can expect a very poor SMT quality at the end of the pipeline.

3.4 Improving transliteration using Arabizi-Arabic word pairs

Next, to reduce the error rate we exploit transliterated *word pairs* extracted from the Arabizi and Arabic sides of our tritext. These can be almost perfectly aligned at the word level (about 6% of the sentence pairs had a mismatching number of words and were discarded), yielding high-precision transliteration candidates. We add these word pairs to the transliteration lexicon used by srilm-disambig, giving them a high score (0.9 versus 0.1 for the other transliteration candidates) so that they will be preferred most of the time over the candidates generated by the character-level SMT system (see bottom of Figure 1). Adding this step to our pipeline results in a decrease of the word-level transliteration error rate from 50% to about 25% on the test sets, see bottom row in Table 3. From a manual inspection of a data sample, we find that a large part of the remaining transliteration errors are due to different possible spellings of English words in Arabic (e.g. *baby* / بابي or بيبي) or different spellings of Arabic dialectal forms (e.g. *when* / امته or امتى), which reveals the difficulty of evaluating Arabizi transliteration.

4 Arabizi-to-English machine translation

We examine the success of the proposed transliteration approaches by running Arabic-to-English SMT experiments, which we describe in Section 4.1 and discuss in Section 4.2.

4.1 Experimental setup

We perform our translation experiments using an in-house state-of-the-art phrase-based SMT system similar to Moses (Koehn et al., 2007). The system is trained on the collection of Arabic-English parallel corpora discussed in Section 2, comprising 1.75M lines (52.9M Arabic tokens) of parallel text. In addition, we use a 5-gram English language model that linearly interpolates different English Gigaword subcorpora with the English side of our bitext.

When no valid Arabic transliteration is found for an Arabizi word, our software component leaves it unchanged. To increase the chances of handling such cases, we exploit our in-house Arabizi-English corpus of web-crawled user comments (see Section 2), on which we train a separate Arabizi-English system. Instead of using this system for the actual translation task, which would suffer from very low coverage, we merge the Arabizi-English phrase translation and phrase reordering models to the main Arabic-English models using a fillup technique (Bisazza et al., 2011). In this way, a non-transliterated word that is not matched by the main Arabic-English models has still a chance of being translated directly by the Arabizi-English models.

We tokenize all Arabic data—training data as well as transliterated Arabizi—using the MADA toolkit (Habash and Rambow, 2005).

4.2 Results

Table 4 shows SMT quality measured with case-insensitive BLEU (Papineni et al., 2002) for a number of transliteration scenarios. First, we see that Arabizi-to-English translation without any preprocessing (top row) results in very poor translation quality. There is, however, a large difference in BLEU between the two test sets, with test set 2 achieving a surprisingly high score given that almost the entire source text is

| | Test set 1 | | Test set 2 | |
Preprocessing scheme	BLEU	% of gold standard	BLEU	% of gold standard
Original Arabizi	1.30	(14.4%)	4.99	(50.5%)
Char.map.+disambig	7.46	(82.6%)	9.42	(95.2%)
Char.map.+disambig+word pairs	8.68	(96.1%)	10.32	(104.3%)
Human transliteration	9.03	(100%)	9.89	(100%)

Table 4: BLEU scores of Arabizi-to-English translation experiments using different preprocessing schemes: no transliteration, two variants of our automatic transliteration pipeline, and human transliteration, respectively. The latter can be considered as a gold standard, so we also present the results relative to what is achieved by human transliteration.

unseen vocabulary. This result can be explained by the large portion of English words and emoticons in test set 2 with respect to test set 1: 25.7% of the source tokens in test set 2 match a target word in their corresponding reference sentence, as opposed to only 16.7% matching tokens in test set 1. English words in the source text are in most cases unknown to the SMT system but will not harm output quality if copied over to the output verbatim. See Table 5 for an example from test set 2 illustrating this observation.

Second, comparison of the two proposed transliteration variants (second and third row) shows that the approach that makes use of Arabizi-Arabic word pairs (third row) achieves better performance than the variant without word-pair information (second row). However, despite the large difference in word-level transliteration error rate between both variants (Table 3), BLEU differences are fairly small.

Finally, we compare our automatic transliteration approaches to human Arabizi-to-Arabic transliteration (bottom row) and notice that BLEU scores of our best automatic method are comparable to those achieved with human transliteration. Interestingly, for test set 2 we achieve higher BLEU scores with the new transliteration approach than with human transliterations. This observation can be explained by the prevalence of English words in the Arabizi source text. We observe numerous sentences where English words in the original Arabizi text were transliterated to Arabic in the human transliteration, leading to phrases that are unknown by the SMT system. In contrast, our transliteration pipeline can in most cases not find a valid Arabic word when transliterating an English word, and hence leaves the English word unchanged, which in turn may lead to correct output in the final translation. See Table 5 for an example that illustrates this scenario.

Preprocessing scheme	SMT input	SMT output
Original Arabizi	mashyyyy okay did you have fun	okay mashyyyy did you have fun
Char.map.+disambig	did you have fun ماشيي كي	in order to did you have fun
Char.map.+disambig+word pairs	did you have fun ماشي أوكي	ok, ok, did you have fun
Human transliteration	ماشي أوكي ضد يا هاف ف ان	ok, ok, against,,

Table 5: SMT input-output example pairs for a sentence containing English words in the original Arabizi text. English reference translation: **fine, okay, did you have fun?**.

5 Related work

In the past years, a few approaches to transliterate Arabizi to Arabic (or other tasks of *deromanizing* text in non-native Romanized script (Irvine et al., 2012)) have been presented, most of which rely to at least some extent on knowledge of experts or native speakers. In contrast, the approach we have presented does not rely on expert knowledge and is constructed using only publicly available data sources.

Chalabi and Gerges (2012) present a transliteration engine that, like our approach, follows the SMT paradigm. However, they complement their method with handcrafted rules.

A similar approach by Darwish (2014) focuses on Arabizi detection as well as conversion to Arabic. The former is important when Arabizi text is alternated with words from other languages, such as French or English, which it regularly is. While our approach leaves unconvertible words unchanged and often yields the right SMT output for English source words, addressing the problem of language detection before transliteration will likely benefit our approach.

Bies et al. (2014) present their work on manually transliterating Arabizi SMS and chat messages to Arabic. Their work is focused on releasing a new resource rather than presenting a transliteration methodology, and naturally yields high-quality transliteration.

Al-Badrashiny et al. (2014) use a weighted finite-state transducer (wFST) approach to converting Arabizi to Arabic in their system "3arrib". They incorporate linguistic information by using CODA, a conventional orthography for Dialectal Arabic (Habash et al., 2012) and morphological analysis, and thus heavily rely on expert knowledge.

All of the above focus on Arabizi-to-Arabic conversion outside the context of SMT from Arabizi. The work by May et al. (2014) is the only that presents an Arabizi-to-English SMT system, in which the authors not only focus on transliterating Arabizi to Arabic, but also evaluate performance in end-to-end Arabizi-to-English SMT experiments. Their transliteration approach uses wFSTs which are constructed by (i) experts, (ii) machine translation, or (iii) semi-automatically. In downstream SMT experiments, the semi-automatic construction performs best but depends partially on expert knowledge. The version of their approach in which wFSTs are constructed fully automatically is very similar to our approach, with a few main differences: While we start using a character mapping with uniform weights, they learn weights from an Arabizi-Arabic bitext. Next, they select the most probable transliteration candidates using Viterbi paths while we use srilm-disambig. Finally, we use Arabizi-Arabic parallel data to guide candidate selection, and Arabizi-English parallel data to enhance our SMT system. Unfortunately, the system of May et al. (2014) is not publicly available, making it impossible to compare performances.

Besides the described work, a few commercial systems for Arabizi conversion exist: Google Ta3reeb, Microsoft Maren, and Yamli. These are, however, not suitable for batch translation as is common in SMT research. Moreover, their approaches have not been published in the research community.

6 Conclusions

A major challenge for SMT of Arabic-to-English user-generated text is the prevalence of text written in *Arabizi*, or Romanized Arabic, which is typically not covered in the SMT models. In this paper we have presented our work on translating Arabizi into English by first transliterating Arabizi into Arabic using an approach that does not require knowledge of experts or native Arabic speakers.

Our transliteration pipeline uses character mapping following the phrase-based SMT paradigm, supplemented with vocabulary-based filtering and contextual disambiguation of candidate Arabic words. In addition, the availability of a small Arabizi-Arabic-English tritext allows us to (i) further improve the transliteration pipeline by prioritizing transliteration options that are supported by Arabizi-Arabic word pairs in the tritext, and (ii) evaluate our method in terms of transliteration error rates and in SMT experiments.

The transliteration pipeline exploiting Arabizi-Arabic word pairs yields considerably lower word-level transliteration error rates, dropping from approximately 50% for the simpler variant without word-pair information to 25% for the extended approach. When evaluating our approach in SMT experiments with two held-out test sets, we see that BLEU scores of the two variants reflect this large difference in error rate only to a limited extent. Furthermore, we have shown that translation quality after automatically transliterating Arabizi to Arabic yields results that are comparable to those achieved after human transliteration.

Finally, we make available for download both the transliteration pipeline software and a web-crawled Arabizi-English bitext of approximately 10,000 sentences.

Acknowledgements

This research was funded in part by the Netherlands Organization for Scientific Research (NWO) under project number 639.022.213. We thank the anonymous reviewers for their thoughtful comments.

References

Mohamed Al-Badrashiny, Ramy Eskander, Nizar Habash, and Owen Rambow. 2014. Automatic transliteration of romanized dialectal Arabic. In *Proceedings of the Eighteenth Conference on Computational Natural Language Learning*, pages 30–38, Ann Arbor, Michigan, June. Association for Computational Linguistics.

Ann Bies, Zhiyi Song, Mohamed Maamouri, Stephen Grimes, Haejoong Lee, Jonathan Wright, Stephanie Strassel, Nizar Habash, Ramy Eskander, and Owen Rambow. 2014. Transliteration of Arabizi into Arabic orthography: Developing a parallel annotated Arabizi-Arabic script sms/chat corpus. In *Proceedings of the EMNLP 2014 Workshop on Arabic Natural Langauge Processing (ANLP)*, pages 93–103.

Arianna Bisazza, Nick Ruiz, and Marcello Federico. 2011. Fill-up versus interpolation methods for phrase-based smt adaptation. In *Proceedings of the 8th International Workshop on Spoken Language Translation*, pages 136–143, San Fransisco, California, December.

Achraf Chalabi and Hany Gerges. 2012. Romanized Arabic transliteration. In *Proceedings of the Second Workshop on Advances in Text Input Methods (WTIM 2)*, pages 89–96.

Kareem Darwish. 2014. Arabizi detection and conversion to Arabic. In *Proceedings of the EMNLP 2014 Workshop on Arabic Natural Language Processing (ANLP)*, pages 217–224.

Nizar Habash and Owen Rambow. 2005. Arabic tokenization, part-of-speech tagging and morphological disambiguation in one fell swoop. In *Proceedings of the 43rd Annual Meeting on Association for Computational Linguistics*, pages 573–580.

Nizar Habash, Mona T Diab, and Owen Rambow. 2012. Conventional orthography for dialectal Arabic. In *LREC*, pages 711–718.

Ann Irvine, Jonathan Weese, and Chris Callison-Burch. 2012. Processing informal, romanized Pakistani text messages. In *Proceedings of the Second Workshop on Language in Social Media*, pages 75–78.

Philipp Koehn, Hieu Hoang, Alexandra Birch, Chris Callison-Burch, Marcello Federico, Nicola Bertoldi, Brooke Cowan, Wade Shen, Christine Moran, Richard Zens, Chris Dyer, Ondrej Bojar, Alexandra Constantin, and Evan Herbst. 2007. Moses: Open source toolkit for statistical machine translation. In *Proceedings of the 45th Annual Meeting of the Association for Computational Linguistics Companion Volume Proceedings of the Demo and Poster Sessions*, pages 177–180, Prague, Czech Republic, June. Association for Computational Linguistics.

Jonathan May, Yassine Benjira, and Abdessamad Echihabi. 2014. An Arabizi-English social media statistical machine translation system. In *Proceedings of the 11th Conference of the Association for Machine Translation in the Americas*, pages 329–341, Vancouver, Canada, October.

Kishore Papineni, Salim Roukos, Todd Ward, and Wei-Jing Zhu. 2002. Bleu: a method for automatic evaluation of machine translation. In *Proceedings of 40th Annual Meeting of the Association for Computational Linguistics*, pages 311–318, Philadelphia, Pennsylvania, USA, July. Association for Computational Linguistics.

Name Variation in Community Question Answering Systems

Anietie Andy
Howard University
anietie.andy@bison.howard.edu

Satoshi Sekine
New York University
sekine@cs.nyu.edu

Mugizi Rwebangira
Howard University
rweba@scs.howard.edu

Mark Dredze
Johns Hopkins University
mdredze@cs.jhu.edu

Abstract

Community question answering systems are forums where users can ask and answer questions in various categories. Examples are Yahoo! Answers, Quora, and Stack Overflow. A common challenge with such systems is that a significant percentage of asked questions are left unanswered. In this paper, we propose an algorithm to reduce the number of unanswered questions in Yahoo! Answers by reusing the answer to the most similar past resolved question to the unanswered question, from the site. Semantically similar questions could be worded differently, thereby making it difficult to find questions that have shared needs. For example, *Who is the best player for the Reds?* and *Who is currently the biggest star at Manchester United?* have a shared need but are worded differently; also, *Reds* and *Manchester United* are used to refer to the soccer team *Manchester United football club*. In this research, we focus on question categories that contain a large number of named entities and entity name variations. We show that in these categories, entity linking can be used to identify relevant past resolved questions with shared needs as a given question by disambiguating named entities and matching these questions based on the disambiguated entities, identified entities, and knowledge base information related to these entities. We evaluated our algorithm on a new dataset constructed from Yahoo! Answers. The dataset contains annotated question pairs, (Q_{given}, [Q_{past}, *Answer*]). We carried out experiments on several question categories and show that an entity-based approach gives good performance when searching for similar questions in entity rich categories.

1 Introduction

In community question answering (CQA) systems, users prefer asking other users questions because (I) their questions are personal and require a direct answer from users with similar experiences or users familiar with the question (II) no single web page can answer their question, and (III) users want to communicate and exchange ideas with other users. One of the challenges with such systems is that some questions are left unanswered because:

- they are short and lack relevant content
- they are not clearly expressed
- they are not appropriately assigned to a user that is able to answer the question

Approximately 15% of incoming English questions in Yahoo! Answers do not receive any answer and leave the user that asked the question (asker) unsatisfied (Shtok et al., 2012). One approach to reducing

Proceedings of the 2nd Workshop on Noisy User-generated Text,
pages 51–60, Osaka, Japan, December 11 2016.

the number of unanswered questions in a CQA is to direct an unanswered question to a user knowledgeable about the question (Dror et al., 2011). Another approach automatically extracts answers from a knowledge base (KB) such as Wikipedia, text passage, or the web (Gyongyi et al., 2007). In certain question categories in Yahoo! Answers, approximately 25% of questions are recurrent (Shtok et al., 2012). A third approach takes advantage of this question recurrence by reusing past resolved questions (PARQ) from within Yahoo! Answers to satisfy unanswered questions. Shtok et al. (2012) used this third approach to satisfy unanswered questions in the *Beauty & Style, Health*, and *Pets* question categories by matching new questions to PARQ's if they had a cosine similarity score above a threshold (0.9); features were then extracted from the new question and PARQ's to train a classifier. Certain question categories such as *Sports* have a high occurrence of named entities and entity name variations. For example, a sports team can be referred to by its official name, the name of the city it plays in or by any of several nicknames. Also, the vocabulary in questions in these categories can be diverse and questions are often very short (Klang and Nugues, 2014; Khalid et al., 2008).

The contribution of this paper is to propose an alternative approach to reducing the number of unanswered questions in question categories that contain a large number of entities by taking advantage of the recent successes in entity linking. We now have systems that can disambiguate named entities to a KB. Matching questions and answers based on these disambiguated entities, entities, and KB information related to these entities finds most of the relevant answers to a given question.

We investigate the validity of using an entity-based approach in entity rich categories by first analyzing 150 questions from each of the following categories *Beauty & Style, Health, Pets, Sports, Entertainment & Music* and *Parenting*.

Question category	Number of questions with named entities or entity variations
Beauty & Style	70
Health	73
Pets	64
Sports	130
Entertainment & Music	135
Parenting	95

Table 1: Number of questions with named entities or entity variations out of 150 questions from each category

Table 1 shows that more questions in the *Sports* and *Entertainment & Music* categories contain named entities and/or entity variations. We annotated 200 question pairs that each exhibit shared needs from the *Sports* and *Entertainment & Music* question categories. We observed that 82% of the relevant annotated question pairs contain either the same named entity or a variation of the entity. This percentage could increase on a larger dataset. We also observed that the cosine similarity score of the relevant question pairs varied i.e. the cosine similarity was high in some relevant question pairs and low in others. Hence, we propose to use an entity-based approach in question categories with high entity usage.

2   Related Work and Background

Yahoo! Answers is one of the largest and most popular CQA sites with more than 20 question categories. In Yahoo! Answers, there are two parts to a question: (I) the title - a brief description of the question, and (II) the content - a detailed description of the question (Dror et al., 2011). Posted questions are assigned to predefined categories, such as *Pets, Sports* and *Entertainment & Music* and these questions can be

answered by any signed-in user. An asked question remains *open* for four days, or for less if the asker
chose a *best answer* within this period. If no *best answer* is chosen by the asker, the task is delegated
to the community, which votes for the *best answer* until a clear winner arises. Only then is the question
considered *resolved*. In case a question is not answered while *open*, it is *deleted* from the site. Registered users may answer a limited number of questions each day, depending on their level (Dror et al.,
2011). Some of the categories of CQA questions are: *factoid, opinion-seeking, recommendation, open-
ended,* and *problem solving* questions. Different approaches have been proposed to reduce the number
of unanswered questions in Yahoo! Answers. Dror et al. (2011) focuses on matching unanswered questions to users that are presumed to be experts in the question topic i.e. "routes the right question to
the right user". This approach uses a multi-channel recommender system technology for associating an
unanswered question with potential answerers that are in an "answering mood". Also in this approach,
a wide variety of content and social signals users regularly provide to the CQA system are exploited
and organized into channels. Gyongyi et al. (2007) automatically generates answers to questions. In this
approach, text passages that may contain the answer to an unanswered question are retrieved and ranked.
The passage with the highest rank is selected to answer the unanswered question. Cao et al. (2011)
proposes an approach to utilizing category information to enhance the performance of question retrieval.
This approach combines the global relevance (the relevance of a query to a category) and the local relevance (the relevance of a query to a question in the category). The intuition behind this approach is that
the more related a category is to a query, the more likely it is that the category contains questions relevant
to the query. The model ranks a historical question based on an interpolation of two relevance scores:
one is a global relevance score between the query and the category containing the historical question, and
the other is a local relevance score between the query and the historical question (Cao et al., 2011). Bian
et al. (2008) attempts to rank past CQA question-answer pairs in response to factual questions. A supervised learning-to-rank algorithm is used to promote relevant past answers to the input question based on
textual properties of the question and the answer, as well as indicators for the answerers quality (Shtok
et al., 2012). In Bian et al. (2008), the goal is to detect if a relevant answer exists, and the scope is not
limited to factual questions. Carmel et al. (2000) proposes to find past questions that are similar to the
target question, based on the hypothesis that answers to similar questions should be relevant to the target
question. This approach ranks past questions using both inter-question and question-answer similarity,
with response to a newly posed questions (Shtok et al., 2012). Jeon et al. (2005) demonstrates that similar
answers are a good indicator of similar questions. Once pairs of similar questions are collected based on
their similar answers, they are used to learn a translation model between question titles to overcome the
lexical chasm when retrieving similar questions (Jeon et al., 2005). Wang et al. (2011) matches similar
questions by assessing the similarity between their syntactic parse tree structure (Shtok et al., 2012). This
approach retrieves semantically similar questions and questions with shared needs. Shtok et al. (2012)
answers unanswered questions by reusing similar PARQ. This approach searches a dataset of PARQ for
similar questions to an unanswered question. The answer to the most similar PARQ is used to answer
the unanswered question. This approach relies on the intuition that even if personal and narrow, some
questions are recurrent enough to allow for at least a few new questions to be answered by past material.
Klang and Nugues (2014) shows that resolving entity disambiguations in question answering systems
helps in retrieving relevant answers to a question from documents or passages. Given a question, (Klang
and Nugues, 2014) uses a named entity disambiguation module to merge entities in a question answering

system. Strings that could be linked to a unique identifier are merged and a list of synonyms with the resulting set is created. The candidate answers to a question were ranked based on their frequency i.e. the number of candidate occurrences after merging. This approach shows that a candidate merging step using a named entity linking module produces high precision results. Khalid et al. (2008) investigates the impact of named entity normalization (NEN) on two specific information access tasks: document and passage retrieval for question answering (QA). These tasks consist in finding items in a collection of documents, which contain an answer to a natural language question. In the NEN task, a system identifies a canonical unambiguous referent for names like Bush or Alabama(Khalid et al., 2008). Two entity normalization methods based on Wikipedia in the context of both passage and document retrieval for question answering were evaluated. It was found that normalization methods lead to improvements of early precision, for both document and passage retrieval.

3 Entity Name Variation in CQA systems

Due to the lack of uniformity in CQA users writing styles (Khalid et al., 2008), the lack of content in some questions, and the frequent use of entity name variations in question categories with a large number of entities, it is necessary to use an entity-based approach to find PARQ with shared needs to a given question. In order to retrieve most of the relevant PARQ to a given question with high precision, it is important to identify the named entities and entity variations in the given question and PARQ. For example, *Q1* and *Q2* below are questions with a shared need referring to *Pro MLB umpire* and *Major League Baseball Umpire* respectively.

- *Q1: How does any one become a Pro MLB umpire?*
- *Q2: How can I become a Major League Baseball Umpire?*

The proposed algorithm, ENTITY-ALCHEMY has 2 stages:

3.1 Stage 1

Given the question pair, (Q_{given}, [Q_{past}, *Answer*]), where Q_{given} represents a given question, Q_{past} represents a past resolved question, and *Answer* is the answer to Q_{past} (Shtok et al., 2012), ENTITY-ALCHEMY identifies named entities in (Q_{given} and Q_{past}) and links these entities to an external KB, using entity linking, to find their name variations and anchor phrases (surface form), textual phrases that potentially link to the entity in the KB (Guo et al., 2013). Using the question-title for retrieval of similar questions in a CQA is of highest effectiveness, while using the question body results in lower Mean Average Precision (MAP) (Shtok et al., 2012). In this stage, we identify named entities and entity variations in the question-title section of Q_{given} and Q_{past}. ENTITY-ALCHEMY selects Q_{past} as a candidate similar question to Q_{given} if both questions have a common entity, entity name variation, or anchor phrases.

3.2 Stage 2

In stage 2, the algorithm extracts features from a pair of Q_{given} and Q_{past}, selected in stage 1. The extracted features are used to score whether the answer to Q_{past} can be used to satisfy the given question, Q_{given}.

3.2.1 Features

Entities and KB information: We collect the following statistics from (Q_{given} and Q_{past}): number of common entities, number of common entity variations, number of common anchor phrases, number of common words or phrases.

Lexical Analysis: We classify words in (Q_{given} and Q_{past}) into their parts-of-speech and extract the number of matching nouns, verbs, and adjectives, if they exist.

Cosine similarity: Cosine similarity is popularly used to show the similarity between documents (Salton and McGill , 1986). We calculate the cosine similarity of the "title" and "title + content" of (Q_{given} and Q_{past}).

Dice coefficient: Misspelled words are common in CQA systems. We use dice coefficient to calculate the string similarity score between identified entities in (Q_{given} and Q_{past}).

Word2vec feature: Mikolov et al. (2013) introduced an efficient implementation of the continuous bag-of-words and skip-gram techniques that can be used for learning high-quality word vectors from huge datasets with billions of words and with millions of words in its vocabulary called word2vec (Mikolov et al., 2013). We trained a word2vec model with a Wikipedia dump and 200 question pairs from Yahoo! Answers.

3.2.2   Classifier model

For learning, we used SVM with a polynomial kernel as implemented by Weka machine learning workbench (Hall et al., 2009). The default SVM parameters were used.

4   Experiments

4.1   Experimental Setup

For this research we used a repository of PARQ from Yahoo! Answers. Since we are interested in finding PARQ with answers that can satisfy a given question, we selected the best answers for each question in the *Sports* and *Entertainment & Music* question categories. We selected these question categories because of the high recurrence of questions and the high occurrence of named entities and named entity variations in these question categories.

4.2   Data Construction and Labeling

The dataset used to train and evaluate our system contains question pairs, (Q_{given}, [Q_{past}, *Answer*]), where Q_{given}, Q_{past}, and *Answer* belong to the Yahoo! Answers repository. Each question pair was associated with a label, described below:

- *Potential answer*: given a question pair, (Q_{given},[Q_{past}, *Answer*]), *Answer* is a "potential answer" if it can be used to satisfy Q_{given}.
- *Similar question*: Q_{past} is similar to Q_{given} if they both refer to the same topic[1], but the answer to Q_{past} cannot be used to satisfy Q_{given}.
- *Related question:* Q_{past} is related to Q_{given} if it contains a common entity as Q_{given}, but refers to a different topic from Q_{given}.

We sampled 1500 resolved questions from the *Sports* and *Entertainment & Music* question categories (750 from each question category) and observed that approximately 20% and 17% respectively of the sampled questions were recurring. To generate the given question and PARQ pair, (Q_{given}, [Q_{past}, *Answer*]), we selected 3000 and 5000 PARQ from the *Sports* and *Entertainment & Music* question categories respectively from the language data section of Yahoo labs Webscope[TM] dataset, and Yahoo!

---

[1] A topic is an activity or event along with all directly related events and activities. A question is on topic when it discusses events and activities that are directly connected to the topic's seminal event

Answers dataset (Chang et al., 2008). Given a question from the selected dataset of PARQ, we selected a candidate similar question in the selected dataset if it had a common named entity, entity variation or anchor phrase as the given question. We had three independent reviewers label the question pairs as either a *potential answer, similar question*, or *related question*. We selected a question pair if at least two of the reviewers agreed on the question pair label. We annotated 500 question pairs from the *Sports* and *Entertainment & Music* question categories. Table 2 shows the number of question pairs and their labels in each of the question categories. Table 4 presents some of the named entities and their variations in our dataset. In each of the question categories, we calculated the reviewer agreements by using Fleiss' kappa[2] Table 3 shows the calculated kappa values. This dataset will be provided to the research community.

We used an entity linking tool, AlchemyAPI (Turian, 2013) to extract named entities, named entity disambiguations, and anchor phrases from a given question and a PARQ. AlchemyAPI extracts anchor phrases from the following KB's, dbpedia and freebase. In our experiments we split our dataset by using 66% for training and 34% for testing. We conducted two baseline experiments on our dataset using SVM described in *Section 3.21*.

Category	Sports	Entertainment & music
Potential answer	130	141
Similar question	64	40
Related question	65	60

Table 2: Number of question pairs in each question pair category

Question Categories	Kappa
Sports	0.579
Entertainment & Music	0.55

Table 3: Fleiss' Kappa calculation in each question category

Named Entity	Entity Name Variation
English Premier League	EPL, premier league
New York City marathon	NYC marathon
Jonas brothers	Jonas bros
Manchester United	Man u, munited

Table 4: Some named entities and their name variations in our dataset

Below are examples of question pairs in each question pair category:

Question pair 1

How do you get on Oprah?

<potential answer>

How do I get on the Oprah Winfrey show?

Question pair 2

how do i win to Germany to watch the FIFA WORLD CUP?

<similar question>

how do i get tickets for Fifa Worldcup 2006 in Germany ?

---

[2] Fleiss kappa assesses the reliability of the agreement between the raters when assigning labels to the question pairs.

Question pair 3

How can I get on the Jay Leno show?

<related question>

how do i get salmas hayek interview with jay leno on march 3 2006?

4.3   Evaluation Metric

We measure the *precision*, *recall*, and *accuracy* of the proposed algorithm.

Precision: the fraction of returned answers that are correct i.e. *potential answers*.

Recall: the fraction of the labelled *potential answer* question pairs that where returned by the system.

Accuracy: the overall fraction of *potential answer* question pairs classified correctly.

4.4   Results

The first baseline, *ENT*, uses AlchemyAPI to extract named entities from a question pair. The extracted entities are not disambiguated to a KB and anchor phrases from the named entities KB entries are not extracted. In this baseline, we aim to find the most similar PARQ with common entities as a given question. *ENT* has two stages: In stage 1, given a question pair, (Q_{given}, [Q_{past}, Answer]), we select Q_{past} if it contains a common named entity as (Q_{given}). In stage two, we extract the features described in *section 3.2.1* from the question pair.

Yahoo! Answers is an informal forum, hence, there is a high prevalence of misspelled words. The second baseline, *ENT-VARIANT* aims to find the most similar PARQ with common entities and minor entity spelling errors as a given question. *ENT-VARIANT* uses AlchemyAPI to identify the named entities in each question in a question pair. *ENT-VARIANT* has two stages. In stage 1, given a question pair, (Q_{given}, [Q_{past}, Answer]), we select Q_{past} if it contains a common named entity as (Q_{given}). Also, dice coefficient is used to compare the identified named entities in Q_{given} and Q_{past}. This comparison helps resolve minor spelling errors in the question pair. In our experiments, two named entities in Q_{given} and Q_{past} respectively, are considered a variation with minor spelling errors if they have a dice coefficient $>$ 0.75. In stage 2 of *ENT-VARIANT*, we extract the features described in *section 3.2.1* from the question pair.

ENTITY-ALCHEMY performed better than both baselines as shown in Table 5. This shows that identifying named entities, disambiguated entities to a KB and, extracting anchor phrases from the identified named entities KB entries finds more relevant PARQ to a given question.

Algorithm	Precision	Recall
ENT	66%	43.05%
ENT-VARIANT	67.1%	44.5%
ENTITY-ALCHEMY	71%	55.15%

Table 5: Precision and recall of ENTITY-ALCHEMY and two baselines

For each of the question categories we measured the accuracy, as defined in *section 4.3*, of the baseline algorithms and ENTITY-ALCHEMY. Table 6 presents the accuracy of ENTITY-ALCHEMY and the two baselines on the *Sports* and *Entertainment & Music* question categories . Most of the entity variations in our dataset are not minor spelling errors, hence the second baseline, ENT-VARIANT did not perform a lot better than the first baseline, ENT.

Algorithm	Sports	Entertainment & music
ENT	54%	40%
ENT-VARIANT	55%	42%
ENTITY-ALCHEMY	60%	62%

Table 6: Accuracy of ENTITY-ALCHEMY and the baselines

We tested ENTITY-ALCHEMY on a question category, *Parenting*, which contains few named entities and entity name variations to see how well it will perform. We extracted 500 questions from the *Parenting* question category of Yahoo! Answers and selected question pairs from this extracted dataset by applying stage 1 of ENTITY-ALCHEMY. Table 7 shows the results of ENTITY-ALCHEMY and cosine similarity on the *Sports* and *Parenting* question categories. ENTITY-ALCHEMY identified 51% of similar questions that exhibited shared needs. We also selected question pairs by conducting cosine similarity and our experiments showed that in this question category, a cosine similarity > 0.5 identified 87% of similar questions that exhibited a shared need. We applied cosine similarity to the *Sports* question category by selecting question pairs that exhibit shared needs from 500 extracted questions from the *Sports* category. Our experiments show that ENTITY-ALCHEMY identified 83% of the similar question pairs that exhibited a shared need and a cosine similarity > 0.5 identified 49% of the similar questions. Hence in question categories with less entity and entity variation usage, a non-entity-based approach such as cosine similarity should be used to find similar questions with shared needs to a given question. Also, in entity rich question categories, an entity-based approach should be used when searching for questions with shared needs.

Algorithm	Sports	Parenting
Cosine Similarity	49%	87%
ENTITY-ALCHEMY	83%	51%

Table 7: Comparing cosine similarity and entity-based approaches in the Sports and Parenting question categories

5   Conclusion

In this paper, we proposed an algorithm, ENTITY-ALCHEMY to reduce the number of unanswered questions in question categories with high entity usage. We evaluated our algorithm on a CQA dataset with a lot of entities and entity variations and our algorithm performed better than two baselines.

In conclusion, reusing PARQ is an effective method for reducing the number of unanswered questions in a CQA system. This paper showed that in question categories with a lot of named entities and entity name variations, using KB information and applying entity linking to identify and disambiguate named entities finds most of the similar PARQ to a given question.

6   Future Work

In the future, we would research time-sensitive questions especially common in *Sports* categories. Also, we would implement an algorithm that can find similar questions to a given question regardless of the question category.

Acknowledgements

This work was supported by the Center for Science of Information (CSoI), an NSF Science and Technology Center, under grant agreement CCF-0939370.

References

American Psychological Association. 1983. *Publications Manual.* American Psychological Association, Washington, DC.

Association for Computing Machinery. 1983. *Computing Reviews*, 24(11):503–512.

Ashok K. Chandra, Dexter C. Kozen, and Larry J. Stockmeyer. 1981. Alternation. *Journal of the Association for Computing Machinery*, 28(1):114–133.

Dan Gusfield. 1997. *Algorithms on Strings, Trees and Sequences.* Cambridge University Press, Cambridge, UK.

Bowman Mic, Debray K. Saumya, and Peterson L. Larry. 1993. *Reasoning About Naming Systems*, volume 15. ACM Trans. Program. Lang. Syst.

Shtok, Anna and Dror, Gideon and Maarek, Yoelle and Szpektor, Idan 2012. *Learning from the past: answering new questions with past answers Proceedings of the 21st international conference on World Wide Web* 759–768

Dror, Gideon and Maarek, Yoelle and Szpektor, Idan 2011. *I want to answer; who has a question?: Yahoo! answers recommender system Proceedings of the 17th ACM SIGKDD international conference on Knowledge discovery and data mining* 1109–1117

Rao, Delip and McNamee, Paul and Dredze, Mark 2013. *Entity linking: Finding extracted entities in a knowledge base Springer Multi-source, multilingual information extraction and summarization* 93–115

Soricut, Radu and Brill, Eric 2004. In *Automatic Question Answering: Beyond the Factoid HLT-NAACL* 57–64

Horowitz, Damon and Kamvar, Sepandar D 2010. *The anatomy of a large-scale social search engine* In *Proceedings of the 19th international conference on World wide web, ACM* 431–440

Voorhees, Ellen M and Tice, DM 2000. *Overview of the TREC-9 Question Answering Track* In *Proceedings of TREC*

Strzalkowski, Tomek and Harabagiu, Sanda 2006. *Advances in open domain question answering*, volume 32 Springer Science & Business Media

Klang, Marcus and Nugues, Pierre 2014. *Named entity disambiguation in a question answering system* In *Proceedings of The Fifth Swedish Language Technology Conference (SLTC 2014)*

Khalid, Mahboob Alam and Jijkoun, Valentin and De Rijke, Maarten 2008. *Advances in Information Retrieval Springer* 705–710

Chang, Ming-Wei and Ratinov, Lev-Arie and Roth, Dan and Srikumar, Vivek 2008. *Importance of Semantic Representation: Dataless Classification* In *proceedings AAAI* 830–835

Salton, Gerard and McGill, Michael J 1986. *Introduction to modern information retrieval* McGraw-Hill, Inc.

Mikolov, Tomas and Chen, Kai and Corrado, Greg and Dean, Jeffrey 2013. *Efficient estimation of word representations in vector space arXiv preprint arXiv:1301.3781*

Liu, Xiaoyong and Croft, W Bruce 2002. *Passage retrieval based on language models* In *Proceedings of the eleventh international conference on Information and knowledge management, ACM* 375–382

Corrada-Emmanuel, Andres and Croft, W Bruce and Murdock, Vanessa 2003. *Passage retrieval based on language models Journal of Center Intell. Inf. Retrieval, Univ. Massachusetts, Amherst, MA, Tech. Rep.{Online}. Available: http://ciir. cs. umass. edu/pubfiles/ir-283. pdf*

Tellex, Stefanie and Katz, Boris and Lin, Jimmy and Fernandes, Aaron and Marton, Gregory 2003. *Quantitative evaluation of passage retrieval algorithms for question answering* In *Proceedings of the 26th annual international ACM SIGIR conference on Research and development in informaion retrieval* 41–47

Guo, Stephen and Chang, Ming-Wei and Kiciman, Emre 2013. *To Link or Not to Link? A Study on End-to-End Tweet Entity Linking HLT-NAACL* 1020–1030

Huang, Anna 2008. *Similarity measures for text document clustering* In *Proceedings of the sixth new zealand computer science research student conference (NZCSRSC2008), Christchurch, New Zealand* 49–56

Mikolov, Tomas and Sutskever, Ilya and Chen, Kai and Corrado, Greg S and Dean, Jeff 2013. *Distributed representations of words and phrases and their compositionality Advances in neural information processing systems* 3111–3119

Mikolov, Tomas and Yih, Wen-tau and Zweig, Geoffrey 2013. *Linguistic Regularities in Continuous Space Word Representations.* *HLT-NAACL* 746–751

Xue, Xiaobing and Jeon, Jiwoon and Croft, W Bruce 2008. *Retrieval models for question and answer archives* In *Proceedings of the 31st annual international ACM SIGIR conference on Research and development in information retrieval, ACM* 475–482

Zhou, Yun and Croft, W Bruce 2007. *Query performance prediction in web search environments* In *Proceedings of the 30th annual international ACM SIGIR conference on Research and development in information retrieval* 543–550

Nadeau, David and Sekine, Satoshi 2007. *A survey of named entity recognition and classification* *Lingvisticae Investigationes*, 30(1):3–26

Gyongyi, Zoltan and Koutrika, Georgia and Pedersen, Jan and Garcia-Molina, Hector 2007. *Questioning yahoo! answers* Stanford InfoLab

Mihalcea, Rada and Csomai, Andras 2007. *Wikify!: linking documents to encyclopedic knowledge* In *Proceedings of the sixteenth ACM conference on Conference on information and knowledge management* 233–242

Hoffart, Johannes and Yosef, Mohamed Amir and Bordino, Ilaria and Fürstenau, Hagen and Pinkal, Manfred and Spaniol, Marc and Taneva, Bilyana and Thater, Stefan and Weikum, Gerhard 2011. *Robust disambiguation of named entities in text* In *Proceedings of the Conference on Empirical Methods in Natural Language Processing* 782–792

Shah, Chirag and Pomerantz, Jefferey 2010. *Evaluating and predicting answer quality in community QA* In *Proceedings of the 33rd international ACM SIGIR conference on Research and development in information retrieval* 411–418

Jeon, Jiwoon and Croft, W Bruce and Lee, Joon Ho 2005. *Finding similar questions in large question and answer archives* In *Proceedings of the 14th ACM international conference on Information and knowledge management* 84–90

Jeon, Jiwoon and Croft, W Bruce and Lee, Joon Ho 2009. *The WEKA data mining software: an update* Journal ACM SIGKDD explorations newsletter, 11(1):10–18

Turian, Joseph 2013. *Using AlchemyAPI for Enterprise-Grade Text Analysis.* Technical report, AlchemyAPI

Yao, Xuchen 2014. *Feature-driven Question Answering with Natural Language Alignment* CreativeSpace Independent Publishing Platform

Cao, Xin and Cong, Gao and Cui, Bin and Jensen, Christian S 2010. *A generalized framework of exploring category information for question retrieval in community question answer archives* In Proceedings of the 19th international conference on World wide web, 181(24):201–210

Wang, Kai and Ming, Zhaoyan and Chua, Tat-Seng 2009. *A syntactic tree matching approach to finding similar questions in community-based qa services* In Proceedings of the 32nd international ACM SIGIR conference on Research and development in information retrieval, 187–194

Bian, Jiang and Liu, Yandong and Agichtein, Eugene and Zha, Hongyuan 2008. *Finding the right facts in the crowd: factoid question answering over social media* In Proceedings of the 19th international conference on World wide web, 181(24):201–210

Carmel, David and Shtalhaim, Menachem and Soffer, Aya 2000. *eResponder: Electronic question responder* Springer, (24):150–161

Whose Nickname is This?
Recognizing Politicians from Their Aliases

**Wei-Chung Wang[†], Hung-Chen Chen[†], Zhi-Kai Ji[*],
Hui-I Hsiao[*], Yu-Shian Chiu[*], Lun-Wei Ku[†]**

[†]Academia Sinica, Taiwan
{anthonywang, hankchen, lwku}@iis.sinica.edu.tw
[*]Data Analytics Technology & Applications Research Institute,
Institute for Information Industry, Taipei, Taiwan
{kevinchi, hhsiao, samuelchiu}@iii.org.tw

Abstract

Using aliases to refer to public figures is one way to make fun of people, to express sarcasm, or even to sidestep legal issues when expressing opinions on social media. However, linking an alias back to the real name is difficult, as it entails phonemic, graphemic, and semantic challenges. In this paper, we propose a phonemic-based approach and inject semantic information to align aliases with politicians' Chinese formal names. The proposed approach creates an HMM model for each name to model its phonemes and takes into account document-level pairwise mutual information to capture the semantic relations to the alias. In this work we also introduce two new datasets consisting of 167 phonemic pairs and 279 mixed pairs of aliases and formal names. Experimental results show that the proposed approach models both phonemic and semantic information and outperforms previous work on both the phonemic and mixed datasets with the best top-1 accuracies of 0.78 and 0.59 respectively.

1 Introduction

Due to the casual nature of social media, there exist a large number of non-standard words in text expressions which make it substantially different from formal written text. It is reported in (Liu et al., 2011b) that more than four million distinct out-of-vocabulary (OOV) tokens occur in the Edinburgh Twitter corpus (Petrovic et al., 2010). This variation poses challenges for natural language processing (NLP) tasks (Sproat et al., 2001). According to (Baldwin et al., 2015), on encountering the many non-standard words, found actually to be unknown named entities, they were obliged to manually eliminate these while normalizing the dataset. Thus, we believe that named entity matching (NEM) is an important problem in noisy text analysis.

NEM is the task of matching the different alias names for entities back to their respective formal names. Many applications benefit from this technique, including name transliteration (Knight and Graehl, 1998), entity linking (Rao et al., 2013), entity clustering (Green et al., 2012), and entity identification for paraphrase mining (Barzilay and Lee, 2003).

This task is different from most in noisy text normalization. While most work on normalization includes two parts—informal word identification and word recovery—this work is different in two ways. First, we focus on the recovery of informal names of named entities, in contrast to the general typo and abbreviation recovery. Second, the identification of these aliases is a named entity recognition (NER) problem, while conventional normalization works search for every OOV words. The challenges of NEM lie in variation, which can be attributed to many factors: nicknames, acronyms, and differences in transliteration. As a result, exact string matching can yield poor results. It is reported (Peng et al., 2015) that

Proceedings of the 2nd Workshop on Noisy User-generated Text,
pages 61–69, Osaka, Japan, December 11 2016.

most tokenization errors are caused by named entities in documents. It is difficult to utilize analysis tools which depend on tokenized text. While most normalization can be achieved using features within words, for example, ('u', 'you') and ('2mr', 'tomorrow'), aliases and formal names may have no graphemic or phonemic connections, for instance, ('Slick Willie', 'Bill Clinton').

In this paper, we propose a novel method to train word models for each named entity with full-connected hidden Markov models (HMMs). We create two datasets of aliases and formal name pairs: one similar-phonemic pair only dataset and one mixed dataset including both similar-phonemic and non-similar-phonemic pairs. In both datasets, our method outperforms all of the baselines, including (Peng et al., 2015). In the mixed dataset, some aliases have no connection with the formal name within words. Combining our model with the statistical PMI measurement improves performance.

Our contributions are as follows. First, we propose a new method to solve the character sequence disorder problem for the NEM task. Second, we propose a new method for pairs of aliases and formal names which contain no graphemic or phonetic similarity. Third, in our experiment, our method outperforms other baselines on both datasets.

Below, we describe in Section 2 the related work for the task and in Section 3 the phonetic similarity formula. The implementation of the word model and the proposed refined version are described in Sections 4 and 5. The dataset collection, evaluation, and error analysis are in Section 6.

2   Related Work

Entity disambiguation is not an uncommon task. Related work such as entity coreferencing (Soon et al., 2001; Ponzetto and Strube, 2006; Moosavi and Strube, 2014) identifies entities which are mentioned more than once in formal documents. The literature contains extensive discussion on the effects of using segmentation, POS taggers, and semantic role labeling, which have achieved considerably high resolution. However, most of those canonical technologies fail to provide accurate information in user-generated text. Normalization on noisy text is also a highly debated topic. Most words must be normalized in this task; this includes abbreviations, non-standard spellings, and phrases prevalent in social media. Rather than considering all parts of speech, our task focuses on aliases of name entities, especially person entities.

Among those different tasks, some useful metrics can be applied to NEM given appropriate refinements. Phonetic similarity is frequently applied in normalization tasks (Li and Liu, 2012; Han and Baldwin, 2011; Xu et al., 2015). Choudhury et al. (2007) represented both non-formal words and formal words in phonemics and word pairs are evaluated on the phonetic level using left-to-right HMM model. Peng et al. (2015) propose a name matching system with a linear SVM model featuring string match methods. They apply string matching at both the character and phonemic levels. Their experiments show that adding phonetic features does improve performance.

Another assumption is that aliases contain strong contextual similarity with normal words. Liu et al. (2012) measures the cosine similarity of the word TF-IDFs in context. Li and Liu (2014) utilize word embeddings in their work.

3   Phonetic Similarity

Most Chinese characters can serve as meaningful words. Each Chinese character contains only one syllable, and each syllable is composed of an initial, a final and a tone. *Initial* refers to the first part of the Chinese syllable, which is a consonant. *Final* refers to the second part of the syllable, which is a vowel with an optional nasal sound. While some Chinese syllables have a null initial which is denoted as $\emptyset$, each syllable has a final. Mandarin Chinese is a tonal language. There are four main tones and one neutral tone, each of which has a distinctive pitch contour. According to (Liu et al., 2011a), frequently misused similar-phonemic characters have one of following features: the same sound and same tone (SS), the same sound but different tones (SD), and similar sounds and the same tone (MS). Similar sounds can be divided into two categories: the same initial (MS-DF) or the same final (MS-DI). Generally, MS-DI is more common than MS-DF. Table 1 lists the four features and some examples. We apply this theory to our word model to create a phonetic similarity character set for each character in our dictionary.

Category	Example
SS (Same sound, Same tone)	(蔡[Tsai4], 菜[Tsai4])
SD (Same sound, Differ in tone [2] and tone [3])	(才[Tsai2], 採[Tsai3])
MS-DF (Similar sound, Differ in final [en] and final [eng])	(人[Jen2], 仍[Jeng2])
MS-DI (Similar sound, Differ in initial [b] and initial [p])	(奔[Ben1], 噴[Pen1])

Table 1: Similar-phonemic features and examples

4 Left-to-right Word Model

A modified version of the word model was proposed by Choudhury et al. (2007). The main idea is to map the formal name to its alias taking into account the graphemic and phonemic aspects. Suppose that word W_1 is composed of a sequence of characters $c_1 c_2 ... c_{l_1}$, where c_i is a character and l_1 is the length of W_1; word W_2 is composed of $t_1 t_2 ... t_{l_2}$, where t_j is a character and l_2 is the length of W_2 Our goal is to measure the transition probability from W_1 to W_2 given the transition probability between c_i and t_j, i and j are indexes of characters. As the problem is a sequence prediction problem, it can be modeled as follows as a left-to-right HMM (Rabiner, 1989).

Each word which consists of l characters is modeled by a word model containing $2l+2$ states. The state set includes a graphemic path with l graphemic states $G_1, G_2, ..., G_l$, a phonemic path with l phonemic states $P_1, P_2, ..., P_l$, a start state, and an end state. The start state $Start$ is appended before G_1 and P_1, and the end state End is appended after G_l and P_l; these denote the start and end of the character sequence.

Each state S, including $Start$, End, P_i and G_j, consists of transition parameters, an emission character set, and emission parameters. The transition parameters denote the probability of a transition from S to the other states. The emission character sets define the candidate characters of S and the emission parameters denote the probability of the emission characters. The implementation details of the left-to-right word model are described as follows.

4.1 Graphemic Path

We define each state G_i as a graphemic state and the path from $Start$ to End through the sequence of graphemic states as the graphemic path. For each graphemic state, we allow three types of emissions: the original character, the deleted character, and typo, which are respectively denoted as $G_i(g_i)$, $G_i(\epsilon)$, and $G_i(@)$. In Figure 1 the process is illustrated for the word "李登輝" [Li3 Deng1 Hui1].

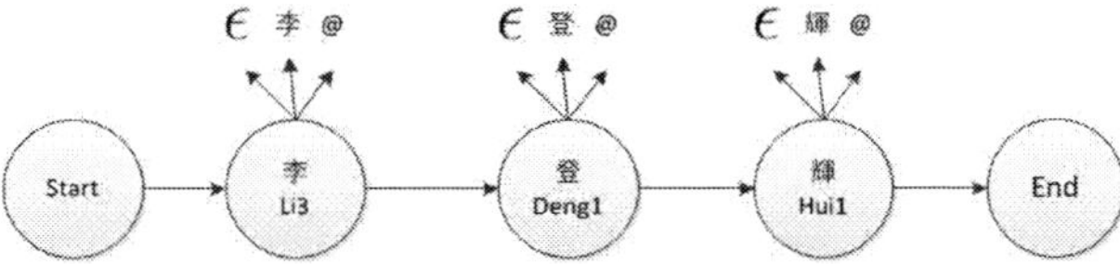

Figure 1: Graphemic path

4.2 Phonemic Path

We define l phonemic states P_1 to P_l, corresponding to the pinyin of each character p_1 to p_l. The emission set of each phonemic state is defined as follows. We construct the set according to the phonetic features of p_i. The emission set thus consists of all the pinyin characters that have the same sounds and tones (SS), the same sounds but different tones (SD), or the same finals but different initials (MS-DI). Take the character "輝" [Hui1] as example: the pinyin of "輝" is [Hui1]. Same-sound and same-tone characters include but are not limited to "輝" [Hui1], "揮" [Hui1], "灰" [Hui1], "徽" [Hui1] and "恢" [Hui1]. Table 2 lists other similar-phonemic types and examples thereof. These similar-phonemic characters compose the emission set of P_i. The emission probability of each character is set uniformly at the beginning. In Figure 2 the process is illustrated for the word "李登輝" [Li3 Deng1 Hui1].

Category	Pinyin	Example
SS	Hui1	輝、揮、灰、徽、恢
SD	Hui2	回、迴、佪、恛、茴
	Hui3	毀、悔、燬、賄、誨
	Hui4	會、惠、繪、匯、檜
MS-DI	Wei1	威、葳、薇、巍、偎
	Zhui1	追、錐、椎、佳、揣
	Cui1	催、崔、摧、墔、璀

Table 2: Phonemic emission set of 輝[Hui1]

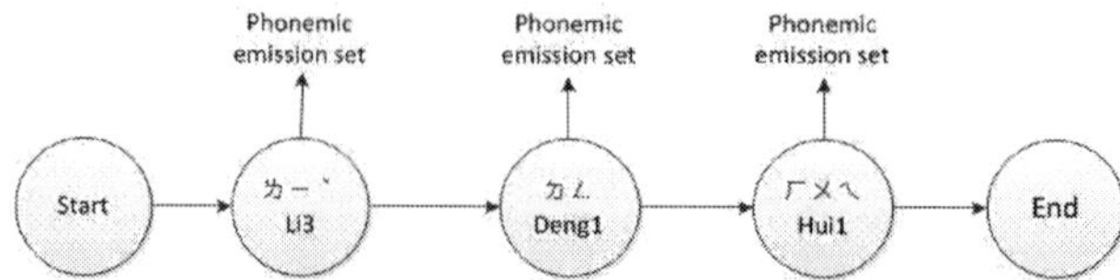

Figure 2: Phonemic path

4.3 Crosslinkages

Most aliases are created from formal names with both similar-graphemic and similar-phonemic characters. For example "李等會" [Li3 Deng3 Hui3] and "李登輝" [Li3 Teng1 Hui1]: these share as the first character the similar-graphemic "李" [Li3]. The second and third characters are similar-phonemic. In order to capture this phenomenon, we model crosslinkages between the graphemic and the phonemic paths. In Figure 3 the process is illustrated again for "李登輝" [Li3 Teng1 Hui1].

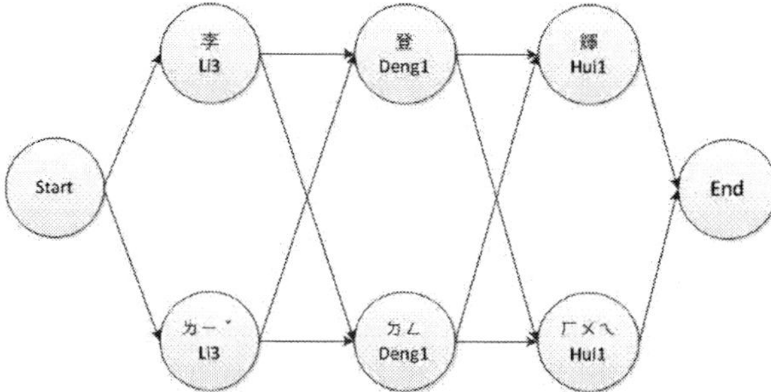

Figure 3: Graphemic and phonemic paths with crosslinks

4.4 Construction of Word HMM

Given a name w, we construct the left-to-right HMM for w as follows. First, the graphemic path is constructed. The pinyin p for w is extracted from a dictionary to construct the phonemic path. Then we create the phonemic emission set which collects the pinyin characters with the similar-phonemic of the word. We construct a left-to-right HMM for each of the 72 politician names, from w_1 to w_{72}, to create the training set. There are three model parameters, $\lambda \equiv (A, B, \pi)$, where A is the state transition probabilities, B is the emission probabilities, and π is the initial state distribution. We initialize the parameters as Choudhury et al. (2007) reported in their work. For each name w_j of the left-to-right HMM, the initial state distribution π_j^0 is defined as

$$\pi(x) = \begin{cases} 1, if X = S_0 \\ 0, otherwise \end{cases} \tag{1}$$

The emission probabilities for each graphemic state are $G_i(g_i) = 0.7$, $G_i(\epsilon) = 0.2$, $G_i(@) = 0.1$.

The emission probabilities of the phonemic states are assigned a uniform distribution. The transition probabilities for the edges from the start state are defined uniformly. For graphemic states, the transition probability to the next graphemic state is set to twice the probability of the transition to the next phonemic state. Similarly, for a phonemic state, the transition probability to another phonemic state is set to twice the probability of the transition to a graphemic state.

4.5 Training Process

Given λ_j^0, we use the Viterbi algorithm (Rabiner, 1989) to find the most likely sequences of states through the HMM for each observation (i.e., aliases in the training set) v_i^j for w_j. We keep count of every transition and emission in the HMM, which is increased by f_i^j (the frequency of the variant v_i^j) if and only if the particular transition or emission is used in the Viterbi path of v_i^j. Once the process is completed for all the variations of w_j, we re-estimate the model parameters of the HMM based on the final counts associated with each transition and emission. Add-α smoothing (Harris, 1985) is used to handle zero counts. We denote this re-estimated model for w_j by α_j^*. It is possible that we lack the training data to train word models for some politician names; for these politicians, we use the initial parameters to predict the probability.

5 Fully Connected HMM

The main disadvantage of the left-to-right HMM is that it fails on prediction when there is no sequence of similar character matches between the alias and formal name; this phenomenon is more common in this task than in canonical normalization. For example, "菊姐" [Ju2 Jie3] is the alias of "陳菊" [Chen2 Ju2]. However, for a left-to-right HMM, the model considers similarity with character mappings between "陳菊" [Chen2 Ju2] and "菊姐" [Ju2 Jie3] as (陳[Chen2], 菊[Ju2]) and (菊[Ju2], 姐[Jie3]). Even if the alias and formal name share several identical characters, simply changing their order can fool the left-to-right HMM. To account for this, we propose a fully connected HMM. We slightly alter the HMM model's parameter settings. We retain the emission parameters, which are independent of the character mapping order. / To achieve this goal, we thus alter the λ initial parameters. The transition probabilities are refined as follows. The transition probabilities from the start to the rest of the states, except the end, are distributed uniformly. For graphemic states, the transition to the next graphemic state is set to 0.5, the transition to the next phonemic state is set to 0.25, and 0.25 is distributed to the rest of the graphemic and phonemic states. Similarly, for a phonemic state, the transition probability to next phonemic state is set to 0.5, the transition to next graphemic state is set to 0.25, and 0.25 is distributed to the rest of the graphemic and phonemic states. After setting all the parameters, we train the fully connected HMM the same way we train the left-to-right HMM.

6 Experiment and Evaluation

We describe in Section 6.1 the dataset creation, and then in Section 6.2 describe the experiment settings and in Section 6.3 the evaluation.

6.1 Experiment Dataset

279 distinct alias and formal name pairs are collected from wikiptt [1].The size of formal name set, which is taken as the candidates for each alias recovery, is 72. From the collection of pairs, we created two datasets: a mixed dataset and a similar-phonemic dataset. To test the power of the phonetic features embedded in our word model, we built a similar-phonemic dataset, a subset of the mixed dataset containing 167 aliases and normal name pairs which were manually identified as bearing phonetic similarity. The mixed and similar-phonemic datasets are described in Table 3.

---

[1] http://zh.pttpedia.wikia.com/wiki/PTT%E6%94%BF%E6%B2%BB%E4%BA%BA%E7%89%A9%E7%B6%BD%E8%99%9F%E5%88%97%E8%A1%A8

	Similar-phonemic dataset	Mixed dataset
Train	104	194
Test	63	85
Total	167	279

Table 3: Similar-phonemic and mixed datasets

6.2 Experiment Settings

We evaluated performance on a ranking task (the setting of (Andrews et al., 2012)). We constructed as the candidates a set of normal names covering all of the entities referred to by aliases. The task is to identify for each alias the best-matched name entity in the normal name set. We acquired two sets of prior knowledge as follows. We collected 114,438 open-source character-to-pinyin mappings from OpenFoundry [2]. The list of possible initials and finals were provided by Weebly [3], a Chinese online remote learning system.

From PTT we collected 478,579 posts discussing of politicians. PTT is a well-known Chinese-language bulletin board system containing 20,000 boards covering a multitude of topics. Users post their opinions on the board. Under each post, other users can add short comments. As with most user-generated text, articles posted on PTT contain extremely short text, out-of-vocabulary tokens, and aliases. We calculated the PMI of each alias and formal name pair at the document level, and then ranked candidates according to their PMI value; the inspiration for this comes from entity clustering (Green et al., 2012), for which related entities tend to be mentioned in the same document.

The experiments were conducted on both the mixed and similar-phonemic datasets. A baseline (Baseline) was implemented based on a statistical character-level transition model. We calculated the frequency of character transitions between aliases and formal names in our training set and handled zero-count transitions using add-α smoothing. We use the pre-trained model (Mingpipe) provided by (Peng et al., 2015) as a comparable setting. The Fixed Order HMM setting denotes the basic left-to-right HMM model. To account for character sequence mismatches between alias and normal name, a simple solution is to rearrange the character order. Thus the (All sequence baseline) and (All sequence HMM) settings try all possible character sequences for each alias with brute force and report the result of the highest matching sequence. The (Fully Connected HMM) denotes a trained fully connected HMM model trained with our dataset and the (Fully connected No training) is a non-trained version. In Tables 4 we compare the rank-one prediction of each setting. The HMM + PMI Hybrid setting ranked candidates according to the average of ranks of PMI and Fully Connected HMM.

6.3 Result and Discussion

In the upper part of the Table 4, we focus on phonetically similar pairs. Applying all sequence metrics improved performance both for the baseline and the HMM model, because different aliases for same formal names tend to contain the same character but in dissimilar order. The Mingpipe model considers several string-matching metrics. It defeats our character-level statistical model but falls behind the basic left-to-right HMM model. This supports our assumption that simple string matching is not the best solution for alias recovery; applying phonetic similarity can greatly improve performance. Fully connected HMM is designed for sequence disorder pairs. It can be improved by learning from the training set, while for different aliases for the same formal name, the trained model tends to contain the same character but in dissimilar order. The trained HMM is hence likely to identify the name entity given the alias if the named entity was seen in the training set. Among the 72 candidates, our proposed model achieved 0.936 at precision @ 5, which is considerably high.

We further investigated each sample and compared our best model with other HMM settings. The Fixed Order left-to-right HMM fails for samples such as (菊姐[Ju2 Jie3], 陳菊[Chen2 Ju2]), (世間

---

[2] https://www.openfoundry.org/of/download_path/cnsphone2010/2016.08.02/CnsPhonetic2016-08_GCIN.cin.zip
[3] http://tzenglaoshi.weebly.com/uploads/6/9/9/2/6992410/pinyin_table.pdf

情[Shi4 Jian1 Qing2], 王世堅[Wang2 Shi4 Jian1]) and (臭青母[Chou4 Qing1 Mu3], 周美青[Zhou1 Mei3 Qing1]). Though using the All sequence HMM setting seems to solve the problem, this setting occasionally goes too far and mistakes (金貝勒[Jin1 Bei4 Le4], 金溥聰[Jin1 Pu3 Cong1]) for (金貝勒[Jin1 Bei4 Le4], 王金平[Wang2 Jin1 Ping2]).

In the lower part of the Table 4, we consider the mixed dataset of common aliases and normal name pairs. The Fully connected HMM model outperforms on the mixed set, but the training process does not yield better performance because the connections of 24 out of 85 pairs require more knowledge than our word model has. For example, "台灣之子" [Tai2 Wan1 Zhi1 Zi3, Son of Taiwan] refers to entity "陳水扁" [Chen2 Shui3 Bian3] because he was the first president of Taiwan who was also born in Taiwan. "大甲王" [Da4 Jia3 Wang2, King of TaChia] refers to entity "顏清標" [Yan2 Qing1 Biao1] because he lived in TaChia, a district located in the middle of Taiwan. These samples are corrected in the setting HMM + PMI Hybrid.

| | Similar-Phonemic Dataset | | | | | | | |
| | Baseline | | Mingpipe | HMM | | | | Hybrid |
	Baseline	All sequence	Mingpipe	Fixed order	All sequence	Fully connected	Fully connected No training	HMM+ PMI
Pre @ 1	0.29	0.32	0.37	0.62	0.65	0.78	0.68	NAN
	Mixed Dataset							
	Baseline		Mingpipe	HMM				Hybrid
	Baseline	All sequence	Mingpipe	Fixed order	All sequence	Fully connected	Fully connected No training	HMM+ PMI
Pre @ 1	0.21	0.19	0.27	0.47	0.49	0.54	0.54	0.59

Table 4: The experiment result with similar-phonemic dataset and mixed dataset

| | HMM | | | | | |
| | Similar-phonemic dataset | | | Mixed dataset | | |
	top 3	top 5	top 10	top 3	top 5	top 10
Correct	57	59	60	59	59	59
Total	63	63	63	85	85	85
Pre @ N	0.90	0.94	0.95	0.69	0.69	0.75

Table 5: Top-N HMM results

6.4 Error Analysis

We conducted an error analysis on our best setting, hoping to provide direction for others who also are interested in alias recovery. There were 39 alias and formal name pairs which were not predicted correctly by Fully connected HMM. Most of these errors were caused by aliases which shared no graphemic and phonemic similarity with the formal entity names. See for instance ("大甲王" [Da4 Jia3 Wang2], "顏清標" [Yan2 Qing1 Biao1]). Also, some politicians' formal names share last names, especially for politicians whose sons are also politicians; for example "馬鶴凌" [Ma3 He4 Ling2], "馬英九" [Ma3 Ying1 Jiu3]. A rare special case is when name entities share the same alias, for example ("黃敏惠" [Huang2 Min3 Hui4], "惠惠" [Hui4 Hui4]) and ("翁啓惠" [Weng1 Qi3 Hui4], "惠惠" [Hui4 Hui4]). In this case our model fails to distinguish the two.

7 Conclusions

In this paper, we proposed a refined HMM for alias recovery of person entities and further improved the model with document-level PMI ranking, which has not been done previously. Both proposed models outperform previous work for both datasets. Our experiments show that considering alias recovery merely as a sequence of character matches yields poor performance.

Acknowledgements

This study is conducted under the "Big Data Technologies and Applications Project (2/4)" of the Institute for Information Industry which is subsidized by the Ministry of Economic Affairs of the Republic of China.

References

Nicholas Andrews, Jason Eisner, and Mark Dredze. 2012. Name phylogeny: A generative model of string variation. In *Proceedings of the 2012 Joint Conference on Empirical Methods in Natural Language Processing and Computational Natural Language Learning*, pages 344–355. Association for Computational Linguistics.

Timothy Baldwin, Young-Bum Kim, Marie Catherine de Marneffe, Alan Ritter, Bo Han, and Wei Xu. 2015. Shared tasks of the 2015 workshop on noisy user-generated text: Twitter lexical normalization and named entity recognition. *ACL-IJCNLP*, 126:2015.

Regina Barzilay and Lillian Lee. 2003. Learning to paraphrase: an unsupervised approach using multiple-sequence alignment. In *Proceedings of the 2003 Conference of the North American Chapter of the Association for Computational Linguistics on Human Language Technology-Volume 1*, pages 16–23. Association for Computational Linguistics.

Monojit Choudhury, Rahul Saraf, Vijit Jain, Animesh Mukherjee, Sudeshna Sarkar, and Anupam Basu. 2007. Investigation and modeling of the structure of texting language. *International Journal of Document Analysis and Recognition (IJDAR)*, 10(3-4):157–174.

Spence Green, Nicholas Andrews, Matthew R Gormley, Mark Dredze, and Christopher D Manning. 2012. Entity clustering across languages. In *Proceedings of the 2012 Conference of the North American Chapter of the Association for Computational Linguistics: Human Language Technologies*, pages 60–69. Association for Computational Linguistics.

Bo Han and Timothy Baldwin. 2011. Lexical normalisation of short text messages: Makn sens a# twitter. In *Proceedings of the 49th Annual Meeting of the Association for Computational Linguistics: Human Language Technologies-Volume 1*, pages 368–378. Association for Computational Linguistics.

Mary Dee Harris. 1985. *Introduction to natural language processing*. Reston Publishing Co.

Kevin Knight and Jonathan Graehl. 1998. Machine transliteration. *Computational Linguistics*, 24(4):599–612.

Chen Li and Yang Liu. 2012. Normalization of text messages using character-and phone-based machine translation approaches. In *INTERSPEECH*, pages 2330–2333.

Chen Li and Yang Liu. 2014. Improving text normalization via unsupervised model and discriminative reranking. In *ACL (Student Research Workshop)*, pages 86–93.

C-L Liu, M-H Lai, K-W Tien, Y-H Chuang, S-H Wu, and C-Y Lee. 2011a. Visually and phonologically similar characters in incorrect chinese words: Analyses, identification, and applications. *ACM Transactions on Asian Language Information Processing (TALIP)*, 10(2):10.

Fei Liu, Fuliang Weng, Bingqing Wang, and Yang Liu. 2011b. Insertion, deletion, or substitution?: normalizing text messages without pre-categorization nor supervision. In *Proceedings of the 49th Annual Meeting of the Association for Computational Linguistics: Human Language Technologies: short papers-Volume 2*, pages 71–76. Association for Computational Linguistics.

Fei Liu, Fuliang Weng, and Xiao Jiang. 2012. A broad-coverage normalization system for social media language. In *Proceedings of the 50th Annual Meeting of the Association for Computational Linguistics: Long Papers-Volume 1*, pages 1035–1044. Association for Computational Linguistics.

Nafise Sadat Moosavi and Michael Strube. 2014. Unsupervised coreference resolution by utilizing the most informative relations. In *Proceedings of COLING 2014, the 25th International Conference on Computational Linguistics: Technical Papers*, pages 644–655, Dublin, Ireland, August. Dublin City University and Association for Computational Linguistics.

Nanyun Peng, Mo Yu, and Mark Dredze. 2015. An empirical study of chinese name matching and applications. In *Proceedings of the 53rd Annual Meeting of the Association for Computational Linguistics and the 7th International Joint Conference on Natural Language Processing (Volume 2: Short Papers)*, pages 377–383, Beijing, China, July. Association for Computational Linguistics.

Sasa Petrovic, Miles Osborne, and Victor Lavrenko. 2010. The edinburgh twitter corpus. In *Proceedings of the NAACL HLT 2010 Workshop on Computational Linguistics in a World of Social Media*, pages 25–26.

Simone Paolo Ponzetto and Michael Strube. 2006. Exploiting semantic role labeling, wordnet and wikipedia for coreference resolution. In *Proceedings of the main conference on Human Language Technology Conference of the North American Chapter of the Association of Computational Linguistics*, pages 192–199. Association for Computational Linguistics.

Lawrence R Rabiner. 1989. A tutorial on hidden markov models and selected applications in speech recognition. *Proceedings of the IEEE*, 77(2):257–286.

Delip Rao, Paul McNamee, and Mark Dredze. 2013. Entity linking: Finding extracted entities in a knowledge base. In *Multi-source, multilingual information extraction and summarization*, pages 93–115. Springer.

Wee Meng Soon, Hwee Tou Ng, and Daniel Chung Yong Lim. 2001. A machine learning approach to coreference resolution of noun phrases. *Computational linguistics*, 27(4):521–544.

Richard Sproat, Alan W Black, Stanley Chen, Shankar Kumar, Mari Ostendorf, and Christopher Richards. 2001. Normalization of non-standard words. *Computer Speech & Language*, 15(3):287–333.

Ke Xu, Yunqing Xia, and Chin-Hui Lee. 2015. Tweet normalization with syllables. In *Proceedings of the 53rd Annual Meeting of the Association for Computational Linguistics and the 7th International Joint Conference on Natural Language Processing (Volume 1: Long Papers)*, pages 920–928, Beijing, China, July. Association for Computational Linguistics.

Towards Accurate Event Detection in Social Media: A Weakly Supervised Approach for Learning Implicit Event Indicators

Ajit Jain, Girish Kasiviswanathan, Ruihong Huang
Department of Computer Science and Engineering
Texas A&M University
College Station, TX 77843
{ajitjain,girishk14,huangrh}@cse.tamu.edu

Abstract

Accurate event detection in social media is very challenging because user generated contents are extremely noisy and sparse in content. Event indicators are generally words or phrases that act as a trigger that help us understand the semantics of the context they occur in. We present a weakly supervised approach that relies on using a single strong event indicator phrase as a seed to acquire a variety of additional event cues. We propose to leverage various types of implicit event indicators, such as props, actors and precursor events, to achieve precise event detection. We experimented with civil unrest events and show that the automatically learnt event indicators are effective in identifying specific types of events.

1 Introduction

Social media data has today evolved into a crowd-sourced knowledge base of real-time happenings, sentiments, and future events. For instance, in a recent natural disaster, rescue volunteers used social media to coordinate their actions and identify survivors (Starbird and Palen, 2011). Accurately identifying a particular class of events in social media will benefit many downstream applications such as event tracking, event time-line generation, and event summarization. However, some critical information is buried within piles of mundane tweets and is hard to detect precisely. In Table 1, we provide some examples of potentially critical content embedded within tweets that our system was able to extract.

Two intuitive approaches have been widely applied to event detection in tweets, first the event keyword matching approach that is far from being perfect with our experiments yielding accuracies as low as 14%, even while using keywords very relevant to a domain. Second, unique to tweets, hashtags, for instance,

Tweet	Critical Content
Public transport suspended in Istanbul as part of authorities precaution to curb #MayDay gatherings in Taksim Square	Real-time warning
Extreme violence of police in Besiktas, Istanbul now! Let the world know	Pleas for help
1km chain of citizens to build a barricade in besiktas, akaretler.	Potential risk in future
An innocent young girl was put into a coma due to tear gas attacks and was later labeled by the government as a terrorist	Consequence of event
This is the craziest I've seen Cairo in the two years I've been here. So many clashes, tear gas everywhere. Insane	Sentiment about event
Dear Policemen, Thank you so much for using bean bag rounds and rubber bullets in Brisbane. I really appreciate your protection of life	Sarcasm

Table 1: A few examples of highly critical tweets that we have detected using the bootstrapping approach and a single high quality event indicator seed "tear gas".

Proceedings of the 2nd Workshop on Noisy User-generated Text,
pages 70–77, Osaka, Japan, December 11 2016.

Trigger Type	Examples
Instruments/Props	barricades, rubber bullets
Sub-events	police pushing, crowd shouting
Precursor events	government bans, arrest of prisoner
Consequences	injury, damaged
Locations	Taksim Square, Ankara
Actors	angry employees

Table 2: Civil unrest event indicators types with examples of extracted phrases. Clustering algorithm is useful towards understanding the semantic types of the learned event indicators.

"#RiseUpOctober" can be used to accurately identify tweets describing the October New York protest in 2015. However, this approach is heavily biased towards already known trending events that are more likely to be "hashtagged", and is often not reliable even to capture tweets referring to a single event.

Tweets belonging to a particular event domain (eg. civil unrest, disaster, presidential election) can be identified by learning various kinds of event indicators or sensors across contexts. In spite of their highly informal and ambiguous nature (Ritter et al., 2011), tweets often mention multiple event characteristic properties and features that act as implicit event cues. An event indicator is defined as any word or phrase that can act as reliable evidence towards detecting an event mention in text. A strong indicator is one that is almost exclusively relevant to the event under consideration (eg. *touchdown* is strong evidence of a sports event). A weak indicator tends to occur in more generic textual contexts and is therefore less useful.

We also observe that these event indicators can be categorized into sub-classes, depending on how they influence the event. Table 2 presents a summary of event indicator types that were prevalent for the civil unrest domain, and corresponding examples of the extracted indicator phrases.

For example, the following tweet,

> *"Police attacking us with plastic bullets and tears gaz in istanbul! 5people died, hundreds injured! Help"*

contains multiple indicators including a sub-event (*police attacking*), instruments (*plastic bullets* and *tears gaz*) and consequential events (*people died* and *hundreds injured*). Some event indicators are so strong that tweets containing one such phrase are almost certainly relevant, for instance *"tear gas"* is a unique type of instrument used in civil unrest events.

Following these observations, we propose a weakly supervised approach to automatically learn such event indicators. The system starts with a single high quality event indicator seed, and extracts an initial set of highly relevant tweets, which are likely to contain other indicators. These potential indicators are then combined with the seed set to grow a collection of indicators. This way, the tweet extraction and collection expansion phases augment each other mutually, the whole process iterates while using empirical thresholds to monitor quality of extraction (Riloff et al., 1999). We then proceed to cluster these indicators based on their contextual similarities, which yield some naturally occurring categories of event triggers as seen in Table 2. Our approach is able to outperform naive keyword matching even without having any prior knowledge or hand labeled data, other than a single seed word. Furthermore, our indicators were able to identify tweets that did not contain a single event keyword.

2 Prior Work

Our research closely follows the multi-faceted event recognition approach (Huang and Riloff, 2013) for news articles which suggests that event facets, namely agents and purposes, supplement event expressions. However, event indicators in tweets are loosely defined and lack phrasal dependencies, hence posing a more challenging problem.

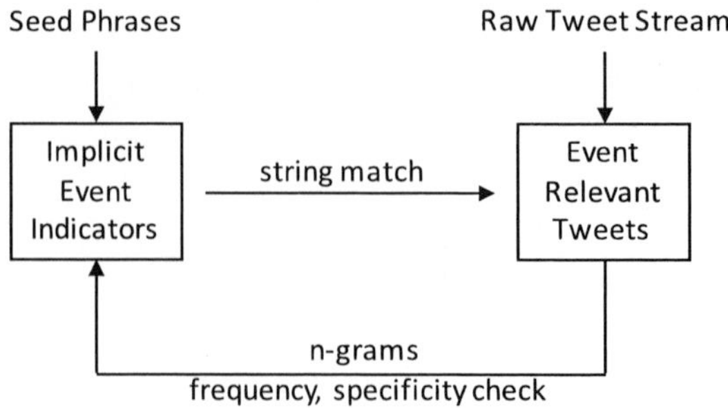

Figure 1: The bootstrapping process iteratively adds event relevant tweets and implicit event indicators.

First, in contrast to event facets, event indicators are loosely defined event properties and features which cover a broader range of implicit event cues. Second, in their proposed bootstrapping system, strict phrasal structures for event facet phrases and dependency relations between event facet phrases and the main event expression are required. Instead, our system is well tailored to event indicator learning in noisy tweets, where learning targets are simply n-grams[1] and we only consider n-grams that strongly correlate with domain-specific tweets as generated through the bootstrapping process.

(Atefeh and Khreich, 2015) summarize the key literature in the spectrum of event detection in Twitter, and establish a taxonomy of these techniques based on type of event, detection task, and detection method. Our weakly supervised approach is capable of detecting both new and retrospective unspecified event types.

(Becker et al., 2011), together with (Sankaranarayanan et al., 2009) and (Petrović et al., 2010), discuss an approach that collects tweets in temporal bins, forms event clusters, and trains a classifier to identify real world events. This approach however is heavily dependent on the incremental clustering criteria, training set of events, and sparse TF-IDF vectors. In this work, we stress on the broader task of extracting tweets that are relevant to a given class of event.

The event extraction task itself most closely resembles that of (Ritter et al., 2012), which presents a hidden variable model for event type discovery on a collection of tweets. Tweets are segregated into discrete event types by first training a sequence model that can identify event triggers, and then using a latent variable model to discover the types implicit within the tweets, and segregating them accordingly. Instead, we focus on improving accuracy of detecting individual tweets that describe a particular type of event by assuming prior knowledge about the event type in the form of a single seed.

This, to the best of our knowledge, is the first attempt to extract events from social media data using a weakly supervised approach.

3 System Overview

Our system broadly comprises of (1) a bootstrapping module for unsupervised learning of event indicators and (2) a clustering module for understanding context of occurrence of these event indicators.

3.1 Bootstrapping

Figure 1 shows the bootstrapping process. We start by selection of initial seed phrases, based on inspection of civil unrest event indicators. Generally, any word that is deemed by a domain expert as being highly relevant to an event, can be used as the seed. We add the seed phrases to the set of implicit event indicators, which are then searched over the raw tweet stream to identify event relevant tweets. From these event relevant tweets, we select n-grams as implicit event indicators for the next iteration, based on frequency and specificity checks.

For our experiment, we used "*tear gas*" as the initial seed word. We used about 200 million tweets that were collected over a period of 6 months in 2013 for bootstrapping implicit event indicators and event

---

[1]We consider 1, 2, 3, 4-grams as candidate event indicators.

relevant tweets. We stop after a couple of iterations as our study is currently in initial phase. We discuss generation of event relevant tweets and implicit event indicators, including filtering steps, redundancy handling, and selection criteria. We also discuss the phrase specificity parameters used for monitoring the quality of extraction.

3.1.1 Event Relevant Tweets

The bootstrapping algorithm first finds all the tweets containing the seed phrases. Redundant tweets drastically impact frequencies and thus selection of event indicators, therefore the algorithm performs a redundancy check for removal of any duplicate tweet texts. This includes removing tweets that are exact matches, substrings, and differing only in use of RTs, preceding and succeeding punctuations, @ and # associations, and web urls. A recursive check is performed as such differences can occur in any order. We then use the non-redundant tweets for determining implicit event indicators for the next iteration. We additionally base selection of tweets on *specificity factor*, which we describe next to generation of implicit event indicators.

3.1.2 Implicit Event Indicators

Our algorithm generates candidate implicit event indicators from newly learned event relevant tweets. For this purpose, we extract n-grams (n=1,2,3,4) from tweets. We use pre-filtering where we discard any n-grams that have frequency less than 5 in the event relevant tweets. This helps us in removal of n-grams less likely to be event indicators. However, this way, we also get a large number of n-grams that are general, i.e., which can occur in any set of random tweets. To handle this, we use the specificity factor, which we describe next.

3.1.3 Specificity Factor

We select both the event relevant tweets and implicit event indicators based on specificity checks. We define specificity factor (sf) as the normalized ratio of frequency of an event indicator occurs in the event relevant tweets and frequency in a random tweet set. To calculate the specificity factor, we use the formula:

$$sf = \frac{(h_c/c_c)}{(h_r/c_r)}$$

where h_c = event indicator hit count in event relevant tweets, c_c = count of tweets in tweet collection, h_r = event indicator hit count in event relevant tweets, c_r = count of tweets in random tweet set

We formed the random tweet set by sampling about 1% i.e. 2 million tweets from the original dataset used for bootstrapping. A general phrase occurs frequently in both the random set and tweet collection. Hence, its specificity factor is low. On the other hand, an event indicator occurs more frequently in the tweet collection as compared to the random set. Only phrases above the set specificity factor thresholds (1000 for unigrams, 5000 for 2,3,4-grams) are retained as event indicators for the next iteration, i.e., for finding event relevant tweets. We also distinguish strong event indicators from relatively weak ones.

Strength	Examples of Event Indicator
Strong Indicators	gas shells, firing tear, clouds fill, disperse protesters, gas canisters, during clashes, water canons, throwing tear, gas attack, gas shot, shooting tear, stun grenades, police disperse, police firing, tear gas, gas clouds, fired by police
Weak Indicators	forces fire, pressurized water, police use, against peaceful, riot police, against protesters, gas bombs, rubber bullets, pressurized, barricades, grenades, anti-government, mercenaries, protesters, demonstrators, clashes, #occupygezi, quell, #bahrain

Table 3: Top event indicators resulting from the bootstrapping approach in descending order of phrase specificities. Different semantic types could be learned starting with a single high quality seed phrase.

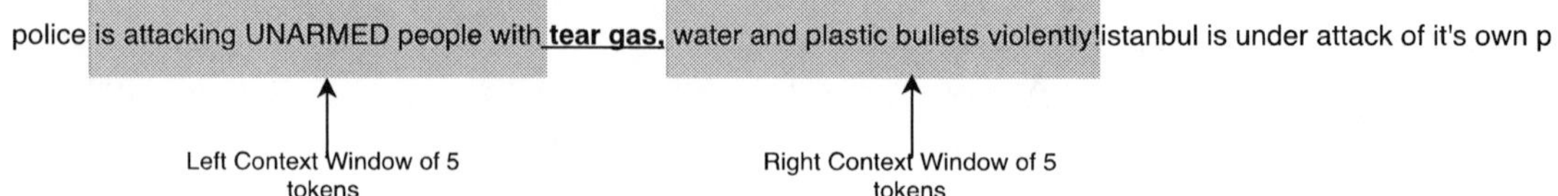

Figure 2: Extraction of context windows from one the tweets containing the learnt phrase 'tear gas'. The tweets are padded on both sides with UNK tokens and a frequency threshold is used to discard unimportant tokens

Strong event indicators have specificity greater than 20000. A tweet is determined to be a relevant tweet if it contains one strong event indicator or two weak event indicators. These thresholds were identified by inspecting specificity factor scores of the n-grams generated from initial couple of iterations. Note that we expect the concrete parameters to change when applying the same system but to learn event indicators for a different event domain, however, tuning the parameters in our experiments based on the generated candidate event indicators from the first one or two iterations is quite manageable. Table 3 shows the top event indicators organized in these two categories.

3.2 Clustering

Upon building a collection of event indicators, we attempt to identify contextual similarities, *i.e* how each phrase acts as a cue for an event, as discussed in Table 2. For each phrase, we accumulate its contexts using a window of 5 words on either side of each tweet in which the phrase occurs, as shown in Figure 2. Next, we build a feature vector to represent the context words of each indicator using two approaches - (1) frequency bag-of-words (2) sum of word embeddings ("tweet-token embedding" to be precise) while clipping stop words and infrequent words. We use the 200-dimensional global vectors (Pennington et al., 2014), pre-trained on 2 billion tweets, covering over 27-billion tokens. We then perform clustering using the affinity-propagation algorithm (Frey and Dueck, 2007).

4 Evaluation

We evaluate the quality of tweets identified by using the automatically learned event indicators over the successive iterations of the bootstrapping phase, as described in Section 3. Table 4 shows the number of event indicator phrases and civil unrest tweets that were collected after each iteration of bootstrapping. Table 5 shows examples of correct and incorrect tweets.

To measure the relevance of the tweets as identified by the event indicators, we sampled 500 tweets from the final set collected after 4 iterations. Further, to verify the capability of our system to learn less prominent indicators such as "cops rounded", "spark clashes", "made demands", we collect an additional 500 tweet sample after filtering out tweets that contain a common event keyword like "protest", "riot", etc.

We also separately collected another random sample of 1000 tweets from the original corpus of 220

Iteration	Event Cues	Relevant Tweets
1	1	1445
2	309	4503
3	719	7555
4	1037	8521

Table 4: Event indicators and relevant tweets accumulate with each iteration. Semantic drift occurs in this process.

<table>
<tr><td>Correct:</td></tr>
<tr><td>Protesters chant 'Stop the IRS' in Cincinnati: CINCINNATI (AP) Tea party activists waving flags and signs, singing pat</td></tr>
<tr><td>Protestors have attacked Al Jazeera TV headquarters in Egypt and have set fire to the building</td></tr>
<tr><td>ISTANBUL - Riot police used tear gas and pressurized water in a dawn raid on Friday to rout a peaceful demonstration by hundreds of peopl</td></tr>
<tr><td>NYC protest at Zuccotti Park in solidarity with #OccupyGezi starting now</td></tr>
<tr><td>CNN: 25 people killed, 70 others wounded as clashes erupted between Iraqi Security Forces and protesters in Hawija, Iraq</td></tr>
<tr><td>Incorrect:</td></tr>
<tr><td>Saudi Arabia postpones crucifixion, firing squad executions: Seven juveniles were arrested for armed robbery</td></tr>
<tr><td>ICYMI: Watch video of my comments on @CTVnews on #Syria and #sarin gas. Iraq WMD deja vu? Or #Assad war crime</td></tr>
</table>

Table 5: Examples of correct and incorrect tweets learned through the bootstrapping process.

million tweets, so as to train a supervised baseline classifier.

Each sample was then annotated by two-annotators to determine if each tweet was actually relevant to civil unrest, with an inter-annotator agreement, $\kappa = 0.81$ (Cohen, 1968), suggesting that our task guidelines are well-defined and unbiased.

We next show the event detection performance of the supervised system and the performance of our event indicator matching approach. In addition, we explain the semantic drift in the bootstrapping process, and demonstrate the results of event indicator clustering.

4.1 Supervised Baseline

To train the baseline model, we used a simple bi-gram model to extract features from each tweet, and trained a Support Vector Machine classifier using a a linear kernel, on the sample of annotated tweets held out exclusively for training purpose.The sample contained 350 relevant tweets.

We then tested this model on the sample set extracted after 4 iterations of our algorithm. The supervised model was able to achieve a precision of 95%, but only yielded a recall of 4%, leading to a poor F-Score of 8%.

The main point to note here is that supervised algorithms are restricted to learning only features that they have been exposed to, and are vulnerable and limited when abundant annotated data is not available.

4.2 Precision and Recall

Table 6 shows accuracies of the event keyword matched tweets and the two tweet samples identified by using learned event indicators. We can see that event keyword alone is very unreliable in detecting tweets that describe a particular type of event and the accuracy is as low as 12%. Using event indicators, we can greatly improve the accuracy of event detection to 66%. The automatically learned event indicators

Methods	Accuracy
Event keyword Matching	12%
Bootstrapped (contain a keyword)	66%
Bootstrapped (contain no keyword)	35%

Table 6: Accuracy of bootstrapping on collected tweets. Our system outperforms the baseline event keyword matching. The automatically learned event indicators is even able to identify the relevant tweets that do not contain an event keyword.

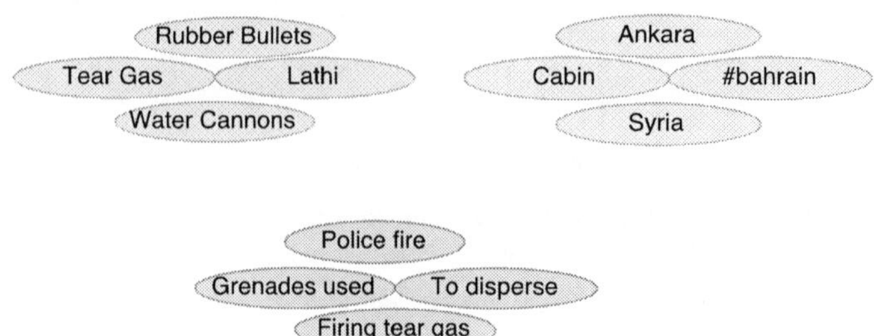

Figure 3: A few examples of the different categories of event indicators our clustering algorithm was able to identify, namely props, locations and actions

can even discover relevant tweets that do not contain a common event keyword, achieving an accuracy of 35%, which is still much better than using the method of keyword matching.

However, we do not analyze recall at this point since it is hard to define a global notion of what subset of the tweets of the entire stream are true positives that our system is expected to detect. We will look into more doable laboratory settings in the future.

4.3 Semantic Drift

While the automatically learned event indicators have significantly improved the accuracy of event detection, the performance is not perfect and many irrelevant tweets were wrongly labeled. Table 5 shows examples of tweets that are truly event relevant tweets and the ones that are errors. Our analysis of the errors shows that the current bootstrapping algorithm suffers from a major drawback, *semantic drift* (Davenport and Cronin, 2000). After each iteration, a conceptual drift in the target collection is triggered, with a few poor indicator phrases propagating error and causing a gradual shift in domain. For instance, there was some noise induced from tweets on police arrests and war crimes. In the future, we are going to investigate techniques for reducing the semantic drift.

4.4 Clustering

While the sparsity and inconsistency of the twitter vocabulary tend to ambiguate the notion of contextual similarity, the final clusters obtained from either feature set (BoW or GloVe), reflected a few interesting patterns, similar to Table 1. For instance, *'tear gas', 'lathi', 'water cannons' and 'pepper spray'* were clustered together, and similarly were *'dispersed', 'violence on', 'sprayed on'*. Hence, clustering can prove useful towards understanding the latent semantic categories of the learnt event indicators. However, we reserve strict evaluation of these clusters for future work, as this task is heavily contingent on our primary task of learning high quality event indicators. Figure 3 shows a few examples of the preliminary clusters we were able to isolate in this setting.

Another interesting observation is that most of the domain-drift inducing indicators discussed in Section 5.2 were grouped together, suggesting that we can filter them out in the future.

5 Future Work

Extracting meaning from tweets is task far more challenging beyond the perspective we have adopted, and requires many more standpoints. The next level of our work is to investigate more event domains as well as to suggest means of eliminating noise propagation in the bootstrapping process. We look to analyze recall using feasible methods. We are also going to further investigate understanding of semantic types through means of clustering.

References

Farzindar Atefeh and Wael Khreich. 2015. A survey of techniques for event detection in twitter. *Computational Intelligence*, 31(1):132–164.

Hila Becker, Mor Naaman, and Luis Gravano. 2011. Beyond trending topics: Real-world event identification on twitter. *ICWSM*, 11:438–441.

Jacob Cohen. 1968. Weighted kappa: Nominal scale agreement provision for scaled disagreement or partial credit. *Psychological bulletin*, 70(4):213.

Elisabeth Davenport and Blaise Cronin. 2000. Knowledge management: semantic drift or conceptual shift? *Journal of Education for library and information Science*, pages 294–306.

Brendan J Frey and Delbert Dueck. 2007. Clustering by passing messages between data points. *science*, 315(5814):972–976.

Ruihong Huang and Ellen Riloff. 2013. Multi-faceted event recognition with bootstrapped dictionaries. In *HLT-NAACL*, pages 41–51.

Jeffrey Pennington, Richard Socher, and Christopher D Manning. 2014. Glove: Global vectors for word representation. In *EMNLP*, volume 14, pages 1532–1543.

Saša Petrović, Miles Osborne, and Victor Lavrenko. 2010. Streaming first story detection with application to twitter. In *Human Language Technologies: The 2010 Annual Conference of the North American Chapter of the Association for Computational Linguistics*, pages 181–189. Association for Computational Linguistics.

Ellen Riloff, Rosie Jones, et al. 1999. Learning dictionaries for information extraction by multi-level bootstrapping. In *AAAI/IAAI*, pages 474–479.

Alan Ritter, Sam Clark, Oren Etzioni, et al. 2011. Named entity recognition in tweets: an experimental study. In *Proceedings of the Conference on Empirical Methods in Natural Language Processing*, pages 1524–1534. Association for Computational Linguistics.

Alan Ritter, Oren Etzioni, Sam Clark, et al. 2012. Open domain event extraction from twitter. In *Proceedings of the 18th ACM SIGKDD international conference on Knowledge discovery and data mining*, pages 1104–1112. ACM.

Jagan Sankaranarayanan, Hanan Samet, Benjamin E Teitler, Michael D Lieberman, and Jon Sperling. 2009. Twitterstand: news in tweets. In *Proceedings of the 17th acm sigspatial international conference on advances in geographic information systems*, pages 42–51. ACM.

Kate Starbird and Leysia Palen. 2011. Voluntweeters: Self-organizing by digital volunteers in times of crisis. In *Proceedings of the SIGCHI Conference on Human Factors in Computing Systems*, pages 1071–1080. ACM.

Unsupervised Stemmer for Arabic Tweets

Fahad Albogamy
School of Computer Science,
University of Manchester,
Manchester, M13 9PL, UK
albogamf@cs.man.ac.uk

Allan Ramsay
School of Computer Science,
University of Manchester,
Manchester, M13 9PL, UK
allan.ramsay@cs.man.ac.uk

Abstract

Stemming is an essential processing step in a wide range of high level text processing applications such as information extraction, machine translation and sentiment analysis. It is used to reduce words to their stems. Many stemming algorithms have been developed for Modern Standard Arabic (MSA). Although Arabic tweets and MSA are closely related and share many characteristics, there are substantial differences between them in lexicon and syntax. In this paper, we introduce a light Arabic stemmer for Arabic tweets. Our results show improvements over the performance of a number of well-known stemmers for Arabic.

1 Introduction

The last few years have seen an enormous growth in the use of social networking platforms such as Twitter in the Arab World. A study prepared and published by Semiocast in 2012 has revealed that Arabic was the fastest growing language on Twitter in 2011. People post about their lives, share opinions on a variety of topics and discuss current issues. There are millions of tweets daily, yielding a corpus which is noisy and informal, but which is sometimes informative. As a result, Twitter has become one of the most important social information mutual platforms. The nature of the text content of microblogs differs from traditional blogs. In Twitter, for example, a tweet is short and contains a maximum of 140 characters. Tweets also are not always written maintaining formal grammar and proper spelling. Slang and abbreviations are often used to overcome their restricted lengths (Java et al., 2007).

Stemming is an essential processing step in a wide range of high level text processing applications such as information extraction, machine translation and sentiment analysis. It is a non trivial problem especially with languages that have rich and complex morphology such as Arabic. The function of a stemmer is to reduce words to their stems by stripping off all affixes (Frakes, 1992). Affixes are syntactic units that do not have free forms, but are instead attached to other words. They use the same alphabet as that of words and are concatenated one after the other with no demarcating marking such as the English apostrophe. Therefore, they are not easily recognisable. Although there have been several studies on developing morphological and stemming tools for Modern Standard Arabic (MSA), a stemmer that can work on Arabic tweets or similar text styles is yet to be developed.

In this study, an unsupervised stemmer for Arabic tweets is proposed, implemented and tested. It applies a light stemming technique on Arabic words to extract their stems. Our Arabic stemming approach is not dictionary based, which is crucial for stemming Arabic tweets, since they have a very open lexicon, and we are able to reach around 78% stemming accuracy. The results are compared with an Arabic stemmer which uses similar approach described in the literature.

The rest of this paper is organised as follows: In Section 2, we give an overview of the related work, followed by the representation of Arabic words in 3. Our approach is presented in Section 4. In Section 5, we discuss the evaluation, results and their analysis. In Section 6, we talk about conclusion and future work.

Proceedings of the 2nd Workshop on Noisy User-generated Text,
pages 78–84, Osaka, Japan, December 11 2016.

2   Related Work

There have been several studies on developing morphological and stemming tools for MSA. These tools can be classified into three categories: manually constructed dictionaries (heavy stemming), light stemming and statistical stemming.

Heavy stemming approaches try to find the stems and roots by using dictionaries. There are many examples of recent research work under this category such as (Buckwalter, 2004), (Khoja and Garside., 1999) and (Algarni et al., 2014). The Buckwalter Arabic Morphological Analyzer (BAMA) is the best known example of such an approach. It is an open-source software package morphological analyser developed by Tim Buckwalter. He developed a set of lexicons of Arabic stems, prefixes, suffixes and a table containing valid morphological combinations in order to produce all possible stems for each word. Khoja stemmer is another example of this class. It based on one dictionary for Arabic roots. It removes the longest suffix and the longest prefix. Then, it matches the remaining word with roots in the dictionary and a list of patterns. This category produces well-formed stems and roots which are potentially correct, but it generates multiple analyses, therefore it has to have some downstream mechanisms for choosing between them and the dictionaries are extremely difficult to maintain.

Light stemming approach is a process of stripping off a set of affixes from a word without trying to recognise patterns and find roots. It is fast, does not need roots or stems dictionaries and plays safe in order to avoid over-stemming errors, but it may produce the stem that may not even be a real Arabic word (Paice, 1994). (Al-Kabi et al., 2015) uses a light stemmer approach but does not cover all affixes in Arabic.

Statistical approach is a process of inducing a list of affixes automatically and using clustering techniques to group word variants. Most statistical approaches require annotated training data such as (Darwish and Oard, 2007) and (De Roeck and Al-Fares, 2000). This data is expensive and is not always available. Although there have been some positive results with un annotated training data for many different languages such as (Goldsmith, 2001) and (Dasgupta and Ng, 2007), it seems likely the complexity of Arabic language makes that kind of approach is infeasible.

On the other hand, there has been relatively little work on building stemmers for Arabic dialect. Most of these works targeted one specific dialect such as (Alamlahi and Ahmed, 2007) and (Al-Gaphari and Al-Yadoumi, 2010).

Our work is, to the best of our knowledge, the first step towards developing a stemmer for Arabic tweets or similar text styles which can benefit a wide range of downstream NLP applications such as information extraction and machine translation. Our approach does not rely on any root dictionary or list of patterns. We use a light stemming approach and shortest stem strategy to extract the stems of the words.

Word	وسيفعلون "wsyfElwn"	
	Arabic	Translit.
Prefixes	و	w
	س	s
	ي	y
Stem	فعل	fEl
Suffixes	ون	wn

Table 1: Example of Arabic Affixes

3   Arabic Word Form

Arabic is a morphologically rich language where the letters are attached together to form a word. A word often conveys complex meanings that can be decomposed into several morphemes (i.e. prefix, stem, suffix). Consequently, it presents significant challenges to many NLP applications such as tagging.

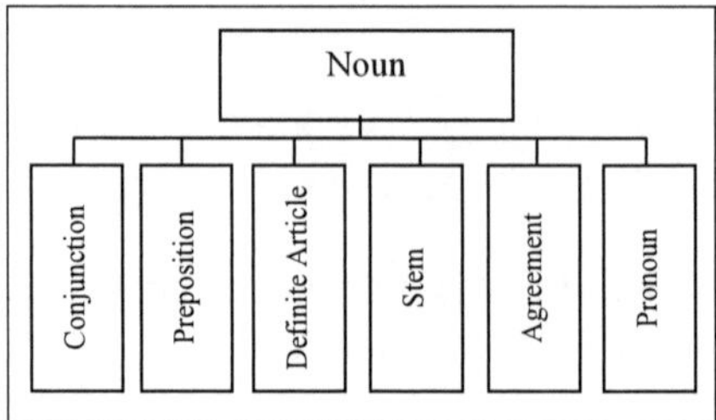

Figure 1: Possible sub-tokens in Arabic nouns

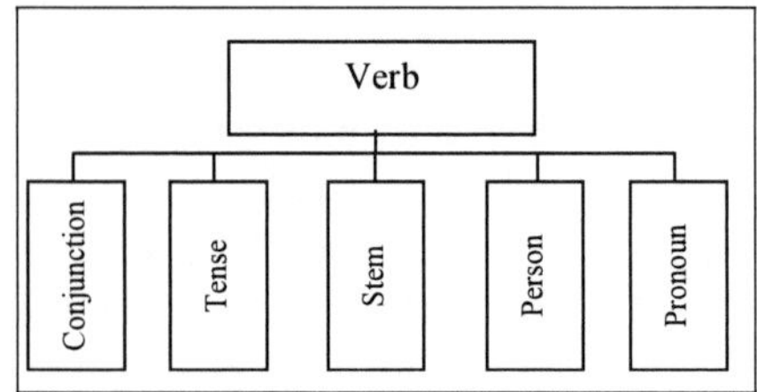

Figure 2: Possible sub-tokens in Arabic verbs

For example, the Arabic word[1] وسيفعلون "wsyfElwn" which means "and they will do", consists of five elements as shown in Table 1. We notice that Arabic affixes (prefixes and suffixes) attach to the base word in a strict order. These affixes are differ based on the word type, but in general we can represent the word as follows:

$$\text{Word} \equiv \text{Prefixes} + \text{Stem} + \text{Suffixes}$$

Arabic morphotactics allow words to have affixes. Affixes themselves can be concatenated one after the other. A noun can comprise up to six sub-tokens as illustrated by Figure1. Similarly a verb can comprise up to five sub-tokens as illustrated by Figure 2. The combination of words with affixes is governed by various rules. These rules are called grammar-lexis specifications (Dichy and Farghaly, 2003). An example of these specifications is a rule that states that the prefix "s", which denotes the future of verbs, is only combined with imperfective verb stems.

4   Our Approach

Although Arabic tweets and MSA are closely related and share many characteristics, there are substantial differences between them in lexicon and syntax (Albogamy and Ramsay, 2015). The lexicon is always evolving and many words in Arabic tweets are not present in MSA. Therefore, dictionary-based stemming approaches will not work for Arabic tweets. The statistical approaches that are used to induce a list of affixes automatically are also not applicable because we predefined a limited set of prefixes and suffixes for Arabic tweets and there is no annotated training data available. In Arabic tweets domain, there are millions of words that need to be stemmed, so stemming approaches that use a set of rules to identify words patterns are not suitable because they consume lots of computational resources (Al-Serhan and Ayesh, 2006).

Based on that, we decided to use a light stemming approach similar to the one that has been used in (Al-Kabi et al., 2015), but we cover all Arabic affixes. We define all possible affixes and write a set of rules of valid prefixes, suffixes and word forms and select the shortest stem of a word as the correct stem. We built our light stemmer by using Python and a basic grammar that we wrote to describe the morphological rules of Arabic noun and verb (see Figure 3). We are interested in two major word types; noun and verb. We defined them as a combination of allowable prefixes, and a word stem which is all letters between the prefix and the end of the string. In case that the word types have suffixes, the stem is defined as all letters between the prefix and the suffix. Our approach has two phases and deals with one word at a time. The first-phase is dedicated to taking the input word and trying it against the definition of its word type in the grammar. Then the stemmer will produce a list of all possible stems. The second-phase is to select the shortest stem as the correct stem. We use the word وباليد "wbalyd" which means "and by the hand" to demonstrate our approach (see Figure 4). The stemmer tried this word gainst the noun type grammar. It produced three possible stems. Then, the shortest stem (analysis 1) was selected 'yd' as the stem for this word. In this particular example, the stem chosen is the correct stem.

---

[1] The word is delimited by a white space

```
patterns = {
"ART": "Al|",
"CONJ": "w|b",
"NSTEM": ".{3,}?",
"VSTEM": ".{2,}?",
"PRON": "y|h|ha|hmA|hm|hn|k|kn|km|kmA|nA",
"VPRON": "PRON|NY",
"NY": "ny",
"PREP": "b|k|l",
"FUT": "s",
"TNS1": "O|n|A|y|t|",
"TENSE": "(FUT)?(TNS1)",
"PERSON": "(?(ON)AGR-ON|(?(AY)AGR-AY|
        (?(t)AGR-T|(?(past)AGR-PAST))))",
"AGR-ON": "",
"AGR-AY": "(A|An|wA|wn|n|)",
"AGR-T": "(yn|An|wn|n| )",
"AGR-PAST": "(tmA|tm|tn|t|A|wA|n|)",
"AGREE": "wn|yn|p|An|At|",
"NOUN": "(CONJ)?(PREP)?(ART)(?P<stem>NSTEM)
        (AGREE)(PRON)?",
"VERB": "(CONJ)?(TENSE)(?P<stem>VSTEM)
        (PERSON)?(VPRON)?"}
```

Figure 3: Combination rules of Arabic noun and verb"

```
Analysis 1:['w', 'b', 'al', 'yd']
          - prefix: ['w', 'b', 'al']
          - stem: yd
Analysis 2:['w', 'b', 'alyd']
          - prefix: ['w', 'b']
          - stem: alyd
Analysis 3:['w', 'balyd']
          - prefix: w
          - stem: balyd
Analysis 4:['wbalyd']
          - stem: wbalyd
```

Figure 4: Possible stems for the word وباليد "wbalyd"

5   Evaluation

As mentioned earlier, we have implemented our proposed stemming approach using Python programming language. The system accepts a text file that includes the Arabic nouns and verbs. Then, it produces the stems of those words. Example of the system's output results are shown in Table 1. Data used to test our stemmer for Arabic tweets, the results and error analysis are shown in the following subsections.

5.1   Experimental Setup

The corpus from which we extract our dataset contains 10 millions tokens taken from Twitter (Albogamy and Ramsay, 2015). They used Twitter Stream API to retrieve tweets from the Arabian Peninsula by using latitude and longitude coordinates of these regions since Arabic dialects in these regions share similar characteristics and they are the closest Arabic dialects to MSA.

To create our test set, we sampled 390 tweets from the above corpus to be used in our experiments. A set of correctly annotated nouns and verbs for this sample (gold standard) is required in order to be able to appraise the outputs of the stemmer. Once we have this, we can compare the outputs of the stemmer with this gold standard. Since there is no publicly available annotated corpus for Arabic tweets, we manually annotated our dataset. The dataset contains 1250 nouns and 692 verbs.

5.2   Results

In our experiments, we used two different settings of stem length: 3-character stem and 2-character stem. In the first experiment, we restricted the length of stems to be at least three characters for nouns and verbs

Word Type	Stem Length	Accuraccy
Nouns	>=3 characters	**78.16 %**
Verbs	>=3 characters	67.19 %

Table 2: Stemming accuracy if stem length is 3 characters and more

Word Type	Stem Length	Accuraccy
Nouns	>=2 characters	76.8 %
Verbs	>=2 characters	**77.45 %**

Table 3: Stemming accuracy if stem length is 2 characters and more

since most of words in MSA have a 3-letter stem. We got 78.16% and 67.19% stemming accuracy for nouns and verbs respectively as shown in Table 2. However, we noticed that for some nouns and verbs their stems were written in two letters. Therefore, they were ignored by the stemmer. In the second experiment, we restricted the length of stems to be at least two characters or more for nouns and verbs to cover all missed cases in the first experiment. The stemming accuracy for verbs was improved by about ten percent whereas the stemming accuracy for noun was decreased by around two percent as shown in Table 3.

Based on the experiments results, we decided to use two different constrains; one for nouns and the other for verbs. the length of stems has to be at least three characters or more for nouns and to be at least two characters or more for verbs. As we can see in Table 4, the best overall stemming performance is achieved when the minimum stem length is three characters for nouns whereas two characters for verbs. The results of the tests on our stemmer yield an accuracy of 77.91% of the whole collection. We have compared our stemming accuracy with (Al-Kabi et al., 2015), (Khoja and Garside., 1999) and (Ghwanmeh et al., 2009). Those three stemmers yield accuracies 75.03%, 74.03% and 67.40% respectively (Al-Kabi et al., 2015). Our results show improvements over the performance of those three well-known stemmers for Arabic. Moreover, we used a light stemming approach whereas they used heavy stemming approaches. We also experimented on Arabic tweets domain which is noisier than MSA. In addition, we are able to extract two and three characters stems length which are most stemmers for Arabic cannot do so.

Stem length	Overall accuracy (nouns and verbs)
>=2 characters	77.03 %
>=3 characters	74.25 %
Verb stem >=2 and noun stem>=3	**77.91 %**

Table 4: Overall stemming accuracy (nouns and verbs)

5.3 Error Analysis

We examined the words that were incorrectly segmented by our system. The errors can be broadly divided into three categories: under-stemming, over-stemming and orthography errors. Under-stemming errors happen when the stemmer does not remove all affixes in the words. For example, the word للمؤمنين "For the believers" the algorithm removes the first letter of the prefix لل but not the second one since it is considered as part of the stem in this case (see Table 5, the first row). Over-stemming errors happen when the stemmer considers part of the words is an affix and removes it. Consider the Arabic word واحد "One", the stemmer removes the original letter و because it looks like a conjunction (see Table 5, the second row). Orthography errors occur when the stemmer removes all affixes and finds the correct stems, but the last letter of the stems have a wrong shape. For example, the word كلمتهم "Their word" the stemmer removes the suffix هم and it considers كلمت as the stem which is correct except that the last letter should be replaced by ة instead of ت (see Table 5, the third row)

Arabic word	Our stemmer	Gold Standard	Error Type
للمؤمنين "For the believers"	لمؤمن	مؤمن	under-stemming
واحد "One"	احد	واحد	over-stemming
كلمتهم "Their word"	كلمت	كلمة	orthography

Table 5: Examples of Stemming errors

6 Conclusion

We have proposed, implemented and evaluated a new stemmer for Arabic tweets. It does not rely on any root dictionary, which is crucial for stemming Arabic tweets, since they have a very open lexicon. It is a light stemming approach that uses shortest stem strategy to extract the stems of the words. It has two phases: phase 1 is dedicated to producing a list of all possible stems by using the grammar, and phase 2 is to select the shortest stem as the correct stem. We compared our stemmer with three Arabic stemmers where one of them uses a similar approach to ours. Results showed that our stemmer is better in terms of accuracy in comparison with other three Arabic stemmers.

Acknowledgments

The authors would like to thank the anonymous reviewers for their encouraging feedback and insights. Fahad would also like to thank King Saud University for their financial support. Allan Ramsay's contribution to this work was partially supported by Qatar National Research Foundation (grant NPRP-7-1334-6 -039).

References

GH Al-Gaphari and M Al-Yadoumi. 2010. A method to convert sana'ani accent to modern standard Arabic. *International Journal of Information Science & Management*, 8(1).

Mohammed N Al-Kabi, Saif A Kazakzeh, Belal M Abu Ata, Saif A Al-Rababah, and Izzat M Alsmadi. 2015. A novel root based Arabic stemmer. *Journal of King Saud University-Computer and Information Sciences*, 27(2):94–103.

Hasan Al-Serhan and Aladdin Ayesh. 2006. A triliteral word roots extraction using neural network for Arabic. In *2006 International Conference on Computer Engineering and Systems*, pages 436–440. IEEE.

Yahya Alamlahi and Fateh Ahmed. 2007. Sanaani dialect to modern standard Arabic: rule-based direct machine translation. *Computer Science Dep., Sanaa University, Sanaa, Yemen*.

Fahad Albogamy and Allan Ramsay. 2015. POS tagging for Arabic tweets. *RECENT ADVANCES IN Natural Language Processing*, page 1.

Mohammed Algarni, Brent Martin, Tim Bell, and Kourosh Neshatian. 2014. Simple Arabic stemmer. In *Proceedings of the 23rd ACM International Conference on Conference on Information and Knowledge Management*, CIKM '14, pages 1803–1806, New York, NY, USA. ACM.

Tim Buckwalter. 2004. Buckwalter Arabic morphological analyzer version 2.0. ldc catalog number ldc2004l02. Technical report, ISBN 1-58563-324-0.

Kareem Darwish and Douglas W Oard. 2007. Adapting morphology for Arabic information retrieval. In *Arabic Computational Morphology*, pages 245–262. Springer.

Sajib Dasgupta and Vincent Ng. 2007. High-performance, language-independent morphological segmentation. In *NAACL HLT 2007: Proceedings of the Main Conference*, pages 155–163.

Anne N De Roeck and Waleed Al-Fares. 2000. A morphologically sensitive clustering algorithm for identifying Arabic roots. In *Proceedings of the 38th Annual Meeting on Association for Computational Linguistics*, pages 199–206. Association for Computational Linguistics.

Joseph Dichy and Ali Farghaly. 2003. Roots & patterns vs. stems plus grammar-lexis specifications: on what basis should a multilingual lexical database centred on Arabic be built. In *The MT-Summit IX workshop on Machine Translation for Semitic Languages, New Orleans*.

W. B. Frakes. 1992. Information retrieval. chapter Stemming Algorithms, pages 131–160. Prentice-Hall, Inc., Upper Saddle River, NJ, USA.

Sameh Ghwanmeh, Ghassan Kanaan, Riyad Al-Shalabi, and Saif Rabab'ah. 2009. Enhanced algorithm for extracting the root of Arabic words. In *Computer Graphics, Imaging and Visualization, 2009. CGIV'09. Sixth International Conference on*, pages 388–391. IEEE.

John Goldsmith. 2001. Unsupervised learning of the morphology of a natural language. *Computational linguistics*, 27(2):153–198.

Akshay Java, Xiaodan Song, Tim Finin, and Belle Tseng. 2007. Why we Twitter: Understanding microblogging usage and communities. In *Proceedings of the 9th WebKDD*, pages 56–65, New York, NY, USA. ACM.

S. Khoja and R. Garside. 1999. Stemming Arabic text. *Computing Department, Lancaster University, Lancaster, UK*.

Chris D. Paice. 1994. An evaluation method for stemming algorithms. In *Proceedings of the 17th Annual International ACM SIGIR Conference on Research and Development in Information Retrieval*, SIGIR '94, pages 42–50, New York, NY, USA. Springer-Verlag New York, Inc.

Topic Stability over Noisy Sources

Jing Su[1], Derek Greene[2] and Oisín Boydell[1]

[1]Centre for Applied Data Analytics Research, University College Dublin
[2]School of Computer Science & Informatics, University College Dublin
{jing.su, derek.greene, oisin.boydell}@ucd.ie

Abstract

Topic modelling techniques such as LDA have recently been applied to speech transcripts and OCR output. These corpora may contain noisy or erroneous texts which may undermine topic stability. Therefore, it is important to know how well a topic modelling algorithm will perform when applied to noisy data. In this paper we show that different types of textual noise can have diverse effects on the stability of topic models. On the other hand, topic model stability is not consistent with the same type but different levels of noise. We introduce a dictionary filtering approach to address this challenge, with the result that a topic model with the correct number of topics is always identified across different levels of noise.

1 Introduction

Topic modelling techniques are widely applied in text retrieval tasks. Frequently these techniques have been applied to explore high-quality texts such as news articles (Newman et al., 2006) and blog posts (Yokomoto et al., 2012) which have low levels of noise (i.e. few missing, misspelled, or incorrect terms and phrases). However, with the reduction in the cost of automatic speech transcription and optical character recognition (OCR) technologies, the range of sources that topic modelling can now be applied to is growing. One challenge with such textual sources is dealing with their inherent noise. In speech to text transcriptions, humans in general manage a WER of 2% to 4% (Fiscus et al., 2007). When transcribing with a vocabulary size of 200, 5000 and 100000 terms, the reported corresponding word error rates are 3%, 7% and 45% respectively. The best accuracy for broadcast news transcription is 13% (Pallet, 2003), but this drops below 25.7% in conference transcription and gets worse in casual conversation (Fiscus et al., 2007). These results indicate that the difficulty of automatic speech recognition increases with vocabulary size, speaker dependency, and level of crosstalk.

Noise aside, many of these newly available sources contain rich and valuable information that can be analysed through topic modelling. For example, automatic speech transcription applied to call centre audio recordings is able to capture a level of detail that is otherwise unavailable unless the call audio is manually reviewed which is infeasible for large call volumes. In this case topic modelling can be applied to transcribed text to extract the key issues and emerging topics of discussion.

In this study we propose a method for simulating various types of transcription errors, for the purpose of examining the effect of noise on topic modelling algorithms. We then test the robustness of probabilistic topic modelling via Latent Dirichlet Allocation (LDA) using a topic stability measure (Greene et al., 2014) over a variety of corpora. The stability of a clustering model refers to its ability to consistently produce similar solutions on data originating from the same source (Lange et al., 2004) (Ben-David et al., 2007). A high level of agreement between the resulting clusterings indicates high stability, in turn suggesting that the current model fits the data well. Consequently, we measure stability of probabilistic topic models over noise-free dataset and its corresponding noisy dataset. A high agreement score indicates an appropriate selection of topic model which is robust against textual noise.

Proceedings of the 2nd Workshop on Noisy User-generated Text,
pages 85–93, Osaka, Japan, December 11 2016.

2   Topic Modelling and Metrics

Topic models aim to discover the latent themes or topics within a corpus of documents, which can be derived by studying the distribution of co-occurrences of words across the documents. Popular approaches for topic modeling have involved the application of probabilistic algorithms such as Latent Dirichlet Allocation (LDA) introduced by Blei et al. (2003). For the evaluation of topic models, we follow the approach by Greene et al. (2014) for measuring topic model agreement. We can denote a topic list as $S = \{R_1, ..., R_k\}$, where R_i is a topic with rank i. An individual topic can be described as $R = \{T_1, ..., T_m\}$, where T_l is a term with rank l belong to the topic. Jaccard index (Jaccard, 1912) compares the number of identical items in two sets, but it neglects ranking order. Average Jaccard (AJ) similarity is a top-weighted version of the Jaccard index used to accommodate ranking information. AJ calculates the average of the Jaccard scores between every pair of subsets in two lists. Based on AJ, we can evaluate the agreement of two sets of ranked lists (topic models). The topic model agreement score between S_1 and S_2 is a mean value of the top similarity scores between each cross pair of R. The agreement score is solved using the Hungarian method (Kuhn, 1955) and is constrained in the range [0,1], where a perfect match between two identical k-way ranked sets results in 1 and a score 0 for non-overlapping sets (Greene et al., 2014).

3   Datasets

In this paper, we make use of two previously-studied text datasets which differ in terms of content and documents lengths. The *bbc* corpus includes 2225 general news articles assigned to five ground truth topics. The *wikilow* corpus is a subset of 4986 Wikipedia articles, where the articles are labeled with 10 fine-grained WikiProject sub-categories. In both datasets the topics consist of distinct vocabularies which we would expect LDA to detect. For example, the topics in *bbc* datasets are *business*, *entertainment*, *politics*, *sport*, and *technology*.

Table 1: Corpora used in the experiments, including the total number of documents n, terms m, and the number of labels k in the associated "ground truth".

Corpus	n	m	$\hat{k}$	Description
bbc	2,225	3,121	5	General news articles from the BBC (Greene and Cunningham, 2005).
wikipedia-low	4,986	15,441	10	A subset of Wikipedia. Articles are labeled with fine-grained WikiProject sub-groups (Greene et al., 2014).

3.1   Simulated Corpus with Word-level Noise

We artificially introduce noise into the above datasets to approximate the performance of topic modelling over naturally noisy sources. We measure noise using word error rate (WER), a common metric for measuring speech recognition accuracy. Moreover, WER has been used as a salient metric in speech quality analytics (Saon et al., 2006) and spoken dialogue system (Cavazza, 2001). WER is defined as the fraction between the sum of the number of substitutions S, the number of deletions D, the number of insertions and the number of terms in reference N:

$$WER = \frac{S + D + I}{N} \tag{1}$$

The experiments investigate the robustness of topic models against each type of noise, and at which noise levels the output of a topic model is consistent with that of the original corpus. *Deletion* noise is introduced by randomly removing a portion of text in the corpus. The proportion of deletion ranges from 0% to 50% and the term selection is based on uniform distribution. *Insertion* is introduced by adding a portion (0% to 50%) of frequent terms from a list of frequent English words with 7726 entries[1]. The probability of sampling of a certain term from the list is based on the term frequency.

---

[1] http://ucrel.lancs.ac.uk/bncfreq/flists.html

3.1.1 Metaphone Replacement

We simulate speech recognition errors using Metaphone, a phonetic algorithm for indexing English words by their pronunciation (Philips, 1990). Here we use the Double Metaphone (Black, 2014) algorithm in replacement and the replacement is on a one-to-one basis. This may not simulate the full range of errors produced by ASR systems, in which the substitution may be a one-to-many or many-to-one mapping, but it was deemed sufficient for the current experiments.

Table 2: Double metaphone dictionary where terms are ranked with descending frequencies.

Metaphone	Matching terms
ANTS	**industry**, units, induced, wound, ...
KRTF	grateful, **creative**, Cardiff, ...

Table 3: An example of 30% metaphone replacement in the *bbc* dataset.

Original text	Replaced text
We **are** hoping to understand the **creative industry** that has a **natural** thirst for **broadband** technology	We **air** hoping to understand the **Cardiff induced** that has a **neutralist** thirst for **portable** technology

In this study we map Metaphone codes to frequent English words (see examples in Table 2). Then in a given text document, we randomly select X percent terms and replace each by a term in the Metaphone map. The candidate terms sharing the same metaphone symbol are selected based on term frequencies. A frequent term has higher probability to be selected over a rare term (see Table 3).

3.2 Simulated Corpus with Image-level Noise

In the last section we simulatde word-level noise with deletion, insertion and metaphone replacement errors. As an alternative, we now introduce image-level random noise and simulate term errors from OCR. *ImageMagick*[2] is a popular software tool which can apply transformations and filters to images. *Tesseract*[3] is a widely-used open source OCR engine. We combine ImageMagick and Tesseract in sequence to generate noisy document images and then re-scan the content from those images. The level of image noise can be specified as a parameter to ImageMagick. The number of error terms from OCR is assumed to be proportional to the level of image noise that has been added. However, we observe that the robustness of OCR is highly influenced by the choice of text font. For instance, Tesseract scans of text in a monospace (fixed-width) font tend to be identical across a range of increasing noise until a certain level is reached, above which almost no characters are retrieved. Therefore, we opt to use variable-width font *Verdana* in this study, as its noise resistance performance is close to linear.

Figure 1 shows two snippets of ImageMagick generated images with noise level 1 and 3. The source texts are from the same document from the *bbc* corpus. The text in the image with level 1 noise remains clearly legibile. However it is rather difficult to read the content from the image with level 3 noise. Figure 2 shows texts scanned by Tesseract from the images of Figure 1. We can observe systematic errors on both images. On Figure 2 (a), `sales` is translated as `saies`, and `Google` is translated as `Googie`. On Figure 2 (b), `which` is retrieved as `wildi`, and `the` is retrieved as `die`. The word `Time` is read as `1Ine`, `Tine` or `The`. These are only part of the errors from OCR output, but they show both one-to-one mapping and one-to-many mapping.

Figure 3 shows the Recall (i.e. how many instances in the scanned texts match the instances of words in original texts) of Tesseract OCR against original texts in *bbc* and *wikilow* corpora. The recall score at each noise level is a mean value of recall from each pair of documents (one original document and its corresponding scanned text). In both corpora the highest recall value is observed from noise level 2.

---

[2] `http://www.imagemagick.org`
[3] `https://github.com/tesseract-ocr`

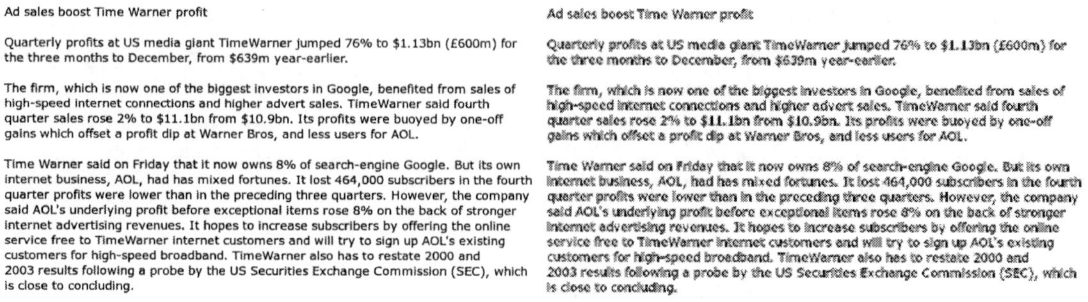

Ad sales boost Time Warner profit

Quarterly profits at US media giant TimeWarner jumped 76% to $1.13bn (£600m) for the three months to December, from $639m year-earlier.

The firm, which is now one of the biggest investors in Google, benefited from sales of high-speed internet connections and higher advert sales. TimeWarner said fourth quarter sales rose 2% to $11.1bn from $10.9bn. Its profits were buoyed by one-off gains which offset a profit dip at Warner Bros, and less users for AOL.

Time Warner said on Friday that it now owns 8% of search-engine Google. But its own internet business, AOL, had has mixed fortunes. It lost 464,000 subscribers in the fourth quarter profits were lower than in the preceding three quarters. However, the company said AOL's underlying profit before exceptional items rose 8% on the back of stronger internet advertising revenues. It hopes to increase subscribers by offering the online service free to TimeWarner internet customers and will try to sign up AOL's existing customers for high-speed broadband. TimeWarner also has to restate 2000 and 2003 results following a probe by the US Securities Exchange Commission (SEC), which is close to concluding.

(a) noise level 1

Ad sales boost Time Warner profit

Quarterly profits at US media giant TimeWarner jumped 76% to $1.13bn (£600m) for the three months to December, from $639m year-earlier.

The firm, which is now one of the biggest investors in Google, benefited from sales of high-speed internet connections and higher advert sales. TimeWarner said fourth quarter sales rose 2% to $11.1bn from $10.9bn. Its profits were buoyed by one-off gains which offset a profit dip at Warner Bros, and less users for AOL.

Time Warner said on Friday that it now owns 8% of search-engine Google. But its own internet business, AOL, had has mixed fortunes. It lost 464,000 subscribers in the fourth quarter profits were lower than in the preceding three quarters. However, the company said AOL's underlying profit before exceptional items rose 8% on the back of stronger internet advertising revenues. It hopes to increase subscribers by offering the online service free to TimeWarner internet customers and will try to sign up AOL's existing customers for high-speed broadband. TimeWarner also has to restate 2000 and 2003 results following a probe by the US Securities Exchange Commission (SEC), which is close to concluding.

(b) noise level 3

Figure 1: Snippets of ImageMagick generated images with noise level 1 (a) and level 3 (b).

Ad saies boost Time Warner profit

Quarterly profits at US media giant TimeWarnerjumped 76% to $1.13bn (£600m) for the three months to December, from $639m year-eariier.

The firm, which is now one of the biggest investors in Googie, benefited from saies of high-speed internet connections and higher advert saies. TimeWarner said fourth quarter saies rose 2% to $11.1bn from $10.9bn. Its profits were buoyed by one-off gains which offset a profit dip at Warner Bros, and iess users for AOL.

Time Warner said on Friday that it now owns 8% of search-engine Googie. But its own internet business, AOL, had has mixed fortunes. It iost 464,000 subscribers in the fourth quarter profits were iower than in the preceding three quarters. However, the company said AOL's underiying profit before exceptionai items rose 8% on the back of stronger internet advertising revenues. It hopes to increase subscribers by offering the oniine service free to TimeWarner internet customers and wiii try to sign up AOL's existing customers for high-speed broadband. TimeWarner aiso has to restate 2000 and 2003 resuits foiiowing a probe by the US Securities Exchange Commission (SEC), which is ciose to conciuding.

(a) noise level 1

Ad sales boost 1Ine Warner profit

Quarterly profits at US meda ¢ant1IneWarnerJunped 75% to $1.13bn{£500m)lor die dI'ee months to December, fi'om $639m year-caller.

The (I'm, wildi is now one oldie biggest Iiyestors Ii Goode, benefited fi'om sales of li¢rspeed IIternet comecdons and li¢ier adyert sales. TIneWarner said lou'di quarter sales rose 2% to $11.1bn fi'om $10.9bn. Its profits were buoyed by one-olf gaIis wildi oll'set a profit q: at Warner Bros, and less users (or AOL.

The Warner said on Friday diat It now owns 8% olseardi-enwe Goode. But Its own IIternet buiness, AOL, liad has mixed loruies. It lost 464,000 swscrlaers Ii die lou'di quarter profits were lower than Ii die precedig dI'ee quarters. Howeyer, die company said AOL's mdel'lyIig profit belore exceptional Items rose 8% on die badt olsironger IIternet adyerding reyenues. It hopes to Iicrease swscrlaers by ollerIig die orIie seryice fi'ee to TIneWarner IIternet customers and wI try to sigi w AOL's exlsiIig customers (or li¢rspeed broadaand. TIneWarner also has to restate 2000 and 2003 restIts lolowIig a probe by die US Secu'Ides Exdiange Commission {SEC}, wildi is dose to condutlig.

(b) noise level 3

Figure 2: Snippets of Tesseract scanned texts with noise level 1 (a) and level 3 (b).

Therefore we drop the assumption that the error rate of scan is linearly scalable to noise levels. Another observation is that recall scores in both corpora are close to each other on each level of image noise, although the contents as well as scan errors of two corpora are quite different.

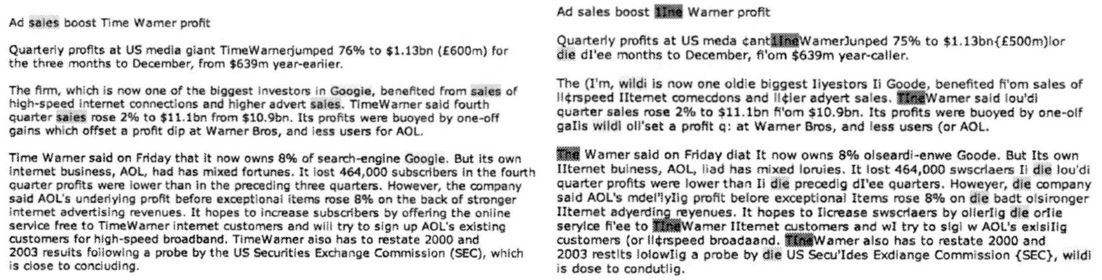

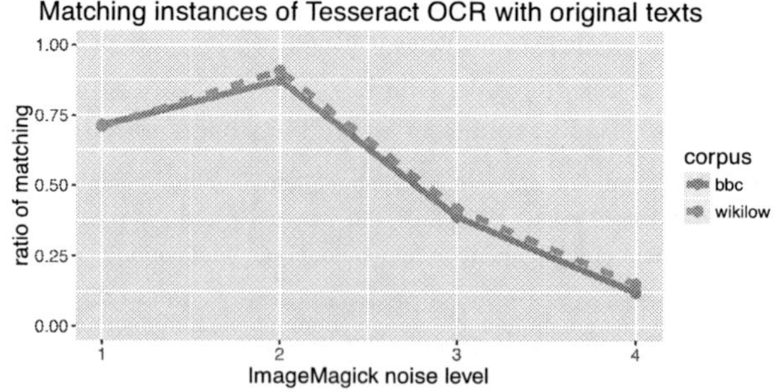

Figure 3: Recall of Tesseract OCR against original texts in *bbc* and *wikilow* corpora

4 Experiments

In our experiments with LDA, we aim to test topic stability over different levels of noise and different numbers of topics. In other words, when there is noise added to a text corpus, would the generated topic models be consistent with those from original corpus? If not, how much discrepancy exists between the two? Two sets of experiments are designed to introduce word-level noise and image-level noise to the original data. Our aim is to find guidelines for topic modelling over real noisy text sources in practice.

Since average Jaccard (AJ) score measures the similarity between two ranked lists (topics), we use AJ as an element in evaluating the similarity of two topic models S_x and S_y. If S_x and S_y each contains

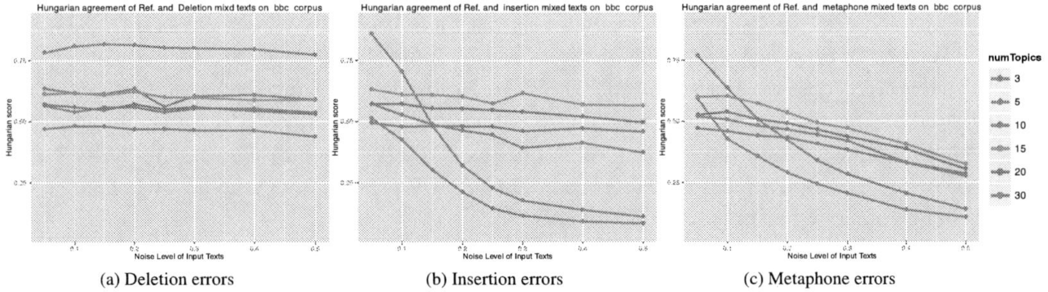

(a) Deletion errors   (b) Insertion errors   (c) Metaphone errors

Figure 4: LDA Hungarian scores against noise levels for the *bbc* corpus (5 reference topics).

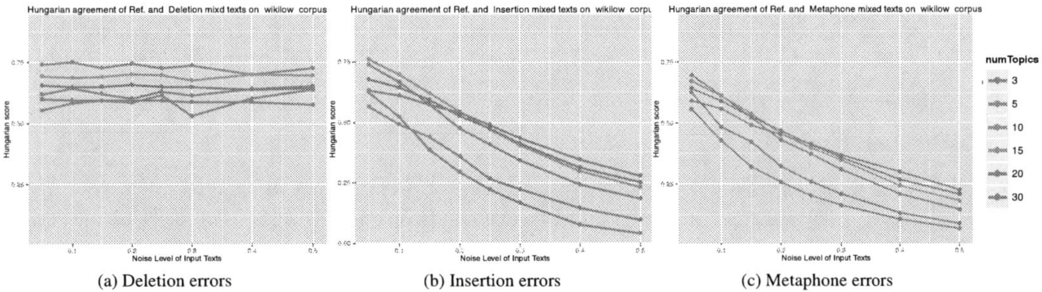

(a) Deletion errors   (b) Insertion errors   (c) Metaphone errors

Figure 5: LDA Hungarian scores against noise levels for the *wikilow* corpus (10 reference topics).

k ranked lists (topics), they are denoted as $S_x = \{R_{x1}, ..., R_{xk}\}$ and $S_y = \{R_{y1}, ..., R_{yk}\}$. We build a $k \times k$ matrix $\mathbf{M}$ to register each similarity score. In this matrix entry M_{ij} indicates the AJ score between topic R_{xi} and topic R_{yj}. The best matching between the rows and columns of $\mathbf{M}$ can be found using the Hungarian method (Kuhn, 1955). The agreement score produced from $\mathbf{M}$ is named as Hungarian agreement score, and is used as a measure of topic model stability in the following experiments.

4.1 LDA with Word-level Noise

In order to produce consistent and repeatable results where each noise generation method relies on a degree of randomness with word deletion, insertion or substitution we generate multiple copies of each modified corpus using 5 random seeds. Similarly we perform 5 iterations of each Mallet LDA (McCallum, 2002) topic model as the algorithm initial state is determined by a random seed. LDA hyperparameters are defined with default values, and each topic is represented by the top 25 terms. The final stability score on each level is a mean value of a number of iterations with fixed seeds.

Figure 4 and Figure 5 show the topic stability achieved by LDA on the *bbc* and *wikilow* corpora, which have 5 and 10 reference topics respectively. For each level of topic model complexity, a downward slope indicates decreasing stability of topic models against increasing noise.

For the *bbc* corpus, the stability measure shows clear differences with different types of noise. The model is especially robust against *Deletion* errors. When noise increases from 5% to 50%, the Hungarian agreement score of output topics only drops about 1% (for the fitted model with $K = 5$ in Figure 4(a)). By inspecting each model in Figure 4(a), we can say that the topic models are robust against random *Deletion* noise in the case of the *bbc* corpus.

In Figure 4(b), the model with 5 topics achieves the highest Hungarian agreement score at noise level 5% and 10%, but it drops significantly afterwards. The best and most stable topic model with noise higher than 15% of *Insertion* errors is the model with 15 topics, which is three times of the reference. Similar trend is observed with *Metaphone* replacement errors in Figure 4(c). The topic model with reference number of topics achieves the highest stability when noise level is low. However, there are differences between Insertion and Metaphone errors in *bbc* corpus tests. With 50% of *Insertion* errors, the model with 15 topics achieves 56.4% agreement with original model, but the agreement is only 32.4% with *Metaphone* errors. In *bbc* corpus *Metaphone* errors are the most challenging case.

For the *wikilow* corpus, we observe similar trends in Figure 4 and Figure 5 on specific types of noise. With *Deletion* errors, the topic model with the reference number of topics is most stable across noise levels. The difference in topic agreement scores is below 2% across the noise levels. With *Insertion* and *Metaphone* errors, the topic model with reference number of topics is almost the best when noise is low, but drops below others when noise is higher than 15%.

Although there are many similarities between Figure 4 and 5, we observe two major differences across corpora. In Figure 5(b) and 5(c), Hungarian scores of different topic models (number of topics) share similar gradient of descending slope. However, a few models for the *bbc* corpus ($K = \{15, 20, 30\}$) achieve quite stable Hungarian scores in Figure *bbc*(b). Another difference is that the most stable topic models against noise levels higher than 20% in Figure 4(b) and 4(c) both have 15 topics, whereas the most stable models in *wikilow* have 30 topics in the same settings. However, if we compare them with corresponding reference topic numbers K, the most stable topic models with high systematic errors all have $K * 3$ topics. Models with topic number higher than $K * 3$ are not optimal in Figure 4(b) and 4(c).

4.1.1 Discussion

In Section 4.1 we considered topic model stability on two corpora with three types of noise. Here we can define a single measurement of topic stability across different settings. If a level of agreement is set as 70%, LDA is robust against Deletion noise up to 50% in both *bbc* and *wikilow* corpora. However, LDA model reaches this agreement level only on 10% Insertion noise and on 5% Metaphone replacement noise. We see that Metaphone replacement and insertion are more severe challenges to topic models vs. deletion.

Regarding deletion errors, we observe that the robustness of a topic model is mostly determined by the number of topics. When this matches the number of reference topics, the topic model is the most stable. However, this does not emerge with insertion and metaphone errors. Reference topic models with 5 (bbc) and 10 (wikilow) topics achieve high stability only when noise is $\leq 10\%$. With higher levels of noise, a more complex topic model exhibits higher stability.

An explanation of the high stability of topic models against *Deletion* error concerns the LDA model. LDA takes term frequency into account. The probability of a word belonging to a topic is high if it appears frequently in one topic and seldom in other topics. Such a word is very likely to be an entry in a topic model. If we randomly delete corpus terms, the scale of frequent terms is influenced trivially and these frequent terms still have a high probability of selection. All rare terms may be removed by deletion, but they have a low chance of appearing in the original topic model anyway. Therefore LDA model has high stability over various levels of deletion errors. *Insertion* and *Metaphone* replacement introduces systematic noise, which changes the distribution of original texts with respect to frequency, thus having more impact on the LDA model. A high portion of general frequent terms may dilute the frequency of characteristic terms and add noisy terms to a topic model. However, a topic model with many more topics than the reference can deal with the effect of systematic errors.

4.2 LDA with Image-level Noise

In Section 3.2 we introduced the concept of image-level random noise. By using this approach, the Tesseract scanned texts contain character-level noise and many of them are systematic errors. For example, many instances of character 1 are retrieved as i in Figure 2. In this section we evaluate the stability of LDA topic models over corpora with substantial systematic errors. Mallet LDA topic model is evaluated over the scanned corpora of noise levels 1 to 4. On each noise level, topic model stability is evaluated with a selection of model complexity (the number of topics ranges from 3 to 30). Since Dirichlet prior of a LDA model is set with a random seed, we test one LDA model three times with 3 fixed seeds and get model stability score from the mean value of three iterations. The number of terms in each topic is 25.

Figure 6(a) and 6(c) show Hungarian agreement scores for LDA topic models, as achieved on the original corpus and a corresponding polluted corpus with image-level noises. Figure 6(a) is from the *bbc*

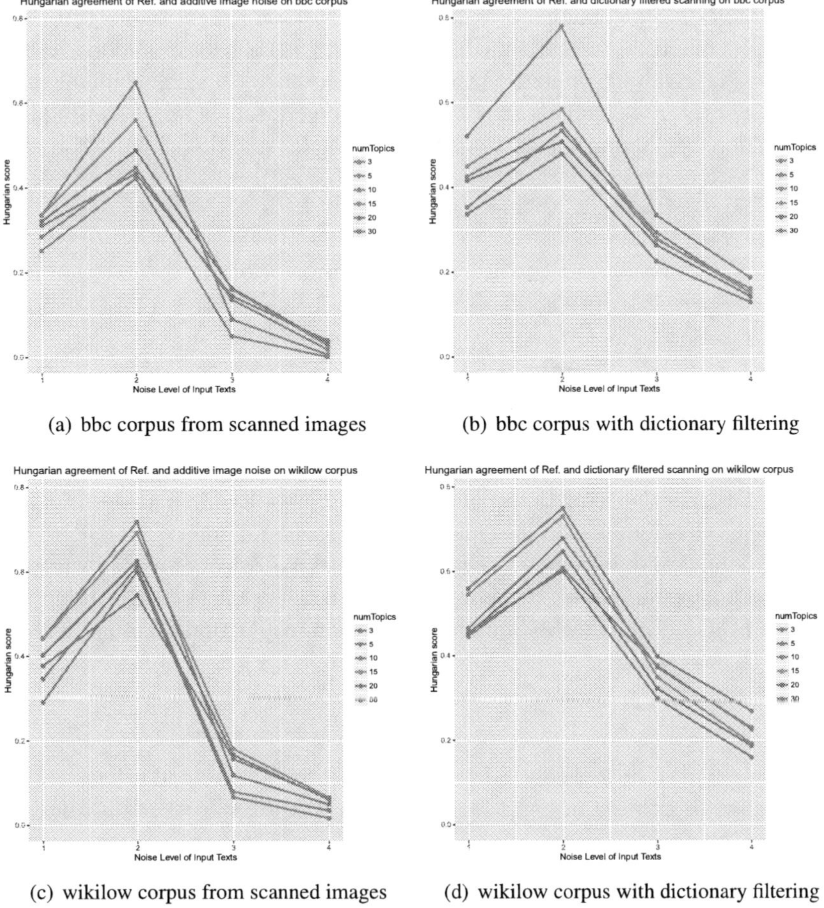

(a) bbc corpus from scanned images   (b) bbc corpus with dictionary filtering

(c) wikilow corpus from scanned images   (d) wikilow corpus with dictionary filtering

Figure 6: LDA Hungarian scores over scanned corpora (a) and (c), and dictionary filtered corpora (b) and (d). In reference dataset, *bbc* corpus has 5 topics and *wikilow* has 10 topics.

corpus and Figure 6(c) is from the *wikilow* corpus. In these two figures Hungarian agreement score drops with increasing image-level noises (noise 2 to 4), but rises from noise 1 to 2. As a comparison, curves in Figure 3 follow similar trends. The stability of LDA model is influenced by character-level noises in the scanned corpus.

For the *bbc* corpus (Figure 6(a)) a model with 5 topics achieves (almost) the highest Hungarian agreement score at noise level 1 and 2, but it drops considerably at noise level 3 and 4. Models with 20 and 30 topics reach the highest Hungarian agreement score at noise level 3 and 4 respectively. For the *wikilow* corpus (Figure 6(c)), the model with 10 topics achieves (almost) the highest scores across noise level 1 to 2, but it drops near to the bottom at noise level 3 and 4. Choosing 15 topics yields the highest Hungarian agreement score at noise level 3 and 4.

4.2.1 Filtering Noisy Corpus with English Dictionary

OCR generates character-level outputs and therefore the scanned corpora contain erroneous terms which are out of English vocabulary (e.g., `saies`). We propose a filtering step over the OCR scanned corpus before the topic modelling step. A general English dictionary with 110k entries is used as a reference set to filter off any undefined terms.

LDA topic models are tested on the dictionary filtered corpora following the same steps used in Section 4.2, and the Hungarian agreement scores are plotted in Figure 6(b) and 6(d). At the first look, we observe similar curves as experiments with unfiltered corpus (Figure 6(a) and 6(c)). However, there are important differences. In Figure 6(b) topic number 5 reaches the highest agreement scores across noise level 1 to 4. In Figure 6(d) topic number 10 reaches the highest agreement scores across noise level 1 to 4. In both corpora, the topic models with the reference number of topics are most stable with the dictionary filtered texts. On each noise level, if we compare the highest agreement scores across two figures side by side, we can see that dictionary filtering brings an increase of model stability over 10% in most cases and it can be as high as 20% on high level noises.

4.2.2 Discussion

We evaluate the stability of topic models over scanned corpus of noisy images, and we find common observations as the experiments in Section 4.1. In general, the stability of LDA models drops with increasing simulated *insertion* and *Metaphone* replacement errors because these errors are not random terms. More consistent systematic errors (e.g., Figure 2) give higher challenge to topic models. Under these challenges, a topic model with reference number of topics performs best at relatively low noise levels. When noise is as large as 4, LDA models with 30 topics (*bbc*) or 15 topics (*wikilow*) are more stable in both corpora.

When we apply dictionary filtering to scanned texts, LDA stability improves considerably. Moreover, the stability of topic models for the reference number of topics is still highest, despite significant levels of noise. There is no more need to increase topic model complexity for better performance. Although there may be a risk that we may remove terms which correspond to names or specialised terminology, this issue could be overcome by augmenting the dictionary with lists of people, organisations, and domain-specific lexicons.

5 Conclusions

In this paper we investigated how transcription errors affect the quality and robustness of topic models produced over a range of corpora, using a topic stability measure introduced *a priori*. We simulated word-level transcription errors from the perspective of word error rate and generated noisy corpora with *deletion*, *insertion* and *Metaphone* replacement. Topic models produced by LDA showed high tolerance to deletion noise up to a reasonably high level, but low tolerance to insertion and metaphone replacement errors. We also simulated image-level OCR transcription errors which are close to real OCR applications.

In general, we found that the robustness of topic models is mainly determined by the extent of systematic errors which modifies the distribution of words in the original texts. With relatively low levels of systematic errors, topic models with reference number of topics were most stable. However, in the case of high level systematic errors, topic models with many more redundant errors were stable.

In order to increase topic model stability when analysing a noisy corpus, we introduced English dictionary-based filtering. Dictionary filtering was shown to be effective in correcting systematic errors across different noise levels, with the result that topics generated from collections of noisy documents were still informative. In future experiments, we aim to explore more approaches in improving topic model stability over noisy sources.

References

Shai Ben-David, Dávid Pál, and Hans Ulrich Simon, 2007. *Stability of k-Means Clustering*, pages 20–34. Springer Berlin Heidelberg, Berlin, Heidelberg.

Paul E. Black. 2014. "double metaphone", in dictionary of algorithms and data structures [online]. `https://xlinux.nist.gov/dads/HTML/doubleMetaphone.html`, May 2014.

David M. Blei, Andrew Y. Ng, and Michael I. Jordan. 2003. Latent dirichlet allocation. *Journal of Machine Learning Research*, 3:993–1022, March.

Marc Cavazza. 2001. An empirical study of speech recognition errors in a task-oriented dialogue system. In *Proceedings of the Second SIGdial Workshop on Discourse and Dialogue - Volume 16*, SIGDIAL '01, pages 1–8, Stroudsburg, PA, USA. Association for Computational Linguistics.

Jonathan G. Fiscus, Jerome Ajot, and John S. Garofolo. 2007. The rich transcription 2007 meeting recognition evaluation. In *Multimodal Technologies for Perception of Humans, International Evaluation Workshops CLEAR 2007 and RT 2007, Baltimore, MD, USA, May 8-11, 2007, Revised Selected Papers*, pages 373–389.

Derek Greene and Pádraig Cunningham. 2005. Producing accurate interpretable clusters from high-dimensional data. In A. Jorge, L. Torgo, P. Brazdi, R. Camacho, and J. Gama, editors, *Proc. 9th European Conference on Principles and Practice of Knowledge Discovery in Databases (PKDD'05)*, pages 486–494. Springer, October.

D. Greene, D. O'Callaghan, and P. Cunningham. 2014. How Many Topics? Stability Analysis for Topic Models. In *Proc. European Conference on Machine Learning (ECML'14)*.

Paul Jaccard. 1912. The distribution of flora in the alpine zone. *New Phytologist*, 11(2):37–50.

H. W. Kuhn. 1955. The hungarian method for the assignment problem. *Naval Research Logistics Quarterly*, 2(1-2):83–97.

Tilman Lange, Volker Roth, Mikio L. Braun, and Joachim M. Buhmann. 2004. Stability-based validation of clustering solutions. *Neural Comput.*, 16(6):1299–1323, June.

Andrew Kachites McCallum. 2002. Mallet: A machine learning for language toolkit. http://mallet.cs.umass.edu.

David Newman, Chaitanya Chemudugunta, Padhraic Smyth, and Mark Steyvers. 2006. Analyzing entities and topics in news articles using statistical topic models. In *Proceedings of the 4th IEEE International Conference on Intelligence and Security Informatics*, ISI'06, pages 93–104, Berlin, Heidelberg. Springer-Verlag.

David S. Pallet. 2003. A look at NIST's benchmark asr tests: Past, present, and future. Technical report, National Institute of Standards and Technology (NIST), Gaithersburg, MD, USA.

Lawrence Philips. 1990. Hanging on the metaphone. *Computer Language*, 7(12 (December)):39.

G. Saon, B. Ramabhadran, and G. Zweig. 2006. On the effect of word error rate on automated quality monitoring. In *Spoken Language Technology Workshop, 2006. IEEE*, pages 106–109, Dec.

Daisuke Yokomoto, Kensaku Makita, Hiroko Suzuki, Daichi Koike, Takehito Utsuro, Yasuhide Kawada, and Tomohiro Fukuhara. 2012. Lda-based topic modeling in labeling blog posts with wikipedia entries. In *Proceedings of the 14th International Conference on Web Technologies and Applications*, APWeb'12, pages 114–124, Berlin, Heidelberg. Springer-Verlag.

Analysis of Twitter Data for
Postmarketing Surveillance in Pharmacovigilance

Julie Pain and **Jessie Levacher** and **Adam Quinquenel**
INSA Rouen
Avenue de l'Université, Saint-tienne-du-Rouvray, France
{julie.pain, jessie.levacher, adam.quinquenel}@insa-rouen.fr

Anja Belz
Computing, Engineering and Mathematics
University of Brighton, Lewes Road, Brighton, UK
a.s.belz@brighton.ac.uk

Abstract

Postmarketing surveillance (PMS) has the vital aim to monitor effects of drugs after release for use by the general population, but suffers from under-reporting and limited coverage. Automatic methods for detecting drug effect reports, especially for social media, could vastly increase the scope of PMS. Very few automatic PMS methods are currently available, in particular for the messy text types encountered on Twitter. In this paper we describe first results for developing PMS methods specifically for tweets. We describe the corpus of 125,669 tweets we have created and annotated to train and test the tools. We find that generic tools perform well for tweet-level language identification and tweet-level sentiment analysis (both 0.94 F1-Score). For detection of effect mentions we are able to achieve 0.87 F1-Score, while effect-level adverse-vs.-beneficial analysis proves harder with an F1-Score of 0.64. Among other things, our results indicate that MetaMap semantic types provide a very promising basis for identifying drug effect mentions in tweets.

1 Introduction

Postmarketing surveillance (PMS) is a vital part of pharmacovigilance, taking place during the final, post-licensing phase of drug development when the effects on larger numbers of users, who may have other conditions and take other medicines than those included in pre-approval tests, can be assessed. PMS is implemented in passive national reporting schemes such as the Yellow Card Scheme in the UK and MedWatch in the US; it is also implemented as active surveillance, e.g. organisations such as the MHRA in the UK and the FDA in the US conduct post-approval studies and postmarketing surveys.

Existing PMS methods either rely on health practitioners and patients to report adverse effects to which only a small (self-selected) proportion of patients in particular will contribute (reporting schemes), or they involve single products and small numbers of participants (surveys). More generally, such methods are more likely to identify (i) very serious problems, and (ii) problems relating to newly released drugs and drugs already under continuous surveillance.

The ultimate goal of our work is to develop text analysis techniques to facilitate automatic, continuous and large-scale monitoring of adverse drug reactions (ADRs), and more generally of effects, beneficial or otherwise, reported for given drugs. There is currently huge interest in such methods in the pharmaceutical industry, in particular where they can be used to monitor what is being said on social media about specific drugs. Automatic PMS methods are also of interest to national regulatory bodies.

The potential benefits of high-precision automatic ADR detection methods for social media are great: such methods would ameliorate the recognised problem of under-reporting of ADRs via existing channels (Lardon et al., 2015), and could inform the design of post-approval studies. Studies have already demonstrated that analysis of social media contents (manual analysis so far) can lead to the discovery of serious side effects, e.g. Abou

Proceedings of the 2nd Workshop on Noisy User-generated Text,
pages 94–101, Osaka, Japan, December 11 2016.

Taam et al. (2014) retrospectively identified a severe side effect on the basis of user content posted months before the drug in question was withdrawn because of the same side effect. The challenge is to automate this process so that suitably large portions of social media can be scanned.

2   Related Research

The main interest has so far been in discovering ADRs, defined by the World Health Organisation as a "a response to a medicinal product which is noxious and unintended and which occurs at doses normally used in [humans] for the prophylaxis, diagnosis or therapy of disease or for the restoration, correction or modification of physiological function" (WHO, No date).

While studies involving manual analysis have confirmed the usefulness of social media content in ADR identification (see previous section), manual analysis is necessarily limited to minute fractions of available online content. Automatic analysis of online content for ADR detection remains a huge challenge, in particular when applied to Twitter, due to the messy and 'un-language-like' nature of tweets, and it remains a small field.

Last year, Lardon et al. (2015) reported the results of a very thorough scoping review of (i) manual and computer-aided identification of ADRs, and (ii) semi-automatic and automatic identification of ADRs, from social media. The authors found just 13 papers on the latter, of which just one paper focused on Twitter data (the remainder used content from online health forums).

That one paper (Bian et al., 2012), among the very earliest on this precise topic, reported the creation and annotation of a corpus of drug-related tweets, and results for training SVM classifiers to detect (a) whether the tweeter was reporting their own experience, and (b) whether a given own-experience tweet contained a mention of an ADR. The study targeted five drugs that were the subject of a pre-approval clinical study during a known time window, and analysed tweets that were posted during the same time window, on the assumption that study participants were likely to tweet about their experience. 489 tweets by 424 users were identified in this way, reduced to 239 users after removal of re-tweets and non-English tweets. Tweets by the same user were concatenated and annotated manually. An SVM classifier was trained to classify texts into (i) users reporting their own experience of taking the drug, and (ii) user reporting someone else's experience; the classifier used 171 features, some based on keywords and word types, hashtags and user names; others based on a MetaMap (Aronson, 2001) analysis of the texts yielding UMLS meta codes. Classification into first-hand vs. second-hand reporting achieved an average accuracy of 0.74, and classification of first-hand-reporting tweets into ADR-mentioning and not ADR-mentioning was also reported as achieving 0.74 accuracy.

Ginn et al. (2014) created a corpus of annotated tweets and results for training classifiers to detect ADR mentions. Two members of the project team with "medical or biological science background" annotated 10,822 tweets related to 74 drugs for mentions of an ADR, indication or beneficial effect, and each ADR/indication/beneficial effect with corresponding UMLS concepts. The 74 drugs included some for which ADRs are well established and some for which they are not. Product names, common names and misspellings were used for each drug; tweets with URLs were removed (deemed to be mostly adverts). Inter-annotator agreement (IAA) was kappa = 0.69. Ginn et al. trained Naive Bayes (NB) and SVM classifiers on the binary annotations (presence/absence of effect mentions), using bag-of-words feature vectors, text normalisation and lemmatisation. Three versions of the corpus were created with different levels of imbalance between positive and negative examples. Best Precision for detecting effects was 0.89 (Recall = 0.695; F-Score=0.78; Accuracy = 0.746) for NB and the exactly balanced version of the corpus; Accuracy was around 0.75 for NB across the three differently balanced corpus versions.

Two members of the Ginn et al. team subsequently reported a larger set of results (Sarker and Gonzalez, 2015), using the Twitter data above, but also data from an online health forum, and an existing corpus of clinical reports. They describe the earlier results as having been obtained by "classification via under-sampling, which yields higher ADR F-scores at the expense of overall accuracy" (Footnote 22). Sarker & Gonzalez decided not to use under-sampling or balancing, and report ADR F-Scores of 0.538 and Accuracy 86.2 for the Twitter data with a different type of SVM than in the earlier work, going up to 0.597 and 90.1, respectively, when the Twitter data is supplemented by the data from the online health forum.

In summary, the tasks for which tools have so far been built under the heading of automatic ADR detection in tweets are all binary (note that the *annotations* in the data sets include a wider variety of information):

- for a given tweet, decide whether it is in English or not (Bian et al., 2012);

- for a given set of tweets by the same Twitter user and a given drug, decide whether or not the user themself is taking (or has taken) the drug (Bian et al., 2012);

- for a given tweet, decide whether or not it contains a mention of an ADR (Bian et al., 2012; Ginn et al., 2014; Sarker and Gonzalez, 2015).

In this paper, we address (i) the first task above (Section 5), (ii) a more general case of the last task above (mentions of all drug reactions, adverse or not, Section 7), as well as two new, non-binary tasks (for this domain): (iii) for a given tweet, decide what its sentiment is (Section 6); and (iv) for a tweet that has been identified as containing a mention of a drug reaction (as in ii above), decide whether the drug reaction is beneficial, adverse or neither (Section 8).

3   Automatic Drug Effect Detection: Task, Annotation, Tools

Automatic drug effect detection for Twitter is something of a worst case scenario for NLP: not only are tweets one of the messiest, most abbreviated forms of short text, for which standard NLP tools do not tend to work well; but automatic ADR detection is also extremely hard, even for very well behaved types of text, due among other factors to the large variety of ways in which the same drug effects can be referred to, and to the complex relationships between drugs and effects.

The research reviewed in the previous section focused on detecting *adverse* drug effects (the annotations in some cases also include other kinds of effects, but the tools were for ADR detection). There are three reasons why we address a wider set of effects: (a) the related research area of automatic drug discovery/development, including our industrial advisory partner, is interested in identifying *all* effects claimed for a given drug/compound; (b) post-marketing drug monitoring, especially by pharmaceutical companies, is

also interested in a wider set of effects; and (c) it may make the detection task harder if one specific subtype of drug effects is targeted only.

To elaborate on that last point, ADRs can be seen as a special case of a more general binary drug-effect relation *has_effect(drug, effect)*. Our corpus (Section 4) contains diverse examples, including the following:[1]

> *has_effect("glucosamine", "got me feeling some typa way")*
> *has_effect("azathioprine", "think I've got #shingles")*
> *has_effect("daunorubicin", "made his wee red")*

Reports of effects, whether positive, negative, or neither, are likely to have similar patterns and cue phrases (e.g. 'I've got', 'got me feeling'). It may be the case that it is easier to identify all reports of effects, not just negative ones, and then classify those into adverse, beneficial, mild, severe, and other dimensions.

We construe drug-effect detection as a knowledge extraction task, where the objective is to identify mentions of drug effects and to fill relation templates such as *has_effect(drug, effect)*. In this general form such mentions can be incorporated into knowledge graphs and combined with other kinds of relations about drugs and health. Such knowledge graphs can be easily visualised, and are used for example in automatic drug discovery research where mentions of drug effects from social media could provide a useful complementary source of information.

In this paper, we report first results towards the above knowledge extraction task. We use the term 'drug effect' to refer to both cases where the effect is specified and cases that might more intuitively be described as 'properties' where there is no specified effect (see also Section 8 below). Section 4 describes how we collected our set of tweets, and the text cleaning and normalisation we perform. Sections 5, 6, and 7 report results from our experiments on language identification, sentiment analysis and drug effect detection in tweets, respectively, while Section 8 reports results from classifying drug effects into beneficial, adverse and other.

---

[1]The text would be mapped to e.g. UMLS codes before being incorporated into knowledge bases, as below.

4 Data Collection

We compiled a list of drug names by extracting all names of approved drugs from DrugBank,[2] 1,999 in total. Next, for each drug name we collected the HTML files of all tweets returned for the search *"Drug Name" OR #DrugName* (e.g. *"Acetic Acid" OR #AceticAcid*), up to a maximum of 100 tweets per drug name, and used Beautiful Soup[3] to extract the information we needed (tweet text, tweet id, timestamp, etc.) from the HTML files containing the search results (tweets).

The results was a corpus[4] of 125,669 tweets, with an average of 62.87 tweets collected for each drug. Figure 1 gives a more detailed picture of number of tweets per drug: most drugs have 70-95 tweets, 19 have none, and 15 have 100 or more. Note that we did not expand the set of drug names with misspelt variants, generic or common names as done in some related research (Ginn et al., 2014).

We used three versions of the tweet texts: (i) in their raw form; (ii) cleaned, with URLs and user names replaced by tags, and hash tags with the '#' removed; and (iii) with hashtags additionally converted to likely strings of words, using a tool made available on StackOverflow.[5]

5 Language Identification

In order to be able to analyse tweets in a meaningful way, moreover using text analysis tools trained for English, it is important that we can reliably filter out non-English tweets. Twitter tags tweets for language, so part of our first set of experiments was to test the reliability of the Twitter language tags, as well as to see how it compared against existing language identification tools. For the latter we chose the three tools that were, combined as an ensemble method, identified by Lui & Baldwin (2014) as the best language identification tools for tweets: langid.py (Lui and Baldwin, 2012), LangDetect,[6] and CLD2.[7]

We randomly selected a subset of 300 tweets (test set A) and manually annotated each for English vs. other. Table 5 shows results for each of the methods tested, as well as for combining

[2]http://www.drugbank.ca/drugs
[3]https://www.crummy.com/software/BeautifulSoup
[4]We will publish the corpus along with this paper.
[5]By anonymous user Generic Human.
[6]Y. Nakatani: http://www.slideshare.net/shuyo/language-detection-library-for-java
[7]Language identification in Google Chrome.

	Twitter	langid.py	CLD2	LangDetect	Majority vote
P	0.995	0.991	0.986	0.973	0.995
R	0.861	0.889	0.877	0.898	0.861
F1	0.923	**0.937**	0.928	0.933	0.923

Table 1: Language identification results for Twitter tags and three language identification tools on test set A of 300 manually annotated tweets (Recall, Precision, F1-Score, for the English class).

langid.py, CLD2 and LangDetect in majority voting. langid.py outperforms the others, including Twitter, slightly on the raw tweets (see end of Section 4). First cleaning/normalising tweets led to a slight improvement for CLD2, and a slight deterioration for languid.py; additionally parsing hashtags led to slight improvement for languid.py, and slight deteriorations for CLD2 and LangDetect. The final best result is an F1-Score of 0.94 for langid.py. This confirms (for this domain) previous results that good language identification tools outperform Twitter language tags (Lui and Baldwin, 2014).

6 Sentiment Analysis

Following the language identification experiments, we filtered out the non-English tweets using langid.py, which left us with 93,697 tweets and an average of 46.87 tweets per drug name. In the experiments in this section, we aim to predict the overall sentiment of an (English) tweet, independently of whether a drug effect is being reported.

For this purpose we selected a different test set of 300 random tweets (test set B) from our corpus and annotated each tweet for positive, negative, or neutral. We tested the 18 sentiment analysis (SA) tools made available in the ifeel package:[8] Afinn, Emolex, Emoticons, EmoticonDS, HappinessIndex, MPQAAdapter, NRCHashtagSentimentLexicon, OpinionLexicon, Panas-t, Sann, SASA, SenticNet, Sentiment140Lexicon, SentiStrengthAdapter, SentiWordNet, SoCal, UmigonAdapter, Vader, and a majority vote by all methods. The ifeel team have reported comparative results for many of these tools (Nunes Ribeiro et al., 2010; Ribeiro et al., 2016). For our task, the methods

[8]http://blackbird.dcc.ufmg.br:1210/ (accessed: 06/2016)

97

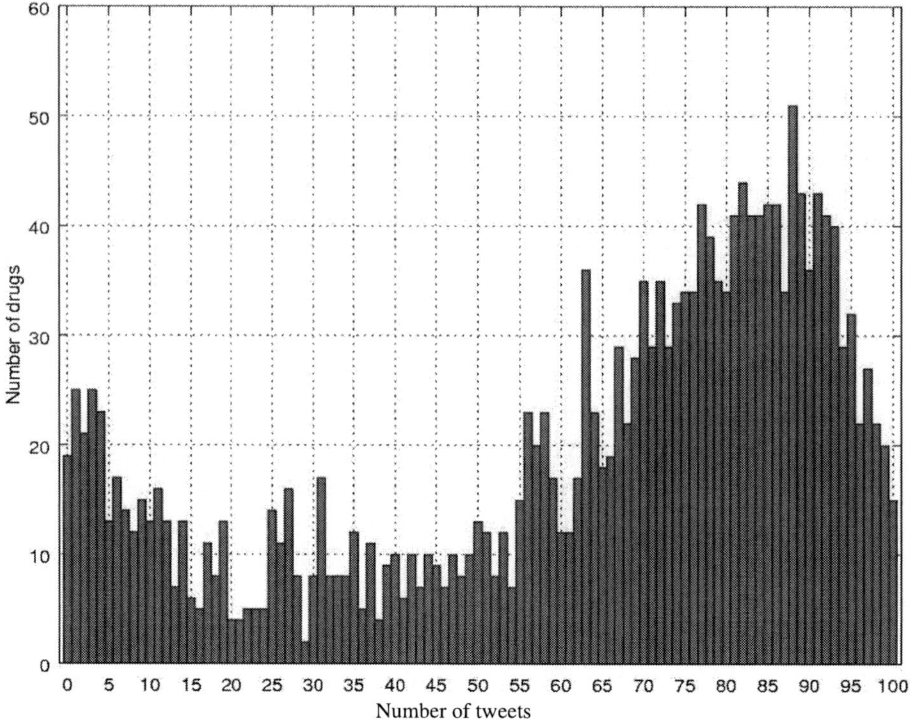

Figure 1: Number of drugs (y) that have a given number of tweets (x). E.g. there are 19 drugs with 0 tweets, and 51 drugs with 88 tweets.

achieved an average F-Score of 0.792, and Accuracy of 0.753. The best three were, by a considerable margin: Emoticons, Panas-t and SANN SA, across all three variants of our corpus. Very briefly, these use the following approaches.

Emoticons: Given lists of positive and neutral emotions, if a text contains an emoticon it is assigned the polarity of the first one, else a text is deemed neutral (Gonçalves et al., 2013a).

Panas-t: Provides association strengths between words and eleven moods including surprise, fear, guilt, joviality, attentiveness, fear, etc. (Gonçalves et al., 2013b).

SANN SA: A dictionary-based rule-based sentiment classifier using the MPQA polarity lexicon (Pappas et al., 2013).

Results for these three classifiers and the majority vote by all 18 systems in ifeel are shown in Table 2; we are only showing results for the raw version of the corpus (see end of Section 4), because results were identical over the three corpus versions, i.e. cleaning, normalising and parsing hashtags did not help with sentiment analysis.

	Emoticons	Panas-t	SANN	Majority vote: (all 18)
F1-measure	**0.941**	0.929	0.920	0.665
Accuracy	**0.936**	0.932	0.932	0.576

Table 2: Tweet-level sentiment analysis results for 3 best sentiment analysis tools on test set B of 300 manually annotated tweets (weighted-average F1-score over POS, NEG and NEU labels; Accuracy).

Out of the 300 tweets in test set B, 259 were annotated as neutral, 22 as positive, and 19 as negative. This gives a very high most-frequent-label baseline of 0.863 Accuracy which the three best classifiers, however, outperform comfortably.

7 Detection of Drug Effect Mentions

We additionally annotated test set B for drug effects with three mention labels: mention of an effect, mention of a property (without specified effect), and none. 81 of the 300 tweets contained an effect mention (sometimes more than one), 10 tweets a property mention, 4 tweets both an effect and a property mention, and 213 contained no mentions.

The experiments in this section were aimed at distinguishing tweets that mention drug effects and properties from tweets that do not. As a starting point we process each of our tweets with MetaMap (Aronson, 2001), a tool for recognising UMLS[9] concepts in text. For a given input text (tweet in our case) MetaMap produces a set of concept vectors as the output, each scored for relevance.

One of the elements in concept vectors indicates 'semantic type' (semtype); semtypes are a set of broad subject categories over all concepts represented in the UMLS metathesaurus. There are 133 different semtypes which fall into six major groupings corresponding to concepts related to organism, anatomical structure, biological function, chemical object, physical object, and idea/concept. For example, a semtype much more commonly seen with tweets that do contain an effect mention is 'Pathologic Function' (83%); examples of semtypes much more commonly seen with tweets that do not contain an effect mention include 'Plant' (96%), 'Receptor' (95%), and 'Laboratory Procedure' (93%).

In this first experiment aimed at detecting effect mentions, we use all 133 semtypes, resulting in binary feature vectors of length 133. We used these paired with the corresponding effect/property labels (+ME = mention of an effect/property, and -ME = none) as training data to train classifiers for this task, using 10-fold cross-validation in testing. The most-frequent-label (-ME) baseline for this task is 0.71 Accuracy.

Table 3 shows results for the three classifiers we tested (Multinomial Naive Bayes, SVM, and Logistic Regression) in terms of overall as well as per-class Recall, Precision and F1-Score. For all classes, SVM performed best with a weighted average F1-Score of 0.873. For the +ME class, the logistic regression classifier did best, with an F1-Score of 0.914. On the -ME class, SVM was best with F1=0.823. Results in Table 3 are for the raw version of the corpus (see end of Section 4); results were identical for the raw and cleaned versions, while additionally parsing hashtags worsened re-

---

[9]The Unified Medical Language System (UMLS) "integrates and distributes key terminology, classification and coding standards, and associated resources" (https://www.nlm.nih.gov/research/umls/).

sults very slightly for the NB classifier only.

Looking at the Precision scores for +ME, which is arguably the most important measure from the perspective of incorporating information into knowledge graphs, all three classifiers performed extremely well. Especially considering we had a tiny training set, this indicates that the MetaMap semtypes form a highly reliable basis for identifying tweets that mention drug effects/properties.

8 Adverse vs. Beneficial Effects

In test set B, we also annotated those tweets with mentions of an effect or property with a further label encoding whether the effect/property was adverse, beneficial or neutral. 23 tweets were labeled as having an effect/property that is adverse, 57 tweets having a beneficial one, and 11 a neutral one, with 5 tweets having more than one of these.

In the experiments in this section, for the subset of tweets which were identified as containing a drug effect/property mention, we wanted to see whether any of the sentiment analysers would be able to predict whether the effect/property mentioned was an adverse, beneficial or neutral one. We tested the same 18 sentiment analysers against the effect sentiment labels (setting adverse=negative, beneficial=positive, and neutral). Some of the sentiment analysers, despite not being designed for this task, did reasonably well at it; the four best ones were the following:

EmoticonsDS: Uses a large sentiment-scored word list based on the co-occurrence of each token with emoticons in a corpus of over 1.5 billion messages (Hannak et al., 2012).

SenticNet: A semantic and affective resource for concept-level sentiment analysis, modelling the polarities of common-sense concepts and relations between them (Cambria et al., 2014).

SentiWordNet: Lexical SA tool based on WordNet using polarity scores associated with WordNet synsets (Baccianella et al., 2010).

AFINN: Twitter based sentiment lexicon providing emotion ratings for words (Nielsen, 2011).

Table 4 shows the results for these four tools. Interestingly, there is no overlap with the three tools that did best at the standard SA task (Table 2), in fact those three methods were the three *worst* ones at this task.

Classifier	Both classes			+ME class			-ME class		
	R	P	F1	R	P	F1	R	P	F1
Multinomial NB	0.847	0.852	0.849	0.848	0.981	0.909	0.961	0.688	0.794
Logistic Regression	0.85	0.851	0.850	**0.855**	0.984	**0.914**	0.969	0.689	0.799
SVM	**0.855**	**0.892**	**0.873**	0.8	**1.0**	0.887	**1.0**	0.71	**0.823**

Table 3: Results for detection of effect mentions (ME) on test set B of 300 manually annotated tweets with 10-fold cross-validation (Recall, Precision, F1-scores for all classes, ME class, and not ME class).

	EmoticonsDS	SenticNet	SentiWordNet	AFINN	Majority vote (all 18)
F1	**0.638**	0.621	0.616	0.615	0.627
Acc	0.592	0.595	0.592	0.597	**0.604**

Table 4: Effect-level sentiment analysis results for 4 best sentiment analysis tools on test set B of 300 manually annotated tweets (weighted-average F1-score over ADV, BEN and NEU labels; Accuracy).

9 Conclusions and Further Work

In this paper we described our new corpus of 125,669 tweets for 1,999 drug names. The corpus includes one randomly selected subset (A) of 300 tweets which is annotated for language, and another set (B) of 300 random tweets which is annotated for overall sentiment and drug effect mentions. The corpus represents many more drug names than in comparable existing corpora, but so far has only a small number of annotated tweets.

We reported results for language identification and sentiment analysis. One of the language identification tools tested (langid.py) outperforms the Twitter language tags in this domain. Tweet-level sentiment analysis achieved a best result of 0.94 weighted average F1-Score (Emoticons method).

Perhaps the most surprising result we report is that a straightforward approach to training a classifier to distinguish tweets that mention drug effects from those that do not, achieves an overall F1-Score of 0.873 and perfect precision for the positive class (+ME). This indicates that MetaMap semtypes are a strong basis for predicting drug effect mentions. However, using sentiment analysis tools for the new task of predicting the polarity of an effect (adverse vs. beneficial vs. neutral) achieved best results of just 0.64 weighted average F1-Score (EmoticonsDS).

In future work, we are planning to expand our annotations to allow more effective training of classifiers in particular to address the latter task, as well as generally to expand our corpus to include tweets containing common, colloquial and generic names and common misspellings of our drug names. In terms of methodology, we are currently working on drug effect extraction, i.e. identifying the span of words in a tweet that describes the effect.

References

M Abou Taam, C Rossard, L Cantaloube, N Bouscaren, G Roche, L Pochard, F Montastruc, A Herxheimer, JL Montastruc, and H Bagheri. 2014. Analysis of patients' narratives posted on social media websites on Benfluorex's (mediator®) withdrawal in france. *Journal of Clinical Pharmacy and Therapeutics*, 39(1):53–55.

Alan R Aronson. 2001. Effective mapping of biomedical text to the umls metathesaurus: the metamap program. In *Proceedings of the AMIA Symposium*, page 17. American Medical Informatics Association.

Stefano Baccianella, Andrea Esuli, and Fabrizio Sebastiani. 2010. Sentiwordnet 3.0: An enhanced lexical resource for sentiment analysis and opinion mining. In *LREC*, volume 10, pages 2200–2204.

Jiang Bian, Umit Topaloglu, and Fan Yu. 2012. Towards large-scale twitter mining for drug-related adverse events. In *Proceedings of the 2012 international Workshop on Smart Health and Wellbeing*, pages 25–32. ACM.

Erik Cambria, Daniel Olsher, and Dheeraj Rajagopal. 2014. Senticnet 3: a common and common-sense knowledge base for cognition-driven sentiment analysis. In *Proceedings of the twenty-eighth AAAI conference on artificial intelligence*, pages 1515–1521. AAAI Press.

Rachel Ginn, Pranoti Pimpalkhute, Azadeh Nikfarjam, Apurv Patki, Karen OConnor, Abeed Sarker, Karen Smith, and Graciela Gonzalez. 2014. Mining twitter for adverse drug reaction mentions: a corpus and classification benchmark. In *Proceedings of the fourth workshop on building and evaluating resources for health and biomedical text processing*.

Pollyanna Gonçalves, Matheus Araújo, Fabrício Benevenuto, and Meeyoung Cha. 2013a. Comparing and combining sentiment analysis methods. In *Proceedings of the first ACM conference on Online social networks*, pages 27–38. ACM.

Pollyanna Gonçalves, Fabrício Benevenuto, and Meeyoung Cha. 2013b. Panas-t: A pychometric scale for measuring sentiments on twitter. *arXiv preprint arXiv:1308.1857*.

Aniko Hannak, Eric Anderson, Lisa Feldman Barrett, Sune Lehmann, Alan Mislove, and Mirek Riedewald. 2012. Tweetin' in the rain: Exploring societal-scale effects of weather on mood. In *ICWSM*. Citeseer.

J. Lardon, R. Abdellaoui, F. Bellet, H. Asfari, J. Souvignet, N. Texier, M.C. Jaulent, M.N. Beyens, A. Burgun, and C. Bousquet. 2015. Adverse drug reaction identification and extraction in social media: A scoping review. *Journal of Medical Internet Research*, 17:171.

Marco Lui and Timothy Baldwin. 2012. langid.py: An off-the-shelf language identification tool. In *Proceedings of the ACL 2012 system demonstrations*, pages 25–30. Association for Computational Linguistics.

Marco Lui and Timothy Baldwin. 2014. Accurate language identification of twitter messages. In *Proceedings of the 5th Workshop on Language Analysis for Social Media (LASM)@ EACL*, pages 17–25.

Finn Årup Nielsen. 2011. A new anew: Evaluation of a word list for sentiment analysis in microblogs. *arXiv preprint arXiv:1103.2903*.

Filipe Nunes Ribeiro, Matheus Araújo, Pollyanna Gonçalves, Fabrício Benevenuto, and Marcos André Gonçalves. 2010. A benchmark comparison of state-of-the-practice sentiment analysis methods. *ACM Transactions on Embedded Computing Systems*, 9(4).

Nikolaos Pappas, Georgios Katsimpras, and Efstathios Stamatatos. 2013. Distinguishing the popularity between topics: A system for up-to-date opinion retrieval and mining in the web. In *International Conference on Intelligent Text Processing and Computational Linguistics*, pages 197–209. Springer.

Filipe N Ribeiro, Matheus Araújo, Pollyanna Gonçalves, Marcos André Gonçalves, and Fabrício Benevenuto. 2016. Sentibench-a benchmark comparison of state-of-the-practice sentiment analysis methods. *EPJ Data Science*, 5(1):1–29.

Abeed Sarker and Graciela Gonzalez. 2015. Portable automatic text classification for adverse drug reaction detection via multi-corpus training. *Journal of biomedical informatics*, 53:196–207.

WHO. No date. World Health Organization English Glossary. Online document, http://www.who.int/medicines/areas/coordination/English_Glossary.pdf. Accessed: 27 July 2016.

Named Entity Recognition and Hashtag Decomposition to Improve the Classification of Tweets

Belainine Billal
Univ. of Quebec in Montreal
201, President Kenney Av.
H2X 3Y7, Montreal-QC, Canada
belainine.billal@courrier.uqam.ca

Alexsandro Fonseca
Univ. of Quebec in Montreal
201, President Kenney Av.
H2X 3Y7, Montreal-QC, Canada
affonseca@gmail.com

Fatiha Sadat
Univ. of Quebec in Montreal
201, President Kenney Av.
H2X 3Y7, Montreal-QC, Canada
sadat.fatiha@uqam.ca

Abstract

In social networks services like Twitter, users are overwhelmed with huge amount of social data, most of which are short, unstructured and highly noisy. Identifying accurate information from this huge amount of data is indeed a hard task. Classification of tweets into organized form will help the user to easily access these required information. Our first contribution relates to filtering parts of speech and preprocessing this kind of highly noisy and short data. Our second contribution concerns the named entity recognition (NER) in tweets. Thus, the adaptation of existing language tools for natural languages, noisy and not accurate language tweets, is necessary. Our third contribution involves segmentation of hashtags and a semantic enrichment using a combination of relations from WordNet, which helps the performance of our classification system, including disambiguation of named entities, abbreviations and acronyms. Graph theory is used to cluster the words extracted from WordNet and tweets, based on the idea of connected components. We test our automatic classification system with four categories: politics, economy, sports and the medical field. We evaluate and compare several automatic classification systems using part or all of the items described in our contributions and found that filtering by part of speech and named entity recognition dramatically increase the classification precision to 77.3 %. Moreover, a classification system incorporating segmentation of hashtags and semantic enrichment by two relations from WordNet, synonymy and hyperonymy, increase classification precision up to 83.4 %.

1 Introduction

The automatic classification of text and the approaches for the extraction of hidden subjects have good performance when there is enough meta-information, the context is extended using knowledge from big collections, like Wikipedia (Sriram et al., 2010) or it uses meta-information from external sources such as Wikipedia (Genc et al., 2011) and include the use of lexical ontologies, like DBPedia (Cano et al., 2013). However, those approaches need online queries, what makes their performance decrease, and the extraction of knowledge from those external collections demand complex algorithms. Moreover, the use of those approaches makes the classification algorithms less general.

We present a classification method that uses offline knowledge extracted from WordNet to disambiguate and enrich information in tweets and also to group semantically connected words of tweets in order to decrease the size of our training matrix.

In Section 2 we present a review of some works on the classification of tweets and short texts in general. In Section 3 we detail the main steps in the pre-processing: tweet normalization, hashtag decomposition and named entity recognition. Section 4 presents our methodology: how WordNet is used

Proceedings of the 2nd Workshop on Noisy User-generated Text,
pages 102–111, Osaka, Japan, December 11 2016.

to disambiguate words in tweets, how we build a graph using the words in tweets and semantic relations extracted from WordNet and how connected components extracted from this graph is used to decrease the number of dimensions in our training matrix. In Section 5 we present the experiments and results obtained in the classification of tweets, in terms of precision. And in Section 6 and Section 7 we present the evaluation and conclusion, respectively.

2   Related Work

Recent works based on machine learning deal with the classification of tweets. Sriram et al. (2010) classify tweets into pre-defined generic classes, e.g. "news", "events", "advertising", etc., using information about the authors and some characteristics, such as abbreviations, words used to express opinion, etc.

Sahami and Heilman (2006) use short texts from tweets in search engines queries in order to increase the information in each tweet. However, those techniques need additional entity disambiguation approaches. For example, even though "jaguar" and "car" are close semantically, a disambiguation in the query results is needed to differentiate the results from "jaguar" as a car and as an animal. Therefore, the intervention of the user is necessary in order to guide the process of tweet expansion.

Genc et al. (2011) propose a method for the classification of tweets using Wikipedia, which calculates the semantic distance between words in a tweet and words in the description of Wikipedia pages to find the most similar page and category. Kinsella et al. (2011) analyze meta-data from objects (Amazon products, YouTube videos, etc.) to which links in tweets are pointing to determine their subjects.

Lee et al. (2011) classify tweets into 18 general categories, such as "sport", "politics", etc. They use two methods: bag of words and a classification based on a network, identifying the most influential users for each category. The number of influential users in common between already classified tweets and a tweet yet to be classified define the category of the new tweet.

Sankaranarayanan et al. (2009) build a news processing system called "TwitterStand" that identifies tweets corresponding to last news. Their objective is to reduce noise and identify tweets classes and groups of interest.

Saif et al. (2012) introduce a method based on the disambiguation of named entities. They add semantic information to the named entity identified (for example, adding "Apple" to "IPhone") and then associate negative/positive sentiment extracted from tweets. Michelson and Macskassy (2010) use Wikipedia to disambiguate, classify named entities found in tweets and identify the subjects of interest to the users and the most frequent categories related to named entities.

Since hashtags are essentials in understanding the subject of a tweet, most systems of analyze of opinions try to incorporate them in their calculations. Asur and Huberman (2010) show how to improve standard techniques of supervised classification by integration of polarity from most frequent hashtags.

Brun and Roux (2014a) show how to extract words from hashtags and use them to improve the detection of polarity in tweets. Their system represents each opinion according to the model proposed by Liu (2010) and compare a system that uses hashtag decomposition with a system that does not use it.

Almeida et al. (2016) present a supervised learning approach dedicated to the biomedical domain for supporting the production of literature on HIV using thesaurus MeSH (Medical Subject Headings).

3   Pre-processing

Our system for the classification of tweets is based on Weka[1] and uses the Twitter API to extract tweets[2].

We use Twitter API[3] to build our training and testing corpus. A language detector (Shuyo, 2010) is used to keep only tweets in English[4]. All tweets containing less than 80% of words in English, only URLs and empty tweets were deleted from the corpus.

Despite the existence of many pre-processing tools for short texts and tweets (e.g. TweetNLP[5]), we

---

1. http://www.cs.waikato.ac.nz/ml/weka
2. https://bitbucket.org/LyesBillal/twitterclassifier/overview
3. https://dev.twitter.com
4. https://github.com/shuyo/language-detection
5. http://www.cs.cmu.edu/ ark/TweetNLP/

have chosen Standford NLP[6] for its robustness.

In the next sections we explain the main pre-processing steps: tweet normalization, hashtag decomposition and named entity recognition.

3.1 Tweet Normalization

Tweet normalization consists in rewriting text in a standard language. It is based on the most common lexical mistakes made in social media and is divided in the following sub-tasks (Han et al., 2013):

1. Suppression of extra letters, e.g. "gooood". We use an English dictionary [7] and regular expressions to detect the closest possible correct word;

2. Minimal orthographic correction for most common mistakes, e.g. substitution of "scoll" for "scroll";

3. Substitution of common words used in social media, e.g. "2day" for "today". We use a dictionary[8] dedicated to this kind of problem.

3.2 Hashtag Decomposition

A hashtag always starts by the character "#", making easy its identification. They are usually composed words created by users and cause a problem for the linguistic analyzes because they are considered unknown words. In a tweet having only 140 characters ignoring the hashtags may cause an enormous loss of information (Brun and Roux, 2014b).

Usually, different hashtags are used for the same subject. For example, for Newsmax_Media we found:

$$\#\text{News\_Media, } \#\text{VanRE, } \#\text{Vancouver}\ldots$$

Those three hashtags are related to the words "Newsmax", "Media", "Vancouver", "VanRE".

Our objective is to extract all words in hashtags and increase their frequency. For example:

$$\#\textbf{Newsmax\_Media} \rightarrow (\textbf{Newsmax}, \textbf{Media})$$
$$\#\textbf{News\_Media} \rightarrow (\textbf{News}, \textbf{Media})$$
$$\#\textbf{Vancouver} \rightarrow (\textbf{Vancouver})$$
$$\#\textbf{VanRE} \rightarrow (\textbf{Van}, \textbf{RE})$$

We propose a recursive algorithm that processes hashtags from left to right and separates the problem in three sub-tasks:

1. When each word in a hashtag start by an uppercase letter, we use a function to separate those words. Example: **#ParisClimateConference**

2. When the words are separated by special characters or by numbers, we use another function. Examples: **#3Novices, #Newsmax_Media**

3. When each word starts by a lowercase letter, we use a third function combined with an English dictionary[9]. This function tries to separate a hashtag in the fewest possible number of words, from left to right. For example, the hashtag **#renewableenergy** can be separated as:
#renewableenergy $\rightarrow$ (**renew**, **able**, **energy**)
#renewableenergy $\rightarrow$ (**renewable**, **energy**)
and we chose (**renewable, energy**), following the human tendency of choosing the longest possible sequence when decodifying a sequence of characters.

---

6. http://nlp.stanford.edu/software/
7. http://gdt.oqlf.gouv.qc.ca/
8. https://github.com/coastalcph/cs_sst/blob/master/data/res/emnlp_dict.txt
9. https://github.com/dwyl/english-words

3.3 Named Entity Recognition

Different users write dates, names of places or people in different ways. For example: "2016-03-10" and "March 10th 2016", "John Kennedy" and "JFK", etc. Named Entity Recognition (NER), a set of techniques to deal with this problem, is used in different projects, such as the Gene/Protein Named Entity Recognition and Normalization Software(GNAT) (Wermter et al., 2009).

Unities of time, distance, currency can be normalized using the Stanford NLP API. A sequence of words that appear with high frequency is kept because they probably represent a unique entity. For the names of location and organization we search in Wordnet for the closest synonyms.

After NER, we remove the stop words, i.e. functional words carrying no meaning[10] and make the lemmatization, i.e. transformation of words into their canonical forms (e.g. nouns from plural to singular, verbs from a conjugated to a infinitive form, etc.), using Standford NLP lemmatizer[11].

4 Methodology

Figure 1 shows the main process in our methodology.

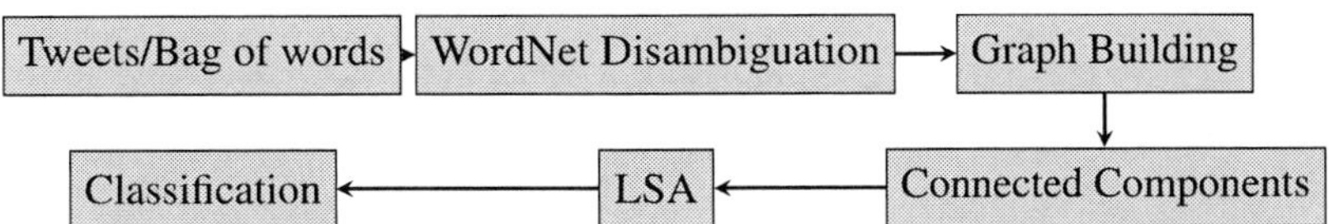

Figure 1: The main processes for building the matrix of connected components.

In the next sections we present the main steps in our methodology. Section 4.1 shows how we use WordNet to disambiguate terms. Section 4.2 presents our method for the construction of a graph of terms in tweets and how we extract connected components from this graph. In Section 4.3, we explain how we use connected components to lower the ranking in our classification matrix. Finally, Section 4.4 shows the classification algorithms used in this work.

4.1 Disambiguation of Tweets Using WordNet

Since we use Wordnet[12] for the tweets expansion, we decided to also use it for the task of disambiguation.

For each word, WordNet suggests many senses, each one containing a synset, i.e. a group of almost synonyms words. We adopt a structural method based on the semantic distance between concepts to choose the correct sense, according to the formula (Navigli, 2009):

$$\hat{S} = \text{argmax}_{S \in Sense(w_i)} \sum_{w_j \in T : w_i \neq w_j} max_{S' \in Sense(w_j)} Score(S, S'). \tag{1}$$

Where T is the set of terms in a tweet, w_i is the term we want to disambiguate, $Sense(w_i)$ is the set of candidates concepts for the term w_i, what in WordNet corresponds to the synsets containing this term, and $Score(S, S')$ is the function used to measure the similarity between two concepts S and S'.

There are many methods for measuring the similarity between concepts S and S'. After many comparisons, we have chosen an approach based on a path formed by the arcs of the graph (Wu and Palmer, 1994), which supposes that the similarity between two concepts depends on the distance between the nodes concerned and their common ancestor (Least Common Concept) in comparison to the distance to a root node in the graph.

To enrich the tweets, we use the technique introduced by (Audeh et al., 2013) from information search for the expansion of queries. The first option is to search for synonyms in the synset selected in the previous step. The second one is to use the synsets of the hypernym of the term.

---

10. http://members.unine.ch/jacques.savoy/clef/englishST.txt
11. http://nlp.stanford.edu/software/
12. http://wordnetcode.princeton.edu/wn3.1.dict.tar.gz

4.2 Graph Building

Once the synset having the closest sense to the context of the tweet is selected, we group the words w extracted from the tweets with their synsets in a graph $G = (V, E)$, defined as follows:

$$
\begin{cases}
V &= \{\forall w \in E_{tweet} / \{w\} \cup Synset_w\} \\[2mm]
E &= \{Synonym,\ Hyperonym \cdots\}
\end{cases}
\tag{2}
$$

In this graph, each word from the corpus and each word in the synsets, as selected by the previous step, is represented by a node V and each relation (synonymy, hyperonymy) between those words, extracted from WordNet, is represented by an arc E. This creates a weakly connected graph that is used to the extraction of connected components.

The next step is to search for the connected components in the graph G. Each component is formed by nodes, corresponding to words, connected by arcs representing the semantic relations. The idea is to cluster the words w_1 and w_2 connected by an arc to another word $w \in \{w_1\} \cup Synset_{w_1}$, having this word w a relation $w \in \{w_2\} \cup Synset_{w_2}$. Mathematically:

$$G' \left(V', E'\right) \text{ a connected component in } G(V\!,E) \ /V' \subset V \wedge \{w_1, w_2\} \in V'$$

Then we have:

$$\{\{w_1\} \cup Synset_{w_1}\} \cap \{\{w_2\} \cup Synset_{w_2}\} \neq \phi \tag{3}$$

A word, called the "representative", is selected to represent each component. The matrix of bag of words becomes a matrix of bags of representatives, or bag of connected components. For example, in Figure 2 the word "football" is the representative of the component:

football ->[football, football game, soccer/sports, association football, soccer]

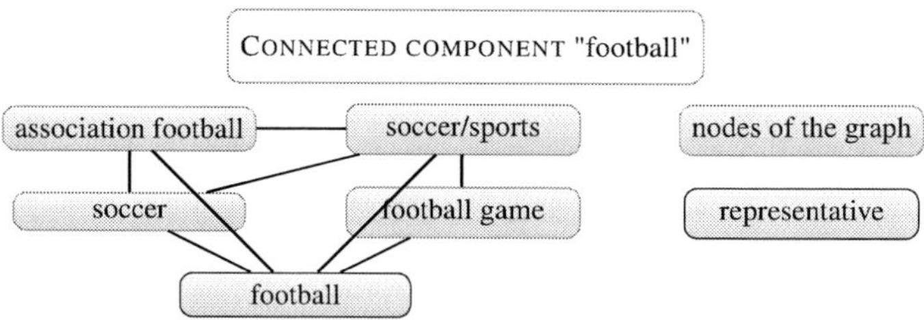

Figure 2: Example of a connected component represented by the word "football" in the vectorial space

Every time we find a word that belongs to this component in a tweet, we increment the frequency of the word "football", which is the representative of this component, leading to a matrix of fewer dimensions.

4.3 Rank Lowering Using Latent Semantic Analysis

Latent Semantic Analysis (LSA) (Bestgen, 2004) is a technique for analyzing the relation between terms and between terms and documents. Each term is represented as a column in a matrix and each document as a row. To represent a corpus of tweets, for example, row_1 represents $tweet_1$, row_2 represents $tweet_2$, etc. Each column represents the frequency or the tf-idf of a term in a tweet. Since tweets are short, most of the columns for a specific tweet are zeros since most of the words present in the entire corpus are not present in each specific tweet. And even in a big corpus, most of the words are rare, appearing only once and their rarity makes them sensible to aleatory variations (Bestgen, 2004).

In this work, we deal with the sparsity of such a matrix by representing the frequency of terms in connected components instead of the frequency or the tf-idf of single terms since we are more interested in the relation of tweets with concepts, represented by the connected components, than the relation of tweets with isolated terms.

Dimension of components / Vectors of tweets	Component$_1$	$\cdots$	Component$_i$	$\cdots$	Component$_n$
Tweet$_1$	$f_{1,1}$	$\cdots$	$f_{1,i}$	$\cdots$	$f_{1,n}$
$\vdots$	$\vdots$	$\vdots$	$\vdots$	$\vdots$	$\vdots$
Tweet$_j$	$f_{j,1}$	$\cdots$	$f_{j,i}$	$\cdots$	$f_{j,n}$
$\vdots$	$\vdots$	$\vdots$	$\vdots$	$\vdots$	$\vdots$
Tweet$_m$	$f_{m,1}$	$\cdots$	$f_{m,i}$	$\cdots$	$f_{m,n}$

Table 1: A matrix representing the frequency of each connected component in each tweet.

Table 1 shows the representation of a matrix of m tweets with the frequencies $f_{j,i}$ of words found in the connected components $Component_i$.

4.4 The Classifier

Liblinear (Fan et al., 2008) is a fast and simple linear classifier and has become one of the most promising machine learning technique for big data.

We use the library LIBLINEAR[13], which is based on the L2-regularized logistic regression (LR), L2-loss and L1-loss SVM linear vectors (Boser et al., 1992). It inherits many characteristics from the SVM library LIBSVM (Chang and Lin, 2011), like a rich documentation and free license (BSD license[14]).

LIBLINEAR is very efficient for training large scale problems: it takes some seconds for a text classification problem. For the same task, a SVM classifier like LIBSVM takes many hours. Furthermore, LIBLINEAR competes with the fastest linear classifiers like Pegasos (Shalev-Shwartz et al., 2007).

5 Experiments and Analysis of Results

We use the Twitter API to build our corpus, passing as queries words related to the chosen domains (sport, politics, economics and medicine). Table 2 presents the number of tweets, terms and lemmas in the corpus for each domain.

	Economy	Medicine	Sport	Politics
Simple Terms	13870	14784	16112	15346
Lemmas	7938	12138	12773	11976
Tweets	2504	2415	2493	2497

Table 2: Number of terms, lemmas and tweets for each category

To test our method we evaluate different criteria in the classification of tweets:

1. Corpus filtered by part-of-speech (POS) vs not filtered by POS. In the corpus filtered by POS, in addition to deleting a regular list of stop words (article, prepositions, etc.), we also delete adverbs and we keep only nouns, verbs and adjectives;

2. Applying vs not applying hashtags segmentation;

3. Using Wordnet relations (synonymy, hyperonymy and synonymy + hyperonymy) for clustering similar words in a graph for the construction of connected components;

4. Applying NER (and using WordNet to disambiguate them) vs not Applying NER.

---

13. http://www.csie.ntu.edu.tw/ cjlin/liblinear
14. The new BSD license (Berkeley Software Distribution License) approved by the Open Source initiative.

Table 3 presents a comparison of the classification results and the gain we obtain when NER is applied.

Filter type	Hashtag segmenta-tion	WordNet relation	Precision w/o ^-NER (%)	Precision with ^+NER (%)	Gain(p.p.)
All words	No	Synonymy	38.3	36.2	-2.1
Only N, V and ADJ	No	Synonymy	68.2	69.7	+1.5
All words	Yes	Synonymy	42.1	41.7	-0.4
Only N, V and ADJ	Yes	Synonymy	73.4	74.8	+1.4
All words	No	Hyperonymy	41.7	40.6	-1.1
Only N, V and ADJ	No	Hyperonymy	70.9	71.3	+0.4
All words	Yes	Hyperonymy	43.2	42.4	-0.8
Only N, V and ADJ	Yes	Hyperonymy	76.4	77.3	+0.9
All words	No	Syn&Hyper	46.8	45.3	-1.5
Only N, V and ADJ	No	Syn&Hyper	72.3	73.2	+0.9
All words	Yes	Syn&Hyper	51.3	50.6	-0.7
Only N, V and ADJ	Yes	Syn&Hyper	81.2	83.4	+1.2

Table 3: Comparison of the precision for different classifications and the gain when named entity recognition is applied.

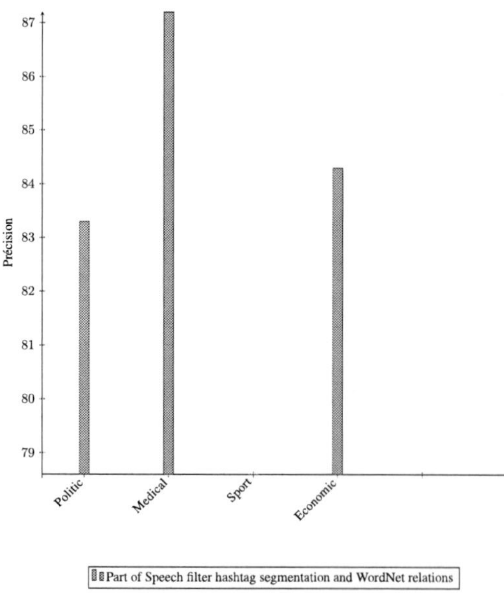

Figure 3: Best results obtained in the classification of each category.

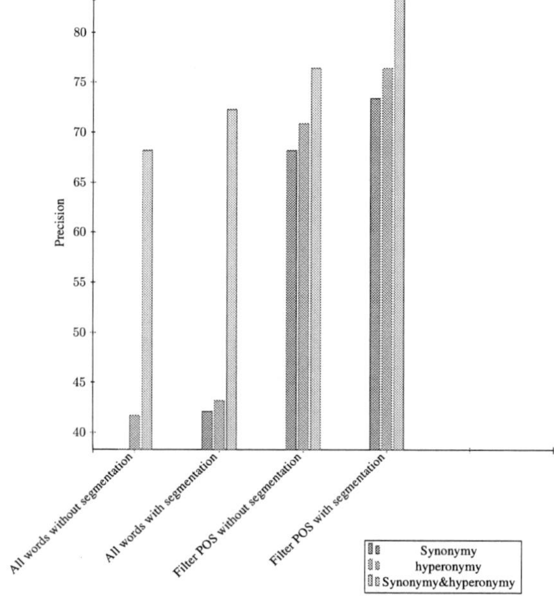

Figure 4: Precisions obtained when applying named entity recognition (NER).

When NER is not applied and we keep only nouns, verbs and adjectives, combined with synonymy, we have a gain of 29.9 p.p. in precision (from 38.3% to 68.2%), which grows to 81.2% when combined with synonymy and hyperonymy. This can be explained by the fact that the words removed, like adverbs, do not contribute for the identification of a tweet subject.

The hashtags segmentation improves the result in 3.8 p.p., when using all the words and 5.2 p.p. when the POS filtering is applied. This is explained by the fact that usually hashtags carries the most significant words for the identification of the subject of a tweet.

The use of hyperonyms gives a better result than the use of synonyms. For example, the precision is 73.4% when we use hashtag segmentation, POS filter and synonyms and it increases to 76.4% when we use hyperonyms instead of synonyms. This can be explained by the fact that hyperonyms by themselves are a better indication of a word group since they represent relations of the type "part-of". Moreover, adding synonyms and hyperonyms together gives the best precision, 81.2%, when using hashtag segmentation and POS filter.

The application of NER increases the precision in the corpus having only nouns, verbs and adjectives, and decreases when the corpus have all words (except stop words).

The histogram in Figure 3 compares the precision in the classification of each category using NER, hashtag segmentation and POS filter.

The histogram in Figure 4 is a graphic representation of the results shown by the column "Precision with NER" in Table 3. We note a progressive increment in precision when segmentation of hashtags and then POS filtering are applied.

6 Evaluation

The hashtags carry important information about the tweets subjects. Moreover, words extracted from them enrich the connected components that contain those words. For example, a tweet that contains the hashtag #ParisClimateConference does not share any word with the following connected component: climate$\rightarrow$ environmental condition, clime, climate. However, after the hashtag segmentation, the word *climate* appears in the vector representing the tweet that contains this hashtag:

$$\text{\#ParisClimateConference} \rightarrow (\text{paris, climate, conference})$$

The tweets containing the word *climate* in their texts or in their hashtags will share the same connected component.

Keeping only verbs, adjectives and adverbs (POS filter) helps improving the classification precision since the sense of the text is usually given by words in those grammatical categories.

Despite the existence of polysemic words, the disambiguation using WordNet, as explained in section 4.1, helps us find the correct sense of a word.

Not all named entities can be detected by WordNet. However, the most common names of people, places and organizations used in tweets can be successfully identified. The application of NER helps increase the precision. For example, in tweets we find "United States of America", "United States" and "USA". Identifying that the three expressions are a unique entity helps understand the connection between the tweets that contain them.

We show how NER can affect the identification of the subject of a text. Without NER, we could have the following connected components:

$$\text{United} \rightarrow \text{unite, unify}$$
$$\text{States} \rightarrow \text{government, authorities, regime}$$

However, NER gives:

$$\text{United States} \rightarrow \text{United States, United States of America, America,}$$
$$\text{the States, US, U.S., USA, U.S.A}$$

Moreover, the detection of the sense of some acronyms using WordNet, for example:

$$\text{FBI} \rightarrow \text{Federal Bureau of Investigation, FBI; or}$$
$$\text{UN} \rightarrow \text{United Nations, UN}$$

helps to connect the sense of a tweet containing *«UN»* with tweets containing *«United Nations»*. Finally, we have a reduction in the number of dimensions in our training matrix.

7 Conclusion

Before discussing results, it is important to stress some limits of this research. First, we use a local WordNet, instead of an online one, due to performance. Second, not all terms or named entities found in our corpus are present in WordNet.

The idea of connected components, based on graph theory, reduces the training matrix based on bag of words, increasing the performance of our classification. Our POS filter improves the precision. And the hashtag segmentation helps us extract more information from tweets and also helps increase the precision of the classification.

NER improves the precision when we keep only nouns, verbs and adjectives. When all words are used, the precision decreases.

In this work we do not consider multiword expressions (MWEs). Finally, the hashtag segmentation does not take into account hashtags written in more than one language, even if one of the languages is English, like, for example, the hashtag #Japanにほん, which is composed by a word in English and another in Japanese.

References

H. Almeida, M. J. Meurs, L. Kosseim, and A. Tsang. 2016. Data sampling and supervised learning for hiv literature screening. *IEEE Transactions on NanoBioscience*, 15(4):354–361, June.

S. Asur and B. A. Huberman. 2010. Predicting the future with social media. In *Web Intelligence and Intelligent Agent Technology (WI-IAT), 2010 IEEE/WIC/ACM International Conference on*, volume 1, pages 492–499, Aug.

Bissan Audeh, Philippe Beaune, and Michel Beigbeder. 2013. Expansion sémantique des requêtes pour un modèle de recherche d'information par proximité. In Chantal Soulé-Dupuy, editor, *INFORSID 2013*, pages pages 83–90, Paris, France, May. https://liris.cnrs.fr/inforsid/?q=Actes

Yves Bestgen, 2004. *Analyse sémantique latente et segmentation automatique des textes*. Cahiers du Cental. Presses universitaires de Louvain, Louvain-la-Neuve.

Bernhard E. Boser, Isabelle M. Guyon, and Vladimir N. Vapnik. 1992. A training algorithm for optimal margin classifiers. In *Proceedings of the Fifth Annual Workshop on Computational Learning Theory*, COLT '92, pages 144–152, New York, NY, USA. ACM.

Caroline Brun and Claude Roux. 2014a. Decomposing hashtags to improve tweet polarity classification (décomposition des « hash tags » pour l'amélioration de la classification en polarité des « tweets ») [in french]. In *Proceedings of TALN 2014 (Volume 2: Short Papers)*, pages 473–478. Association pour le Traitement Automatique des Langues.

Caroline Brun and Claude Roux. 2014b. Decomposing hashtags to improve tweet polarity classification (décomposition des « hash tags » pour l'amélioration de la classification en polarité des « tweets ») [in french]. In *Proceedings of TALN 2014 (Volume 2: Short Papers)*, pages 473–478. Association pour le Traitement Automatique des Langues.

Amparo E. Cano, Andrea Varga, Matthew Rowe, Fabio Ciravegna, and Yulan He. 2013. Harnessing linked knowledge sources for topic classification in social media. In *Proceedings of the 24th ACM Conference on Hypertext and Social Media*, HT '13, pages 41–50, New York, NY, USA. ACM.

Chih-Chung Chang and Chih-Jen Lin. 2011. Libsvm: A library for support vector machines. *ACM Trans. Intell. Syst. Technol.*, 2(3):27:1–27:27, May.

Rong-En Fan, Kai-Wei Chang, Cho-Jui Hsieh, Xiang-Rui Wang, and Chih-Jen Lin. 2008. Liblinear: A library for large linear classification. *J. Mach. Learn. Res.*, 9:1871–1874, June.

Yegin Genc, Yasuaki Sakamoto, and Jeffrey V. Nickerson, 2011. *Discovering Context: Classifying Tweets through a Semantic Transform Based on Wikipedia*, pages 484–492. Springer Berlin Heidelberg, Berlin, Heidelberg.

Bo Han, Paul Cook, and Timothy Baldwin. 2013. Lexical normalization for social media text. *ACM Trans. Intell. Syst. Technol.*, 4(1):5:1–5:27, February.

Sheila Kinsella, Alexandre Passant, and John G. Breslin, 2011. *Topic Classification in Social Media Using Metadata from Hyperlinked Objects*, pages 201–206. Springer Berlin Heidelberg, Berlin, Heidelberg.

Kathy Lee, Diana Palsetia, Ramanathan Narayanan, Md. Mostofa Ali Patwary, Ankit Agrawal, and Alok Choudhary. 2011. Twitter trending topic classification. In *Proceedings of the 2011 IEEE 11th International Conference on Data Mining Workshops*, ICDMW '11, pages 251–258, Washington, DC, USA. IEEE Computer Society.

Bing Liu, 2010. *Sentiment analysis and subjectivity*, chapter 26, pages 627–666. Chapman and Hall/CRC, second edition, February.

Matthew Michelson and Sofus A. Macskassy. 2010. Discovering users' topics of interest on twitter: A first look. In *Proceedings of the Fourth Workshop on Analytics for Noisy Unstructured Text Data*, AND '10, pages 73–80, New York, NY, USA. ACM.

Roberto Navigli. 2009. Word sense disambiguation: A survey. *ACM Comput. Surv.*, 41(2):10:1–10:69, February.

Mehran Sahami and Timothy D. Heilman. 2006. A web-based kernel function for measuring the similarity of short text snippets. In *Proceedings of the 15th International Conference on World Wide Web*, WWW '06, pages 377–386, New York, NY, USA. ACM.

Hassan Saif, Yulan He, and Harith Alani, 2012. *Semantic Sentiment Analysis of Twitter*, pages 508–524. Springer Berlin Heidelberg, Berlin, Heidelberg.

Jagan Sankaranarayanan, Hanan Samet, Benjamin E. Teitler, Michael D. Lieberman, and Jon Sperling. 2009. Twitterstand: News in tweets. In *Proceedings of the 17th ACM SIGSPATIAL International Conference on Advances in Geographic Information Systems*, GIS '09, pages 42–51, New York, NY, USA. ACM.

Shai Shalev-Shwartz, Yoram Singer, and Nathan Srebro. 2007. Pegasos: Primal estimated sub-gradient solver for svm. In *Proceedings of the 24th International Conference on Machine Learning*, ICML '07, pages 807–814, New York, NY, USA. ACM.

Nakatani Shuyo. 2010. Language detection library for java.

Bharath Sriram, Dave Fuhry, Engin Demir, Hakan Ferhatosmanoglu, and Murat Demirbas. 2010. Short text classification in twitter to improve information filtering. In *Proceedings of the 33rd International ACM SIGIR Conference on Research and Development in Information Retrieval*, SIGIR '10, pages 841–842, New York, NY, USA. ACM.

Joachim Wermter, Katrin Tomanek, and Udo Hahn. 2009. High-performance gene name normalization with geno. *Bioinformatics*, 25(6):815–821.

Zhibiao Wu and Martha Palmer. 1994. Verbs semantics and lexical selection. In *Proceedings of the 32Nd Annual Meeting on Association for Computational Linguistics*, ACL '94, pages 133–138, Stroudsburg, PA, USA. Association for Computational Linguistics.

Exploring Word Embeddings for Unsupervised Textual User-Generated Content Normalization

Thales Felipe Costa Bertaglia
ICMC-USP / São Carlos – Brazil
thales.bertaglia@usp.br

Maria das Graças Volpe Nunes
ICMC-USP / São Carlos – Brazil
gracan@icmc.usp.br

Abstract

Text normalization techniques based on rules, lexicons or supervised training requiring large corpora are not scalable nor domain interchangeable, and this makes them unsuitable for normalizing user-generated content (UGC). Current tools available for Brazilian Portuguese make use of such techniques. In this work we propose a technique based on distributed representation of words (or word embeddings). It generates continuous numeric vectors of high-dimensionality to represent words. The vectors explicitly encode many linguistic regularities and patterns, as well as syntactic and semantic word relationships. Words that share semantic similarity are represented by similar vectors. Based on these features, we present a totally unsupervised, expandable and language and domain independent method for learning normalization lexicons from word embeddings. Our approach obtains high correction rate of orthographic errors and internet slang in product reviews, outperforming the current available tools for Brazilian Portuguese.

1 Introduction

The huge amount of data currently available on the Web allows computer-based knowledge discovery to thrive. The growth in recent years of user-generated content (UGC) – especially the one created by ordinary people – brings forth a new niche of promising practical applications (Krumm et al., 2008). Textual UGC, such as product reviews, blogs, and social network posts, often serves as a base for natural language processing (NLP) tasks. This type of content may be used for business intelligence, targeted marketing, prediction of political election results, analysis of sociolinguistic phenomena, among many other possibilities. Despite its wide range of application, UGC is hard for NLP to handle.

Most of the natural language processing tools and techniques are developed from and for texts of standard language (Duran et al., 2015). From basic components of a NLP-based system, such as taggers, to complex tools aiming to tackle more significant problems, there is a reliance on well structured textual information in order to achieve a proper behavior. However, user generated content does not necessarily follow the structured form of standard language. This type of text is often full of idiosyncrasies, which represent noise for NLP purposes. Beyond the context of NLP, textual UGC may also represent an obstacle for end-users. Specially on social networks, where a domain-specific and context reliant language is used, users not familiar to its particularities may have difficulties to fully grasp the expressed content. Considering the aforementioned problems, it is relevant to identify noises in UGC for purposes which include a simple identification of the noise, its typification, eventually its substitution for another word or expression. These actions aim to both enhance NLP tools performance and facilitate end-user text comprehension, besides to provide an overview of the linguistics practices on the web.

The process of identifying noise and suggesting possible substitutions is known as text normalization. Non-standard words (NSWs) are often regarded as noise, but the precise definition of what constitutes them depends on the application domain. Some examples that might be seen as deviations from standard language and that should be normalized include spelling errors, abbreviations, mixed case words, acronyms, internet slang, hashtags, and emoticons. In general, NSWs are words which properties and meaning cannot be derived directly from a lexicon (Sproat et al., 2001). The term "lexicon" in this context does not necessarily mean the list of words that are formally recognized in a language, but rather

Proceedings of the 2nd Workshop on Noisy User-generated Text,
pages 112–120, Osaka, Japan, December 11 2016.

a set of words that are considered treatable by the specific application. Therefore, it is not possible to clearly state what is noise and what should be normalized.

In contrast to standardized language, UGC is often informal, with less adherence to conventions regarding punctuation, spelling, and style (Ling et al., 2013). Therefore, it is considerably noisy, containing *ad-hoc* abbreviations, phonetic substitutions, customized abbreviations, and slang language (Hassan and Menezes, 2013). Considering the specificity of such content, traditional techniques – such as lexicon-based substitution – are not capable to properly handle with many types of noise. Thus, in order to achieve satisfactory results, it is necessary to deeply analyze UGC and develop specific methods aimed at normalizing it.

Conventional string similarity measures (such as edit distance) are not, by themselves, capable of accurately correcting many errors found in UGC. Abbreviations and shorthands found in informal texts, specially on social networks, may contain a large number of edits often resulting in low string similarity – discouraging the use of traditional techniques.

More recently, the interest in techniques based on distributed representations of words (also called word embeddings) has increased. These representations are able to generate continuous numeric vectors of high-dimensionality to represent words. The vectors explicitly encode many linguistic regularities and patterns, as well as syntactic and semantic word relationships (Mikolov et al., 2013a). Words that share semantic similarity are represented by similar vectors. For example, the result of a vector calculation vec("King") - vec("Man") + vec("Woman") is closer to vec("Queen") than to any other word vector. Another strong characteristic of distributed representations is their capability of capturing the notion of contextual similarity – which is essential for textual normalization. The models used for learning these vectors, such as Skip-grams, are totally unsupervised and can be implemented efficiently. In this work, we exploit this set of advantages, combined with lexical similarity measures, in order to capture contextual similarity and learn normalization lexicons based on word embeddings.

2 Related work

Early work handled text normalization as a noisy channel model. This model consists of two components: a source model and a channel model (Shannon, 1948). It assumes that a signal is transferred through a medium and gets corrupted. The source model indicates the canonical form of the signal, and the channel model represents how the signal gets corrupted. (Brill and Moore, 2000) defined the spelling correction problem as finding $argmax_w P(w|s)$, being s the canonical word, which was sent by the source model, and w the received corrupted word. Applying Bayes' Theorem, the noisy channel model is obtained as $argmax_w P(s|w)P(w)$. This model presented significant performance improvements compared to previously proposed models, achieving up to 98% correction accuracy on well-behaved noisy text. However, this approach requires supervised training data for both canonical and corrupted words.

Log-linear models also have been applied as unsupervised statistical models for text normalization. (Yang and Eisenstein, 2013) proposed a model in which the relationship between standard and non-standard words may be characterized by a log-linear model with arbitrary features. The weights of these features can then be trained in maximum-likelihood frameworks. The use of this type of model requires a study of the problem to get the most significant features. From the definition of the features, the training process in conducted to optimize the weights. The advantage of these models is the easy incorporation of new features and the optimization is performed according to an objective function. Although not being highly dependent of resources and context-driven, the log-linear approach requires well-defined features – which are not easily identifiable in UGC. Another disadvantage is the total reliance on statistical observations on the corpus. Hence, the model does not satisfactorily represents the highly semantic specificity of the noise found in UGC, which can occur with low frequency thus not having a significant statistical impact. Considering these issues, this type of model is not enough to deal with generic domain and high context and semantic dependency found is UGC noise.

More recently, social media text normalization was tackled by using contextual graph random walks. (Hassan and Menezes, 2013) proposed a method that uses random walks on a contextual similarity bipartite graph constructed from n-gram sequences on large unlabeled text corpus to build a normalization lexicon. They obtained a precision of 92.43% and, using the method as a preprocessing step, improved translation quality of social media text by 6%. (Han et al., 2012) also presented an approach for unsupervised construction of normalization lexicons based on context information. Instead of a graph representation, this approach uses string similarity measures between word within a given context. (Ling et al., 2013) proposed a supervised learning technique for learning normalization rules from machine translations of a parallel corpus of microblog messages. They built two models that learn generalizations of the normalization process – one on the phrase level and the other on the character level. The approach was shown able to improve multiple machine translation systems.

Our technique is most similar to (Sridhard, 2015), since we implement an adaptation of the method presented in the mentioned work. The method proposed by (Sridhard, 2015) aims to learn distributed representations of words to capture the notion of contextual similarity and subsequently learn normalization lexicons from these representations in a completely unsupervised manner. The lexicons are represented as finite-state machines (FSMs) and the process of normalization is performed by transducing the noisy words from the FSMs. Our work makes use of different distributed representation of words, different scoring function for candidate generation and hash structures (dictionaries) instead of FSMs. We also introduce a method for automatically expanding the learned lexicons.

Regarding Brazilian Portuguese, some studies have been performed considering noises in specific domains, such as reviews of products (Duran et al., 2014), and some tools have been developed specifically for that same domain. The normalizer described in (Duran et al., 2015) is, as far as we know, the only tool for text normalization available for Brazilian Portuguese. The proposed lexicon-based normalizer considers that errors found in UGC are divided into six categories: **Common misspellings:** context-free orthographic errors, often phonetically-motivated. **Real-word misspellings:** contextual orthographic errors. Words that are contained in the language lexicon, but are wrong considering the context they appear. **Internet slang**: abbreviations and expressions often used informally by internet users. **Case use (proper names and acronyms)**: proper names and acronyms wrongly or not at all capitalized. **Case use (start of sentence)**: sentences starting with a lower case word. **Glued words**: agglutinated words that should be split. **Punctuation**: wrong use of sentence delimiters.

Since a large part of misspellings found in UGC is phonetically-motivated, (Duran et al., 2015) proposed a phonetic-based speller for correcting such errors. The speller combines edit distance and several specific phonetic rules for Portuguese in order to generate correction candidates. The correction of internet slang and proper name and acronyms capitalization is based on a set of lexicons. Each lexicon contains many pairs of wrong–correct form of words. The correction is performed by looking up the noisy word in the lexicon and substituting it by the correct version. Despite this technique achieving good results in the product review domain, it is not scalable and is too restricted, since there is no form of automatic lexicon-learning. Therefore, it is not suitable for a generic, domain-free normalizer. The results obtained by (Duran et al., 2015) will be further discussed, as they are the main source of comparison for our work.

Another technique specially designed for Brazilian Portuguese is the one proposed by (de Mendonça Almeida et al., 2016). The work presents two approaches for dealing with spelling correction of UGC. The first approach makes use of three phonetic modules, composed by the Soundex algorithm, a grapheme-to-phoneme converter and a set of language-specific phonetic rules. The second one combines grapheme-to-phoneme conversion and a decision tree classifier. The classifier is trained on a corpus of noisy text and employs 14 features (including string and phonetic similarity measures) to identify and correct different classes of orthographic errors. The approach achieves average correction accuracy of 78%, however requires training on an annotated corpus and feature extraction – making it less scalable than an unsupervised technique.

3   Distributed Representation of Words

Distributed representations of words in a vector space, also known as word embeddings, are able to capture lexical, semantic, syntactic, and even contextual similarity between words. This idea has been recently applied to a wide range of NLP tasks with surprising results (Sridhard, 2015). The Skip-gram model, introduced by (Mikolov et al., 2013a), brought forth an efficient method for learning high-quality vector representations of words from large amounts of unstructured text data. This model, unlike previous ones, does not involve dense matrix multiplications – making the training optimized and efficient.

Figure 1: The Skip-gram model architecture (Mikolov et al., 2013a).

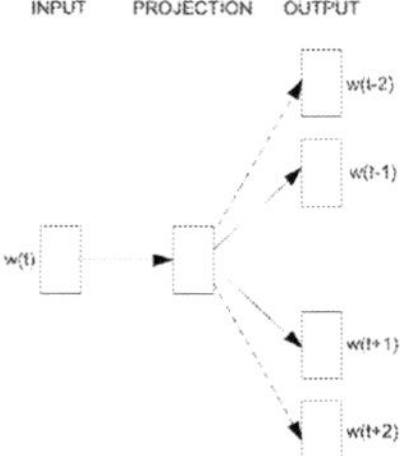

The Skip-gram model, graphically represented in Figure 1, tries to maximize classification of a word based on another word in the same sentence. Each current word is used as input to a log-linear classifier and predicts words in a windows before and after the current one. More formally, the goal of the Skip-gram model is to maximize the average log probability given by:

$$\frac{1}{T} \sum_{t=1}^{T} \sum_{-c < j < c, j \neq 0} \log p(w_{t+j} | w_t) \tag{1}$$

where c is the size of the training context, centered on word w_t (Mikolov et al., 2013b). In practice, word embeddings can be trained using many frameworks that already implement the training process. We used the Gensim [1] framework for Python. The process and parameters we used to train the embeddings will be explained in the next section.

For training distributed representations of words, two sources of data were used in our work. One is a large corpus of product reviews containing both noisy and correct texts. A complete description of the corpus can be found in (Hartmann et al., 2014). The other one is a corpus of Twitter posts (tweets) written in Portuguese. The tweets were extracted using a crawler developed by the authors and the data cannot be distributed due to license restrictions. Most of that content is noisy, considering that the tweets are limited by a maximum of 140 characters and that Twitter is, in general, an informal medium of content generation.

Both corpora had to be preprocessed in order to improve the text quality. First, the Twitter corpus was tokenized using Twokenizer [2], a specific tokenizer for tweets. User names, hashtags and hyperlinks were removed. The product review corpus was tokenized using a simple word tokenizer and predefined tags contained in the reviews (such as "What I liked about this product:") were removed. Next, the sentences were segmented by using the tool provided by (Duran et al., 2015). After segmentation, we obtained 6.8 million sentences from the Twitter corpus and 20 million from the product reviews corpus.

4   Similarity Measures

In order to find candidates for normalizing noisy words, some similarity measures were employed. The cosine distance between two D-dimensional vectors u and v can be used to determine how similar are two word embeddings. It is defined as:

$$\text{cosine similarity} = \frac{\sum_{i=1}^{D} u_i \times v_i}{\sqrt{\sum_{i=1}^{D} (u_i)^2 \times \sum_{i=1}^{D} (v_i)^2}} \tag{2}$$

---

[1] https://radimrehurek.com/gensim/index.html
[2] http://www.cs.cmu.edu/~ark/TweetNLP/#pos

To illustrate the representation power of word embeddings, the following image shows the 25 nearest neighbors (closest cosine similarity) of word 'você' (you) obtained from our word embedding model:

Figure 2: 25 nearest neighbors for word 'você' (you) found in our word embedding model.

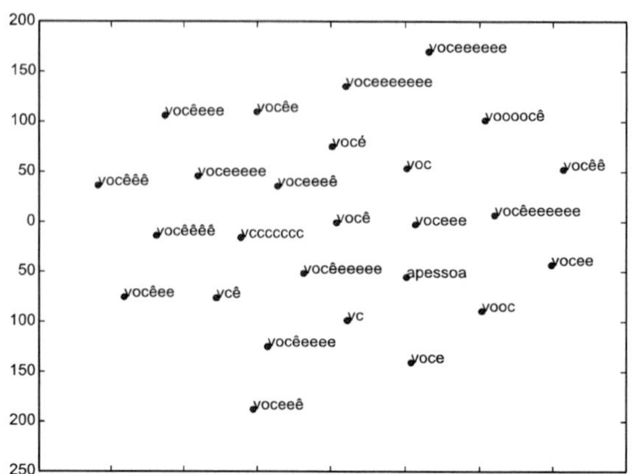

In Figure 2, the canonical form of the word (bold) is located at the center. Around it, there are many noisy variations found in the embedding model. In order to find the canonical form parting from a noisy word, it is also necessary to consider the lexical similarity. We compute its value using an adaptation of the definition presented in (Hassan and Menezes, 2013), as:

$$\text{lexical similarity}(w_1, w_2) = \begin{cases} \frac{LCSR(w_1,w_2)}{MED(w_1,w_2)}, & \text{if} MED(w_1, w_2) > 0 \\ LCSR(w_1, w_2), & \text{otherwise} \end{cases} \tag{3}$$

where w_1 and w_2 are two given words and $MED(w_1, w_2)$ is the modified edit distance between them, calculated as $MED(w_1, w_2) = ED(w_1, w_2) - DS(w_1, w_2)$. $DS(w_1, w_2)$ is the *diacritical symmetry* between w_1 and w_2 – *i.e*, the number of characters from a word that are aligned with versions of itself with diacritical marks in the other word. For instance, the diacritical symmetry between *maçã* (apple) and *maca* (stretcher) is 2. This measure is employed due to the fact that many misspellings in Portuguese happen because of a single diacritic, thus this modification improves the correction of such errors. $LCSR$ refers to Longest Common Subsequence Ratio and is calculated, in our modified version, as:

$$LCSR(w_1, w_2) = \frac{LCS(w_1, w_2) + DS(w_1, w_2)}{\text{max length}(w_1, w_2)} \tag{4}$$

where LCS refers to Longest Common Subsequence, being usually obtained through a dynamic programming approach. The lexical similarity measure indicates how similar two words are, ranging from 0 (no similarity) to 1 (identical).

5 Learning Normalization Lexicons

Having obtained the set of word embeddings, the method requires a list of canonical words as input. This list may be a lexicon of words recognized by a language, but may also be a list of words considered treatable by the application. We used the UNITEX-PB [3] lexicon for Brazilian Portuguese, removing words with frequency below 100 on Corpus Brasileiro [4] frequency list. This pruning step removes words that probably do not appear in UGC, reducing the lexicon size and improving performance. The next step obtains the K-nearest neighbors, excluding words contained in the lexicon, in the vector space for

---

[3] http://www.nilc.icmc.usp.br/nilc/projects/unitex-pb/web/dicionarios.html
[4] http://corpusbrasileiro.pucsp.br/cb/Acesso.html

each canonical word contained in the lexicon. We used K = 25, following (Sridhard, 2015) experiments. This step creates a list of possible corruptions (noisy versions) for every canonical word w_c. Considering the vector space V, the lexicon L and w_c every word $\in L$, the list of noisy versions is obtained as:

$$\text{noisy versions}[w_c] = \forall_{w \in V, V \notin L} \max_k \text{cosine similarity}(w_c, w) \tag{5}$$

After obtaining the list of noisy versions, it is necessary to invert it, because we must find the canonical version given a noisy word – therefore, the noisy version must index a list of correction candidates to it. In order to do so, we loop through every noisy versions list. We create a new structure to store each noisy word w_n as index to a list of canonical words that contain w_n in its noisy versions list. We then store a tuple $(w_c, score(w_n, w_c))$ as a candidate to correct w_n. The score is calculated as:

$$score(w_n, w_c) = n \times \text{lexical similarity}(w_n, w_c) + (1 - n) \times \text{cosine similarity}(w_n, w_c) \tag{6}$$

Different from (Sridhard, 2015), our approach considers the cosine similarity at the score function, because some corrections have low lexical similarity but appear in the same context, specially for abbreviations – for instance, $d+$ as abbreviation for *demais* (too much). The term n is a value between 0 and 1 that indicates the weight (or importance) given to the lexical similarity. In our experiments, n was set as 0.8. The learned lexicon is stored as a hash structure, indexed by w_n, where each entry contains the list of candidate corrections for the respective noisy word. To determine the best candidate to correct w_n, we simply compute $\max(score(w_n, w_c))$. Algorithm 1 summarizes the lexicon learning process.

Input: list of canonical words L, word embedding model V, number of K nearest neighbors
Output: learned lexicon T where $T[w_n]$ is the list of candidates for correcting noisy word w_n
for *each* $w \in L$ **do**
    for *each* $v \in V$ **do**
        if $v \notin L$ **then**
            compute cosine similarity(w, v)
        end
        store top K neighbors in $C(w)$
    end
end
for *each* $w \in C$ **do**
    for *each* $w' \in C[w]$ **do**
        $T[w'] \Leftarrow (w, score(w', w))$
    end
end

Algorithm 1: Unsupervised Lexicon Learning

5.1 Expanding the Learned Lexicon

Given that only the K-nearest neighbors of a canonical word are added to the lexicon, some very infrequent noisy words may not be a top neighbor of any canonical word. In this case, the approach presented above cannot find any correction candidates. In order to solve this issue, we added an expansion step to the method. If a given noisy w_n is not in the learned lexicon, that is, $w_n \notin T$, then we find the canonical word from L which is most similar to w_n, and add it as a correction candidate. Thus, the expansion step can be defined as:

$$\text{If } w_n \notin T : T[w_n] \Leftarrow \max_{w_c \in L} \text{lexical similarity}(w_n, w_c) \tag{7}$$

Despite its simplicity, the expansion step improved the overall correction recall.

5.2 Representing Context

Thus far, our framework has scored candidates deterministically, based solely on lexical information. In this case, correction candidates will always be the same for a given noisy word, independent from the context it appears. This idea might be enough for correcting internet slang, since equal abbreviations are seldom used for different words. However, ignoring contextual information makes it impossible to handle contextual orthographic errors (also called real-word errors or RWEs). This type of error occurs when a given word is in the recognized lexicon (so it is not *per se* a noisy word) but is incorrect due to the context it appears. In Portuguese, cases of real-word errors caused by missing a single diacritic are frequent and can only be corrected by considering the context. In order to do so, we used a language model (LM) (with trigrams) trained on a Wikipedia sample consisting of 3841834 sentences. We trained our LM using the KenLM framework, which employs modified Kneser-Ney smoothing for estimation (Heafield, 2013). The estimated trigram probabilities were normalized to fit the range of the other measures and then added to the scoring function. The correction of RWEs relies only on similarity measures and on the language model, because it maps a canonical (but inadequate to the context) word to another canonical word – therefore the learned lexicon based on word embeddings does not include it.

6 Evaluation

In order to evaluate the proposed method and compare it to already existing tools for Brazilian Portuguese, two annotated samples of product reviews written by users were used. Each sample contains 60 reviews, with every error manually annotated by a specialist. The annotation considers the six categories of noise proposed by (Duran et al., 2015), but our technique can only be applied to the correction of orthographic errors and internet slang.

First, we conducted experiments in order to determine the best word embedding model. We trained both Skip-gram and Continuous bag-of-words (Cbow) models, implemented in Gensim, to learn the embeddings. We used a context window of size 5, *i.e* 2 words before and 2 after the center, and used hierarchical sampling for reducing the vocabulary size during training, considering only words with a minimum count of 10 occurrences. We generated embeddings with 100, 300 and 500 dimensions. For each dimension size, we trained the embeddings on two different sets of data: the first one, referred as Noisy, is exactly as described in Section 3, and the second one, referred as Hybrid, includes an additional dataset containing 38 million sentences from Wikipedia. Table 1 shows the recall measure obtained for the correction of orthographic errors (O) (without the LM probabilities) and internet slang (I) (with the best setup) using each embedding model trained.

Table 1: Results for error correction obtained from each word embedding model

Model	Dimensions					
	100		300		500	
	O	I	O	I	O	I
Cbow Hybrid	67.2%	64.5%	72.3%	64.5%	72.1%	64.5%
Cbow Noisy	70.7%	54.8%	74.7%	64.5%	76.0%	64.5%
Skip-gram Hybrid	63.8%	77.4%	74.2%	71.0%	76.0%	71.0%
Skip-gram Noisy	77.3%	64.5%	78.6%	67.7%	**78.6%**	**77.4%**

The Skip-gram model with 500 dimensions showed the best results. Therefore, further experiments were conducted using these embeddings. In order to better evaluate the framework, we performed experiments using three different learned lexicons models. The only difference between them is the word embedding model employed. The first one, referred as *Noisy*, uses embeddings trained on data preprocessed exactly as described in Section 3. The second model, referred as *Clean*, uses embedding trained on data with an additional preprocessing step: every symbol that is not either a letter or a number is removed. Both are Skip-gram models with 500 dimensions. The third model is an *Ensemble* containing the previous ones. Its output is defined as $max(output(Clean), output(Noisy))$. We have found empirically that the *Noisy* model is better for internet slang correction, the *Clean* model is better for orthographic errors and the *Ensemble* joins the best of both. In Tables 2 and 3 we compare the three lexicon models with UGCNormal, the tool proposed by (Duran et al., 2015). The tables follow the format $X/Y = Z$, being X the total of corrections performed by each model, Y the total of annotated errors in the sample and Z the obtained recall measure.

Table 2: Results for orthographic errors correction

Model	Corrections
Noisy	129/164 = 78.6%
Clean	135/164 = 82.3%
Ensemble	137/164 = 83.5%
Ensemble+Expansion Step	149/164 = 90.9%
Ensemble+Expansion Step+LM	**151/164 = 92.1%**
Expansion Step+LM (RWEs)	**84/115 = 73.0%**
UGCNormal	137/164 = 83.5%
UGCNormal (RWEs)	39/115 = 33.9%

Table 3: Results for internet slang correction

Model	Corrections
Noisy	20/31 = 64.5%
Clean	17/31 = 54.8%
Ensemble	22/31 = 71.0%
Ensemble+Expansion Step	23/31 = 74.2%
Ensemble+Expansion Step+LM	**24/31 = 77.4%**
UGCNormal	19/31 = 61.3%

The results show that the ensemble model with expansion step and context representation (LM) outperforms every other model, including UGCNormal. For RWEs, the combination of expansion step and language model outperforms UGCNormal by a large margin.

7 Conclusion

We presented an unsupervised method for learning normalization lexicons based on similarity measures and distributed representation of words. Our approach does not require sets of rules or domain-specific lexicons, but only a lexicon containing a list of canonical words. Therefore, it can be easily expanded and adapted according to the needs of each specific application. We trained distributed representations using the Skip-gram model on a large corpus of both Twitter posts and product reviews. The results indicate that the method for both internet slang and orthographic error correction surpasses the results obtained from already existing tools for Brazilian Portuguese. The expansion step, despite being simple, improved the correction significantly. As future work, different methods of context representation must be explored. Methods for dealing with multiword expressions, such as acronyms for internet slang, must be added to our framework. Despite being rare in Brazilian Portuguese, such language constructs are commonly find on internet slang, mainly derived from English. Correcting more categories of noise, either by expanding this technique or investigating new approaches, is the following step for this project.

References

Eric Brill and Robert C. Moore. 2000. An improved error model for noisy channel spelling correction. In *Proceedings of the 38th Annual Meeting on Association for Computational Linguistics*, ACL '00, pages 286–293, Stroudsburg, PA, USA. Association for Computational Linguistics.

Gustavo Augusto de Mendonça Almeida, Lucas Avanço, Magali Sanches Duran, Erick Rocha Fonseca, Maria das Graças Volpe Nunes, and Sandra Maria Aluísio. 2016. Evaluating phonetic spellers for user-generated content in brazilian portuguese. In *Computational Processing of the Portuguese Language: 12th International Conference, PROPOR 2016, Tomar, Portugal, July 13-15, 2016, Proceedings*, pages 361–373. Springer International Publishing.

Magali Sanches Duran, Lucas Avanço, Sandra M Aluisio, Thiago A S Pardo, and M Graças Volpe Nunes. 2014. Some issues on the normalization of a corpus of products reviews in Portuguese. *Proceedings of the EACL 2014 9th Web as Corpus Workshop (WAC-9)*, pages 22–27.

Magali Sanches Duran, Lucas Avanço, and M Graças Volpe Nunes. 2015. A Normalizer for UGC in Brazilian Portuguese. *Proceedings of the ACL 2015 Workshop on Noisy User-generated Text*, pages 38–47.

Bo Han, Paul Cook, and Timothy Baldwin. 2012. Automatically constructing a normalisation dictionary for microblogs. In *EMNLP-CoNLL 2012 - 2012 Joint Conference on Empirical Methods in Natural Language Processing and Computational Natural Language Learning, Proceedings of the Conference*, pages 421–432.

Nathan Hartmann, Lucas Avanço, Pedro Balage, Magali Duran, Maria Das Graças Volpe Nunes, Thiago Pardo, and Sandra Aluísio. 2014. A large corpus of product reviews in portuguese: Tackling out-of-vocabulary words. In *Proceedings of the Ninth International Conference on Language Resources and Evaluation (LREC'14)*, Reykjavik, Iceland, may. European Language Resources Association (ELRA).

Hany Hassan and Arul Menezes. 2013. Social text normalization using contextual graph random walks. *Proceedings of the 51st Annual Meeting of the Association for Computational Linguistics (ACL 2013)*, pages 1577–1586.

Kenneth Heafield. 2013. Scalable modified kneser-ney language model estimation. In *In Proceedings of the 51st Annual Meeting of the Association for Computational Linguistics*.

John Krumm, Nigel Davies, and Chandra Narayanaswami. 2008. User-generated content. *Ieee Cs*, 7:10–11.

Wang Ling, Chris Dyer, W. Alan Black, and Isabel Trancoso. 2013. Paraphrasing 4 Microblog Normalization. *Proceedings of the 2013 Conference on Empirical Methods in Natural Language Processing*, pages 73–84.

Tomas Mikolov, Kai Chen, Greg Corrado, and Jeffrey Dean. 2013a. Distributed Representations of Words and Phrases and their Compositionality. *Nips*, pages 1–9.

Tomas Mikolov, Kai Chen, Greg Corrado, and Jeffrey Dean. 2013b. Efficient estimation of word representations in vector space. *ArXiv Preprint*.

Claude E. Shannon. 1948. A Mathematical Theory of Communication. *The Bell System Technical Journal*, 27(3):379–423.

Richard Sproat, Alan W. Black, Stanley Chen, Shankar Kumar, Mari Ostendorf, and Christopher Richards. 2001. Normalization of non-standard words. *Computer Speech & Language*, 15(3):287–333.

K. R. Vivek Sridhard. 2015. Unsupervised Text Normalization Using Distributed Representations of Words and Phrases. *Proceedings of the 2015 Conference of the North American Chapter of the Association for Computational Linguistics: Human Language Technologies*, pages 8–16.

Yi Yang and Jacob Eisenstein. 2013. A Log-Linear Model for Unsupervised Text Normalization. *Emnlp*, (October):61–72.

How Document Pre-processing affects Keyphrase Extraction Performance

Florian Boudin and **Hugo Mougard** and **Damien Cram**
LINA - UMR CNRS 6241, Université de Nantes, France
`firstname.lastname@univ-nantes.fr`

Abstract

The SemEval-2010 benchmark dataset has brought renewed attention to the task of automatic keyphrase extraction. This dataset is made up of scientific articles that were automatically converted from PDF format to plain text and thus require careful preprocessing so that irrevelant spans of text do not negatively affect keyphrase extraction performance. In previous work, a wide range of document preprocessing techniques were described but their impact on the overall performance of keyphrase extraction models is still unexplored. Here, we re-assess the performance of several keyphrase extraction models and measure their robustness against increasingly sophisticated levels of document preprocessing.

1 Introduction

Recent years have seen a surge of interest in automatic keyphrase extraction, thanks to the availability of the SemEval-2010 benchmark dataset (Kim et al., 2010). This dataset is composed of documents (scientific articles) that were automatically converted from PDF format to plain text. As a result, most documents contain irrelevant pieces of text (e.g. muddled sentences, tables, equations, footnotes) that require special handling, so as to not hinder the performance of keyphrase extraction systems. In previous work, these are usually removed at the preprocessing step, but using a variety of techniques ranging from simple heuristics (Wang and Li, 2010; Treeratpituk et al., 2010; Zervanou, 2010) to sophisticated document logical structure detection on richly-formatted documents recovered from Google Scholar (Nguyen and Luong, 2010). Under such conditions, it may prove difficult to draw firm conclusions about which keyphrase extraction model performs best, as the impact of preprocessing on overall performance cannot be properly quantified.

While previous work clearly states that efficient document preprocessing is a prerequisite for the extraction of high quality keyphrases, there is, to our best knowledge, no empirical evidence of how preprocessing affects keyphrase extraction performance. In this paper, we re-assess the performance of several state-of-the-art keyphrase extraction models at increasingly sophisticated levels of preprocessing. Three incremental levels of document preprocessing are experimented with: raw text, text cleaning through document logical structure detection, and removal of keyphrase sparse sections of the document. In doing so, we present the first consistent comparison of different keyphrase extraction models and study their robustness over noisy text. More precisely, our contributions are:

- We show that performance variation across keyphrase extraction systems is, at least in part, a function of the (often unstated) effectiveness of document preprocessing.

- We empirically show that supervised models are more resilient to noise, and point out that the performance gap between baselines and top performing systems is narrowing with the increase in preprocessing effort.

Proceedings of the 2nd Workshop on Noisy User-generated Text,
pages 121–128, Osaka, Japan, December 11 2016.

- We compare the previously reported results of several keyphrase extraction models with that of our re-implementation, and observe that baseline performance is underestimated because of the inconsistence in document preprocessing.

- We release both a new version of the SemEval-2010 dataset[1] with preprocessed documents and our implementation of the state-of-the-art keyphrase extraction models[2] using the `pke` toolkit (Boudin, 2016) for use by the community.

2   Dataset and Preprocessing

The SemEval-2010 benchmark dataset (Kim et al., 2010) is composed of 244 scientific articles collected from the ACM Digital Library (conference and workshop papers). The input papers ranged from 6 to 8 pages and were converted from PDF format to plain text using an off-the-shelf tool[3]. The only preprocessing applied is a systematic dehyphenation at line breaks[4] and removal of author-assigned keyphrases. Scientific articles were selected from four different research areas as defined in the ACM classification, and were equally distributed into training (144 articles) and test (100 articles) sets. Gold standard keyphrases are composed of both author-assigned keyphrases collected from the original PDF files and reader-assigned keyphrases provided by student annotators.

Long documents such as those in the SemEval-2010 benchmark dataset are notoriously difficult to handle due to the large number of keyphrase candidates (i.e. phrases that are eligible to be keyphrases) that the systems have to cope with (Hasan and Ng, 2014). Furthermore, noisy textual content, whether due to format conversion errors or to unusable elements (e.g. equations), yield many spurious keyphrase candidates that negatively affect keyphrase extraction performance. This is particularly true for systems that make use of core NLP tools to select candidates, that in turn exhibit poor performance on degraded text. Filtering out irrelevant text is therefore needed for addressing these issues.

In this study, we concentrate our effort on re-assessing keyphrase extraction performance on three increasingly sophisticated levels of document preprocessing described below.

Level 1: We process each input file with the Stanford CoreNLP suite (Manning et al., 2014)[5]. We use the default parameters and perform tokenization, sentence splitting and Part-Of-Speech (POS) tagging.

Level 2: Similarly to (Nguyen and Luong, 2010; Lopez and Romary, 2010), we retrieve[6] the original PDF files from the ACM Digital Library. We then extract the enriched[7] textual content of the PDF files using an Optical Character Recognition (OCR) system[8], and perform document logical structure detection using ParsCit (Kan et al., 2010)[9]. We use the detected logical structure to remove author-assigned keyphrases and select only relevant elements: title, headers, abstract, introduction, related work, body text[10] and conclusion. We finally apply a systematic dehyphenation at line breaks and run the Stanford CoreNLP suite.

Level 3: As pointed out by (Treeratpituk et al., 2010; Nguyen and Luong, 2010; Wang and Li, 2010; Eichler and Neumann, 2010; El-Beltagy and Rafea, 2010), considering only the keyphrase dense parts of the scientific articles allows to improve keyphrase extraction performance. Accordingly we follow previous work and further abridge the input text from level 2 preprocessed documents to the following: title, headers, abstract, introduction, related work, background and conclusion. Here, the idea is to achieve the best compromise between search space (number of candidates) and maximum performance (recall).

---

[1] https://github.com/boudinfl/semeval-2010-pre
[2] https://github.com/boudinfl/pke
[3] pdftotext, http://www.foolabs.com/xpdf/
[4] Valid hyphenated forms may have their hyphen removed by this process.
[5] Use use Stanford CoreNLP v3.6.0.
[6] To ensure consistency, articles were manually collected.
[7] Additional information such as font format or spacial layout is also extracted.
[8] We use Omnipage v18, http://www.nuance.com/omnipage
[9] We use ParsCit v110505.
[10] We further filter out tables, figures, captions, equations, notes, copyright and references.

Table 1 shows the average number of sentences and words along with the maximum possible recall for each level of preprocessing. The maximum recall is obtained by computing the fraction of the reference keyphrases that occur in the documents. We observe that the level 2 preprocessing succeeds in eliminating irrelevant text by significantly reducing the number of words (-19%) while maintaining a high maximum recall (-2%). Level 3 preprocessing drastically reduce the number of words to less than a quarter of the original amount while interestingly still preserving high recall.

	Lvl 1	Lvl 2	Lvl 3
Avg. sentences	399	347	101
Avg. words	9 772	7 874	1 922
Max. recall	83.9%	81.8%	70.9%

Table 1: Statistics computed at the different levels of document preprocessing on the training set.

3   Keyphrase Extraction Models

We re-implemented five keyphrase extraction models : the first two are commonly used as baselines, the third is a resource-lean unsupervised graph-based ranking approach, and the last two were among the top performing systems in the SemEval-2010 keyphrase extraction task (Kim et al., 2010). We note that two of the systems are supervised and rely on the training set to build their classification models. Document frequency counts are also computed on the training set[11]. Stemming[12] is applied to allow more robust matching. The different keyphrase extraction models are briefly described below:

TF×IDF: we re-implemented the TF×IDF n-gram based baseline computed by the task organizers. We use 1, 2, 3-grams as keyphrase candidates and filter out those shorter than 3 characters, containing words made of only punctuation marks or one character long[13].

Kea (Witten et al., 1999): keyphrase candidates are 1, 2, 3-grams that do not begin or end with a stopword[14]. Keyphrases are selected using a naïve bayes classifier[15] with two features: TF×IDF and the relative position of first occurrence.

TopicRank (Bougouin et al., 2013): keyphrase candidates are the longest sequences of adjacent nouns and adjectives. Lexically similar candidates are clustered into topics and ranked using TextRank (Mihalcea and Tarau, 2004). Keyphrases are produced by extracting the first occurring candidate of the highest ranked topics.

KP-Miner (El-Beltagy and Rafea, 2010): keyphrase candidates are sequences of words that do not contain punctuation marks or stopwords. Candidates that appear less than three times or that first occur beyond a certain position are removed[16]. Candidates are then weighted using a modified TF×IDF formula that account for document length.

WINGNUS (Nguyen and Luong, 2010): keyphrase candidates are simplex nouns and noun phrases detected using a set of rules described in (Kim and Kan, 2009). Keyphrases are then selected using a naïve bayes classifier with the optimal set of features found on the training set[17]: TF×IDF, relative position of first occurrence and candidate length in words.

---

[11] For more reliable estimates, we rely on level 2 counts when experimenting with level 3.

[12] We use the Porter stemmer in nltk.

[13] This filtering process is also applied to the other models.

[14] We use the stoplist in nltk, http://www.nltk.org

[15] We use the Multinomial Naive Bayes classifier from scikit-learn with default parameters, http://scikit-learn.org

[16] To better see the impact of preprocessing, we do not consider the cutoff parameter in our experiments. The least allowable seen frequency parameter is set to 2 which is the optimal value found on the training set.

[17] The optimal set of features in (Nguyen and Luong, 2010) also include the term frequency of substrings, but we observed a significant drop in performance when this feature is included.

Each model uses a distinct keyphrase candidate selection method that provides a trade-off between the highest attainable recall and the size of set of candidates. Table 2 summarizes these numbers for each model. Syntax-based selection heuristics, as used by TopicRank and WINGNUS, are better suited to prune candidates that are unlikely to be keyphrases. As for KP-miner, removing infrequent candidates may seem rather blunt, but it turns out to be a simple yet effective pruning method when dealing with long documents. For details on how candidate selection methods affect keyphrase extraction, please refer to (Wang et al., 2014).

Model	Lvl 1		Lvl 2		Lvl 3	
TF×IDF	80.2%	7 837	78.2%	6 958	67.8%	2 270
Kea	80.2%	3 026	78.2%	2 502	67.8%	912
TopicRank	70.9%	742	69.2%	627	57.8%	241
KP-Miner	64.0%	724	61.8%	599	48.7%	212
WINGNUS	75.2%	1 355	73.0%	1 007	63.0%	403

Table 2: Maximum recall and average number of keyphrase candidates for each model.

Apart from TopicRank that groups similar candidates into topics, the other models do not have any redundancy control mechanism. Yet, recent work has shown that up to 12% of the overall error made by state-of-the-art keyphrase extraction systems were due to redundancy (Hasan and Ng, 2014; Boudin, 2015). Therefore as a post-ranking step, we remove redundant keyphrases from the ranked lists generated by all models. A keyphrase is considered redundant if it is included in another keyphrase that is ranked higher in the list.

4 Experiments

4.1 Experimental settings

We follow the evaluation procedure used in the SemEval-2010 competition and evaluate the performance of each model in terms of f-measure (F) at the top N keyphrases[18]. We use the set of combined author- and reader-assigned keyphrases as reference keyphrases. Extracted and reference keyphrases are stemmed to reduce the number of mismatches.

4.2 Results

The performances of the keyphrase extraction models at each preprocessing level are shown in Table 3. Overall, we observe a significant increase of performance for all models at levels 3, confirming that document preprocessing plays an important role in keyphrase extraction performance. Also, the difference of f-score between the models, as measured by the standard deviation σ_1, gradually decreases with the increasing level of preprocessing. This result strengthens the assumption made in this paper, that performance variation across models is partly a function of the effectiveness of document preprocessing.

Somewhat surprisingly, the ordering of the two best models reverses at level 3. This showcases that rankings are heavily influenced by the preprocessing stage, despite the common lack of details and analysis it suffers from in explanatory papers. We also remark that the top performing model, namely KP-Miner, is unsupervised which supports the findings of (Hasan and Ng, 2014) indicating that recent unsupervised approaches have rivaled their supervised counterparts in performance.

In an attempt to quantify the performance variation across preprocessing levels, we compute the standard deviation σ_2 for each model. Here we see that unsupervised models are more sensitive to noisy input, as revealed by higher standard deviations. We found two main reasons for this. First, using multiple discriminative features to rank keyphrase candidates adds inherent robustness to the models. Second, the supervision signal helps models to disregard noise.

In Table 4, we compare the outputs of the five models by measuring the percentage of valid keyphrases that are retrieved by all models at once for each preprocessing level. By these additional results, we aim

---

[18]Scores are computed using the evaluation script provided by the SemEval-2010 organizers.

	Model	Lvl 1	Lvl 2	Lvl 3	σ_2
Unsup.	TopicRank	12.2	12.5	$14.5^{\alpha,\beta}$	1.25
	TF×IDF	16.0	16.4	$19.3^{\alpha,\beta}$	1.80
	KP-Miner	20.2	19.8	$\mathbf{22.5}^{\alpha,\beta}$	1.46
Sup.	Kea	19.2	19.3	21.2^{α}	1.13
	WINGNUS	**20.5**	**20.3**	21.8^{β}	0.82
	σ_1	3.51	3.26	3.22	

Table 3: F-scores computed at the top 10 extracted keyphrases for the unsupervised (Unsup.) and supervised (Sup.) models at each preprocessing level. We also report the standard deviation across the five models for each level (σ_1) and the standard deviation across the three levels for each model (σ_2). α and β indicate significance at the 0.05 level using Student's t-test against level 1 and level 2 respectively.

to assess whether document preprocessing smoothes differences between models. We observe that the overlap between the outputs of the different models increases along with the level of preprocessing. This suggests that document preprocessing reduces the effect that the keyphrase extraction model in itself has on overall performance. In other words, the singularity of each model fades away gradually with increase in preprocessing effort.

	Lvl 1	Lvl 2	Lvl 3
% valid keyphrases	19.9%	23.1%	25.1%

Table 4: Percentage of valid keyphrases found by all five keyphrase extraction models at each preprocessing level.

4.3 Reproducibility

Being able to reproduce experimental results is a central aspect of the scientific method. While assessing the importance of the preprocessing stage for five approaches, we found that several results were not reproducible, as shown in Table 5.

Model	Ori.	Lvl 1	Lvl 2	Lvl 3
TopicRank	12.1	+0.1	+0.4	+2.4
TF×IDF	14.4	+1.6	+2.0	+4.9
KP-Miner	23.2	−3.2	−3.4	−0.7
WINGNUS	24.7	−4.2	−4.4	−2.8

Table 5: Difference in f-score between our re-implementation and the original scores reported in (Hasan and Ng, 2014; Bougouin et al., 2013).

We note that the trends for baselines and high ranking systems are opposite: compared to the published results, our reproduction of top systems under-performs and our reproduction of baselines over-performs. We hypothesise that this stems from a difference in hyperparameter tuning, including the ones that the preprocessing stage makes implicit. Competitors have strong incentives to correctly optimize hyperparameters, to achieve a high ranking and get more publicity for their work while competition organizers might have the opposite incentive: too strong a baseline might not be considered a baseline anymore.

We also observe that with this leveled preprocessing, the gap between baselines and top systems is much smaller, lessening again the importance of raw scores and rankings to interpret the shared task results and emphasizing the importance of understanding correctly the preprocessing stage.

5 Additional experiments

In the previous sections, we provided empirical evidence that document preprocessing weighs heavily on the outcome of keyphrase extraction models. This raises the question of whether further improvement might be gained from a more aggressive preprocessing. To answer this question, we take another step beyond content filtering and further abridge the input text from level 3 preprocessed documents using an unsupervised summarization technique. More specifically, we keep the title and abstract intact, as they are the two most keyphrase dense parts within scientific articles (Nguyen and Luong, 2010), and select only the most content bearing sentences from the remaining contents. To do this, sentences are ordered using TextRank (Mihalcea and Tarau, 2004) and the less informative ones, as determined by their TextRank scores normalized by their lengths in words, are filtered out.

Finding the optimal subset of sentences from already shortened documents is however no trivial task as maximum recall linearly decreases with the number of sentences discarded. Here, we simply set the reduction ratio to 0.865 so that the average maximum recall on the training set does not lose more than 5%. Table 6 shows the reduction in the average number of sentences and words compared to level 3 preprocessing.

	Lvl 4	Δ Lvl 3
Avg. sentences	71	−30.0%
Avg. words	1 470	−23.5%
Max. recall	65.9%	−7.0%

Table 6: Statistics computed at level 4 of document preprocessing on the training set. We also report the relative difference with respect to level 3 preprocessing.

The performances of the keyphrase extraction models at level 4 preprocessing are shown in Table 7. We note that two models, namely TopicRank and TF×IDF, lose on performance. These two models mainly rely on frequency counts to rank keyphrase candidates, which in turn become less reliable at level 4 because of the very short length of the documents. Other models however have their f-scores once again increased, thus indicating that further improvement is possible from more reductive document preprocessing strategies.

	Model	Lvl 4	Δ Lvl 3
Unsup.	TopicRank	13.7	−0.8
	TF×IDF	18.5	−0.8
	KP-Miner	23.2	+0.7
Sup.	Kea	21.7	+0.5
	WINGNUS	22.5	+0.7

Table 7: F-scores computed at the top 10 extracted keyphrases for the unsupervised (Unsup.) and supervised (Sup.) models at level 4 preprocessing. We also report the difference in f-score with level 3 preprocessing.

6 Conclusion

In this study, we re-assessed the performance of several keyphrase extraction models and showed that performance variation across models is partly a function of the effectiveness of the document preprocessing. Our results also suggest that supervised keyphrase extraction models are more robust to noisy input.

Given our findings, we recommend that future works use a common preprocessing to evaluate the interest of keyphrase extraction approaches. For this reason we make the four levels of preprocessing used in this study available for the community.

References

Florian Boudin. 2015. Reducing over-generation errors for automatic keyphrase extraction using integer linear programming. In *Proceedings of the ACL 2015 Workshop on Novel Computational Approaches to Keyphrase Extraction*, pages 19–24, Beijing, China, July. Association for Computational Linguistics.

Florian Boudin. 2016. pke: an open source python-based keyphrase extraction toolkit. In *Proceedings of COLING 2016: System Demonstrations*, Osaka, Japan, December.

Adrien Bougouin, Florian Boudin, and Béatrice Daille. 2013. Topicrank: Graph-based topic ranking for keyphrase extraction. In *Proceedings of the Sixth International Joint Conference on Natural Language Processing*, pages 543–551, Nagoya, Japan, October. Asian Federation of Natural Language Processing.

Kathrin Eichler and Günter Neumann. 2010. Dfki keywe: Ranking keyphrases extracted from scientific articles. In *Proceedings of the 5th International Workshop on Semantic Evaluation*, pages 150–153, Uppsala, Sweden, July. Association for Computational Linguistics.

Samhaa R. El-Beltagy and Ahmed Rafea. 2010. Kp-miner: Participation in semeval-2. In *Proceedings of the 5th International Workshop on Semantic Evaluation*, pages 190–193, Uppsala, Sweden, July. Association for Computational Linguistics.

Kazi Saidul Hasan and Vincent Ng. 2014. Automatic keyphrase extraction: A survey of the state of the art. In *Proceedings of the 52nd Annual Meeting of the Association for Computational Linguistics (Volume 1: Long Papers)*, pages 1262–1273, Baltimore, Maryland, June. Association for Computational Linguistics.

Min-Yen Kan, Minh-Thang Luong, and Thuy Dung Nguyen. 2010. Logical structure recovery in scholarly articles with rich document features. *Int. J. Digit. Library Syst.*, 1(4):1–23, October.

Su Nam Kim and Min-Yen Kan. 2009. Re-examining automatic keyphrase extraction approaches in scientific articles. In *Proceedings of the Workshop on Multiword Expressions: Identification, Interpretation, Disambiguation and Applications*, pages 9–16, Singapore, August. Association for Computational Linguistics.

Su Nam Kim, Olena Medelyan, Min-Yen Kan, and Timothy Baldwin. 2010. Semeval-2010 task 5 : Automatic keyphrase extraction from scientific articles. In *Proceedings of the 5th International Workshop on Semantic Evaluation*, pages 21–26, Uppsala, Sweden, July. Association for Computational Linguistics.

Patrice Lopez and Laurent Romary. 2010. Humb: Automatic key term extraction from scientific articles in grobid. In *Proceedings of the 5th International Workshop on Semantic Evaluation*, pages 248–251, Uppsala, Sweden, July. Association for Computational Linguistics.

Christopher Manning, Mihai Surdeanu, John Bauer, Jenny Finkel, Steven Bethard, and David McClosky. 2014. The stanford corenlp natural language processing toolkit. In *Proceedings of 52nd Annual Meeting of the Association for Computational Linguistics: System Demonstrations*, pages 55–60, Baltimore, Maryland, June. Association for Computational Linguistics.

Rada Mihalcea and Paul Tarau. 2004. Textrank: Bringing order into texts. In Dekang Lin and Dekai Wu, editors, *Proceedings of EMNLP 2004*, pages 404–411, Barcelona, Spain, July. Association for Computational Linguistics.

Thuy Dung Nguyen and Minh-Thang Luong. 2010. Wingnus: Keyphrase extraction utilizing document logical structure. In *Proceedings of the 5th International Workshop on Semantic Evaluation*, pages 166–169, Uppsala, Sweden, July. Association for Computational Linguistics.

Pucktada Treeratpituk, Pradeep Teregowda, Jian Huang, and C. Lee Giles. 2010. Seerlab: A system for extracting keyphrases from scholarly documents. In *Proceedings of the 5th International Workshop on Semantic Evaluation*, pages 182–185, Uppsala, Sweden, July. Association for Computational Linguistics.

Letian Wang and Fang Li. 2010. Sjtultlab: Chunk based method for keyphrase extraction. In *Proceedings of the 5th International Workshop on Semantic Evaluation*, pages 158–161, Uppsala, Sweden, July. Association for Computational Linguistics.

Rui Wang, Wei Liu, and Chris Mcdonald. 2014. How preprocessing affects unsupervised keyphrase extraction. In *Proceedings of the 15th International Conference on Computational Linguistics and Intelligent Text Processing - Volume 8403*, CICLing 2014, pages 163–176, New York, NY, USA. Springer-Verlag New York, Inc.

Ian H. Witten, Gordon W. Paynter, Eibe Frank, Carl Gutwin, and Craig G. Nevill-Manning. 1999. Kea: Practical automatic keyphrase extraction. In *Proceedings of the Fourth ACM Conference on Digital Libraries*, DL '99, pages 254–255, New York, NY, USA. ACM.

Kalliopi Zervanou. 2010. Uvt: The uvt term extraction system in the keyphrase extraction task. In *Proceedings of the 5th International Workshop on Semantic Evaluation*, pages 194–197, Uppsala, Sweden, July. Association for Computational Linguistics.

Japanese Text Normalization with Encoder-Decoder Model

Taishi Ikeda, Hiroyuki Shindo and Yuji Matsumoto
Graduate School of Information Science
Nara Institute of Science and Technology
8916-5 Takayama, Ikoma, Nara, 630-0192, Japan
{ikeda.taishi.io7, shindo, matsu}@is.naist.jp

Abstract

Text normalization is the task of transforming lexical variants to their canonical forms. We model
the problem of text normalization as a character-level sequence to sequence learning problem
and present a neural encoder-decoder model for solving it. To train the encoder-decoder model,
many sentences pairs are generally required. However, Japanese non-standard canonical pairs
are scarce in the form of parallel corpora. To address this issue, we propose a method of data
augmentation to increase data size by converting existing resources into synthesized non-standard
forms using handcrafted rules. We conducted an experiment to demonstrate that the synthesized
corpus contributes to stably train an encoder-decoder model and improve the performance of
Japanese text normalization.

1 Introduction

With the rapid spread of the social media, many texts have been uploaded to the internet. As such, social
media texts are considered important language resources owing to an increasing demand for information extraction and text mining (Lau et al., 2012; Aramaki et al., 2011). However, these texts include
lexical variants such as insertions, phonetic substitutions and internet slangs. These non-standard forms
adversely affect language analysis tools that are trained on a clean corpus. Since Japanese has no explicit boundaries between words, word segmentation and part-of-speech (POS) tagging are extremely
important in Japanese language processing. For example, the output obtained using the Japanese morphological analyzer: MeCab [1] for a non-standard sentence: "このあぷりすげえええ！" is as follows:

Input:このあぷりすげえええ！ (*kono apuri sugeee*; This app is greeeat!)

Output:この (This, Prenominal adjective) / あ (a, Filler) / ぷりすげえええ (UNK) / ！ (Symbol)
where the slashes indicate word boundaries. Although "アプリ" (*apuri*; app) is originally written in
Katakana form, it is written in Hiragana form "あぷり" (*apuri*; app) in this example. Japanese has several
writing scripts: Kanji, Hiragana and Katakana. Such interchanging between scripts in social media texts
often occurs. Furthermore, "すげえええ" (*sugeeee*; greeeat) is derived from "すごい" (*sugoi*; great) by
changing some vowels from /oi/ to /eee/. These non-standard forms such as "あぷり" and "すげえええ"
are not registered in the morphological analysis dictionary. For this reason, if a word does not exist in the
morphological analysis dictionary, the traditional system cannot predict the correct word segmentation
or POS tags. If we could normalize all non-standard forms, then the canonical sentence is considerd as
"このアプリすごい！". As a result, we can obtain the correct result of morphological analysis for this
normalized sentence as follows:

Input:このアプリすごい！ (*kono apuri sugoi*; This app is great!)

Output:この (This, Prenominal adjective) / アプリ (app, Noun) / すごい (great, Adjective) / ！(Symbol)
As the above example shows, we would expect improvement in the result of the morphological analysis
by transforming non-standard forms into their standard ones.

In this work, we adopt the character-level encoder-decoder model as a method of Japanese text normalization. Since the encoder-decoder model was proposed in the field of machine translation, it has

---

[1]http://taku910.github.io/mecab/

Proceedings of the 2nd Workshop on Noisy User-generated Text,
pages 129–137, Osaka, Japan, December 11 2016.

achieved good results in morphological inflection generation and error correction (Bahdanau et al., 2015; Luong et al., 2015; Sutskever et al., 2015; Cho et al., 2014; Manaal et al., 2016; Barret et al., 2016). As these models are capable of capturing sequential patterns, it is possible to apply the encoder-decoder model to Japanese text normalization. As mentioned previously, Japanese has no explicit boundaries between words. Thus, Japanese text normalization is naturally posed to a character-level sequence to sequence learning.

Although the encoder-decoder model has been shown its effectiveness in large datasets, it is much less effective for small datasets such as low-resource languages (Barret et al., 2016). Unfortunately, contrary to machine translation, Japanese non-standard canonical pairs are scarce in the form of parallel corpora. To address this issue, we propose a method of data augmentation to increase the data size by converting existing resources into synthesized non-standard forms using handcrafted rules. We conducted an experiment to demonstrate that the synthesized corpus provides stable training of the encoder-decoder model and improves the performance of Japanese text normalization.

The contributions of this research can be summarized by citing two points. First, the proposed data augmentation methods can provide stable training of the encoder-decoder model. Second, it can improve the performance of Japanese text normalization by adding the synthesized corpus. The rest of this paper is organized as follows. Section 2 describes the related work to our research including Japanese text normalization and the neural encoder-decoder model. Section 3 introduces the model architecture in this research. Section 4 describes how to construct a synthesized corpus. Section 5 discusses experiments that we have performed and our corresponding analyses of the experimental results. Section 6 concludes the paper with a brief summary and a mention of future work.

2   Related Work

In this section, we mainly describe text normalization for Japanese. Furthermore, we explain some related works with regard to the encoder-decoder model in the field of machine translation.

2.1   Text Normalization

Several studies for joint modeling of morphological analysis and text normalization have been conducted (Saito et al., 2014; Kaji and Kitsuregawa, 2014; Sasano et al., 2013). Saito et al. (2014) extracted non-standard tokens from Twitter and blog texts, and manually annotated their standard forms. They automatically generated derivational patterns based on the character-level alignment between non-standard tokens and their standard forms, then included these patterns to a morphological lattice. Kaji et al. (2014) similarly proposed a joint modeling for morphological analysis and text normalization via their construction of a normalization dictionary using handcrafted rules that were similar to those used in (Sasano et al., 2013) to derive non-standard forms from the entries already registered in a dictionary. Sasaki et al. (2013) solved Japanese text normalization as a character-level sequential labeling problem. Specifically, they extracted one-to-one character alignment from non-standard canonical pairs. Then, they performed character-level Conditional Random Fields (CRF) to normalize a non-standard sentence by assigning a tag to each character. In their work, the sequence labeler specifies the class of rules such as *delete*, *replace* and *no edit*. While these methods need feature engineering, our approach uses character vectors as features instead of discrete features of a surface character sequence. In our approach, a canonical text is generated as a sequence of characters from all character vocabularies, which is different from the approaches that assign tags from a fixed tag set.

2.2   The Encoder-Decoder Model

In this work, we normalize non-standard sentences using the neural encoder-decoder model. The encoder-decoder model has been shown effective in the field of machine translation (Bahdanau et al., 2015; Luong et al., 2015; Sutskever et al., 2015; Cho et al., 2014). It consists of two neural networks: the encoder network and the decoder network. The encoder maps the input sentence to a fixed-dimensional vector and the decoder generates the output sentence. Although the encoder-decoder model has been shown effective with large datasets, it is much less effective in small datasets of low-resource lan-

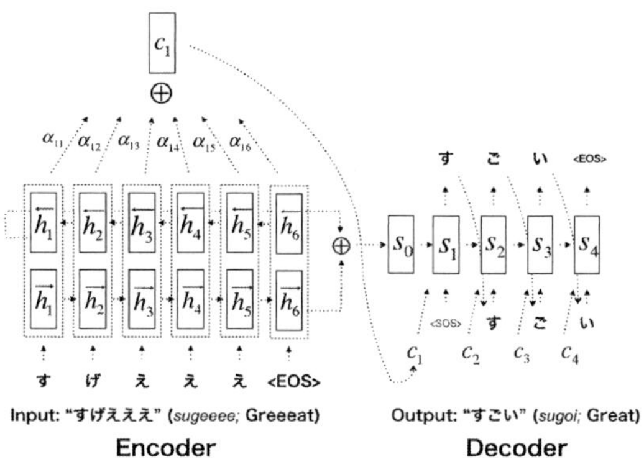

Figure 1: The encode-decoder architecture for Japanese text normalization

guages (Barret et al., 2016). As a solution to this issue, we propose a method of data augmentation to increase data size. Our approach converts existing resources into synthesized non-standard forms with handcrafted rules.

Our model is also inspired by character-level models of error correction and morphological inflection (Manaal et al., 2016; Ziang et al., 2016). However, the character set used in Japanese is numerous much larger than that in English, which makes the encoder-decoder model challenging. For example, there are about 3,500 Kanji character types used in a Japanese newspaper corpus. On the contrary, the character set used in English includes at most 100 characters; lower alphabet, upper alphabet, numerals and special symbols.

3 The Model Architecture

In this section, we briefly describe the architecture of our model. Our neural network model consists of the encoder and decoder networks. The encoder maps the input sentence to a fixed-dimensional vector with bidirectional recurrent neural network. The decoder is also a recurrent neural network (RNN) that uses a content-based attention mechanism (Bahdanau et al., 2015) to attend to the encoded representation, and generate the output sentence one character at a time. Figure 1 shows our text normalization architecture. Our model performs at a character-level process in the encoder as well as the decoder. The encoder reads the input $x = (x_1, x_2, \ldots, x_N)$, where $x_i \in \mathbb{R}^V$ is an input vector of length V. The length V is equal to the vocabulary size of all characters in the training data. x_i is represented as a one-hot vector that corresponds to a character. N is the length of the input sentence. The decoder generates the output $y = (y_1, y_2, \ldots, y_M)$, where $y_i \in \mathbb{R}^V$ is an output vector of length V. y_i is represented as a one-hot vector that corresponds to a character. M is the length of the output sentence. Then, the task of text normalization is formularized as follows:

$$P(\boldsymbol{y}|\boldsymbol{x};\theta) = \prod_{t=1}^{M} p(y_t|y_1, y_2, \ldots, y_{t-1}, \boldsymbol{x}) \tag{1}$$

To summarize, we map a non-standard sentence $\boldsymbol{x}$ to a canonical sentence $\boldsymbol{y}$ with the encoder-decoder model.

3.1 The Encoder Network

The encoder maps the input sentence to a fixed-dimensional vector h with a bidirectional RNN. The bidirectional RNN has two parallel layers in two directions, and these two layers memorize the information of the sentences from both forward and backward direction (Schuster et al., 1997). More specifically, given the input vector $\boldsymbol{x}$, the forward and backward hidden vectors are computed by using an RNN as follows:

$$\overrightarrow{h}_t = \mathrm{GRU}(x_t, \overrightarrow{h}_{t-1}) \tag{2}$$

$$\overleftarrow{h}_t = \text{GRU}(x_t, \overleftarrow{h}_{t+1}) \tag{3}$$

where $\overrightarrow{h}_t \in \mathbb{R}^l$ is a forward hidden vector at time t and GRU denotes the gated recurrent unit function that is similar to long short-term memory units (LSTMs), which have shown to improve the performance of RNN (Cho et al., 2014). GRU allows the retention of information from time steps in the distant past. GRU has two gates: the update gate and the reset gate. These gates control how much each hidden unit remembers or forgets the information while reading a sequence. Finally, in the encoder we get $h_t = [\overrightarrow{h}_t, \overleftarrow{h}_t]$ by concatenating the forward hidden state $\overrightarrow{h}_t$ and the backward one $\overleftarrow{h}_t$ for each time.

3.2 The Decoder Network

The decoder network is also GRU based on a recurrent neural network. The decoder is trained to predict the next output y_t, given the encoded $h = [h_1, h_2, \ldots, h_N]$ and all the previously predicted outputs $y_1, y_2, \ldots, y_{t-1}$.

$$y_t = \text{Decoder}(y_1, y_2, \ldots, y_{t-1}, h) \tag{4}$$

Specifically, the decoder is conditioned on the encoded representation c_t which is the weighted sum of the encoded hidden states h_t by an attention mechanism. The attention mechanism is computed as:

$$c_t = \sum_{j=1}^{N} \alpha_{tj} h_j \tag{5}$$

$$\alpha_{tj} = \frac{\exp(e_{tj})}{\sum_{k=1}^{N} \exp(e_{tk})} \tag{6}$$

$$e_{tj} = v_a^t \tanh(W_a s_{t-1} + U_a h_j + b_a) \tag{7}$$

The attention mechanism decides which parts of the input characters to be paid attention. Then, a hidden state of the decoder s_t is computed as:

$$s_t = \text{GRU}(s_{t-1}, y_{t-1}, c_t) \tag{8}$$

In the decoder, we compute the hidden layer s_t at time t and feed this into a softmax layer to obtain the conditional probability of the output character y_t as:

$$o_t = \text{softmax}(W_s s_t + b_s) \tag{9}$$

Finally, we obtain the max probability of o_t as the output character y_t at time t.

3.3 Training

We use the cross-entropy per time step summed over the output sequence $\boldsymbol{y}$ as a loss function. Given the training data of the non-standard sentence $\boldsymbol{x}$ and the canonical sentence $\boldsymbol{y}$, the goal is to optimize the parameters set θ by minimizing the loss function $E(\theta)$.

$$E(\theta) = - \sum_{(\boldsymbol{x}, \boldsymbol{y}) \in D} \log P(\boldsymbol{y}|\boldsymbol{x}; \theta) \tag{10}$$

We minimize the loss function $E(\theta)$ using stochastic gradient-based optimization techniques.

4 Construction of Synthesized Corpus

To address the problem of a small dataset, a method of data augmentation to increase data size is proposed. To achieve the increase in data size, our approach focuses on converting existing resources into synthesized non-standard forms using handcrafted rules. Specifically, we convert a morpheme in the canonical form from the newswire portion of Balanced Corpus of Contemporary Written Japanese (BC-CWJ) (Maekawa et al., 2014) into a non-standard form with handcrafted rules. We use some rules from the work of (Sasano et al., 2013). Our proposed synthesized rules are explained below in detail.

rules	part-of-speech	vowel	original canonical form	transformed non-standard form
(1)	adjective	i	かわいい (*kawaii*; cute)	かわいー (*kawaii*)
(2)	auxiliary verb	i	たい (*tai*; want)	てええ (*teee*)
(3)	adjective	i	美味しい (*oishii*; delicious)	美味しぃ (*oishii*)
(4)	sentence-end particle	a	な (*na*)	なぁ (*naa*)
(5)	auxiliary verb	a	です (*desu*)	で〜す (*deesu*)
(6)	interjection	u	ありがとう (*arigatou*; Thank you)	ありがと (*arigato*)

Table 1: Examples of transforming canonical forms into their non-standard forms

Rule 1: Substitution of vowel characters with long sound symbols

Japanese vowel characters "あ"(a), "い"(i), "う"(u), "え"(e) and "お"(o) are substituted by long sound symbols "ー" or "〜". For example, a vowel character "う" in the morpheme "どう" (*dou*; how) is substituted by "ー" and this morpheme is transformed as "どー" (*doo*).

Rule 2: Substitution of an end of the word with a common non-standard form

For example, "すげえええ" (*sugeeee*; greeeat) is derived from "すごい" (*sugoi*; great) by changing the vowels from /oi/ to /eee/, where changing vowels are observed in Japanese social media texts. Thus, we substitute the end of the word of canonical forms with common non-standard form such as changing vowels.

Rule 3: Substitution with lowercases

Some hiragana characters, such as "あ"(a), "い"(i), "う"(u), "え"(e), "お"(o) and "わ"(wa) are substituted by their lowercases: "ぁ", "ぃ", "ぅ", "ぇ", "ぉ" and "ゎ".

Rule 4: Insertion of vowel characters or double consonants

Japanese vowel characters (their lowercases) or double consonants "っ" are inserted into a morpheme.

Rule 5: Insertion of long sound symbols

Long sound symbols "ー" or "〜" are inserted into a morpheme.

Rule 6: Abbreviation

Abbreviate some characters from a morpheme. For example, we drop "い" from this canonical form"している"(*shiteiru*; to be doing), which results in "してる"(*shiteru*) as the non-standard form.

Table 1 shows examples of the application of our rules to the newswire portion of BCCWJ. To apply our rules, we would first check the POS, surface form and vowel of a morpheme from a sentence in BCCWJ; Then, we would employ the appropriate rules to the morpheme. Note that the rules are not applicable to some sentences in the corpus.

5   Experiments

To evaluate the effectiveness of our normalization method, we conducted experiments on a microblog data to confirm the effectiveness of our model. For the experiments, we used the Microblog corpus and the Synthesized corpus for training. Both corpora consist of canonical and non-standard sentence pairs. The Synthesized corpus comprised 213,618 non-standard and canonical sentences pairs. The Microblog corpus was constructed from Japanese Twitter data by Kaji and Kitsuregawa (2014). They collected 17,386 Japanese tweets using the Twitter Api. Among these, 1000 tweets were randomly selected, and they annotated the 1831 sentences with canonical forms and morphological information. In our work, we extracted 506 sentences that included at least one non-standard form from the Microblog corpus. These extracted sentences comprised 697 non-standard canonical pairs. In the preprocessing, repetitions of more than one character of long sound symbols, namely "ー", "〜" and the double consonant "っ" are reduced back to one character, whereas the others are reduced to three characters. We used these sentences as the Microblog corpus.

method	test CER(%)
No-operation	17.15
Rule-based	15.07
CRF (Microblog corpus)	13.71
CRF (Synthesized corpus)	13.63
CRF (Combined corpus)	**13.43**
EncDec (Microblog corpus)	87.07
EncDec (Synthesized corpus)	13.54
EncDec (Combined corpus)	**13.43**

Table 2: Results for test sets on CER

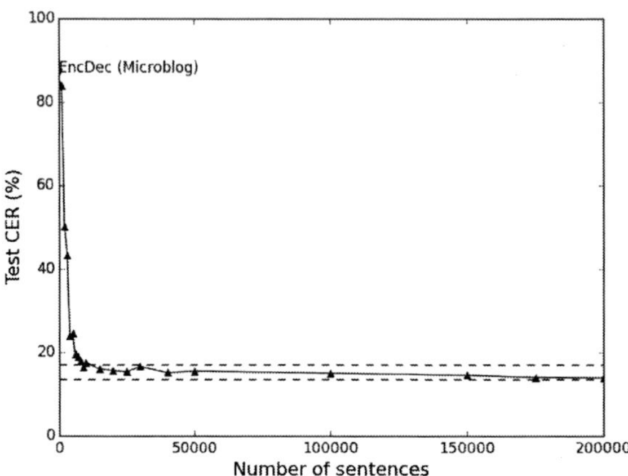

Figure 2: Scatter plot of the relationship between Test CER and the training data size

5.1 Compared Methods

We compared our method with two baseline methods listed in Table 2. Rule-based is a method of applying simple rules to a non-standard sentence in order to normalize it. In particular, we use the following rules: "Substitution of long sound symbols with vowel characters" and "Deletion of long sound symbols or lowercases". CRF is a method of tagging each character with normalization rules proposed by (Sasaki et al., 2013). Specifically, we extracted one-to-many character alignments from non-standard canonical pairs of the training data. Then, we assigned each character the class of rules such as "delete", "replace with arbitrary characters" and "no edit". The features we used in CRF were "the current characters including window size of 2" and "the binary value indicating whether the current character is a vowel character or not".

EncDec is our proposed method. Across all the encoder-decoder models described in this paper, we used the following hyperparameters. We used the Adam optimizer with a learning rate of 0.0002 (Diederik Kingma and Jimmy Ba, 2014). In both the encoder and decoder models, we used a single layer GRU with the hidden vector of size 500. The size of the character embedding vector was 250. The minibatch size was 32. While models are trained for 50 epochs, the parameters set was selected with the lowest character error rate on the development set. All results were obtained by using a beam search with a beam width of 10. Our models were implemented using Theano (Theano Development Team, 2016). In decoding, characters with the exception of Hiragana, Katakana, Kanji and long sound symbols are directly to the output.

We explain how to use the training datasets on each method in Table 2. In the case of Rule-based, the training data is not used at all. In the case of CRF (Microblog corpus) and EncDec (Microblog corpus), we used only the Microblog corpus as the training data. In the case of CRF (Synthesized corpus)

	sentences
input sentence	ラルクって海外でも人気すげーな☆ (L'Arc is greeatly popular in the world ☆)
target sentence	ラルクって海外でも人気すごいな☆ (L'Arc is greatly popular in the world ☆)
EncDec (Microblog)	一近と一一中ちゃんとうらみたとう☆ (*This sentence doesn't make sense.*)
EncDec (Synthesized)	ラルクって海外でも人気すごいな☆ (L'Arc is greatly popular in the world ☆)

Table 3: System output examples: The training of EncDec on the different training data sets

	sentences
input sentence (1)	おごりっすか？ (isit your treat?)
target sentence (1)	おごりですか？ (Is it your treat?)
Rule-based	おごりっすか？ (isit your treat?)
CRF (Microblog)	おごりっすか？ (isit your treat?)
EncDec (Combined)	おごりですか？ (Is it your treat?)
input sentence (2)	久々にＴｗｉｔｔｅｒ浮上したなぁ。 (I've not been on twitter for a long time.)
target sentence (2)	久々にＴｗｉｔｔｅｒ浮上したな。 (I've not been on twitter for a long time.)
Rule-based	久々にＴｗｉｔｔｅｒ浮上したな。 (I've not been on twitter for a long time.)
CRF (Microblog)	久々にＴｗｉｔｔｅｒ浮上したな。 (I've not been on twitter for a long time)
EncDec (Combined)	久久々にＴｗｉｔｔｅｒ浮上したな。 (I've not been on twitter for a long long time.)
input sentence (3)	車離れが捗りますなーw (It makes people turning away from driving.)
target sentence (3)	車離れが捗りますなw (It makes people turning away from driving.)
Rule-based	車離れが捗りますなw (It makes people turning away from driving.)
CRF (Microblog)	車離れが捗りますなw (It makes people turning away from driving.)
EncDec (Combined)	車離れが暇りますなw (It makes free turning away from driving.)

Table 4: System output examples: Comparison between our method and the baselines

and EncDec (Synthesized corpus), we used only the Synthesized corpus as the training data, while the Microblog corpus is only used as the development data. In the case of EncDec (Combined corpus) and CRF (Combined corpus), we used the Microblog corpus and the Synthesized corpus together as the training data and then termed both as the Combined corpus.

5.2 Evaluation

As our evaluation metric, we used a character error rate (CER), which is defined as the Levenshtein edit distance between the predicted character sequence x and the target character sequence y, normalized by the total number of characters in the target. CER indicates the closeness of the normalized sentence toward the target sentence.

In the experiments, we performed 5-fold cross validation. By dividing the Microblog corpus into the test data, development data and training data, we tested on only the Microblog corpus to evaluate the effectiveness of each method on all the microblog data.

5.3 Results and Discussion

Table 2 shows the results of our experiments on test CER. No-operation indicates a baseline that leaves the input sentence unchanged. This demonstrates that the input sentence has about two non-standard characters in itself. As shown in Table 2, the Rule-based method reduces errors by 2.08 %, as compared with No-operation. CRF trained on only the Microblog corpus: CRF (Microblog corpus) reduces errors by 3.44 %, as compared with No-operation. With these results, when the encoder-decoder model trained on only the Microblog corpus, we found that the EncDec (Microblog corpus) is worse than No-operation, then the results in CER from 17.15 % to 87.07 %. As Table 3 shows, it generated entirely different strings of the input sentence. This indicates that the Microblog corpus is too small for training the encoder-decoder model; however, the Synthesized corpus contributes to the stable training of the encoder-decoder model. Additionally, EncDec (Synthesized corpus) is able to normalize the non-standard form "すげー" (*sugee*; greeat) into the canonical form "すごい" (*sugoi*; great) without generating different strings of the input sentence. Figure 2 shows the relation between test CER and the training data size for the encoder-decoder model. The first dotted line indicates that it needs more than 10,000 sentences to reduce the error rate than No-operation. The second dotted line represents that about 200,000 sentences reach CER on CRF (Microblog corpus). As we have combined the Microblog corpus and the Synthesized corpus, the Combined corpus contributes to improving the performance of Japanese text normalization in CRF and EncDec. Both methods are able to reduce errors by 3.72 %, as compared with No-operation. Other examples of our normalization system output are illustrated in Table 4. Example (1) shows that our method is able to normalize the spoken form "っす" (*ssu*; is) into its canonical form "です" (*desu*; is). Examples (2) and (3) demonstrate that our method is inability to generate correct normalization sentence. Example (2) shows an incorrect example of over-translation, which generates the same character repeatedly: The Kanji character "久" was generated twice. Example (3) shows an incorrect example of the low frequency of a character: The Kanji character "捗" appears once in the training data. Thus, the wrong character "暇" was generated instead of "捗" in this example.

6   Conclusions and Future Work

In this work, we modeled the problem of text normalization as a character-level sequence to sequence learning problem. To address the problem of a small dataset, we proposed a method of data augmentation to increase data size, which converts existing resources into synthesized non-standard forms using hand-crafted rules. We found that the proposed data augmentation methods could provide a stable training of the encoder-decoder model, and it improved the performance of Japanese text normalization by adding the synthesized corpus. For our future work, we plan to extend the encoder-decoder model by incorporating a copy mechanism (Gu et al., 2016; Miltiadis et al., 2016) to address the issues of over-translation and low frequency of a character.

Acknowledgements

We thank the anonymous reviewers for their helpful comments. This work was partially supported by JST CREST and JSPS KAKENHI Grant Number 15K16053, 26240035.

References

Dzmitry Bahdanau, Kyunghyun Cho, and Yoshua Bengio. 2015. Neural machine translation by jointly learning to align and translate. In *Proceedings of the 3rd International Conference on Learning Representations (ICLR)*.

Minh-Thang Luong, Pham Hieu, and Christopher D. Manning. 2015. Effective approaches to attention-based neural machine translation. In *Proceedings of the 2015 Conference on Empirical Methods in Natural Language Processing (EMNLP)*, pages 1412-1421.

Ilya Sutskever, Oriol Vinyals, and Quoc V. Le 2014. Sequence to sequence learning with neural networks. In *Proceedings of Conference on Advances in Neural Information Processing Systems (NIPS)*, pages 3104-3112.

Kyunghyun Cho, Bart Van Merriënboer, Caglar Gulcehre, Dzmitry Bahdanau, Fethi Bougares, Holger Schwenk, and Yoshua Bengio. 2014. Learning Phrase Representations using RNN Encoder-Decoder for Statistical Machine Translation. In *Proceedings of the 2014 Conference on Empirical Methods in Natural Language Processing (EMNLP)*, pages 1724-1734.

Nobuhiro Kaji and Masaru Kitsuregawa. 2014. Accurate Word Segmentation and POS Tagging for Japanese Microblogs: corpus Annotation and Joint Modeling with Lexical Normalization. In *Proceedings of the 2014 Conference on Empirical Methods in Natural Language Processing (EMNLP)*, pages 99-109.

Itsumi Saito, Sadamitsu Kugatsu, Hisako Asano, and Yoshihiro Matsuo. 2014. Morphological Analysis for Japanese Noisy Text based on Character-level and Word-level Normalization. In *Proceedings of the 25th International Conference on Computational Linguistics (COLING)*, pages 1773-1782.

Ryohei Sasano, Sadao Kurohashi, and Manabu Okumura. 2013. A Simple Approach to Unknown Word Processing in Japanese Morphological Analysis. In *Proceedings of the Sixth International Joint Conference on Natural Language Processing (IJCNLP)*, pages 162-170.

Kazushi Ikeda, Tadashi Yanagiharaand, Kazunori Matsumoto, and Yasuhiro Takishima. 2009. Unsupervised text normalization approach for morphological analysis of blog documents. In *Proceedings of Australasian Joint Conference on Advances in Artificial Intelligence*, pages 401-411.

Akira Sasaki, Junta Mizuno, Naoaki Okazaki, and Kentaro Inui. 2013. Normalization of text in microblogging based on machine learning (in japanese). In *Proceedings of The 27th Annual Conference of the Japanese Society for Articial Intelligence.*

Faruqui Manaal, Yulia Tsvetkov, Graham Neubig, and Chris Dyer. 2016. Morphological inflection generation using character sequence to sequence learning. In *Proceedings of the 2016 Conference of the North American Chapter of the Association for Computational Linguistics (NAACL).*

Zoph Barret, Deniz Yuret, Jonathan May, and Kevin Knight. 2016. Transfer Learning for Low-Resource Neural Machine Translation. In *Proceedings of the 2016 Conference on Empirical Methods in Natural Language Processing (EMNLP).*

Xie Ziang, Anand Avati, Naveen Arivazhagan, Dan Jurafsky, and Andrew Y Ng. 2016. Neural language correction with character-based attention. *arXiv preprint arXiv:1603.09727*, http://arxiv.org/pdf/1603.09727v1.

Kikuo Maekawa, Makoto Yamazaki, Toshinobu Ogiso, Takehiko Maruyama, Hideki Ogura, Wakako Kashino, Hanae Koiso, Masaya Yamaguchi, Makiro Tanaka, and Yasuharu Den. 2014. Balanced corpus of contemporary written Japanese. *Language Resources and Evaluation* 48 (2), pages 345-371.

Sanae Fujita, Hirotoshi Taira, Tessei Kobayashi, and Takaaki Tanaka. 2014. Japanese Morphological Analysis of Picture Books. *The Association for Natural Language Processing*, volume 21 number 3, pages 515-539.

Naoaki Okazaki. 2007. CRFsuite: a fast implementation of Conditional Random Fields (CRFs). http://www.chokkan.org/software/crfsuite/.

Theano Development Team. 2016. Theano: A Python framework for fast computation of mathematical expressions. *arXiv e-prints*, abs/1605.02688, http://arxiv.org/abs/1605.02688.

Grzegorz Chrupaa. 2014. Normalizing tweets with edit scripts and recurrent neural embeddings. In *Proceedings of the 52nd Annual Meeting of the Association for Computational Linguistics (ACL)*, pages 680-686.

Bo Han and Timothy Baldwin. 2011. Lexical normalisation of short text messages: Makn sens a #twitter. In *Proceedings of the 49th Annual Meeting of the Association for Computational Linguistics (ACL)*, pages 368-378.

Taku Kudo, Kaoru Yamamoto, and Yuji Matsumoto. 2004. Applying conditional random fields to Japanese morphological analysis. In *Proceedings of the 2004 Conference on Empirical Methods in Natural Language Processing (EMNLP)*, pages 230-237.

Sadao Kurohashi, Toshihisa Nakamura, Yuji Matsumoto, and Makoto Nagao. 1994. Improvements of japanese morphological analyzer juman. In *Proceedings of The International Workshop on Sharable Natural Language Resources*, pages 22-38.

Graham Neubig, Yousuke Nakata, and Shinsuke Mori. 2011. Pointwise prediction for robust adaptable Japanese morphological analysis. In *Proceedings of the 49th Annual Meeting of the Association for Computational Linguistics: Human Language Technologies (ACL)*, pages 529-533.

Mike Schuster and Paliwal, Kuldip K. 1997. Bidirectional recurrent neural networks. *IEEE Transactions on Signal Processing* volume 45 number 11, pages 2673-2681.

Jey Han Lau and Nigel Collier, and Timothy Baldwin. 2012. On-line Trend Analysis with Topic Models: # twitter Trends Detection Topic Model Online. In *Proceedings of the 24th International Conference on Computational Linguistics (COLING)*, pages 1519-1534.

Eiji Aramaki, Sachiko Maskawa, and Mizuki Morita. 2011. Twitter catches the flu: detecting influenza epidemics using Twitter. In *Proceedings of the 2011 Conference on Empirical Methods in Natural Language Processing (EMNLP)*, pages 1568-1576.

Diederik Kingma and Jimmy Ba. 2015. Adam: A method for stochastic optimization. In *Proceedings of 5th International Conference on Learning Representations (ICLR).*

Jiatao Gu, Zhengdong Lu, Hang Li, and Victor O.K. Li. 2016. Incorporating copying mechanism in sequence-to-sequence learning. In *Proceedings of the 54nd Annual Meeting of the Association for Computational Linguistics (ACL)*, pages 1631-1640.

Allamanis Miltiadis, Hao Peng, and Charles Sutton. 2016. Convolutional Attention Network for Extreme Summarization of Source Code. In *Proceedings of The 33rd International Conference on Machine Learning (ICML)*, pages 2091-2100.

Results of the WNUT16 Named Entity Recognition Shared Task

Benjamin Strauss, Bethany E. Toma, Alan Ritter, Marie-Catherine de Marneffe, Wei Xu
The Ohio State University OH, USA
{strauss.105,toma.18,ritter.1492,demarneffe.1,xu.1265}@osu.edu

Abstract

This paper presents the results of the Twitter Named Entity Recognition shared task associated with W-NUT 2016: a named entity tagging task with 10 teams participating. We outline the shared task, annotation process and dataset statistics, and provide a high-level overview of the participating systems for each shared task.

1 Introduction

The increasing flood of user-generated text on social media has created an enormous opportunity for new data analysis techniques to extract and aggregate information about breaking news (Ritter et al., 2012), disease outbreaks (Paul and Dredze, 2011), natural disasters (Neubig et al., 2011), cyber-attacks (Ritter et al., 2015) and more. Named entity recognition is an important first step in most information extraction pipelines. However, performance of state-of-the-art NER on social media still lags behind well edited text genres. This motivates the need for continued research, in addition to new datasets and tools adapted to this noisy text genre.

In this paper, we present the development and evaluation of a shared task on named entity recognition in Twitter, which was held at the 2nd Workshop on Noisy User-generated Text (W-NUT 2016) and attracted 10 participating teams, 7 of which described their approach in peer-reviewed papers. This is a re-run of the NER task from W-NUT 2015, with an updated test set. The new test set consists of tweets annotated with named entities from a later time period than the data from 2015. The new test set developed for the 2016 iteration of the task consists of 3,856 tweets; this roughly doubles the amount of annotated data available for Twitter named entity recognition. We hope this new data will help to advance research on named entity recognition in noisy text.

A major development as compared to 2015 is the increased use of neural network methods by participants. Several teams, including the winning team, CambridgeLTL, used bidirectional LSTMs. Other teams achieved competitive performance by integrating a broad range of linguistic and knowledge-based features using conditional random fields (e.g., NTNU) or learning to search methods (Talos).

Another new development for 2016 was the inclusion of small amounts of domain-specific data into the test set. The motivation was to test whether Twitter named entity taggers targeting general-domain suffer a drop in performance when applied to tweets on specific types of events. For this purpose we annotated 350 tweets related to cyber-attacks and 500 related to mass shooting events. Note that no data from these domains was specifically included in the training or development data.

In the following sections, we describe details of the task including training and development datasets in addition to the newly annotated test data for 2016. We briefly summarize the systems developed by selected teams, and conclude with results.

2 Named Entity Recognition over Twitter

Named entity recognition is a crucial component in many information extraction pipelines. However, the majority of available NER tools were developed for newswire text and these tools perform poorly on informal text genres such as Twitter. While performance on named entity recognition in newswire is

Proceedings of the 2nd Workshop on Noisy User-generated Text,
pages 138–144, Osaka, Japan, December 11 2016.

quite high[1] (Tjong Kim Sang and De Meulder, 2003), state-of-the-art performance on Twitter data lags far behind.

The diverse and noisy style of user-generated content presents serious challenges. For instance tweets, unlike edited newswire text, contain numerous nonstandard spellings, abbreviations, unreliable capitalization, etc. Because of these issues, off-the-shelf named entity recognition tools tuned for newswire suffer a severe performance degradation when applied to noisy Twitter data. But tweets often contain more up-to-date information than news, in addition the increased volume of text offers opportunities to exploit redundancy of information which is very beneficial for information extraction (Downey et al., 2005). To exploit the opportunities for information extraction on top of social media, there is a crucial need for in-domain annotated data to train and evaluate named entity recognition systems on this noisy style of text.

Twitter processing has the additional challenge that the language people use on Twitter changes over time (Dredze et al., 2010; Fromreide et al., 2014). The previous edition of this task (Baldwin et al., 2015) addressed this issue by evaluating on a test set collected from a later time period then the training and development data. This year we take a similar approach, providing a new test dataset of tweets gathered from 2016. In addition to enabling research on adapting named entity recognition to new language over time, we hope this new dataset will be useful for adapting future Twitter named entity recognition systems, improving their performance on up-to-date data.

Additionally, this year we address the issue of topic distribution by including evaluation data from two specific domains (cybersecurity events and mass shootings) along with general domain data. Both the time period and topic selection of the evaluation data were not announced to participants until the (unannotated) test data was released at the beginning of the evaluation period. Teams had 7 days to submit their results on the test data, which were subsequently scored and gold annotations were released to participants. Evaluating the NER systems on these domains specific Twitter data provides information about possible system weakness.

2.1 Training and Development Data

The training and development data for our task was taken from prior work on Twitter NER (Ritter et al., 2011; Baldwin et al., 2015), which distinguishes 10 different named entity types (see Table 1 for the set of types). The training data was created from the union of the training and development data from the 2015 task (Baldwin et al., 2015).

The data was split into 2,394 annotated tweets for training and 1,000 as a development set. We also provided an additional 425 annotated tweets from the 2015 development data set (Baldwin et al., 2015).

2.2 Test Data Annotation

The data set we created for testing is new for this shared task. We collected general Twitter data and domain specific Twitter data. In real world situations people want to run taggers on a specific subset of the twitter stream. To simulate these situations we collected and tested on two example domains. The domain specific data sets are mass shooting events and cybersecurity events. General domain test data was randomly sampled from December 2014 through February 2015. Shooting domain data was collected by searching for tweets that are referring to a shooting event. To collect tweets from the mass shooting domain used www.gunviolencearchive.org's mass shooting event database for information about shooting events; including date, location, victim, and perpetrators of shooting events. Using this information, we searched for tweets that occur on the same day as a mass shooting and include the key word "shooting" and the location of the shooting event. The shooting domain contains 8,963 tokens with 751 phrases. Computer hacking events were found by searching for tweets including the keyword "breach". The breach domain contains 5,537 tokens with 603 phrases.

The additional data annotated this year was completed by a single annotator instructed to follow the annotation guidelines of the prior annotations. The annotator was presented with a set of simple guidelines[2] that cover common ambiguous cases and was also instructed to refer to the September 2010 data

---

[1] For example, the Stanford named entity tagger (Finkel et al., 2005) achieves an F1 score of 0.86 on the CoNLL data set.
[2] http://bit.ly/1FSP6i2

for reference (Ritter et al., 2011). The BRAT tool[3] was used for annotation. Figure 1 is a screenshot of the interface presented to the annotators. To ensure that the new annotations were consistent with the earlier annotations, 100 tweets were annotated in both tasks to calculate agreement. The new annotator proved a high agreement with the old data set with a F1 score of 67.67.

Table 1 presents the count of each of the 10 named entity types labeled by the annotators in the training, development and test sets created for this shared task.

	Train	Dev	Test
company	171	39	621
facility	104	38	253
geo-loc	276	116	882
movie	34	15	34
musicartist	55	41	191
other	225	132	584
person	449	171	482
product	97	37	246
sportsteam	51	70	147
tvshow	34	2	33
Total	1496	661	3473

Table 1: Named entity type counts in the train, development and test sets.

Figure 1: Annotation interface.

[3]http://brat.nlplab.org/

Team ID	Affiliation
CambridgeLTL	University of Cambridge
Talos	Viseo R&D
akora	University of Manchester
NTNU	Indian Institute of Technology Patna
ASU	Ain Shams University, Cairo, Egypt
DeepNNNER	Honda Research Institute Japan
DeepER	University of Illinois at Urbana-Champaign
hjpwhu	Wuhan University
UQAM-NTL	Université du Québec à Montréal
LIOX	The Hong Kong Polytechnic University

Table 2: Team ID and affiliation of the named entity recognition shared task participants.

	POS	Orthographic	Gazetteers	Brown clustering	Word embedding	ML
BASELINE	–	✓	✓	–	–	CRFsuite
CambridgeLTL	–	–	–	–	–	LSTM
akora	–	–	–	–	–	LSTM
NTNU	✓	✓	✓	–	–	CRF
Talos	✓	✓	✓	✓	GloVe	L2S
DeepNNNER	–	–	–	–	Multiple	LSTM-CNN
ASU	–	–	✓	✓	–	LSTM
UQAM-NTL	✓	✓	✓	–	–	CRF

Table 3: Features and machine learning approach taken by each team.

2.3 System Descriptions

This section briefly describes the approach taken by each team. Overall we noticed different trends between the types of systems submitted this year and last year. The most notable change is the use of LSTM-based systems. Four of the seven submissions were LSTM-based as opposed to zero submissions last year. The previous year Conditional Random Fields was the most popular ML technique for extracting named entities.

CambridgeLTL (Limsopatham and Collier, 2016) The system uses bidirectional LSTM to automatically induce and leverage orthographic features for performing Named Entity Recognition in Twitter messages.

akora (Kurt Junshean Espinosa and Ananiadou, 2016) This system uses bidirectional LSTM networks and exploits weakly annotated data to bootstrap sparse entity types.

NTNU (Sikdar and Gambäck, 2016) This system is based on classification using Conditional Random Fields, a supervised machine learning approach. The system utilizes a large feature set developed specifically for the task, with eight types of features based on actual characters and token internal data, five types of features built through context and chunk information, and five types of features based on lexicon-type information such as stop word matching, word frequencies, and entries in the shared task lexicon and Babelfy (Moro et al., 2014).

Talos (Ioannis Partalas and Kalitvianski, 2016) The system uses three types of features: lexical and morpho-syntactic features, contextual enrichment features using Linked Open Data, and features based on distributed representation of words. The system also exploits words clustering to enhance performance. The learning algorithm was solved by using Learning to search (L2S) that resembles a reinforcement learning algorithm.

DeepNNNER (Dugas and Nichols, 2016) The system uses a bidirectional LSTM-CNN model with word embedding trained on a large scale Web corpus. Additionally, the system uses automatically constructed lexicons with a partial matching algorithm and text normalization to handle the large vocabulary problem in Web texts.

	Precision	Recall	F1
CambridgeLTL	60.77	46.07	52.41
Talos	58.51	38.12	46.16
akora	51.70	39.48	44.77
NTNU	53.19	32.13	40.06
ASU	40.58	37.58	39.02
DeepNNNER	54.97	28.16	37.24
DeepER	45.40	31.15	36.95
hjpwhu	48.90	28.76	36.22
UQAM-NTL	40.73	23.52	29.82
LIOX	40.15	12.69	19.26

Table 4: Results segmenting and categorizing entities into 10 types.

	Precision	Recall	F1
CambridgeLTL	73.49	59.72	65.89
NTNU	64.18	62.28	63.22
Talos	70.53	52.58	60.24
akora	64.75	54.28	59.05
ASU	57.55	52.98	55.17
DeepER	63.17	43.31	51.38
DeepNNNER	70.66	36.14	47.82
hjpwhu	63.00	37.06	46.66
UQAM-NTL	53.21	37.95	44.30
LIOX	58.18	31.33	40.73

Table 5: Results on segmentation only (no types)

	Acc	P	R	F1
CambridgeLTL	90.57	69.75	51.24	59.08
Talos	89.36	60.49	41.13	48.96
akora	88.42	54.21	36.32	43.50
hjpwhu	88.21	59.79	28.86	38.93
ASU	87.76	42.22	32.84	36.94
NTNU	87.72	51.89	27.36	35.83
DeepNNNER	87.66	62.88	23.88	34.62
DeepER	84.32	40.23	22.89	29.18
UQAM-NTL	85.64	37.97	16.75	23.25
LIOX	84.41	30.08	6.63	10.87

Table 6: Results for the Cyber domain data on segmenting and categorizing entities into 10 types.

	Acc	P	R	F1
CambridgeLTL	93.00	66.25	56.72	61.12
Talos	92.03	68.53	49.00	57.14
DeepER	91.96	64.01	51.40	57.02
akora	91.54	58.89	49.40	53.73
NTNU	91.14	61.36	42.08	49.92
DeepNNNER	91.22	59.88	41.15	48.78
hjpwhu	90.83	53.71	41.41	46.77
ASU	90.74	45.40	47.94	46.63
UQAM-NTL	89.38	45.80	33.42	38.65
LIOX	88.35	55.77	23.17	32.74

Table 7: Results for the Shooting domain on segmenting and categorizing entities into 10 types.

ASU (Michel Naim Gerguis and Gerguis, 2016) The system shows an experimental study on using word embeddings, Brown clusters, part-of-speech tags, shape features, gazetteers, and local context to create a feature representation along with a set of experiments for the network design. A Wikipedia-based classifier framework was adopted to extract lists of fine-grained entities out of few input examples to be used as gazetteers. The model uses the LSTM algorithm to learn a NE classifier from the feature representation.

UQAM-NTL (Ngoc Tan LE and Sadat, 2016) The system is based on supervised machine learning and trained with a sequential labeling algorithm, using Conditional Random Fields to learn a classifier for Twitter NE extraction. The model uses 6 different categories of features including (1) orthographic, (2) lexical and (3) syntactic features as well as (4) part-of-speech tags, (5) polysemy count and (6) longest n-gram length in order to create a feature representation.

3 Summary

In this paper, we presented a shared task for Named Entity Recognition in Twitter data. We detailed the task setup and datasets used in the respective shared tasks, and also outlined the approach taken by the participating systems. The shared task included larger data sets than prior shared task (Baldwin et al., 2015). The evaluation data included new tweets collected from 2016. First, we are able to draw stronger conclusions about the true potential of different approaches in the latest Twitter data. Second, through analyzing the results of the participating systems, we are able to suggest potential research directions for both future shared tasks and noisy text processing in general.

Acknowledgments

This material is based upon work supported by the National Science Foundation under Grant No. IIS-1464128. Alan Ritter and Benjamin Strauss are supported by the Office of the Director of National Intelligence (ODNI) and the Intelligence Advanced Research Projects Activity (IARPA) via the Air Force Research Laboratory (AFRL) contract number FA8750-16-C-0114. The U.S. Government is authorized to reproduce and distribute reprints for Governmental purposes notwithstanding any copyright annotation thereon. Disclaimer: The views and conclusions contained herein are those of the authors and should not be interpreted as necessarily representing the official policies or endorsements, either expressed or implied, of ODNI, IARPA, AFRL, or the U.S. Government.

References

Timothy Baldwin, Young-Bum Kim, Marie Catherine de Marneffe, Alan Ritter, Bo Han, and Wei Xu. 2015. Shared tasks of the 2015 workshop on noisy user-generated text: Twitter lexical normalization and named entity recognition. *ACL-IJCNLP*, 126:2015.

Doug Downey, Oren Etzioni, and Stephen Soderland. 2005. A probabilistic model of redundancy in information extraction. In *Proceedings of the 19th international joint conference on Artificial intelligence*.

Mark Dredze, Tim Oates, and Christine Piatko. 2010. We're not in kansas anymore: detecting domain changes in streams. In *Proceedings of the 2010 Conference on Empirical Methods in Natural Language Processing*, pages 585–595. Association for Computational Linguistics.

Fabrice Dugas and Eric Nichols. 2016. Deepnnner: Applying blstmcnns and extended lexicons to named entity recognition in tweets. In *proceedings of W-NUT 2016*, Osaka, Japan.

Jenny Rose Finkel, Trond Grenager, and Christopher Manning. 2005. Incorporating non-local information into information extraction systems by gibbs sampling. In *Proceedings of the 43rd Annual Meeting on Association for Computational Linguistics*, ACL '05, pages 363–370, Stroudsburg, PA, USA. Association for Computational Linguistics.

Hege Fromreide, Dirk Hovy, and Anders Søgaard. 2014. Crowdsourcing and annotating ner for twitter# drift. *European language resources distribution agency*.

Nadia Derbas Ioannis Partalas, Cédric Lopez and Ruslan Kalitvianski. 2016. Learning to search for recognizing named entities in twitter. In *proceedings of W-NUT 2016*, Osaka, Japan.

Riza Theresa BatistaNavarro Kurt Junshean Espinosa and Sophia Ananiadou. 2016. Learning to recognise named entities in tweets by exploiting weakly labelled data. In *proceedings of W-NUT 2016*, Osaka, Japan.

Nut Limsopatham and Nigel Collier. 2016. Bidirectional lstm for named entity recognition in twitter messages. In *proceedings of W-NUT 2016*, Osaka, Japan.

M. Watheq El-Kharashi Michel Naim Gerguis, Cherif Salama and Michel Naim Gerguis. 2016. Asu: An experimental study on applying deep learning in twitter named entity recognition. In *proceedings of W-NUT 2016*, Osaka, Japan.

Andrea Moro, Alessandro Raganato, and Roberto Navigli. 2014. Entity linking meets word sense disambiguation: a unified approach. *Transactions of the Association for Computational Linguistics*, 2:231–244.

Graham Neubig, Yuichiroh Matsubayashi, Masato Hagiwara, and Koji Murakami. 2011. Safety information mining-what can nlp do in a disaster-. In *IJCNLP*.

Fatma Mallek Ngoc Tan LE and Fatiha Sadat. 2016. Uqam-ntl: Named entity recognition in twitter messages. In *proceedings of W-NUT 2016*, Osaka, Japan.

Michael J Paul and Mark Dredze. 2011. You are what you tweet: Analyzing twitter for public health. *ICWSM*.

Alan Ritter, Sam Clark, Oren Etzioni, et al. 2011. Named entity recognition in tweets: an experimental study. In *Proceedings of the Conference on Empirical Methods in Natural Language Processing*, pages 1524–1534. Association for Computational Linguistics.

Mausam Ritter, Alan, Oren Etzioni, and Sam Clark. 2012. Open domain event extraction from twitter. In *Proceedings of the 18th ACM SIGKDD international conference on Knowledge discovery and data mining*.

Alan Ritter, Evan Wright, William Casey, and Tom Mitchell. 2015. Weakly supervised extraction of computer security events from twitter. In *Proceedings of the 24th International Conference on World Wide Web*.

Utpal Kumar Sikdar and Björn Gambäck. 2016. Feature-rich twitter named entity recognition and classification. In *proceedings of W-NUT 2016*, Osaka, Japan.

Erik F Tjong Kim Sang and Fien De Meulder. 2003. Introduction to the conll-2003 shared task: Language-independent named entity recognition. In *Proceedings of the seventh conference on Natural language learning at HLT-NAACL 2003-Volume 4*, pages 142–147. Association for Computational Linguistics.

Bidirectional LSTM for Named Entity Recognition in Twitter Messages

Nut Limsopatham and **Nigel Collier**
Language Technology Lab
Department of Theoretical and Applied Linguistics
University of Cambridge
Cambridge, UK
`{nl347,nhc30}@cam.ac.uk`

Abstract

In this paper, we present our approach for named entity recognition in Twitter messages that we used in our participation in the Named Entity Recognition in Twitter shared task at the COLING 2016 Workshop on Noisy User-generated text (WNUT). The main challenge that we aim to tackle in our participation is the short, noisy and colloquial nature of tweets, which makes named entity recognition in Twitter messages a challenging task. In particular, we investigate an approach for dealing with this problem by enabling bidirectional long short-term memory (LSTM) to automatically learn orthographic features without requiring feature engineering. In comparison with other systems participating in the shared task, our system achieved the most effective performance on both the 'segmentation and categorisation' and the 'segmentation only' sub-tasks.

1 Introduction

Named entity recognition (NER), which is one of the first and important stages in a natural language processing (NLP) pipeline, is to identify mentions of entities (e.g. persons, locations and organisations) within unstructured text. Traditionally, most of the effective NER approaches are based on machine learning techniques, such as conditional random field (CRF), support vector machine (SVM) and perceptrons (Lafferty et al., 2001; McCallum and Li, 2003; Settles, 2004; Luo et al., 2015; Ju et al., 2011; Ratinov and Roth, 2009; Segura-Bedmar et al., 2015). For instance, Ratinov and Roth (2009) effectively learned a perceptron model using features, including word classes induced using Brown clustering (Liang, 2005), and gazetteer extracted from Wikipedia.

Twitter NER is an NER task that aims to identify mentions of entities in Twitter messages (i.e. tweets) (Baldwin et al., 2015; Ritter et al., 2011). Twitter NER is particularly challenging because of the unique characteristics of tweets. For instance, tweets are typically short as the number of characters in a particular tweet is restricted to 140; hence, the contextual information is limited. In addition, the use of colloquial language makes it difficult for existing NER approaches a general domain, such as newswire to be reused (Baldwin et al., 2015). Consequently, state-of-the-art NER software (e.g. Standford NER) is less effective on Twitter NER tasks (Derczynski et al., 2015).

For our participation in the Named Entity Recognition in Twitter shared task at the COLING 2016 Workshop on Noisy User-generated text (WNUT) (Strauss et al., 2016), we aim to investigate a novel approach that allows neural network to explicitly learn and leverage orthographic features. We focus on orthographic features as they have shown to be effective and widely used in several NER systems. Importantly, orthographic features are used by majority of the systems (including the best system) participating in the Twitter NER shared task at the 2015 WNUT workshop (Baldwin et al., 2015).

Proceedings of the 2nd Workshop on Noisy User-generated Text,
pages 145–152, Osaka, Japan, December 11 2016.

Social Media Sentence	Orthographic Sentence
14th MENA FOREX EXPO announced!!	nncc CCCC CCCCC CCCC ccccccccpp
Nintendo 3DS released in north America	Cccccccc nCC cccccccc cc cccc Ccccccc
END!! Cowboys 28, Eagles 24	CCCpp Ccccccc nnp Cccccc nn
@NutLims c u 2mor	pCccCccc c c nccc
The Hobbit is on TV now!!	Ccc Cccccc cc cc CC cccpp

Table 1: Examples of social media sentences and their corresponding orthographic sentence.

2   Related Work

Conditional random field (CRF) is one of the most effective approaches (Lafferty et al., 2001; McCallum and Li, 2003; Settles, 2004) for NER, as it achieved state-of-the-art performances on several NER tasks, such as CoNLL03 (Tjong Kim Sang and De Meulder, 2003) or Twitter NER (Baldwin et al., 2015). In particular, CRF learns latent structures of an input sequence by using a undirected statistical graphical model. Nevertheless, the performance of CRF mainly depends on hand-crafted features designed specifically for a particular task or domain. Consequently, these hand-crafted features are difficult to develop and maintain. Examples of hand-crafted features are orthographic features (Bikel et al., 1999), which are based on patterns of characters contained in a given word. In this work, we investigate an approach for could automatically inducing and leveraging orthographic features for named entity recognition for Twitter messages.

Neural networks have recently shown to be effective for several NLP tasks, such as NER (Chiu and Nichols, 2015), POS tagging (Huang et al., 2015), sentiment analysis (Limsopatham and Collier, 2016b) and grounding (Limsopatham and Collier, 2016c; Limsopatham and Collier, 2015). For example, Collobert et al. (2011) designed a feed-forward neural network that learned to identify entities in a sentence by using contexts within a fixed number of surrounding words. Chiu and Nichols (2015) showed that modelling both character and word embeddings within a neural network for NER further improve the performance. Huang et al. (2015) introduced a more complex model based on bidirectional LSTM could also take into account hand-crafted features. In this work, we investigate an application of our novel approach (Limsopatham and Collier, 2016a) that enables bidirectional LSTM to automatically induce orthographic features rather than feeding hand-crafted features into the model, when performing Twitter NER.

3   Bidirectional LSTM for Twitter NER

In this section, we describe our end-to-end neural network approach for Twitter NER. In particular, our approach consists of three main components: (1) orthographic sentence generator, (2) word representations as input vectors, (3) bidirectional LSTM.

3.1   Orthographic Sentence Generator

Our orthographic sentence generator creates an *orthographic sentence*, which contains orthographic pattern of words in each input sentence. In particular, for a given social media sentence (e.g. '14th MENA FOREX EXPO announced!!'), we generate an orthographic sentence (e.g. 'nncc CCCC CCCCC CCCC ccccccccpp') by using a set of rules, where each of the upper-case characters, lower-case characters, numbers and punctuations, are replaced with C, c, n and p, respectively. Examples of orthographic sentences generated from social media sentences are shown in Table 1. This orthographic sentence allows bidirectional LSTM to explicitly induce and leverage orthographic features automatically.

3.2   Input Vectors for Bidirectional LSTM

Our approach uses word representations extracted from both character and word levels. To do so, we create vectors of character-based word representation (Section 3.2.1) and word representation (Section 3.2.2) for both social media sentence and its orthographic sentence, as follows:

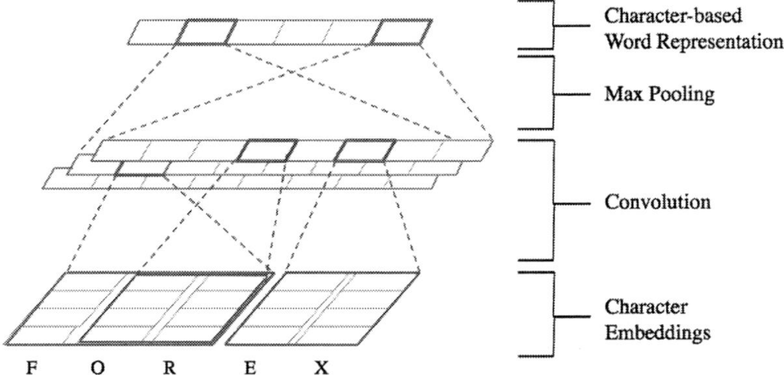

Figure 1: Our CNN architecture for inducing word representation from a character level.

3.2.1 Character-based Word Representation

We use CNN to induce word representation from character embeddings of a given word, as shown in Figure 1. Specifically, for a given word of length l characters, we create a word matrix $\mathbf{M} \in \mathbb{R}^{d \times l}$ as:

$$\mathbf{M} = \begin{bmatrix} | & | & | & & | \\ \mathbf{x}_1 & \mathbf{x}_2 & \mathbf{x}_3 & ... & \mathbf{x}_l \\ | & | & | & & | \end{bmatrix} \tag{1}$$

where each column of $\mathbf{M}$ is the d-dimensional vector (i.e. character embedding) $\mathbf{x}_i \in \mathbb{R}^d$ of each character in the given word, which are initialised randomly.

To learn patterns of characters in a given word, a convolution operation with a filter $\mathbf{w} \in \mathbb{R}^{d \times h}$ is applied to a window of h characters. In particular, a filter $\mathbf{w}$ is convolved over the sequence of characters in the word matrix $\mathbf{M}$, which results in a feature matrix $\mathbf{C}$. Specifically, each feature c_i in feature matrix $\mathbf{C}$ is extracted from a window of words $\mathbf{x}_{i:i+h-1}$, as follows:

$$c_i = f(\mathbf{w} \cdot \mathbf{x}_{i:i+h-1} + b) \tag{2}$$

where f is an activation function, e.g. sigmoid and tanh, and $b \in \mathbb{R}$ is a bias. In this work, we use 200 different filters with window size $h = 3$.

Then, we follow Collobert et al. (2011) and apply max pooling to capture the most important feature from each filter. Indeed, max pooling takes the maximum value of each row in the matrix $\mathbf{C}$:

$$\mathbf{c}_{max} = \begin{bmatrix} max(\mathbf{C}_{1,:}) \\ \vdots \\ max(\mathbf{C}_{d,:}) \end{bmatrix} \tag{3}$$

We use $\mathbf{c}_{max}$ vector as a character-based word representation in bidirectional LSTM (Section 3.3), as it captures important features of a given word induced from a character level.

3.2.2 Word Representation

Existing studies, e.g. (Mikolov et al., 2013; Pennington et al., 2014), have shown that word embeddings induced from a large corpus could effectively capture semantic and syntactic information of words. Hence, we also use pre-trained word embeddings as word representation. However, any randomly generated word embeddings can also be used.

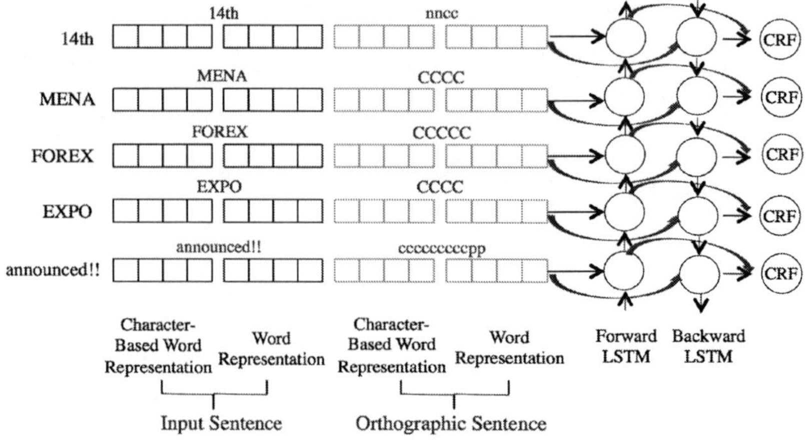

Figure 2: Our bidirectional LSTM for Twitter NER.

3.3 Bidirectional LSTM

In this work, we use bidirectional LSTM for modelling social media sentences, as existing work (e.g. (Huang et al., 2015; Dyer et al., 2015; Dyer et al., 2015; Bengio et al., 1994)) has shown that bidirectional LSTM could effectively deal with the variable lengths of sentences. In addition, it could capture past (from the previous words) and future (from the next words) information effectively (Huang et al., 2015; Dyer et al., 2015).

Our bidirectional LSTM for Twitter NER is shown in Figure 2. For a given a social media sentence and its orthographic sentence, we firstly extract both character-based word representation and word vector representation corresponding to each word in the social media sentence and the orthographic sentence, by using the approaches previously described in Sections 3.2.1 and 3.2.2.[1] Word representations associated to the same words are then concatenated and sequentially fed into bidirectional LSTM to learn contextual information of words in the sentence. At the output layer, we optimise the CRF log-likelihood, which is the likelihood of labelling the whole sentence correctly by modelling the interactions between two successive labels using the Viterbi algorithm, as suggested by Huang et al. (2015).

4 Experimental Setup

4.1 Datasets

The Twitter NER shared task datasets consist of *training set* (i.e. '2015 train'+'2015 dev'), *development set* (i.e. '2015 test'), *additional set* (i.e. additional 'dev 2015') and *test set*, respectively. The numbers of tweets and tokens of each set are shown in Table 2. The shared task focuses on finding 10 types of target entities, including company, facility, geo-location, movie, music-artist, other, person, product, sport team and TV show. In particular, the shared task can be divided to to sub-tasks: 'segmentation only' and 'segmentation and categorisation'. The former focuses only on finding the boundaries of entities; meanwhile, the latter requires both the boundaries of entities and the correct categories of entity types.

4.2 Training Regime

To learn bidirectional LSTM, we use only the four datasets (see Table 2) provided by the workshop organisers. In particular, we use the combination of *training set* and *development set* as training data, and use *additional set* as validation data, when generating the test models. Note that we train two different models for the two sub-tasks, i.e. 'segmentation and categorisation' (10-type) and 'segmentation only' (no-type).

---

[1] Note that we use separated set of word and character embeddings for the input sentence and the orthographic sentence.

	Training Set	Development Set	Additional Set	Test Set
# tweets	2,349	1,000	419	3,850
# tokens	46,469	16,261	6,789	61,908
# entity tokens	2,462	1,128	439	5,955
# Company entity tokens	207	49	64	886
# Facility entity tokens	209	77	13	619
# Geo-loc entity tokens	325	158	62	1,101
# Movie entity tokens	80	30	5	82
# MusicArtist entity tokens	116	76	22	331
# Other entity tokens	545	229	91	1,140
# Person entity tokens	664	266	113	782
# Product entity tokens	177	158	15	746
# SportsTeam entity tokens	74	83	46	195
# TvShow entity tokens	65	2	8	73

Table 2: Statistics of the WNUT 2016 NER shared task datasets.

To tune hyper-parameters of the model, we optimise the performance on the *development set* when training on the *training set*.

4.3 Embeddings

4.3.1 Word Embeddings

As discussed in Section 3.2.2, our approach uses word embeddings as inputs when learning an NER model. For input sentences, we use pre-trained word embeddings of Godin et al. (2015)[2], which consists 400-dimensional vectors of 3.04 million unique words induced from 400 million Twitter messages using the Skip-gram model from the word2vec tool (Mikolov et al., 2013). For the words that do not exist in the pre-trained embeddings, we use a vector of random values sampled from $[-\sqrt{\frac{3}{dim}}, +\sqrt{\frac{3}{dim}}]$ where dim is the dimension of embeddings as suggested by He et al. (2015).

For orthographic sentences, we represent each word using a 200-dimensional randomly generated vector, where each dimension is also uniformly sampled from $[-\sqrt{\frac{3}{dim}}, +\sqrt{\frac{3}{dim}}]$.

4.3.2 Character Embeddings

We use 30-dimensional character embeddings for representing each character when inducing the character-based word representation (Equation (1) in Section 3.2.1) from both social media and orthographic sentences. The 30-dimensional character embeddings are initialised using uniform samples from $[-\sqrt{\frac{3}{dim}}, +\sqrt{\frac{3}{dim}}]$. Note that we have a separated embedding for each set of characters in the social media and orthographic sentences.

4.4 Parameter Optimisation

We implement our bidirectional LSTM using the Theano library (Bergstra et al., 2010). Parameter optimisation is done by mini-batch stochastic gradient descent (SGD) where back-propagation is performed using Adadelta update rule (Zeiler, 2012). The mini-batch size is 50. In addition, we allow the learner to fine-tune both word and character embeddings when performing gradient updates during training. Moreover, we follow Pascanu et al. (2013) and use a gradient clipping of 5.0, in order to reduce gradient exploding.

To avoid overfitting, we apply L_2 regularisation on the weight vectors and dropout (Srivastava et al., 2014) on hidden units in all layers in our models. Dropout rate is set to 0.5. We also use early stopping (Giles, 2001) based on the performance achieved on the development sets.

Approach	Segmentation and Categorisation (10-Type)			Segmentation Only (No-Type)		
	F1	Precision	Recall	F1	Precision	Recall
Our approach	**52.41**	**60.77**	**46.07**	**65.89**	**73.49**	59.72
Talos	46.16	58.51	38.12	60.24	70.53	52.58
akora	44.77	51.70	39.48	59.05	64.75	54.28
NTNU	40.06	53.19	32.13	63.22	64.18	**62.28**
ASU	39.02	40.58	37.58	55.17	57.55	52.98
DeepNNNER	37.24	54.97	28.16	47.82	70.66	36.14
DeepER	36.95	45.40	31.15	51.38	63.17	43.31
hjpwhu	36.22	48.90	28.76	46.66	63.00	37.06
UQAM-NTL	29.82	40.73	23.52	44.30	53.21	37.95
LIOX	19.26	40.15	12.69	40.73	58.18	31.33

Table 3: Performances in terms of F1, precision and recall of our approach and the participating systems on the 'segmention and categorisation' (10-type) and the 'segmentation only' (no-type) sub-tasks.

Type	F1	Precision	Recall
company	57.22	69.84	48.47
facility	42.42	51.70	35.97
geo-loc	72.61	75.21	70.18
movie	10.91	14.29	8.82
musicartist	9.48	26.83	5.76
other	31.66	49.45	23.29
person	58.99	52.06	68.05
product	20.12	36.96	13.82
sportsteam	52.41	53.15	51.70
tvshow	5.88	100.00	3.03
Overall	52.41	60.77	46.07

Table 4: Performances of our approach broken down by entity types.

5   Experimental Results

Next, we discuss the performance of our proposed approach. Table 3 compares the performances of our approach with the other systems participating in the Twitter NER shared task at the 2016 WNUT workshop, in terms of F1, precision and recall measures, on both the 'segmentation and categorisation' and 'segmentation only' sub-tasks.

From Table 3, we observed that our approach achieved the best F1 score for both sub-tasks. In particular, our approach attains F1 scores of 52.41 and 65.89 for the 'segmentation and categorisation' and 'segmentation only' sub-tasks, respectively. Importantly, for the 'segmentation and categorisation' sub-task, our approach significantly outperformed the second best system (namely, Talos) by 6.2 F1 score. Table 4 showed the performance of our approach broken down into entity types. Our approach performed effectively on entities related to *geo-location*, *person* and *company*. Meanwhile, it was less effective on the entity types *tvshow*, *musicartist* and *movie*.

6   Conclusions

In this paper, we describe our novel approach used in the Twitter NER shared task at the WNUT 2016 workshop. Our approach deals with the noisy and colloquial of tweets by leveraging word representations of input sentence and orthographic sentence in bidirectional LTSM. In particular, our approach automatically induce and leverage orthographic features when performing NER. Importantly, we show that without requiring hand-crafted features, our approach is highly effective for the Twitter NER tasks, as it achieves the best performance among all of the participating systems. For future work, we aim to investigate approaches for enabling neural networks to automatically induce other hand-crafted features, such as gazetteers.

Acknowledgements

The authors wish to thank funding support from the EPSRC (grant number EP/M005089/1).

References

Timothy Baldwin, Young-Bum Kim, Marie Catherine de Marneffe, Alan Ritter, Bo Han, and Wei Xu. 2015. Shared tasks of the 2015 workshop on noisy user-generated text: Twitter lexical normalization and named entity recognition. *ACL-IJCNLP*, 126:2015.

Yoshua Bengio, Patrice Simard, and Paolo Frasconi. 1994. Learning long-term dependencies with gradient descent is difficult. *IEEE transactions on neural networks*, 5(2):157–166.

James Bergstra, Olivier Breuleux, Frédéric Bastien, Pascal Lamblin, Razvan Pascanu, Guillaume Desjardins, Joseph Turian, David Warde-Farley, and Yoshua Bengio. 2010. Theano: a cpu and gpu math expression compiler. In *Proceedings of the Python for Scientific Computing Conference (SciPy)*.

Daniel M. Bikel, Richard Schwartz, and Ralph M. Weischedel. 1999. An algorithm that learns what‘s in a name. *Mach. Learn.*, 34(1-3):211–231, February.

Jason PC Chiu and Eric Nichols. 2015. Named entity recognition with bidirectional lstm-cnns. *arXiv preprint arXiv:1511.08308*.

Ronan Collobert, Jason Weston, Léon Bottou, Michael Karlen, Koray Kavukcuoglu, and Pavel Kuksa. 2011. Natural language processing (almost) from scratch. *J. Mach. Learn. Res.*, 12:2493–2537, November.

Leon Derczynski, Diana Maynard, Giuseppe Rizzo, Marieke van Erp, Genevieve Gorrell, Raphaël Troncy, Johann Petrak, and Kalina Bontcheva. 2015. Analysis of named entity recognition and linking for tweets. *Information Processing & Management*, 51(2):32–49.

Chris Dyer, Miguel Ballesteros, Wang Ling, Austin Matthews, and Noah A Smith. 2015. Transition-based dependency parsing with stack long short-term memory. *arXiv preprint arXiv:1505.08075*.

Rich Caruana Steve Lawrence Lee Giles. 2001. Overfitting in neural nets: Backpropagation, conjugate gradient, and early stopping. In *Advances in Neural Information Processing Systems 13: Proceedings of the 2000 Conference*, volume 13, page 402. MIT Press.

Fréderic Godin, Baptist Vandersmissen, Wesley De Neve, and Rik Van de Walle. 2015. Multimedia lab@ acl w-nut ner shared task: Named entity recognition for twitter microposts using distributed word representations. *ACL-IJCNLP 2015*, page 146.

Kaiming He, Xiangyu Zhang, Shaoqing Ren, and Jian Sun. 2015. Delving deep into rectifiers: Surpassing human-level performance on imagenet classification. In *Proceedings of the IEEE International Conference on Computer Vision*, pages 1026–1034.

Zhiheng Huang, Wei Xu, and Kai Yu. 2015. Bidirectional lstm-crf models for sequence tagging. *arXiv preprint arXiv:1508.01991*.

Zhenfei Ju, Jian Wang, and Fei Zhu. 2011. Named entity recognition from biomedical text using svm. In *Bioinformatics and Biomedical Engineering,(iCBBE) 2011 5th International Conference on*, pages 1–4. IEEE.

John Lafferty, Andrew McCallum, and Fernando Pereira. 2001. Conditional random fields: Probabilistic models for segmenting and labeling sequence data. In *Proceedings of the eighteenth international conference on machine learning, ICML*, volume 1, pages 282–289.

Percy Liang. 2005. *Semi-supervised learning for natural language*. Ph.D. thesis, Massachusetts Institute of Technology.

Nut Limsopatham and Nigel Collier. 2015. Adapting phrase-based machine translation to normalise medical terms in social media messages. In *Proceedings of the 2015 Conference on Empirical Methods in Natural Language Processing*, pages 1675–1680, Lisbon, Portugal, September. Association for Computational Linguistics.

Nut Limsopatham and Nigel Collier. 2016a. Learning orthographic features in bi-directional lstm for biomedical named entity recognition. In *Proceedings of the 2016 biennial Workshops on Building and Evaluating Resources for Biomedical Text Mining*. Association for Computational Linguistics.

Nut Limsopatham and Nigel Collier. 2016b. Modelling the combination of generic and target domain embeddings in a convolutional neural network for sentence classification. In *Proceedings of the 15th Workshop on Biomedical Natural Language Processing*. Association for Computational Linguistics.

Nut Limsopatham and Nigel Collier. 2016c. Normalising medical concepts in social media texts by learning semantic representation. In *Proceedings of the 54th Annual Meeting of the Association for Computational Linguistics (Volume 1: Long Papers)*, pages 1014–1023, Berlin, Germany, August. Association for Computational Linguistics.

Gang Luo, Xiaojiang Huang, Chin-Yew Lin, and Zaiqing Nie. 2015. Joint entity recognition and disambiguation. In *Proceedings of the 2015 Conference on Empirical Methods in Natural Language Processing*, pages 879–888, Lisbon, Portugal, September. Association for Computational Linguistics.

Andrew McCallum and Wei Li. 2003. Early results for named entity recognition with conditional random fields, feature induction and web-enhanced lexicons. In *Proceedings of the seventh conference on Natural language learning at HLT-NAACL 2003-Volume 4*, pages 188–191. Association for Computational Linguistics.

Tomas Mikolov, Ilya Sutskever, Kai Chen, Greg S Corrado, and Jeff Dean. 2013. Distributed representations of words and phrases and their compositionality. In *NIPS*, pages 3111–3119.

Razvan Pascanu, Tomas Mikolov, and Yoshua Bengio. 2013. On the difficulty of training recurrent neural networks. *ICML (3)*, 28:1310–1318.

Jeffrey Pennington, Richard Socher, and Christopher D Manning. 2014. GloVe: Global vectors for word representation. In *EMNLP*, pages 1532–1543.

Lev Ratinov and Dan Roth. 2009. Design challenges and misconceptions in named entity recognition. In *Proceedings of the Thirteenth Conference on Computational Natural Language Learning*, pages 147–155. Association for Computational Linguistics.

Alan Ritter, Sam Clark, Oren Etzioni, et al. 2011. Named entity recognition in tweets: an experimental study. In *Proceedings of the Conference on Empirical Methods in Natural Language Processing*, pages 1524–1534. Association for Computational Linguistics.

Isabel Segura-Bedmar, Víctor Suárez-Paniagua, and Paloma Martínez. 2015. Exploring word embedding for drug name recognition. In *SIXTH INTERNATIONAL WORKSHOP ON HEALTH TEXT MINING AND INFORMATION ANALYSIS (LOUHI)*, page 64.

Burr Settles. 2004. Biomedical named entity recognition using conditional random fields and rich feature sets. In *Proceedings of the International Joint Workshop on Natural Language Processing in Biomedicine and its Applications*, pages 104–107. Association for Computational Linguistics.

Nitish Srivastava, Geoffrey E Hinton, Alex Krizhevsky, Ilya Sutskever, and Ruslan Salakhutdinov. 2014. Dropout: a simple way to prevent neural networks from overfitting. *Journal of Machine Learning Research*, 15(1):1929–1958.

Benjamin Strauss, Bethany E. Toma, Alan Ritter, Marie Catherine de Marneffe, and Wei Xu. 2016. Results of the wnut16 named entity recognition shared task. In *Proceedings of the Workshop on Noisy User-generated Text (WNUT 2016)*, Osaka, Japan.

Erik F Tjong Kim Sang and Fien De Meulder. 2003. Introduction to the conll-2003 shared task: Language-independent named entity recognition. In *Proceedings of the seventh conference on Natural language learning at HLT-NAACL 2003-Volume 4*, pages 142–147. Association for Computational Linguistics.

Matthew D Zeiler. 2012. Adadelta: an adaptive learning rate method. *arXiv preprint arXiv:1212.5701*.

Learning to recognise named entities in tweets
by exploiting weakly labelled data

Kurt Junshean Espinosa[1,2]   **Riza Batista-Navarro**[1]   **Sophia Ananiadou**[1]

[1]School of Computer Science, University of Manchester, United Kingdom

[2]Department of Computer Science, University of the Philippines Cebu, Philippines

kurtjunshean.espinosa@postgrad.manchester.ac.uk

{riza.batista, sophia.ananiadou}@manchester.ac.uk

Abstract

Named entity recognition (NER) in social media (e.g., Twitter) is a challenging task due to the noisy nature of text. As part of our participation in the W-NUT 2016 Named Entity Recognition Shared Task, we proposed an unsupervised learning approach using deep neural networks and leverage a knowledge base (i.e., DBpedia) to bootstrap sparse entity types with weakly labelled data. To further boost the performance, we employed a more sophisticated tagging scheme and applied dropout as a regularisation technique in order to reduce overfitting. Even without hand-crafting linguistic features nor leveraging any of the W-NUT-provided gazetteers, we obtained robust performance with our approach, which ranked third amongst all shared task participants according to the official evaluation on a gold standard named entity-annotated corpus of 3,856 tweets.

1   Introduction

Named entity recognition (NER) is one of the most fundamental natural language processing (NLP) tasks that is central to understanding unstructured, textual data. Popular approaches (Chieu and Ng, 2002; Florian et al., 2003; Ratinov and Roth, 2009; Luo et al., 2015) mainly rely on hand-crafted features and gazetteers which require knowledge about the domain. Recently, there has been a surge in terms of interest in applying deep learning techniques to NLP tasks. These methods, together with substantial amount of annotated data, can learn features automatically and have been reported to outperform traditional methods on certain NLP tasks (Ma and Hovy, 2016; Lample et al., 2016; Chiu and Nichols, 2016). However, in spite of the perceived success of deep learning methods particularly in NER in newswire (Ma and Hovy, 2016), performance on social media content, particularly that from Twitter, has been lagging behind (Baldwin et al., 2015).

There are two state-of-the-art deep learning methods for newswire NER, namely, those proposed by Chiu and Nichols (2016) and Ma and Hovy (2016). Considering that the former requires hand-crafted features (e.g., word matches against gazetteers) and yet obtains only a small boost in performance over the latter which does not rely on any such features, we took the approach of Ma and Hovy (2016) and applied it on microblog posts from the Twitter platform, i.e., tweets. Based on the results of our initial experiments, we observed suboptimal performance relative to that on newswire. Informed by the error analysis that we carried out, we employed a distant supervision method exploiting an external lexical resource, i.e., DBpedia (Daiber et al., 2013), in order to generate weakly labelled data for low-frequency named entity types. We also investigated the effect of using different token-level tagging schemes and confirmed that improved performance can be obtained by applying the finer-grained BIOES scheme rather than the more popularly used BIO convention. Furthermore, we explored the use of generic placeholders to address out-of-embedding-vocabulary (OOEV) words, although this approach did not lead to better performance.

2   Related Work

Named entity recognition—the automatic demarcation of named mentions within text and their classification according to predefined semantic types—is a fundamental NLP task that has attracted the attention

153

Proceedings of the 2nd Workshop on Noisy User-generated Text,
pages 153–163, Osaka, Japan, December 11 2016.

of many researchers. Several efforts (Chieu and Ng, 2002; Florian et al., 2003; Ratinov and Roth, 2009), tackle this problem by hand-crafting linguistic features and presenting them to a machine learning algorithm, which will then discriminate between various semantic types based on those features. This particular approach, however, is usually done ad hoc making it very tedious to adapt features to other domains. Recently, extensions to this approach have been introduced (Godin et al., 2015; Cherry and Guo, 2015; Toh et al., 2015) by considering word embeddings as sources of features for classification. Other studies (Luo et al., 2015; Yamada123 et al., 2015) combined this machine learning-based approach with entity linking methods which exploit knowledge bases (e.g., Wikipedia) to detect named mentions. With the NLP research community's continuously surging interest in deep learning, approaches based on deep neural networks have also been applied to NER. While they take away the burden that comes with hand-crafting linguistic features, they require huge amounts of data. Nevertheless, they have been proven to be effective for the NER task (Godin et al., 2015; Chiu and Nichols, 2016; Ma and Hovy, 2016; Lample et al., 2016). For instance, state-of-the-art NER systems for newswire were built upon deep learning-based approaches (Ma and Hovy, 2016; Chiu and Nichols, 2016). It has been shown, however, that even such state-of-the-art methods tend to underperform when applied to other domains, particularly on social media content, e.g., tweets (Baldwin et al., 2015). Challenges in this domain include noise inherent in the data, the many new terms—neologisms—introduced in social media over time, and changes in linguistic conventions in general, also known as language drift (Dredze et al., 2010; Ritter et al., 2011; Eisenstein, 2013; Fromreide et al., 2014).

In this paper, we describe our methods addressing the above-mentioned challenges in the context of the 2016 Named Entity Recognition in Twitter Task (Strauss et al., 2016) organised as part of the Second Workshop on Noisy User-generated Text (W-NUT). For our contribution to the said shared task, we combined deep learning-based approaches with distant supervision methods for generating weakly labelled data, and further optimised performance by exploring the use of different tagging schemes and word embeddings.

3 Methodology

We cast the NER task as a sequence labelling problem: every tweet is a sequence of tokens, each of which is automatically assigned a label (or tag) that is indicative of its membership to a semantic type or category. In learning and applying token labels, two different tagging schemes were compared in order to confirm previously reported observations that employing more sophisticated tagging schemes leads to better predictions (Ratinov and Roth, 2009; Dai et al., 2015). According to the popular begin-inside-outside (BIO) scheme, each token is tagged as any of 'B', 'I' or 'O' depending on whether it is at the *beginning*, *inside* or *outside* a named entity, respectively. The more fine-grained BIOES scheme, however, additionally makes use of 'E' and 'S' to also distinguish tokens at the *end* and those comprising *single-token* entities.

Approaches to sequence labelling based on the conditional random fields (CRF) algorithm are known to demonstrate strong performance (McCallum and Li, 2003; Leaman et al., 2008; Finkel and Manning, 2009). CRFs find the most probable label sequence given a sequence of tokens encoded using features, e.g., surface forms, lemma, part-of-speech tags, surrounding tokens, morphology (Sang and Veenstra, 1999). Meanwhile, convolutional neural networks (CNNs) are sparse feed-forward neural networks which have been shown to effectively extract morphological features such as word prefixes and suffixes (Chiu and Nichols, 2016). One can thus explore the combination of the ability of CRFs to model relations between labels of tokens in a tweet, and the effectiveness of CNNs to extract morphological features of words. CNNs, however, suffer from one drawback, i.e., failure to capture the contextual information surrounding a word. To alleviate this issue, we instead employed recurrent neural networks (RNNs) (Rumelhart et al., 1988). RNN models make use of the sequential information found in structured input (e.g., in a sentence). It is called *recurrent* because it performs the same computation for every element in a sequence with inputs as the only difference. RNN models use the backpropagation algorithm throughout all of the time steps (i.e., from the current word to the nth preceding word). During backpropagation, the gradient is computed, which is the measure of how much the cost (i.e., the difference between the expected and the actual value) changes with a change in weight or bias value. The gradient is computed from the output layer (i.e., the current word) and is propagated back to the first layer (i.e., the nth preceding word). Since the gradient at a particular point (e.g., current/output layer) is a product of the gradients up to that point (e.g., from the first up to the current layer), the product becomes much smaller or bigger depending on the gradient value. This is called the vanishing/exploding gradient problem common in deep backpropagation investigated more deeply in Bengio et al. (1994) and Pascanu et al. (2013). To remedy this problem, we use a variant of RNNs known as the Long-Short-Term Memory (LSTM) network (Hochreiter and Schmidhuber, 1997). LSTM addresses the shortcomings of vanilla RNNs by allowing the network to capture information for an extended number of time steps. Furthermore, we incorporate the findings of Dyer et al. (2015) that bi-directional LSTM (BLSTM) provides more benefits since it allows access to both the past and future contexts, i.e., m words to each of the left and right sides of a given word, where m is the window size.

3.1   Neural Network Architecture

The input to the network is a concatenation of character representations of words extracted from a convolutional neural network and word embeddings, which will be described in Section 3.3. The inputs are fed into a bi-directional LSTM (BLSTM) and the outputs are concatenated and fed into the CRF layer to jointly decode the best label sequence. For a schematic diagram depicting this neural network architecture, we refer the reader to the work by Ma and Hovy (2016), who first proposed this method for NER in newswire. In our work, the same architecture is applied to the task of NER in tweets.

We also sought to tune the hyperparameters of the neural network, specifically, learning rate and dropout. However, in the interest of time, only a local search within a small interval was carried out, setting the other parameters to arbitrarily determined fixed values. Learning rate controls the step size in gradient descent optimisation: a very small learning rate could lead to longer training time, and potentially to being trapped in a local minimum. Meanwhile, choosing too big a learning rate could lead to overshooting the global optimum. Hence, one way to determine the optimal learning rate is to observe the performance based on a range of different learning rates and selecting the one yielding the maximum performance. Meanwhile, tuning the other important hyperparameter, dropout, has been found to be useful to prevent overfitting. Serving as a means for regularisation, dropout disables units in the network (along with their connections) during training. It is based on a value p which indicates the probability that a unit is retained, typically determined using a validation data set. Dropout thus reduces the problem of overfitting and at the same time, provides a way for exploring an exponential number of different neural network architectures efficiently (Srivastava et al., 2014).

3.2   Distant supervision for augmenting training data

We carried out an analysis of the corpus that was provided by the task organisers to participants containing 2,394 and 1,000 tweets in the training and development sets, respectively. The training set is composed of tweets collected in 2010 while those in the development set were collected between 2014 and 2015 (Baldwin et al., 2015). Examining the training set, we observed that whilst 3.6% of the tweets are retweets, 74.2% of the tokens are unique. This same pattern was also observed in the development set: it contains a similar proportion of unique tokens (74.6%), although with much fewer retweets (0.4%). Prepositions, punctuations, articles and pronouns account for many of the repeated tokens in both data sets.

In terms of named entity type distribution, around 96% in each data set correspond to non-named entity tokens. The remaining 4% were distributed unevenly across the 10 entity categories. Based on our frequency analysis, shown in Table 1, we observed that the *person* entity type is the most prevalent in both the training set (449 out of 1,496 entities or 30%) and development set (171 out of 661 entities or 26%) while both *tvshow* and *movie* entity types were consistently the most sparse entities in both the training set (both 34 out of 1491 entities or 2%) and development set (2 out of 661 entities or 0.3%, 15 out of 661 entities or 2%), respectively.

To mitigate the data sparsity of some entity types as observed in the data set, we sought to increase their number of annotated samples. To this end, we leveraged DBpedia Spotlight (Daiber et al., 2013), a

Training Set (1,496 entities)			Development Set (661 entities)		
Entity Type	**Count**	**Percentage**	**Entity Type**	**Count**	**Percentage**
person	449	30.01	**person**	171	25.87
geo-loc	276	18.45	other	132	19.97
other	225	15.04	geo-loc	116	17.55
company	171	11.43	sportsteam	70	10.59
facility	104	6.95	musicartist	41	6.20
product	97	6.48	company	39	5.90
musicartist	55	3.68	facility	38	5.75
sportsteam	51	3.41	product	37	5.60
movie	34	2.27	**movie**	15	2.27
tvshow	34	2.27	**tvshow**	2	0.30

Table 1: Entity type distribution in training and development sets

Entity Type	DBpedia Categories
company	Website, Company, Software, BroadcastNetwork, RadioStation
facility	EducationInstitution, InternationalOrganisation, PublicTransitSystem, ArchitecturalStructure, SportsClub
geo-loc	PopulatedPlace, WorldHeritageSite
other	Non-ProfitOrganisation, Event, SportsLeague, PoliticalParty, MilitaryUnit
movie	Film
musicartist	MusicArtist
person	Person, Athlete, Celebrity, Cleric, Coach, BeautyQueen, BusinessPerson, Criminal, Economist, Engineer, FictionalCharacter, Journalist, Judge, Lawyer, Model, Monarch, MovieDirector, Noble, OrganisationMember, Politician, PoliticianSpouse, Royalty, Scientist, SportsManager, TelevisionDirector, TelevisionPersonality, Writer, OfficeHolder
product	VideoGame, Device, MeanOfTransportation, Food, LineOfFashion, ProgrammingLanguage
tvshow	TelevisionShow, TelevisionSeason, TelevisionEpisode
sportsteam	SportsTeam

Table 2: Proposed mapping between W-NUT entity types and DBpedia categories

tool for linking mentions in text to DBpedia entries, which in our case was employed to weakly annotate our own collection of tweets, gathered between July and August 2016. The tool can be configured in order to define the resulting entity matches. For example, there are configuration parameters, e.g., confidence and contextual score, which can be specified to control the quality of the output (Mendes et al., 2011). Confidence is a parameter for disambiguation, ranging from 0 to 1, which takes into account factors such as topical pertinence and contextual ambiguity. The confidence threshold setting instructs the tool to exclude low-ranking annotations at the risk of losing potentially correct ones. For example, a confidence level of 0.7 will eliminate 70% of low-ranking candidates. Meanwhile, contextual score is the cosine similarity between term vectors weighted by the Term Frequency Inverse Candidate Frequency (TF*ICF) measure introduced by Mendes et al. (2011). ICF is based on the idea that the discriminative power of a word is inversely proportional to the number of DBpedia resources it is associated with. The above parameters provide the tool with a way to rank the list of candidates.

In applying DBpedia Spotlight on our own collection of tweets, we initially set the confidence and contextual score parameters to 0.7. Fuzzy string matching heuristics were also employed, to enable the matching of lexical variants in tweets (e.g., those which differ in length by at most two characters)

Pre-trained Word Embeddings	Description	Text Type
Twitter	2B tweets, 27B tokens, 1.2M vocabulary words, uncased, 100 dimensions	Tweets
Common Crawl	840B tokens, 2.2M vocabulary words, cased, 300 dimensions	Web Pages
Wikipedia 2014 + Gigaword 5	6B tokens, 400K vocabulary words, uncased, 100 dimensions	Wiki pages + newswire

Table 3: Description of word embeddings pre-trained using GloVe

against DBpedia entries. The tool assigns matched entities with semantic labels that come from DBpedia's ontology, which defines a hierarchy of types. In order to categorise these entities according to the shared task's categories of interest, we defined the mappings shown in Table 2, informed by the annotation guidelines provided by the shared task organisers. For many entities, DBpedia Spotlight provides multiple hierarchical labels. For example, the entity "Justin Bieber" is labelled by the tool as both *Person* and *MusicArtist*, which map to W-NUT's *person* and *musicartist*, respectively. In such cases, we take the most specific entity type (e.g., *musicartist*) as the final label. Furthermore, if an entity match x is subsumed by another match y, we disregard x and retain the longer matching entity y with its corresponding type. For example, if a tweet contains three entity matches such as "New York USA", "New York" and "USA", we disregard the two shorter entity matches ("New York", "USA") and choose the entity with the longer span of tokens ("New York USA").

The above techniques, however, did not result in better performance. With the threshold of 0.7, which turned out to be too low, even named entities that DBpedia Spotlight was not very confident about were included in the training set, thus introducing noise. This corresponds to token sequences which were recognised as entities of a certain type when in reality they are actually non-entities or fall under a different entity type. This noise is compounded as the bi-directional LSTM models we employed made use of the context surrounding the wrongly recognised entities to learn the segmentation and classification tasks. To resolve these issues, we increased the required level of confidence in weakly annotated named entity types, from 0.7 to 0.9. Furthermore, we added weakly annotated data only to the entity types for which our models have obtained poor performance based on our initial experiment, namely: *product, movie, musicartist, tvshow*. In this way, we avoid adding unexpected noise with respect to the other named entity types.

3.3 Exploiting different types of word embeddings

Word embeddings are n-dimensional continuous-valued representations of a word where n is an arbitrarily chosen number of dimensions. In contrast to one-hot representations whose number of dimensions would be equal to the vocabulary size V, distributed representations such as word embeddings represent a word in n dimensions where n is much smaller than V (i.e., $n \ll V$). Aside from avoiding sparse representations, word embeddings are shown to capture a word's semantic and syntactic information (Mikolov et al., 2013). Specifically, since word embeddings are generated based on co-occurrence information, co-occurring words share the same context and are thus expected to have similar values.

There are a number of implementations for generating word embeddings such as word2vec (Mikolov et al., 2013) and GloVe (Pennington et al., 2014). Pennington et al. (2014) have shown that GloVe produces better results over word2vec (i.e., using CBOW and Skip-gram models) on word similarity and named entity recognition tasks. They also provided pre-trained word embeddings generated based on three different corpora: Common Crawl, Twitter, and Wikipedia 2014+Gigaword 5. Based on the comparison presented in Table 3, it can be observed that Common Crawl has the largest vocabulary size.

Word embeddings have been employed as features for the NER task (Baldwin et al., 2015). As our study is based on unsupervised learning, i.e., neural networks, in which the feature set is learned auto-

Word	Wikipedia+Gigaword	Twitter	Common Crawl
IV	64.66 (9,620)	65.88 (9,802)	**70.65 (10,512)**
OOEV	35.34 (5,258)	34.12 (5,076)	29.35 (4,366)

Table 4: Percentage distribution of IV and OOEV words in the pre-trained embeddings

Category	Percentage
@username	39.31
http://url	21.19
words	19.87
#hashtags	12.15
punctuations	5.43
numbers	2.19

Table 5: OOEV word categories and their distribution

matically, we instead use word embeddings as representations of input words. In this paper, we observe the effect on NER performance, of using each of the three different pre-trained word embeddings.

3.4 Representing Out-of-Embedding Vocabulary (OOEV) Words

Words for which there are no embeddings, i.e., out-of-embedding vocabulary (OOEV) words, commonly occur in the given data set, accounting for around 30% of all words. Table 4 presents the frequency of words with embeddings, i.e., in-vocabulary (IV) words, and OOEV words in the different pre-trained embeddings. We analysed the most frequently occurring OOEV words and categorised them, as shown in Table 5. We observed that the most prevalent type of OOEV words correspond to Twitter usernames of the pattern "@username" as well as URLs, comprising around 60% of the words with no embedding values. Out of the OOEV words, only 10% are named entities, with the rest accounting for context words. Table 6 shows the percentage of named entities with word embeddings (i.e., IV words) and the percentage OOEV words in the training and test sets, respectively.

One way of representing OOEV words is by randomly initialising embeddings with values uniformly sampled from a specified range $[-\sqrt{3/dim}, +\sqrt{3/dim}]$ where dim is the dimension of embeddings (He et al., 2015). In this work, we compare that method with the use of placeholder values to replace OOEV words, e.g., by substituting rare words with *'UNK'* (Nam et al., 2016). We applied this on the following OOEV categories: usernames, URLs, punctuations, numbers and hashtags. Furthermore, to account for OOEV words which are potentially lexical variants of IV words (e.g., *'gud'* vs *'good'*, *'#Twitter'* vs *'Twitter'*), we employed string similarity measures based on the edit distance metric (Contractor et al., 2010) to find the IV word most similar to a given OOEV word. This technique was applied on hashtags, punctuations and words. Whilst GloVe comes with its own script for normalisation[1], we chose to implement our own in order to incorporate string similarity measures.

4 Results and Discussion

In this section, we present the results of our evaluation of the methods described above. We investigated the impact on performance of employing different tagging schemes and word embeddings, as well as the substitution of OOEV words with placeholders. We then analysed the extent to which the use of different hyperparameter values and weakly labelled named entities, contributed to NER performance.

As a first step, a decision was made on the data sets to be used for training our models and subsequently evaluating performance. Noting that the shared task-provided training and development data came from disjoint time periods, i.e., 2010 and 2014-2015 respectively, we were interested in determining whether the use of a more temporally heterogeneous set of tweets for training our models could lead to better results. To this end, we formed our own training and development data partitions out of the original data

---

[1] http://nlp.stanford.edu/projects/glove/preprocess-twitter.rb

Data Set	Total Named Entities	IV	OOEV
Training Set	80.83 (2,902)	93.34 (2,709)	**6.06 (193)**
Test Set	19.17 (688)	95.49 (657)	**4.5 (31)**

Table 6: Percentage distribution of named entities with IV and OOEV words

Tagging Scheme	Precision	Recall	F-score
BIO	**61.76**	53.17	57.14
BIOES	60.99	**57.25**	**59.06**

Table 7: Comparison of performance when using different tagging schemes

sets. Firstly, we combined the tweets from the provided training and development sets. The resulting collection was then partitioned into two: 80% of the tweets became part of a new training set while the remaining 20% formed a new development set. We then ran an experiment to compare the performance obtained when using this new partition, against using the original training and development sets. Our results show that utilising our own data partition yields better performance. This confirms previous observations by Fromreide et al. (2014) that language drift is prevalent in tweets: models trained on relatively older tweets (i.e., from 2010) perform suboptimally on more recent ones (i.e., from 2014-2015). Our own training and development data partitions were thus used in the rest of the experiments described below, together with the following hyperparameter values for the neural network: dropout = 0.6, learning = 0.013 and number of epochs = 63. The value for each hyperparameter was determined by comparing performance across a small number of options: {0.3, 0.4, 0.5, 0.6, 0.7} for dropout, {0.01, 0.013, 0.015, 0.017, 0.02} for learning rate and values within the interval [1, 1500] for number of epochs.

Table 7 compares the performance obtained by employing the BIO tagging convention versus that using the finer-grained BIOES tagging scheme. As in previous studies (Ratinov and Roth, 2009; Dai et al., 2015), our results show that adopting the BIOES scheme leads to better performance. This can be attributed to the additional information obtained by distinguishing tokens at the end ('E') of entities and those comprising single-token ('S') entities.

We next observed the differences in performance brought about by varying the set of word embeddings (between pre-trained Common Crawl, Twitter and Wikipedia+Gigaword embeddings) used as input to the neural network. It is slightly surprising that optimum performance was obtained with word embeddings learned based on Common Crawl rather than Twitter (Table 8). This, however, can be attributed to Common Crawl's much larger vocabulary (i.e., five times more than Wikipedia+Gigaword and twice the size of the Twitter corpus). We plan to carry out more experiments (as part of future work) to further investigate the effect of exploiting different pre-trained word embeddings.

Contrary to our expectations, embeddings generated by substituting OOEV words with placeholders did not yield better performance compared to randomly initialised embeddings (see Table 9 below). It is highly probable that replacing OOEV words with placeholders weakened the discriminative power of CNNs, which take into consideration character-level features. Similarly, the string similarity-based measures did not have a noticeable impact on performance as the affected words account for only a very small percentage of the OOEV words.

We then evaluated the contribution of augmenting the sparse entity types in the training data with weakly labelled named entities. As presented in Table 10, performance noticeably increased for all en-

GloVe Pretrained Vectors	Precision	Recall	F-score
Twitter	59.83	51.22	55.19
Common Crawl	63.20	54.88	**58.75**
Wikipedia 2014 + Gigaword 5	58.46	46.34	51.70

Table 8: Comparison of performance based on different pre-trained word embeddings

Embedding Strategy	Precision	Recall	F-score
Randomly initialised embeddings (baseline)	63.20	54.88	**58.75**
Randomly initialised embeddings (words) + placeholder(all others)	64.13	51.84	57.34
string sim (words, hashtags, punctuations) + placeholder(url, @username, number)	62.28	51.11	56.14
string sim (words, hashtags) + placeholder(url, @username, number, punctuations)	62.92	50.86	56.25

Table 9: Performance of different embedding strategies for representing OOEV words

Entity Type	Training Set only	Training Set + Weakly Labelled entities for sparse types
tvshow	44.44	**44.44**
product	40	**41.38**
musicartist	28.57	**46.15**
movie	0	**16.67**

Table 10: Effect on the F-scores after adding weakly labelled data to sparse entity types

tity types except in the case of *tvshow*, in which no improvement was obtained. The effect is especially high for *movie* and *musicartist*—entity types for which the F-scores were previously zero. This demonstrates that the incorporation of weakly labelled data in training the neural network can lead to significant improvement with respect to sparse entity types.

Informed by the above results, we trained our final NER model on our training data partition augmented with weakly labelled named entities, using: (1) the BIOES tagging scheme; (2) pre-trained Common Crawl word embeddings; and (3) randomly initialised word embeddings for OOEV words. Model training took two hours on an Nvidia M2050 GPU processor.

Underpinned by the final NER model, our system ("akora") was applied on the shared task's test data, yielding an overall precision = 51.70, recall = 39.48, and F-score = 44.77. It ranked third amongst participating systems (Strauss et al., 2016) as shown in Table 11. Details of the evaluation results according to entity type are presented in Table 12.

Unfortunately, we have been unable to carry out a performance-wise comparison with the systems that participated in the previous edition of the W-NUT NER task. Their performance results were reported based on a data set that formed part of the development data set that we used to fine-tune our neural network architecture's hyperparameters and optimise our approach's performance. Thus, reporting our system's results on the same data set would not have given a fair comparison.

A model for the W-NUT's named entity segmentation task was trained in the same way as above, but with the entity type labels removed from the training data. When applied on the official test data, this model obtained an F-score of 59.05 (precision = 64.75, recall = 54.28).

System Name	Precision	Recall	F-score
CambridgeLTL	60.77	46.07	52.41
Talos	58.51	38.12	46.16
akora	51.70	39.48	44.77
NTNU	53.19	32.13	40.06
ASU	40.58	37.58	39.02

Table 11: Performance of our NER system, akora, compared to other top-ranking W-NUT 2016 systems

Entity Type	Precision	Recall	F-score
company	67.11	32.53	43.82
facility	48.03	28.85	36.05
geo-loc	61.41	65.31	63.30
movie	10.00	2.94	4.55
musicartist	21.05	4.19	6.99
other	37.23	23.97	29.17
person	47.97	58.71	52.80
product	33.33	12.60	18.29
sportsteam	38.89	38.10	38.49
tvshow	10.00	3.03	4.65
Overall	51.70	39.48	**44.77**

Table 12: Named entity recognition performance on the official evaluation data set

5 Conclusion and Future Work

Our experiments have shown that taking advantage of weakly annotated data to alleviate data sparsity of some named entity types resulted in increased performance in the respective entity types. In contrast, mitigating OOEV words by using placeholders did not result in better performance. Future work includes performing further error analysis by means of hidden layer visualisation to enable us to investigate representations created at each layer. Moreover, Bayesian optimisation of parameters can be done as proposed by Rasmussen (2006). Finally, considering the language drift inherent in social media content, looking into word sense disambiguation may help improve performance.

Acknowledgement

We thank our anonymous reviewers for their invaluable feedback, as well as Piotr Przybyła for his comments on the final draft. The first author gratefully acknowledges financial support from the University of the Philippines System Doctoral Studies Fund.

References

Timothy Baldwin, Young-Bum Kim, Marie Catherine de Marneffe, Alan Ritter, Bo Han, and Wei Xu. 2015. Shared tasks of the 2015 workshop on noisy user-generated text: Twitter lexical normalization and named entity recognition. *ACL-IJCNLP*, 126:2015.

Yoshua Bengio, Patrice Simard, and Paolo Frasconi. 1994. Learning long-term dependencies with gradient descent is difficult. *IEEE transactions on neural networks*, 5(2):157–166.

Colin Cherry and Hongyu Guo. 2015. The unreasonable effectiveness of word representations for Twitter named entity recognition. In *Proc. NAACL*.

Hai Leong Chieu and Hwee Tou Ng. 2002. Named entity recognition: a maximum entropy approach using global information. In *Proceedings of the 19th international conference on Computational linguistics-Volume 1*, pages 1–7. Association for Computational Linguistics.

Jason PC Chiu and Eric Nichols. 2016. Named entity recognition with bidirectional LSTM-CNNs. *Transactions of the Association for Computational Linguistics*, 4:357–370.

Danish Contractor, Tanveer A Faruquie, and L Venkata Subramaniam. 2010. Unsupervised cleansing of noisy text. In *Proceedings of the 23rd International Conference on Computational Linguistics: Posters*, pages 189–196. Association for Computational Linguistics.

Hong-Jie Dai, Po-Ting Lai, Yung-Chun Chang, and Richard Tzong-Han Tsai. 2015. Enhancing of chemical compound and drug name recognition using representative tag scheme and fine-grained tokenization. *Journal of cheminformatics*, 7(1):1.

Joachim Daiber, Max Jakob, Chris Hokamp, and Pablo N. Mendes. 2013. Improving efficiency and accuracy in multilingual entity extraction. In *Proceedings of the 9th International Conference on Semantic Systems (I-Semantics)*.

Mark Dredze, Tim Oates, and Christine Piatko. 2010. We're not in Kansas anymore: detecting domain changes in streams. In *Proceedings of the 2010 Conference on Empirical Methods in Natural Language Processing*, pages 585–595. Association for Computational Linguistics.

Chris Dyer, Miguel Ballesteros, Wang Ling, Austin Matthews, and Noah A Smith. 2015. Transition-based dependency parsing with stack long short-term memory. *arXiv preprint arXiv:1505.08075*.

Jacob Eisenstein. 2013. What to do about bad language on the internet. In *HLT-NAACL*, pages 359–369.

Jenny Rose Finkel and Christopher D. Manning. 2009. Joint parsing and named entity recognition. In *Proceedings of Human Language Technologies: The 2009 Annual Conference of the North American Chapter of the Association for Computational Linguistics*, pages 326–334. Association for Computational Linguistics.

Radu Florian, Abe Ittycheriah, Hongyan Jing, and Tong Zhang. 2003. Named entity recognition through classifier combination. In *Proceedings of the seventh conference on Natural language learning at HLT-NAACL 2003-Volume 4*, pages 168–171. Association for Computational Linguistics.

Hege Fromreide, Dirk Hovy, and Anders Sgaard. 2014. Crowdsourcing and annotating NER for Twitter# drift. In *LREC*, pages 2544–2547.

Frderic Godin, Baptist Vandersmissen, Wesley De Neve, and Rik Van de Walle. 2015. Multimedia Lab@ ACL W-NUT NER Shared Task: Named Entity Recognition for Twitter Microposts using Distributed Word Representations. *ACL-IJCNLP 2015*, page 146.

Kaiming He, Xiangyu Zhang, Shaoqing Ren, and Jian Sun. 2015. Delving deep into rectifiers: Surpassing human-level performance on imagenet classification. In *Proceedings of the IEEE International Conference on Computer Vision*, pages 1026–1034.

Sepp Hochreiter and Jürgen Schmidhuber. 1997. Long short-term memory. *Neural computation*, 9(8):1735–1780.

Guillaume Lample, Miguel Ballesteros, Sandeep Subramanian, Kazuya Kawakami, and Chris Dyer. 2016. Neural architectures for named entity recognition. *arXiv preprint arXiv:1603.01360*.

Robert Leaman, Graciela Gonzalez, and others. 2008. BANNER: an executable survey of advances in biomedical named entity recognition. In *Pacific symposium on biocomputing*, volume 13, pages 652–663.

Gang Luo, Xiaojiang Huang, Chin-Yew Lin, and Zaiqing Nie. 2015. Joint named entity recognition and disambiguation. In *Proc. EMNLP*.

Xuezhe Ma and Eduard Hovy. 2016. End-to-end Sequence Labeling via Bi-directional LSTM-CNNs-CRF. *arXiv preprint arXiv:1603.01354*.

Andrew McCallum and Wei Li. 2003. Early results for named entity recognition with conditional random fields, feature induction and web-enhanced lexicons. In *Proceedings of the seventh conference on Natural language learning at HLT-NAACL 2003-Volume 4*, pages 188–191. Association for Computational Linguistics.

Pablo N Mendes, Max Jakob, Andrés García-Silva, and Christian Bizer. 2011. Dbpedia spotlight: shedding light on the web of documents. In *Proceedings of the 7th international conference on semantic systems*, pages 1–8. ACM.

Tomas Mikolov, Kai Chen, Greg Corrado, and Jeffrey Dean. 2013. Efficient estimation of word representations in vector space. *arXiv preprint arXiv:1301.3781*.

Jinseok Nam, Eneldo Loza Menca, and Johannes Frnkranz. 2016. All-in Text: Learning Document, Label, and Word Representations Jointly. In *Thirtieth AAAI Conference on Artificial Intelligence*.

Razvan Pascanu, Tomas Mikolov, and Yoshua Bengio. 2013. On the difficulty of training recurrent neural networks. *ICML (3)*, 28:1310–1318.

Jeffrey Pennington, Richard Socher, and Christopher D Manning. 2014. Glove: Global vectors for word representation. In *EMNLP*, volume 14, pages 1532–43.

Carl Edward Rasmussen. 2006. Gaussian processes for machine learning. MIT Press.

Lev Ratinov and Dan Roth. 2009. Design challenges and misconceptions in named entity recognition. In *Proceedings of the Thirteenth Conference on Computational Natural Language Learning*, pages 147–155. Association for Computational Linguistics.

Alan Ritter, Sam Clark, Oren Etzioni, and others. 2011. Named entity recognition in tweets: an experimental study. In *Proceedings of the Conference on Empirical Methods in Natural Language Processing*, pages 1524–1534. Association for Computational Linguistics.

David E Rumelhart, Geoffrey E Hinton, and Ronald J Williams. 1988. Learning representations by back-propagating errors. *Cognitive modeling*, 5(3):1.

Erik F Sang and Jorn Veenstra. 1999. Representing text chunks. In *Proceedings of the ninth conference on European chapter of the Association for Computational Linguistics*, pages 173–179. Association for Computational Linguistics.

Nitish Srivastava, Geoffrey E Hinton, Alex Krizhevsky, Ilya Sutskever, and Ruslan Salakhutdinov. 2014. Dropout: a simple way to prevent neural networks from overfitting. *Journal of Machine Learning Research*, 15(1):1929–1958.

Benjamin Strauss, Bethany E. Toma, Alan Ritter, Marie Catherine de Marneffe, and Wei Xu. 2016. Results of the wnut16 named entity recognition shared task. In *Proceedings of the Workshop on Noisy User-generated Text (WNUT 2016)*, Osaka, Japan.

Zhiqiang Toh, Bin Chen, and Jian Su. 2015. Improving twitter named entity recognition using word representations.

Ikuya Yamada123, Hideaki Takeda, and Yoshiyasu Takefuji. 2015. Enhancing Named Entity Recognition in Twitter Messages Using Entity Linking. *ACL-IJCNLP 2015*, page 136.

Feature-Rich Twitter Named Entity Recognition and Classification

Utpal Kumar Sikdar and **Björn Gambäck**
Department of Computer and Information Science
Norwegian University of Science and Technology
Trondheim, Norway
{sikdar.utpal, gamback}@idi.ntnu.no

Abstract

Twitter named entity recognition is the process of identifying proper names and classifying them into some predefined labels/categories. The paper introduces a Twitter named entity system using a supervised machine learning approach, namely Conditional Random Fields. A large set of different features was developed and the system was trained using these. The Twitter named entity task can be divided into two parts: i) Named entity extraction from tweets and ii) Twitter name classification into ten different types. For Twitter named entity recognition on unseen test data, our system obtained the second highest F_1 score in the shared task: 63.22%. The system performance on the classification task was worse, with an F_1 measure of 40.06% on unseen test data, which was the fourth best of the ten systems participating in the shared task.

1 Introduction

Social media such as Twitter has become an everyday part of many people's lives, and play a major role in modern society. There are currently 1.65 billion monthly active users on Facebook (Facebook, 2016) and 310 million on Twitter (Twitter, 2016). The number of people involved leads to a vast amount of data being shared, with almost 500 million short messages, *tweets*, being produced daily on Twitter (Internet Live Stats, 2016). Due to the ease and spontaneity of the message creation, and the restriction of a maximum length of 140 characters on the tweets, the language used on Twitter is often very noisy, with tweets containing many grammatical and spelling mistakes, short form of the words, multiple words merged together, special symbols and characters inserted into the words, etc. Hence it is difficult to analyse and monitor all types of tweets, and to sift through the vast number of tweets: specific tweets may need to be filtered out from millions of tweets. Named entity extraction plays a vital role when filtering out relevant tweets from a collection. It is also useful as a pre-processing step in many other language processing tasks, such as machine translation and question-answering.

Several approaches to Twitter named entity extraction have already been tried, but it is still a challenging task due to noisiness of the texts. Liu et al. (2011) proposed a semi-supervised learning framework to identify Twitter names. They used a k-Nearest Neighbors (kNN) approach to label the Twitter names and gave these labels as an input feature to a Conditional Random Fields (CRF) classifier, achieving almost 80% accuracy on their own annotated data. A supervised model was proposed for Twitter named entity recognition by Ritter et al. (2011) who applied Labeled LDA (Ramage et al., 2009) to recognize the possible types of Twitter names, and also showed that part-of-speech and chunk information are important components in Twitter named identification. Li et al. (2012) introduced an unsupervised Twitter named entity extraction strategy based on dynamic programming.

The present work addresses the second version of a Twitter named entity shared task that first was organized at the ACL 2015 workshop on noisy user-generated text (Baldwin et al., 2015), with two sub-tasks: Twitter named entity identification and classification of those named entities into ten different types. Of the eight systems participating in the first workshop, the best (Yamada et al., 2015) achieved an F_1 score of 70.63% for Twitter name identification and 56.41% for classification, by combining supervised machine learning with high quality knowledge obtained from several open knowledge bases such as Wikipedia. Another team, (Akhtar et al., 2015) used a strategy based on differential evolution, getting F_1 scores of 56.81% for Twitter name identification and 39.84% for the classification task.

Proceedings of the 2nd Workshop on Noisy User-generated Text,
pages 164–170, Osaka, Japan, December 11 2016.

A related shared task on Twitter named entity recognition and linking to DBpedia was held in conjunction with the 2016 WWW conference at #Microposts2016 (Cano et al., 2016). Five teams submitted their systems to the workshop, with the best (Waitelonis and Sack, 2016) achieving recall, precision and F-measure values of 49.4%, 45.3% and 47.3%. In that system, each token is mapped to gazetteers developed from the DBpedia database. Tokens are discarded if they match stop words or are not nouns.

The present paper outlines a supervised machine learning approach to Twitter named entity identification and classification. A Conditional Random Field (Lafferty et al., 2001) classifier was trained on a rich set of features and used for identification of Twitter names from the tweets, giving an F_1 score of 63.22%. In order to classify the named entities into ten different types, we developed two models and combined their output, achieving an F-measure of 40.06%. The rest of the paper is organized as follows: The Twitter name identification methodology and the different features used are introduced in Section 2. Results are presented and discussed in Section 3, while Section 4 addresses future work and concludes.

2 Twitter Named Entity Recognition

The Twitter Named Entity Recognition shared task (Strauss et al., 2016) at W-NUT 2016, the COLING workshop on noisy user-generated text, was divided into two subtasks: 'notypes' and '10types'. In the 'notypes' subtask, named entities should just be identified in the tweets, while in the '10types' subtask the aim was to identify and classify Twitter names into ten different categories: *facility, geo-loc, movie, musicartist, person, company, product, sportsteam, tvshow*, and *other*. We hence first identify the Twitter names from the tweets, and then in a second step classify the names according to the ten given labels.

2.1 Twitter Named Entity Identification for 'notypes'

The Twitter named entities were first extracted from the tweets using a supervised machine learning approach, namely Conditional Random Fields, CRFs (Lafferty et al., 2001). We used the C^{++} based CRF^{++} package,[1] a simple, customizable, and open source implementation of CRF for segmenting or labelling sequential data. The 'notypes' system is shown at the top of Figure 1.

A range of different features were developed for identifying the Twitter names. These features are described below. Note that some of the feature types are implemented as several different features and that the first five types mainly are lexicon-based, while the last five types primarily relate to the context. The eight feature types in the middle of the list are predominantly word internal and character-based. The contributions of these three different groups of feature types will be compared to each other in the experimental section (Section 3).

Lexicon-based features

    Lexical data: This binary feature was extracted from the lexical data supplied by the shared task organisers. The feature is set to 1 if the current word belongs to the lexical data, otherwise 0.

    Babelfy named entities: Each tweet was passed to the Babelfy (Moro et al., 2014) named entity recognition system for recognizing Twitter names. If the current word belongs to the Babelfy named entities, this binary feature is set.

    Part-of-speech (POS): The TweeboParser[2] was used for generating part-of-speech tags for each token in the tweets and the POS tag of the current word was used as a feature. The POS tags of the previous two tokens and following two tokens were also used as features, so in total there are five POS tag features for each token.

    Stop word match: All tokens are checked against a stop word list collected from the web.[3] The binary feature is set if the current token matches one of these stop words.

    Word frequency: Less frequent words were found to often belong to named entities. If the pre-calculated frequency from the training data of the current word is less than a certain threshold, this binary feature is set.

---

[1] `http://crfpp.sourceforge.net`
[2] `http://www.cs.cmu.edu/~ark/TweetNLP/`
[3] `http://www.ranks.nl/stopwords`

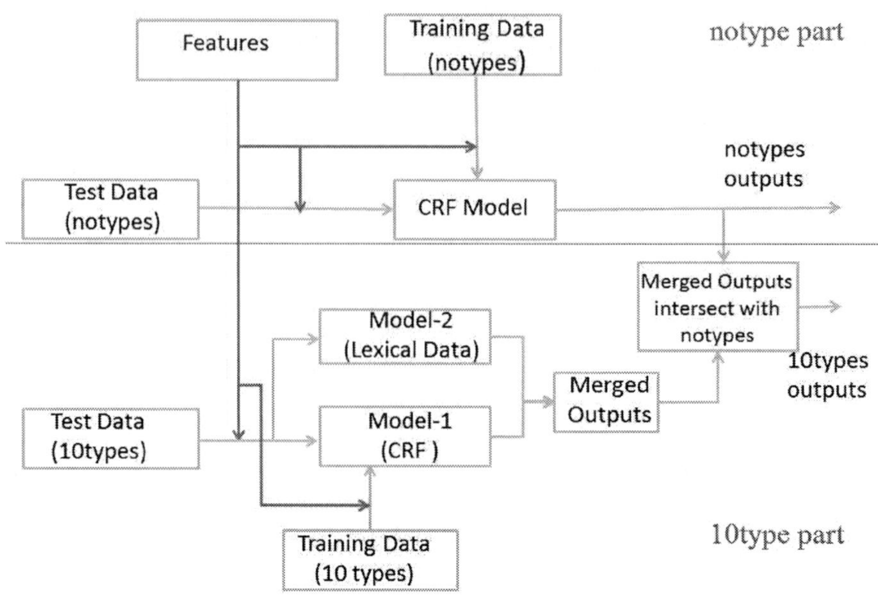

Figure 1: Twitter Named Entity Recognition system(s)

Character-based features

Numeric: Many Twitter names were found to contain numeric characters, so this binary feature shows whether the current token contains numeric characters or not.

Initial capital: Proper nouns in general tend to start with capital letters, so this feature flags if the current word has an initial capital letter.

Inner capital: This feature is set if the token contains any capital letter in a word-internal position.

Word normalisation: The word mapped to its equivalent class: each capital letter in the token is mapped to 'A', all lower-case letters to 'a', and digits to '0'. Other characters are kept unaltered.

Special character followed by token: Many Twitter names follow certain special characters (e.g., '@' and '#'). The feature checks if the token is following any special character or not.

Word length: If the current word's length is greater than some threshold, this binary feature is set.

Word suffix and prefix: A fixed maximum number of characters are stripped from the beginning and the end of the current word, with the remainder parts being used as two features.

Context-based features

Local context: Local contexts play an important role in identifying Twitter names. Here we used the three previous and the three next words as local contexts (so there are six context features).

Chunk information: Chunk information was collected using annotated chunk data from the OSU Twitter NLP Tools.[4] A CRF-based chunk model was developed using prefix, suffix and part-of-speech information. Each tweet was passed to the chunk model and chunk labels generated for that tweet. This information was then used as a feature for the current token. In addition, the chunk information of the previous token and the following token were also used as features.

First word: This binary feature checks if the current token is at the beginning of a sentence or not.

Last word: This binary feature is set if the current token is the last word of a sentence, without considering sentence ending symbols and punctuation marks (i.e., '.', '?', '!', etc.).

Previous label: Finally, the previous token's calculated named entity label was used as a feature.

---

[4]`https://github.com/aritter/twitter_nlp/blob/master/data/annotated/chunk.txt`

Dataset	Tweets	Named Entities
Training	2,814	1,768
Development	1,000	661
Test	3,850	3,473

Table 1: Number of tweets and named entities in the W-NUT 2016 datasets

For the actual named entity system, some of the limits used for the features were set based on testing on the training data. Hence, the thresholds for the word frequency and word length features were empirically set to ≥ 10 and ≥ 5, respectively, while the prefix and suffix strip lengths were fixed to four characters.

2.2 Twitter Named Entity Classification for '10types'

For the '10types' subtask, the goal was to identify and classify Twitter names into ten given categories. Two models were developed for the Twitter name classification, as follows:

Model-1: In Model-1, the tokens are classified into ten categories using CRF. The same features were utilised as described in Section 2.1 above.

Model-2: This model was based on the lexical data given by the shared task organisers (Strauss et al., 2016): the Twitter named entity classes are categorized into 10types based on the supplied file 'dictionaries.conf'. In addition, Twitter names were extracted from the training data and merged with the lexical data for each category. All tokens were passed to the lexical data and classified into the ten categories.

The output of these two models was first merged and the merged output was later checked as to whether it belonged to 'notypes' or not. When merging the output from the models, highest priority was given to Model-2, if the two models generated different named entity classes for a particular token. For example, 'Washington Navy Yard' is recognized as belonging to the *other* category by the Model-1, but Model-2 recognizes it as *facility*. So the category actually assigned to this entity by the overall system will be *facility*, as suggested by Model-2. If an entity matches more than one class in Model-2, we randomly assign the class of the entity among the matched classes.

Next, the merged output was compared to the 'notypes' entities. If the merged output belongs to those 'notypes' entities (fully matched), the output entity is considered to be a Twitter name, otherwise it is discarded. For example, the entity 'Nobu Restaurant' is classified as *other*, but this entity is not identified by 'notypes', so it is not considered as a Twitter named entity. The '10types' system is outlined in Figure 1, and consists of processes shown mainly in the lower half of the figure, but thus also utilises the 'notype' subsystem (the upper part of the figure).

3 Experiments and Discussion

A range of experiments were conducted based on the datasets provided by the shared task organizers (Strauss et al., 2016). The statistics of the datasets are given in Table 1.

3.1 The 'notypes' Named Entity Identification Task

For the 'notypes' task, the system was developed on the training data and evaluated on the development data. The 'notypes' model was initially developed using all the training data, but that gave low recall in relation to the precision. To increase the recall performance, the tweets that did not contain any named entities were removed from the training data, and a new model was built using all the features described in Section 2. This system achieved recall, precision and F-measure values of 68.68%, 65.14% and 66.86%, respectively. This final F-measure value represents an increase by almost 7% compared to the model which was built using all the training data, as can be seen in Table 2.

Training Data	Recall	Precision	F_1
all training data	54.01	67.74	60.10
removing tweets without Twitter names	68.68	65.14	66.86

Table 2: Performance on the development data for Twitter Named Entity Identification ('notypes')

Features	Recall	Precision	F_1
Lexical	57.19	49.48	53.05
Word internal	44.18	49.32	46.61
Context	16.79	57.81	26.03

Table 3: Feature class contributions to Twitter Named Entity Identification ('notypes' development data)

Team	Accuracy	Recall	Precision	F_1
CambridgeLTL	95.34	73.49	59.72	65.89
NTNU	94.38	64.18	62.28	63.22
Talos	94.54	70.53	52.58	60.24
akora	94.51	64.75	54.28	59.05
ASU	94.08	57.55	52.98	55.17

Table 4: Comparison of results (top five systems) for 'notypes' on the unseen test data

Table 3 looks at the feasibility of the different groups of features, that is, how much each feature group actually contribute in isolation. In the table, the features are sorted into three different classes: 'lexical', 'word internal' and 'context'. Referring to Section 2, the 'lexical' group consists of the features lexical data, babelfy, POS, stopword and word frequency. The 'word internal' (character-based) feature group contains the alphanumeric, initial/inner capital, normalisation, special character, word length and pre-/suffix features, while the 'context' group is made up of the context window words features, chunk, first/last words, and the previous token's label.

As can be seen in Table 3, the context features do not contribute much at all to improving the recall, but are the most helpful features for improving the precision. The lexical and word internal features contribute roughly equally to the precision score, but the lexical features very clearly are the most useful for achieving good recall.

The full-feature set 'notypes' model built only on the tweets with named entities was entered in the shared task as the named entity extraction system 'NTNU'. When applied to the unseen test data it achieved state-of-the-art results by obtaining the second highest score in the task. The comparable test data results (top five of the ten participating systems) are reported in Table 4. The NTNU system achieved recall, precision and F_1 values of respectively 64.18%, 62.28% and 63.22%, and thus scored over 2 points less on F-measure than the best performing system, but on the other hand scored 3 points more than the third ranked system.

3.2 The '10types' Named Entity Classification Task

For the '10types' classification task, we developed the two models described in Section 2.2 and also merged their output. The results are shown in Table 5. When using all the feature classes (lexical, word internal and context), Model-1 produced the best recall (28.74%) with an F-measure of 37.40%. Model-2 generated a better precision (85.16%), but due to bad recall still had a lower F_1: 27.63%. Combining the two models boosted the results on the development data on all measures, giving a 43.81% F-score.

Table 6 indicates the contribution from each of the three types of feature sets to the performance of Model-1. Just as for the identification task, it is also for classification clear that the context features are most helpful for boosting precision, while the lexical features help the recall most.

Classification Model	Recall	Precision	F_1
Model-1	28.74	53.52	37.40
Model-2	16.49	85.16	27.63
Combined Model	35.10	58.29	43.81

Table 5: Results for Twitter Named Entity Classification ('10types') on the development data

Features	Recall	Precision	F_1
Lexical	22.39	34.58	27.18
Word internal	15.13	49.50	23.17
Context	6.20	95.35	11.65

Table 6: Feature contributions to Model-1 for Named Entity Classification ('10types' development data)

Team	Test Data			
	Accuracy	Recall	Precision	F_1
CambridgeLTL	93.52	60.77	46.07	52.41
Talos	92.95	58.51	38.12	46.16
akora	92.73	51.70	39.48	44.77
NTNU	92.48	53.19	32.13	40.06
ASU	92.42	40.58	37.58	39.02

Table 7: Comparison of results (top five systems) for '10types' on the unseen test data

Applying the NTNU '10types' model to the previously unseen test data, it achieved recall, precision and F-measure values of 53.19%, 32.13% and 40.06%, respectively. The system came in fourth place in this subtask and the results of the top five systems are shown in Table 7. One of the main reasons why our system is outperformed by the top systems is that not all the named entities identified by the system were classified into any of the ten categories.

3.3 Error Analysis

The outputs were analysed in order to understand the nature of the errors encountered. In the 'notypes' Twitter named entity extraction subtask, several named entities were not identified by the system, while many tokens were wrongly identified as names by the system. The probable reason for this is that the system could not find enough relevant examples in the training data.

In the '10types' classification task, very few of the entities were identified and classified into the ten categories. In the development data, only 398 entities were identified out of the 661 named entities that actually were in the data, and out of those 398, only 232 entities were correctly identified. Again, this may be due to insufficient number of relevant training instances in the training data.

4   Conclusion

This paper has proposed a system for Twitter named entity identification and classification. A range of different features were developed to extract Twitter names from the tweets. Two systems were built, one for the 'notypes' named entity extraction task and the other for the '10types' classification task. The systems were built around a CRF-based classifier and lexical data, and both systems achieved state-of-the-art results. In the future, we will analyse the errors in more detail and aim to use external resources (e.g., DBpedia and Wikipedia) to reduce the misclassification of the tokens, as well as to identify more entities from the tweets. We will also try to generate more models and later ensemble these model to improve the system performance.

References

Md Shad Akhtar, Utpal Kumar Sikdar, and Asif Ekbal. 2015. IITP: Multiobjective differential evolution based Twitter named entity recognition. In Wei Xu, Bo Han, and Alan Ritter, editors, *Proceedings of the ACL 2015 Workshop on Noisy User-generated Text*, pages 106–110, Stroudsburg, PA, USA, July. Association for Computational Linguistics.

Timothy Baldwin, Marie Catherine de Marneffe, Bo Han, Young-Bum Kim, Alan Ritter, and Wei Xu. 2015. Shared tasks of the 2015 workshop on noisy user-generated text: Twitter lexical normalization and named entity recognition. In Wei Xu, Bo Han, and Alan Ritter, editors, *Proceedings of the ACL 2015 Workshop on Noisy User-generated Text*, pages 126–135, Stroudsburg, PA, USA, July. Association for Computational Linguistics.

Amparo E. Cano, Daniel Preoţiuc-Pietro, Danica Radovanović, Katrin Weller, and Aba-Sah Dadzie. 2016. #Microposts2016 — 6th workshop on 'making sense of microposts'. In *Proceedings of the 25th World Wide Web Conference (WWW'16)*, volume Companion, pages 1041–1042, Montréal, Canada, April. Association for Computing Machinery.

Facebook. 2016. Company Information. `http://newsroom.fb.com/company-info/`.

Internet Live Stats. 2016. Twitter Usage Statistics. `http://www.internetlivestats.com/twitter-statistics`.

John Lafferty, Andrew McCallum, and Fernando CN Pereira. 2001. Conditional random fields: Probabilistic models for segmenting and labeling sequence data. In *Proceedings of the 18th International Conference on Machine Learning*, pages 282–289, San Francisco, CA, USA. Morgan Kaufmann.

Chenliang Li, Jianshu Weng, Qi He, Yuxia Yao, Anwitaman Datta, Aixin Sun, and Bu-Sung Lee. 2012. TwiNER: Named entity recognition in targeted Twitter stream. In *Proceedings of the 35th International ACM SIGIR Conference on Research and Development in Information Retrieval*, pages 721–730, New York, NY, USA. Association for Computing Machinery.

Xiaohua Liu, Shaodian Zhang, Furu Wei, and Ming Zhou. 2011. Recognizing named entities in tweets. In *Proceedings of the 49th Annual Meeting of the Association for Computational Linguistics: Human Language Technologies*, volume 1, pages 359–367, Stroudsburg, PA, USA. Association for Computational Linguistics.

Andrea Moro, Alessandro Raganato, and Roberto Navigli. 2014. Entity linking meets word sense disambiguation: a unified approach. *Transactions of the Association for Computational Linguistics*, 2:231–244.

Daniel Ramage, David Hall, Ramesh Nallapati, and Christopher D. Manning. 2009. Labeled LDA: A supervised topic model for credit attribution in multi-labeled corpora. In *Proceedings of the 2009 Conference on Empirical Methods in Natural Language Processing*, volume 1, pages 248–256, Stroudsburg, PA, USA. Association for Computational Linguistics.

Alan Ritter, Sam Clark, Mausam, and Oren Etzioni. 2011. Named entity recognition in tweets: An experimental study. In *Proceedings of the 2011 Conference on Empirical Methods in Natural Language Processing*, pages 1524–1534, Stroudsburg, PA, USA. Association for Computational Linguistics.

Benjamin Strauss, Bethany E. Toma, Alan Ritter, Marie Catherine de Marneffe, and Wei Xu. 2016. Results of the WNUT16 named entity recognition shared task. In Bo Han, Alan Ritter, Leon Derczynski, Wei Xu, and Timothy Baldwin, editors, *Proceedings of the Workshop on Noisy User-generated Text (WNUT 2016)*, Stroudsburg, PA, USA, December. Association for Computational Linguistics.

Twitter. 2016. Company Information. `https://about.twitter.com/company`.

Jörg Waitelonis and Harald Sack. 2016. Named entity linking in #tweets with KEA. In Daniel Preoţiuc-Pietro, Danica Radovanović, Amparo E. Cano-Basave, Katrin Weller, and Aba-Sah Dadzie, editors, *Proceedings of 6th Workshop on Making Sense of Microposts (#Microposts2016)*, pages 61–63, Montréal, Canada, April. Sun SITE Central Europe (CEUR) Workshop Proceedings.

Ikuya Yamada, Hideaki Takeda, and Yoshiyasu Takefuji. 2015. Enhancing named entity recognition in Twitter messages using entity linking. In Wei Xu, Bo Han, and Alan Ritter, editors, *Proceedings of the ACL 2015 Workshop on Noisy User-generated Text*, pages 136–140, Stroudsburg, PA, USA, July. Association for Computational Linguistics.

Learning to Search for Recognizing Named Entities in Twitter

Ioannis Partalas, Cédric Lopez, Nadia Derbas and Ruslan Kalitvianski
Viseo R&D
Grenoble, France
`firstname.lastname@viseo.com`

Abstract

This paper describes our participation in the shared task *Named Entity Recognition in Twitter* organized as part of the 2nd Workshop on Noisy User-generated Text. The shared task comprises two sub-tasks, concerning a) the detection of the boundaries of entities and b) the classification of the entities into one of 10 possible types. The proposed approach is based on Linked Open Data for extracting rich features along with standard ones which are then used by a learning to search algorithm in order to build the tagger. The submitted system scored 46.16 and 60.24 in terms of F-measure and ranked 2nd and 3rd for the classification and segmentation tasks respectively.

1 Introduction

Named-Entity Recognition (NER) is a well-studied task for over two decades now with notable success for noise-free and grammatically well-structured documents. The final goal of a NER system is to classify textual segments in a predefined set of categories, for example persons, organizations, and locations. While current NER systems achieve very high performance for a narrow set of entities, in applications like in Twitter[1] where text is short, using an informal style and with an unreliable use of capitalization, the recognition of entities becomes a challenging task (Marrero et al., 2013; Ritter et al., 2011; Derczynski et al., 2015). For example, in the 2015 *NER in Twitter* competition the best system achieved an F-score of around 56% for ten entities (Baldwin et al., 2015).

In this context, the shared task for *Named-Entity Recognition in Twitter* has been organized in order to provide standard benchmarks for this task. In this paper we describe our participation in the 2nd edition of the *Named-Entity Recognition in Twitter* shared task which was organized in the framework of the Workshop on Noisy User-generated Text.[2] We cast the problem as a sequence labeling task and used a learning to search approach for solving it. The proposed system, called Talos,[3] combines an approach based on Linked-Open Data for extracting rich contextual features along with standard ones that are usually included in NER systems.

A total of 3,814 annotated tweets were provided by the organizers while the test set contained 3,850 examples. Our system ranked second in the classification and third in the segmentation (only detecting the boundaries) sub-tasks achieving F-scores of 46.16 and 60.24 respectively. In the following sections we present a description of the method we developed for tackling the tasks and provide evaluations of its performance.

2 Approach

In this section we detail our approach for the NER task. More specifically, we provide the different features that were extracted from the textual data as well as from external resources. Later, we present

---

[1]For example, one would like to track certain entities as a step towards influence detection, see SOMA project http://www.somaproject.eu/

[2]http://noisy-text.github.io/2016/

[3]In Greek mythology, Talos was a giant automaton constructed by the god Hepheastus and had as mission to protect Europa in Crete. https://en.wikipedia.org/wiki/Talos

Proceedings of the 2nd Workshop on Noisy User-generated Text,
pages 171–177, Osaka, Japan, December 11 2016.

the learning algorithm we used and finally an ensemble of rules that were applied on the predictions of the learned model in order to correct inconsistencies in the tagging.

2.1 Feature Engineering

We divide the extracted features into three major categories: a) lexical and morphosyntactic features for word units in the textual data, b) features using Linked Open Data (LOD) and c) features based on distributed representations of words.

2.1.1 Lexical and Morphosyntactic Features

The word-level features that we employ are the following:

- Current token w in its original form and words around it, $w[-n : n]$ for $n = 2$.

- Suffixes and prefixes of the current token of size 3 (empirically defined).

- Boolean features regarding the capitalization of the current token:
    - The token starts with capital letter.
    - All letters in the token are capital.
    - Previous words are capitalized.
    - The token contains a capitalized letter.

- Lexical features (is digit, is punctuation etc., starts with @, is hashtag, contains capital letter).

The presence of the current token in a standard English dictionary as well as in Wordnet are used as features along with the probability of its bigram prefix in order to be able to distinguish entities with rare n-grams (e.g. for XBOX the probability of encountering XB as a character bigram is zero). In the same line, we also included the presence of each token in the gazetters provided by the organizers.

Finally, we use the Stanford taggers in order to obtain the part-of-speech (POS) tag of the current and the previous tokens as well as the 3-class named-entity tag (location, person and organization) for a window of one token around the word (Kristina Toutanova, 2003). Both POS and named-entity tags have improved the performance of our system.

2.1.2 Contextual Enrichment Features

As tweets are limited to 140 characters, the context is often not sufficient to disambiguate the mentions they contain. To overcome this constraint we propose to add context in a two fold manner: 1) using more tweets that contain the same mention, 2) using external LOD resources.

Regarding the first point, we used the Twitter API[4] and for each mention in the tweet we obtained a maximum of 100 tweets which is the limit imposed by Twitter API. For each set of tweets, we compute a score based on the presence of the immediate context (that is the two words before and after) in lexical fields defined for each class of entities. For instance, `fan`, `sing`, `dj` and `musician` are words contained in the `musicartist` lexical field. Such lexical fields were created manually from Wikipedia pages. We called this feature ***enrichTweetsImmediateContext (ETIC)***. A variant of this feature is ***enrichTweets (ET)***, that considers all the words in the tweet.

Concerning the second point, we generated features inspired from Entity Linking approaches. Indeed, Yamada et al. (2015) obtained the best results in the last edition of the challenge considering entity linking results as features dedicated to enhance the NER performance. For each tweet, whenever a mention is not provided, we generated all the possible n-grams of words (with $n \leq 5$). We directly use the DBpedia SPARQL endpoint in order to request the presence of each n-gram as an entry of this knowledge base, taking into account:

---

[4]We used the Twitter4J Java library: $http://twitter4j.org/en/$

- ***Exact Matching** (EM)*. We search the type (`rdf:type`[5]) of the DBpedia ressource built according to the standard URI format (`http://dbpedia.org/resource/+Entity`). For instance, we obtain `<http://dbpedia.org/resource/Olympique_de_Marseille>` `rdf:type dbo:SportsTeam`.

- ***Redirection** (EM)*. In order to deal with common misspelling, abbreviation and acronym cases, we also consider the `dbo:wikiPageRedirects`[6] predicate. For instance, "'L'oheme'" or "'Olympic de Marseille'" refers to the same URI namely `dbo:Olympique_de_Marseille`.

- ***Disambiguation** (D)*. As most of the mentions are ambiguous, we use the `dbo:wikiPageDisambiguates`.[7] For instance, "OM" could be the Russian river `dbo:Om_River` or a television show `dbo:Om_(2003_film)`.

In these three cases, the mention receives a boolean value according to each category in the classification task (movie, geo-loc, person, etc.): 1 if a `rdf:type` corresponds to one of the 10 categories, 0 otherwise.

2.1.3 Word Clusters

We exploited unlabeled data using word representations which have been proved to enhance performance for a variety of NLP tasks (Ritter et al., 2011; Owoputi et al., 2012; Cherry et al., 2015). In this line, we used Brown clusters (Brown et al., 1992) as well as word clusters on top of GloVe word representations from external resources and a set of tweets collected in several periods between July and September 2016 resulting to a corpus of around 39 million tweets. The collection has been biased to include tweets in the context of each of the ten entity classes. For example, for the class `musicartist` we used the following keywords, {`band, musicgroup, livemusic, concert, musician, musical`}.

Regarding the external resources we used pre-trained Brown clusters from TweetNLP[8](Owoputi et al., 2012) and pre-trained GloVe word vectors of Wikipedia and Twitter collections[9] which were grouped in 1,000 clusters using K-means (Pennington et al., 2014). Several dimensions for the word vectors were tested, ranging from 50 to 200, and the best results were obtained with the 100 dimensional ones. For the collected tweets, around 36 million English tweets were selected using langpid.py (Lui and Baldwin, 2012). Then, we trained Brown clusters to partition the words in 1,000 classes with a minimum frequency of appearance in the collection of 10 times (Liang, 2005).

2.2 Learning Algorithm

The learning problem was cast as a sequence labeling one, and for solving it we used a learning to search (L2S) approach, which represents a family of algorithms for structured prediction tasks (Daumé III et al., 2014; Chang et al., 2015). These methods decompose the problem in a search space with states, actions and policies and then learn a hypothesis controlling a policy over the state-action space. In this case, each example in the training data is used as a reference policy (labels to be assigned at each token) and the learning algorithm tries to approximate it. This technique resembles reinforcement learning methods, with the difference that in the latter one is not provided with a reference policy but discovers it through trial-and-error.

The L2S framework is highly modular as it reduces structured problems to cost-sensitive multi-class classification ones. This allows us to use state-of-the-art algorithms for multi-class classification.

2.3 Post-application of Rules

The annotations produced by our system contained inconsistencies which we corrected with a post-processing step. For instance, in the BIO encoding, a label "I" can not exist if the previous label is not a "B". In order to avoid such cases, we applied the following rules:

---

[5]$http://www.w3.org/1999/02/22 - rdf - syntax - ns\#type$
[6]$http://dbpedia.org/ontology/wikiPageRedirects$
[7]$http://dbpedia.org/ontology/wikiPageDisambiguates$
[8]http://www.cs.cmu.edu/ ark/TweetNLP/
[9]http://nlp.stanford.edu/projects/glove/

1. $O-\mathbf{I} \Rightarrow O-\mathbf{B}$ or $B-\mathbf{I}$ or $B-I-\mathbf{I}$ or $B-I-I-\mathbf{I}$ regarding the presence of capital letters in previous words.

2. $I-\mathbf{B} \Rightarrow I-\mathbf{I}$

3. $B-\mathbf{B} \Rightarrow B-\mathbf{I}$

Concerning the last two rules, we take into account the fact that the phenomenon of composition (when an entity is included in another entity) is not frequently present in the training set.

3   Experiments

3.1   Data

The organizers provided a training set with 2,814 tweets and a development set of 1,000 tweets which corresponds to the test set of the 2015 edition of the challenge. Table 1 presents the distribution for each entity type in the training and development sets. We observe that `person`, `geo-loc` and `other` are the dominating classes in both sets.

type	train	dev	test
company	204	39	621
facility	111	38	253
person	522	171	482
musicartist	68	41	191
geo-loc	322	116	882
movie	37	15	34
other	272	132	584
product	106	37	246
sportsteam	86	70	147
tvshow	40	2	33

Table 1: Size for each class of entities in the training, development and test sets.

Tweets were already tokenized and we applied normalization in order to reduce noise induced by spelling errors or the use of abbreviations and slang. There are three kinds of token normalizations (Baldwin et al., 2015):

- one-to-one normalization, when one out-of-vocabulary (OOV) token is replaced by one in-vocabulary equivalent,

- one-to-many (OTM), when one token is replaced by several,

- many-to-one (MTO), when several tokens are replaced by one.

In this work we perform a simple one-to-one normalization, by substituting OOV terms for which a normalized equivalent exists in the W-NUT normalization shared task corpus of 2015 by their normalized counterparts (Baldwin et al., 2015). This has the advantage of not requiring to perform a token-level alignment between the unnormalized tweet and the potentially longer (or shorter) tweet that would result from an OTM or MTO normalization.

No further preprocessing has been applied to the data. Nevertheless, during an inspection of the data we observed some inconsistencies in the annotation of some entities like for example "Justin Bieber" which was annotated as `person` in the training data while in the test set as `musicartist`. During development, we decided not to alter these annotations although it could have slightly improved the performance of our system.

It is interesting to note here that the intersection of the unique entities between the `train` and `dev` sets is around 14.6% while the corresponding ratio for `train + dev` and the `test` set is around 8.3%. This means that we should expect a harder prediction task than this of 2015 which will test the generalization capabilities of our approach.

Namespace	Segmentation	Classification
LM	$w_{-2:2}$, $N_{-1:1}$, $POS_{-1:0}$, $Cap_{-1:0}$, $Lexical$	$w_{-2:2}$, $N_{-1:1}$, $POS_{-1:0}$, $Cap_{-1:0}$, $\alpha_0^{\pm 3}$, $Lexical$
LOD	LOD_{EM}, LOD_R, LOD_D	LOD_{ETIC} LOD_{ET}, LOD_R, LOD_{EM}, LOD_R, LOD_D
WordClusters	$B_0, B_0^{indomain}, GV_0^{wiki}, GV_0^{tweets}$	$B_0, B_0^{indomain}, GV_0^{wiki}, GV_0^{tweets}$

Table 2: Template features for the two tasks. w corresponds to the word, N to the 3-class **NER** tag, Cap to the capitalization features and α to the affix.

3.2 Setup

We trained two different systems for the corresponding tasks, that is the detection of boundaries and the classification of types of entities. Note, that we use the predictions of the system that detects the boundaries in order to extract the Linked Open Data features discussed in Section 2.1.2. While this approach can have a low recall rate, it has the advantage of being very fast and precise and thus not injecting noise in the features. On the other hand, one could have generated all the n-grams from left to right for each tweet, letting the system increase the coverage of the entities but with a high computational cost and a low precision rate. Table 2 presents the templates we used for each of the two tasks where w, N, Cap, $Lexical$ and α refer to the form of word, named-entity obtained by the Stanford tagger, lexical features and affixes of a word. For each feature, a subscript denotes the slice that has been used around the current token. For the word clusters B and $B^{indomain}$ refer to the pre-trained brown clusters and the ones learned over our collection of tweets (see Section 2.1.3). Finally, GV clusters correspond to the trained clusters for Wikipedia and tweets GloVe vectors respectively.

For both tasks, parameter tuning was performed through a random search with cross-validation for the estimation of the performance. In order to evaluate the performance of our system with respect to the results of the 2015 edition of the competition, we performed the tuning only on the training set and then test on the development set. For our final submission the same procedure was repeated on the union of the train and development sets.

We used the Vowpal Wabbit[10] suite, which implements several L2S algorithms and provides a framework for compiling structured learning tasks. We tune the following parameters for L2S: *learning_rate* $\in [0.05, 0.3]$, *passes* $\in [2, 20]$ and *history_length* $\in \{1, 2, 3\}$. The parameter for the hash function was optimized beforehand and kept fixed to 29 bits throughout the experiments. Finally, we used the default setting for solving the multi-class cost-sensitive classification problems.

3.3 Results

Tables 3 and 4 present the results for the segmentation and classification tasks respectively. As the development set for 2016 corresponds to the test set of 2015 edition of the challenge, we include the best two systems of 2015 for comparison, namely **Ousia** (Yamada et al., 2015) and **NLANGP** (Toh et al., 2015). Our system, Talos, was ranked third and second respectively for the two tasks.

Regarding the segmentation task, Talos achieved a high precision score but with a lower recall in both the development and the test sets.

Table 4 presents the results in the same fashion as previously for the entities classification task. We include a version of our system without using the LOD features and a version without normalization in order to assess their contribution. Talos achieved a high F-score in the test set and ranked second in this task. We also observe that on the development set it outperformed the best system of the 2015 edition of the challenge. However, noticeably we note the lower scores in the test set for the best systems with respect to the results of 2015. This could come from the fact that many mentions never appear in the training data and thus stressing the generalization capabilities of the systems. Also, as tweets come from different periods of time one should account for concept-drift phenomena, which we did not consider in our case.

---

[10] http://hunch.net/vw

System	dev 2016			test		
	P	R	F	P	R	F
Talos	71.29	55.98	62.71	70.53	52.58	60.24
1st-2016	-	-	-	73.49	59.72	65.89
2nd-2016	-	-	-	64.18	62.28	63.22
Ousia	72.20	69.14	70.63	-	-	-
NLANGP	67.74	54.31	60.29	-	-	-

Table 3: Results for the no-types task in terms of Precision, Recall and F-score. The development test of 2016 corresponds to the test set of 2015 for which we present the best two systems.

Concerning LOD features, we note that they improve considerably the performance of the system showing how rich contextual features can compensate for the lack of context. Finally, considering normalization, we observe an increase in both the development test set F-scores. Nevertheless, one should be careful as in some cases normalization may change semantics in the text and thus deteriorate the performance.

System	dev 2016			test		
	P	R	F	P	R	F
Talos	63.64	51.89	57.17	58.51	38.12	46.16
Talos_no_LOD	62.90	44.63	52.21	54.32	36.37	43.57
Talos_no_norm	63.55	51.44	56.86	58.19	37.83	45.86
1st-2016	-	-	-	60.77	46.07	52.41
3rd-2016	-	-	-	51.70	39.48	44.77
Ousia	57.66	55.22	56.41	-	-	-
NLANGP	63.62	43.12	51.40	-	-	-

Table 4: Results for the no-entity task. The development test of 2016 corresponds to the test set of 2015 for which we present the best two systems.

Table 5 presents the results per entity class for Talos. As expected, the system performs well for the person, company and geo-loc classes which are the most populated ones.

Type	Precision	Recall	F
company	64.51	36.88	46.93
facility	60.67	21.34	31.58
geo-loc	71.31	65.65	68.36
movie	20.00	2.94	5.13
musicartist	45.00	4.71	8.53
other	50.94	18.49	27.14
person	46.12	59.13	51.82
product	33.33	6.91	11.45
sportsteam	42.42	28.57	34.15
tvshow	0.00	0.00	0.00

Table 5: Results per entity type for Talos.

4 Conclusion

We presented in this work our participation in the "2nd Named Entity Recognition for Twitter" shared task. The task has been cast as a sequence labeling one and we employed a learning to search approach in order to tackle it. We also leveraged LOD for extracting rich contextual features for the named-entities. Our submission achieved F-scores of 46.16 and 60.24 for the classification and the segmentation tasks and ranked 2nd and 3rd respectively. The post-analysis showed that LOD features improved substantially the performance of our system as they counter-balance the lack of context in tweets.

The shared task gave us the opportunity to test the performance of NER systems in short and noisy textual data. The results of the participated systems shows that the task is far to be considered as a solved one and methods with stellar performance in normal texts need to be revised.

5   Acknowledgments

We would like to thank the organizers of the shared-task for their time and effort that they allocated in order to provide a standard benchmark. This work has been supported by the SOMA Eurostars program 9292/12/19892.

References

Timothy Baldwin, Young-Bum Kim, Marie Catherine De Marneffe, Alan Ritter, Bo Han, and Wei Xu. 2015. Shared tasks of the 2015 workshop on noisy user-generated text: Twitter lexical normalization and named entity recognition. In *Association for Computational Linguistics (ACL)*. ACL Association for Computational Linguistics, August.

Peter F. Brown, Peter V. deSouza, Robert L. Mercer, Vincent J. Della Pietra, and Jenifer C. Lai. 1992. Class-based n-gram models of natural language. *Computational Linguistics*, 18:467–479.

Kai-Wei Chang, He He, Hal Daumé III, and John Langford. 2015. Learning to search for dependencies. *CoRR*, abs/1503.05615.

Colin Cherry, Hongyu Guo, and Chengbi Dai. 2015. Nrc: Infused phrase vectors for named entity recognition in twitter. In *Proceedings of the Workshop on Noisy User-generated Text*, pages 54–60, Beijing, China, July. Association for Computational Linguistics.

Hal Daumé III, John Langford, and Stéphane Ross. 2014. Efficient programmable learning to search. *CoRR*, abs/1406.1837.

Leon Derczynski, Diana Maynard, Giuseppe Rizzo, Marieke van Erp, Genevieve Gorrell, Raphal Troncy, Johann Petrak, and Kalina Bontcheva. 2015. Analysis of named entity recognition and linking for tweets. *Information Processing & Management*, 51(2):32 – 49.

Christopher D. Manning Yoram Singer Kristina Toutanova, Dan Klein. 2003. Feature-rich part-of-speech tagging with a cyclic dependency network. In *In Proceedings of NAACL*.

Percy Liang. 2005. Semi-supervised learning for natural language. In *PhD Thesis, MIT*.

Marco Lui and Timothy Baldwin. 2012. Langid.py: An off-the-shelf language identification tool. In *Proceedings of the ACL 2012 System Demonstrations*, ACL '12, pages 25–30. Association for Computational Linguistics.

Mónica Marrero, Julián Urbano, Sonia Sánchez-Cuadrado, Jorge Morato, and Juan Miguel Gómez-Berbís. 2013. Named entity recognition: fallacies, challenges and opportunities. *Computer Standards & Interfaces*, 35(5):482–489.

Olutobi Owoputi, Chris Dyer, Kevin Gimpel, and Nathan Schneider. 2012. Part-of-speech tagging for twitter: Word clusters and other advances. Technical report, CMU.

Jeffrey Pennington, Richard Socher, and Christopher D. Manning. 2014. Glove: Global vectors for word representation. In *Empirical Methods in Natural Language Processing (EMNLP)*, pages 1532–1543.

Alan Ritter, Sam Clark, Mausam, and Oren Etzioni. 2011. Named entity recognition in tweets: An experimental study. In *Proceedings of the Conference on Empirical Methods in Natural Language Processing*, EMNLP '11, pages 1524–1534.

Zhiqiang Toh, Bin Chen, and Jian Su. 2015. Improving twitter named entity recognition using word representations. In *Proceedings of the Workshop on Noisy User-generated Text*, pages 141–145, Beijing, China, July. Association for Computational Linguistics.

Ikuya Yamada, Hideaki Takeda, and Yoshiyasu Takefuji. 2015. Enhancing named entity recognition in twitter messages using entity linking. In *Proceedings of the Workshop on Noisy User-generated Text*, pages 136–140, Beijing, China, July. Association for Computational Linguistics.

DeepNNNER: Applying BLSTM-CNNs and Extended Lexicons to Named Entity Recognition in Tweets

Fabrice Dugas
École Polytechnique de Montréal
faberice.dugas@gmail.com

Eric Nichols
Honda Research Institute Japan Co.,Ltd.
e.nichols@jp.honda-ri.com

Abstract

In this paper, we describe the DeepNNNER entry to The 2nd Workshop on Noisy User-generated Text (WNUT) Shared Task #2: Named Entity Recognition in Twitter. Our shared task submission adopts the bidirectional LSTM-CNN model of Chiu and Nichols (2016), as it has been shown to perform well on both newswire and Web texts. It uses word embeddings trained on large-scale Web text collections together with text normalization to cope with the diversity in Web texts, and lexicons for target named entity classes constructed from publicly-available sources. Extended evaluation comparing the effectiveness of various word embeddings, text normalization, and lexicon settings shows that our system achieves a maximum F1-score of 47.24, performance surpassing that of the shared task's second-ranked system.

1 Introduction

Named entity recognition (NER) is an important part of natural language processing. It is a challenging task that requires robust recognition to detect common entities over a large variety of expressions and vocabularies. These problems are intensified when targeting Web texts because of challenges such as differences in spelling and punctuation conventions, neologisms, and Web markup (Baldwin et al., 2015).

Traditional approaches to NER on newswire texts has been dominated by machine learning methods that rely heavily on manual feature engineering and external knowledge sources (Ratinov and Roth, 2009; Lin and Wu, 2009; Passos et al., 2014). Recently, neural network models – especially those that use recursive models – have shown that state of the art performance can be achieved with little feature engineering (Collobert et al., 2011; Santos et al., 2015; Chiu and Nichols, 2016). However, despite their popularity for NER on newswire texts, neural networks have not been widely adopted for NER on Web texts, with the exception of the feed-forward neural network (FFNN) model of Godin et al. (2015).

In this paper, we present the DeepNNNER entry to the WNUT 2016 Shared Task #2: Named Entity Recognition in Twitter. Our shared task submission is based on the model of Chiu and Nichols (2016), a hybrid model of bidirectional long short-term memory (BLSTM) networks and convolutional neural networks (CNN) that automatically learns both character- and word-level features, and which holds the current state-of-the-art on both newswire texts (CoNLL 2003) and diverse corpora including Web texts (OntoNotes 5.0). In contrast to CRFs, FFNNs, and other windowed models, the BLSTM gives our model effectively infinite context on both sides of a word during sequential labeling. The character-level CNN allows our model to learn relevant features from the orthography of words, which is important in task where unseen words are commonplace. Finally, it also encodes partial lexicon matches in neural networks, allowing it to make effective use of lexical knowledge.

Our primary contribution is adapting the model of Chiu and Nichols (2016) to Twitter data by developing a text normalization method to effectively apply word embeddings to large vocabulary Web texts and automatically constructing lexicons for the shared task's target NE classes from publicly-available sources. The rest of our paper is organized as follows. In Section 2, we describe the adaptations made to Chiu and Nichols (2016)'s model. In Section 3, we describe the evaluation methodology. In Section 4, we discuss the results and present an error analysis. In Section 5, we summarize related research. Finally, in Section 6, we give concluding remarks.

Proceedings of the 2nd Workshop on Noisy User-generated Text,
pages 178–187, Osaka, Japan, December 11 2016.

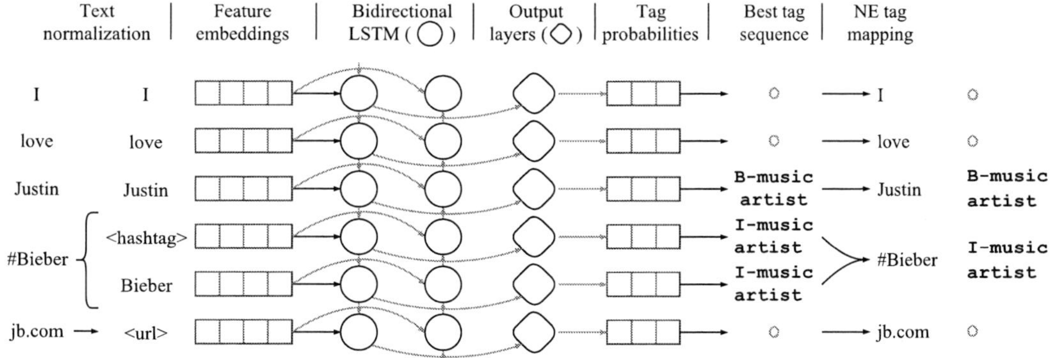

Figure 1: Our proposed system architecture for NER. Feature embeddings are constructed following Section 2.1. The output from both the forward and the backward LSTM are fed through a linear and a log-softmax layer before being added together (shown as "Output layers") to produce the tag scores.

2 Model

In this section, we describe the architecture of our shared task submission. An overview is given Figure 1. Our system is based on the BLSTM-CNN model of Chiu and Nichols (2016), and, unless otherwise noted, follows their training and tagging methodology, which the reader is referred to for more details.

2.1 Features

Feature embeddings for words are constructed by concatenating together the features listed here.

2.1.1 Word Embeddings

Word embeddings are critical for high-performance neural networks in NLP tasks (Turian et al., 2010). In this paper, we compare six publicly available pre-trained word embeddings. The embeddings are described in detail in Table 3. The neural embeddings of Collobert et al. (2011) were chosen because Chiu and Nichols (2016) reported them to be the highest performing on both CoNLL-2003 and OntoNotes 5.0 datasets. To evaluate embeddings trained on data closer to the WNUT dataset, we also selected the GloVe embeddings of Pennington et al. (2014), trained on both Web text and tweets, and word2vec embeddings trained on Google News data (Mikolov et al., 2013) and on tweets (Godin et al., 2015).

Preliminary evaluation on the Dev1 data showed that GloVe 27B outperformed Collobert's embeddings (see Table 5) and word2vec 3B, so they were used in our submission. Following Collobert et al. (2011), we use lookup tables to extract embeddings and every word is lower cased before lookup.

2.1.2 CNN-extracted Character Features

Following Chiu and Nichols (2016), we use a CNN to extract features from 25 dim. character embeddings randomly-initialized from a uniform distribution between -0.5 and 0.5. To accommodate text normalization, we added embeddings for the normalization symbols described in Section 2.2, namely `<url>`, `<user>`, `<smile>`, `<lolface>`, `<sadface>`, `<neutralface>`, `<heart>`, `<number>` and `<hashtag>`. All experiments were conducted with the same character embeddings.

2.1.3 Lexicon Features

Prior knowledge in the form of lexicons (also known as "gazetteers") has been shown to be essential to NER (Ratinov and Roth, 2009; Passos et al., 2014). This section describes how the lexicons employed by our system were constructed. We designed the lexicon categories to be as close as possible to the shared task NE classes by extracting corresponding descendants from the DBpedia ontology (Auer et al., 2007). The lexicon used by our system contains 2.2 million entries over 9 different categories, as shown in Table 1. While most of the lexicons were extracted using only one descendant from the ontology, `Misc`, `Music`, and `Product` were constructed using multiple classes.

Text	Steve	King	on	ObamaCare	and	Constitution	Day
Company	–	–	–	–	–	–	–
Location	–	S	–	–	–	–	–
Misc	–	–	–	–	–	B	E
Movie	–	–	–	–	–	–	–
Music	–	–	–	–	–	–	–
Person	B	E	–	–	–	–	–
Product	–	–	–	–	–	–	–
SportsTeam	–	–	–	–	–	–	–
TVShow	–	–	–	–	–	–	–
WNUT Gold	B-person	E-person	O	O	O	B-other	E-other

Figure 2: Example of lexicon partial matching. The BIE tags indicate whether the token matched the beginning, inside or end of a lexical entry, and the S tag indicate an exact match with a single entry.

Category	Entries	DBpedia Classes
Company	57,856	Company
Location	710,704	Place
Misc	132,055	Work + Event - Movie - TVShow
Movie	87,234	Movie
Music	74,816	Band + MusicalArtist
Person	1,074,384	Person
Product	37,820	Device + WNUT:Product
SportsTeam	28,155	SportsTeam
TVShow	29,272	TelevisionShow
Total	2,232,295	

Table 1: Number of entries for each lexical category and their corresponding DBpedia classes.

Hyper-parameter	Final	Range
Convolution width	5	$[3, 9]$
CNN output size	51	$[15, 85]$
LSTM state size	200	$[100, 525]$
LSTM layers	1	$[1, 5]$
Learning rate	0.0138	$[10^{-3}, 10^{-1.8}]$
Epochs	50	-
Dropout	0.56	$[0.25, 0.75]$
Mini-batch size	9	-

Table 2: Hyper-parameter search space and final values used for all experiments.

First, in order to match entries such as festivals, holidays, songs, and more from the other class, we constructed the Misc lexicon from Event and Work types in the DBpedia ontology excluding Movie and TelevisionShow to avoid overlap with other classes. Second, in order to deal with inconsistencies between person and musicartist classes as discussed in Section 3, the Music lexicon is a combination of the subtypes Band and MusicalArtist[1]. Finally, in order to maximize coverage, the Product lexicon is a combination of the subtype Device from the DBpedia ontology and the lexicon *product* distributed with WNUT dataset. Every other category is as described in Table 1.

To generate lexicon features, we apply the partial matching algorithm of Chiu and Nichols (2016) to the input text, as shown in Figure 2. Each lexicon and match type (BIOES) is associated with a randomly-initialized 5 dim. embedding. The embeddings for all lexicons are concatenated together to produce the lexicon feature for each word in the input. To facilitate matching, all entries were stripped of parentheses and tokenized with the Penn Treebank tokenization script.

2.1.4 Capitalization Feature

Following Chiu and Nichols (2016), we used different symbols for word-level capitalization feature each assigned a randomly initialized embedding: allCaps, upperInitial, lowercase, mixedCaps and noinfo. Similar symbols were used for character-level (upper case, lower case, punctuation, other).

2.2 Text Normalization

In order to maximize word embedding lookup coverage, we modify the publicly available GloVe preprocessing script[2] to normalize irregular spelling and replace special symbols with special embeddings: <url>, <user>, <smile>, <lolface>, <sadface>, <neutralface>, <heart>, <number> and <hashtag>. Repeated punctuation is also removed.

When processing hashtags, the hashtag body is split on capital letters, distributing the NE tag across the resulting tokens. This helps increase word embedding coverage. Refer to Figure 1 for an example.

---

[1]Because MusicalArtist is a subtype of Person, both lexicons overlap, but experiments showed that the system still performed better when MusicalArtist was in both lexicons.

[2]http://nlp.stanford.edu/projects/glove/preprocess-twitter.rb

Word Embeddings	Data (Size)	Dims.	Vocab.	Types		Tokens	
				-	+norm.	-	+norm
Collobert	RCV1 + Wikipedia (850M words)	50	130K	51.43%	75.31%	84.63%	82.18%
GloVe 6B	Gigaword5 + Wikipedia (6B words)	50	400k	54.22%	82.71%	86.02%	84.17%
GloVe 27B	Twitter microposts (27B words)	50	1.2M	57.47%	90.47%	83.67%	**97.66%**
GloVe 42B	Common Crawl (42B words)	300	1.9M	62.14%	90.86%	**89.09%**	86.21%
word2vec 3B	Google News (3B words)	300	3M	55.65%	86.00%	74.95%	72.62%
word2vec 400MT	Twitter microposts (400M *tweets*)	400	3M	**63.36%**	**91.08%**	87.23%	85.79%

Table 3: A comparison of word embedding type and token coverage with and without text normalization.

Additionally, we attempted to correct the most obvious spelling irregularities where letters in a word are repeated more than twice, consulting a dictionary to decide wether to keep one or two occurrences of that repeated letter. When consulting the dictionary, we prioritized shorter matches when the repeated letter appeared at the end of the word and longer matches otherwise.

For evaluation of the final system, we mapped the NE tags onto the original test data tokens, as shown in Figure 1. Because of the tokenization, some of the original entries could end up with more than one tag. In this case, we prioritize entity over non-entity tags, and keep the most frequent tag. Prioritizing entity over non-entity tags was meant to improve recall, albeit at the expense of precision.

Initial experiments on Dev1 comparing word2vec 3B, Collobert, and GloVe 27B embeddings showed that text normalization improved performance for word2vec 3B and GloVe 27B but not Collobert[3] (Table 5); that word type coverage increased drastically for all embeddings; and that while word token coverage greatly increased for GloVe 27B, it slightly decreased for other embeddings (see Table 4). We thus selected GloVe 27B embeddings for our submission due to their superior performance and coverage.

2.3 Training and Inference

We follow the training and inference methodology of Chiu and Nichols (2016), training our neural network to maximize the sentence-level log-likelihood from Collobert et al. (2011). Training is done by mini-batch SGD with a fixed learning rate, and we apply dropout (Pham et al., 2014) to the output nodes. All feature representations are "unfrozen" and allowed to be updated by the training algorithm.

We used the IOB tag scheme to annotate named entities. We also explored the BIOES tag scheme[4], as it was reported to outperform IOB (Ratinov and Roth, 2009), however, IOB outperformed BIOES in preliminary experiments. We suspect that data sparsity prevented the model from learning meaningful representations for the extra tags. Our shared task submission's model trained in approximately 90 minutes and tags the test set in approximately 20 seconds, with memory usage peaking at 350MB[5].

2.4 Hyper-parameter Optimization

To maximize performance, we perform hyper-parameter optimization using Optunity's implementation of particle swarm (Claesen et al., 2014), as there is some evidence that it is more efficient than random search (Clerc and Kennedy, 2002). The hyper-parameters of our model and final selected values are given in Table 2. We evaluated 800 hyper-parameter settings in total. The search used 5-fold validation to maximize the influence of the entire dataset, as it was small, and we kept the best performing setting.

3   Evaluation

The WNUT 2016 dataset consists of user-generated tweets tagged with 10 types of named entities: `company`, `facility`, `geo-loc`, `movie`, `musicartist`, `other`, `person`, `product`, `sportsteam`, and `tvshow`. Table 4 shows the train, dev and test set data splits. Compared to the well-researched CoNLL-2003 (Tjong Kim Sang and De Meulder, 2003) or the OntoNotes 5.0 dataset (Pradhan et al., 2013), the WNUT dataset contains a lot of spelling irregularities and special symbols. For example, *Christmas* written as *xmas*, *Guys* written as *Gaiiissss*, emoticons such as *":-)"*, *":("*, *"<3"*

---

[3]Neither difference was statistically significant.

[4]BIOES stands for `Begin`, `Inside`, `Outside`, `End`, `Single`, indicating the position of the token in the entity.

[5]Our models were trained on a 2.7 GHz 12-Core Intel Xeon E5 CPU, with a maximum of 4 cores being used at once.

	Train	Dev1	Dev2	Test
Sentences	1,795	599	420	3,850
Tokens	34,899	11,570	6,790	61,908
Entities	1,140	356	272	3,473

Table 4: The WNUT 2016 dataset.

Settings	Dev1		
	Prec.	Recall	F1
Collobert	**56.92**	47.33	51.63 (±2.11)
Collobert + norm	55.80	45.84	50.24 (±1.52)
GloVe 27B	54.89	49.07	51.78 (±1.91)
GloVe 27B + norm	54.41	**49.86**	**51.96** (±1.25)
word2vec 3B	54.21	46.74	50.08 (±2.98)
word2vec 3B + norm	54.94	47.44	50.81 (±2.42)

Table 5: Dev1 preliminary evaluation.

Model	Test			
	Prec.	Recall	F1	Rank*
CambridgeLTL	**60.77**	**46.07**	**52.41**	1
Talos	58.51	38.12	46.16	2
akora	51.70	39.48	44.77	3
NTNU	53.19	32.13	40.06	4
ASU	40.58	37.58	39.02	5
Submitted model	**54.97**	28.16	37.24	6
*Fixed model	52.04	39.63	44.97	3
**Best model	54.02	**42.06**	**47.24**	2

Table 6: F1-scores for our submitted, fixed, and best 10 tag models. *Rank** is the retroactive rank.

Settings	Test		
	Prec.	Recall	F1
Collobert	50.52	38.00	43.37 (±0.47)
+ norm	51.44	38.13	43.73 (±0.66)
+ lex	51.50	39.73	44.82 (±0.79)
+ norm + lex	51.72	40.46	45.39 (±1.15)
GloVe 6B	50.26	38.90	43.84 (±1.08)
+ norm	52.21	38.10	43.96 (±1.19)
+ lex	51.14	38.95	44.19 (±0.63)
+ norm + lex	51.73	38.73	44.24 (±0.44)
GloVe 27B	48.44	38.44	42.86 (±1.06)
+ norm	49.35	39.66	43.92 (±0.99)
+ lex	51.13	39.12	44.31 (±1.14)
*+ norm + lex	52.04	39.63	44.97 (±0.65)
GloVe 42B	51.81	40.87	45.59 (±0.71)
+ norm	52.91	41.60	46.53 (±0.84)
+ lex	52.27	41.50	46.22 (±0.93)
**+ norm + lex	**54.02**	**42.06**	**47.24** (±0.70)
word2vec 3B	51.71	38.56	44.11 (±0.47)
+ norm	53.92	37.82	44.39 (±1.28)
+ lex	51.37	39.01	44.31 (±0.68)
+ norm + lex	52.64	39.53	45.10 (±0.91)
word2vec 400MT	50.62	40.92	45.22 (±0.76)
+ norm	51.95	40.41	45.45 (±0.76)
+ lex	53.23	41.45	46.59 (±0.92)
+ norm + lex	53.87	41.78	47.03 (±0.97)

Table 7: F1-scores with different word embeddings evaluated on test set with final settings.

and so on are commonplace. Such examples illustrate the diversity of the dataset's vocabulary, motivating us to perform text normalization as described in Section 2.2.

Some inconsistencies were found between Dev2 and the other data. The most obvious one is where singers previously tagged as `person` in Train were tagged as `musicartist` in Dev2. This is easily verifiable by comparing tags for the entity *Justin Bieber* in those datasets. These tag inconsistencies make it difficult to learn a robust model for those classes, so we manually retagged all person entities, keeping the most precise tag (i.e. tagging all singers as `musicartist`). We did so by searching for every person entity with Google and used the surrounding context to determine the most precise tag, replacing a total of 82 `person` entities out of 664. Other local inconsistencies were not corrected as not enough evidence was found. In Section 4.3.2 we explore inconsistencies in common tagging errors.

For each experiment, we report the average for precision and recall, and the average and standard deviation for f1-score for 10 successful trials. Minor inconsistencies in reported f1-scores and precision and recall result from those scores being averaged independently. Statistical significance is calculated using the Wilcoxon rank sum test, due to its robustness against small sample sizes with unknown distributions.

4 Results and Discussion

In this section, we (1) compare the performance of different word embeddings, (2) analyze the influence of our lexicon over the performance of our final model, and (3) perform error analysis of various aspects of both our system and the dataset. Table 7 shows the final results for different settings. Following Cherry et al. (2015), we compare our system settings to other shared task entries (Strauss et al., 2016) and present their retroactive ranks. While our submitted system uses GloVe embeddings trained on Twitter (GloVe 27B), we found that GloVe embeddings trained on Common Crawl (GloVe 42B) with text normalization and lexicons was our best performing setting, achieving a retroactive rank of second place.

4.1 Word Embeddings

Table 7 shows that GloVe embeddings trained on Common Crawl (GloVe 42B) outperformed all other embeddings by over 2 f1 points. Comparing Tables 4 and 7, we see that word type coverage is correlated

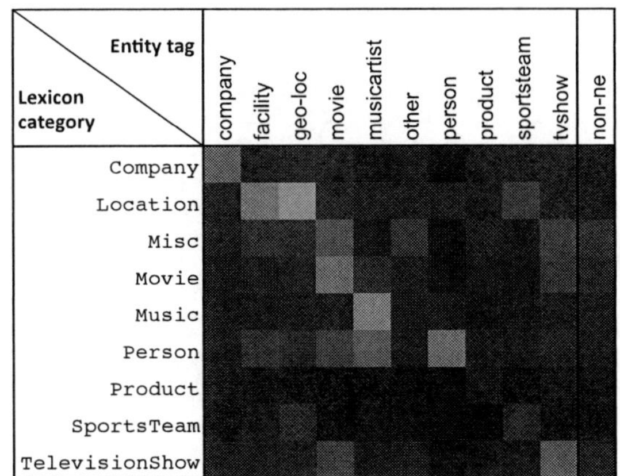

Gold Tag \ Predicted Tag	company	facility	geo-loc	movie	music...	other	person	product	Sports...	tvshow	O
company	328	17	48	2	1	75	25	15	3	0	452
facility	19	234	101	0	5	22	43	22	0	1	194
geo-loc	9	41	770	0	0	12	45	0	8	1	355
movie	1	0	0	5	2	10	1	0	1	4	72
musicartist	0	2	0	0	50	31	112	5	0	0	177
other	39	23	64	3	6	311	31	7	11	6	772
person	4	0	5	1	14	6	606	0	0	0	169
product	13	0	6	5	24	57	28	88	5	0	650
sportsteam	4	3	42	0	2	17	7	0	69	0	96
tvshow	0	4	3	2	0	6	2	1	0	7	64
O	50	34	66	1	19	95	61	40	27	2	32207

Figure 3: Left: fraction of named entities of each class matched by entries in each lexicon category. White = higher fraction. Right: entity-level confusion matrix with outliers highlighted.

with performance for GloVe and word2vec embeddings[6]. Note that word type coverage appears to be more important than token coverage. It could be the case that NEs are more likely to contain low-frequency words, necessitating a large token vocabulary. GloVe 42B's increased performance over GloVe 27B could be explained thus, though it is also possible that its larger, more diverse dataset is responsible.

It is interesting to point out that Collobert was able to outperform embeddings trained on much larger datasets with much larger vocabularies. While all embeddings improved with text normalization, only GloVe 27B and 42B got statistically significant[7] increases.

Finally, in order to save time on training, we reduced the vocabulary of the word embedding lookup table to contain only words from the training data. This allowed us to reduce the network's training time by half and reduce its memory usage by over 90%. However, due to a bug, words outside of the train and dev set vocabulary were treated as unknown, considerably degrading our system's performance. When the vocabulary bug is fixed, our submission setting achieves performance with a retroactive rank of third place. See Table 6 for a comparison to other shared task entries taken from Strauss et al. (2016).

4.2 Lexicon Features

Usage of lexicons greatly improved performance, providing a statistically significant increase in f1-score for Collobert[8], GloVe 27B[9], GloVe 42B[10], and word2vec-400MT[11] embeddings (see Tables 7 and 8).

Figure 3 (left) shows a heat map of lexical coverage. As many of the cells along the diagonal are bright, it shows that we were able to produce lexicons for many categories with high coverage and low ambiguity. However, there are some notable exceptions, such as the `Location` lexicon showing high coverage on both `facility` and `geo-loc`, and both `Music` and `Person` lexicons showing high coverage on `musicartist`. This lexical overlap likely contributes to misclassification errors; the confusion matrix in Figure 3 (right) shows that misclassifications between `facility` and `geo-loc` and `musicartist` and `person` are quite frequent. Some lexical overlap makes sense considering the fact that sports teams will often include city names such as *Montreal Canadiens* or *Philadelphia Eagles*.

Table 8 compares our fixed shared task submission's entity-level f1-scores with and without lexicons. These results show that while many lexicons were effective – particularly `company`, `geo-loc`, and

---

[6] It is surprising that word2vec-400MT underperforms Glove 42B, despite its superior word type coverage, but this could be due to differences in training algorithm, preprocessing (word2vec-400MT used Ritter et al. (2011)'s Twitter NLP Tools), or casing (word2vec-400MT preserved case, while Glove 42B did not). We also evaluated 300 dim. GloVe embeddings trained on 840B words of Common Crawl data with a vocabulary size of 2.2M, however, they underperformed the GloVe 42B embeddings.

[7]Wilcoxon rank sum test, $p < 0.05$.

[8]Wilcoxon rank sum test, $p < 0.005$.

[9]Wilcoxon rank sum test, $p < 0.05$.

[10]Wilcoxon rank sum test, $p < 0.05$.

[11]Wilcoxon rank sum test, $p < 0.01$.

NE	com.	fac.	geo-loc	movie	musicartist	other	person	product	sportsteam	tvshow
− lex	38.94	29.00	61.16	3.43	28.68	26.54	55.75	8.48	35.34	10.77
+ lex	45.74	29.87	64.13	4.18	23.06	27.84	55.01	9.04	35.20	9.76
Δ	+6.80	+0.87	+2.97	+0.75	−5.63	+1.30	−0.74	+0.57	−0.13	−1.01

Table 8: Per-category comparison of our fixed shared task submission settings with and without lexicons.

<table>
<tr><td rowspan="3">(1)</td><td rowspan="3">Don't</td><td rowspan="3">be</td><td rowspan="3">biased</td><td>B-sports</td><td rowspan="3">destroyed</td><td rowspan="3">them</td><td rowspan="3">...</td></tr>
<tr><td>Argentina</td></tr>
<tr><td>B-geo-loc</td></tr>
<tr><td rowspan="3">(2)</td><td>O</td><td>B-sports</td><td>I-sports</td><td rowspan="3">struggle</td><td rowspan="3">to</td><td rowspan="3">beat</td><td rowspan="3">FCS</td><td rowspan="3">...</td></tr>
<tr><td>#SunDevils</td><td>Sun</td><td>Devils</td></tr>
<tr><td>O</td><td>O</td><td>O</td></tr>
<tr><td rowspan="3">(3)</td><td>O</td><td rowspan="3"></td><td>O</td><td rowspan="3">,</td><td>B-company</td><td rowspan="3">...</td></tr>
<tr><td>#Fedex</td><td>#microsoft</td><td>#Twitter</td></tr>
<tr><td>O</td><td>O</td><td>O</td></tr>
</table>

Figure 4: Examples of (1) contextual ambiguity (2) tagging inconsistencies and (3) hashtags inconsistencies. The upper tag is gold annotation. The lower tag is our system's prediction.

`other` – the lexicons `MusicArtist`, `Person`, `SportsTeam`, and `TVShow` were detrimental to NER performance. As noted above, the `MusicArtist` and `Person` lexicons had substantial overlap, most likely contributing to poor performance.

4.3 Error Analysis

In this section, we describe different sources of errors from a subsample of mistagged test set entities.

4.3.1 Unseen Entities

One of the biggest source of errors when trying to tag noisy Web-text is the amount of unseen entities the system will face. In the WNUT dataset, roughly 40% of the entities present in the test set are not in the train or dev datasets. This underscores the importance of high-coverage word embeddings, lexicon construction, and lexical matching, since the tagger has not encountered almost half of the entities.

4.3.2 Contextual Ambiguity

With fine-grained entities such as the ones defined for this task, our system tends to make errors due to confusion between entity classes. Figure 3 shows the confusion matrix when the system is evaluated over the test dataset. One common error occurs between `geo-loc` and other classes, more specifically `company`, `facility` and `sportsteam`. We extracted 50 examples for each type of confusion and found out that place names were mostly being tagged as `geo-loc` even though context indicates otherwise. Figure 4 shows a few examples.

Another important class ambiguity is between `musicartist` and `person`. In a subsample of 64 examples, 49 were tagged as `person`. Furthermore, the entity matched both entity's lexicons in 59% of the cases. This is also supported by the confusion matrix where music artists get tagged as `person` more than twice as often as they get tagged correctly. This contextual ambiguity seems to have led to a few tagging inconsistencies that could also explain lower overall performance. Either from train to test set or within the same set, entities sometimes ended up with multiple tags or no tags at all. Such examples are: singers like *Justin Bieber* being tagged as `person` in the training set and `musicartist` in the test set; devices such as *BlackBerry* being tagged either as `company` or `product`. Some of these inconsistencies are understandable because most of the time more than one tag could fit[12]. Refining lexicons to maximize coverage while minimizing ambiguity remains an essential area of future work.

4.3.3 Hashtags

In tweets, hashtags are omnipresent. They are a way to highlight relevant keywords or phrases making it easier to categorize the tweets they are in. It then becomes important to be able to retrieve important

---

[12]It could also be explained by the fact that the dataset consists of data constructed with different time periods and annotators.

information from those relevant keywords. From the subsample we observed that most entities containing a hashtag were not tagged at all. This can be explained by the fact that only 4% of hashtags are part of entities in the training set making our network biased against tagging hashtags. This likely lead to more errors on the test set where more than 15% of hashtags are part of entities.

5   Related Research

Named entity recognition is a task with a long history, dating back to MUC-7 (Chinchor and Robinson, 1997). In this section, we describe the NER research that influenced our system and give an overview of the work on NER for Twitter. For a more detailed survey, see (Chiu and Nichols, 2016).

Most recent approaches to NER have been characterized by the use of CRF, SVM, and perceptron models, where performance is heavily dependent on feature engineering. Ratinov and Roth (2009) used non-local features, a gazetteer extracted from Wikipedia, and Brown-cluster-like word representations. Lin and Wu (2009) used phrase features obtained by performing k-means clustering over a private database of search engine query logs in place of a lexicon. Passos et al. (2014) proposed a model that infused word embeddings with lexical knowledge. In order to combat the problem of sparse features, Suzuki et al. (2011) performed feature reduction with large-scale unlabelled data.

Recently, the state-of-the-art for NER neural networks have overtaken other approaches to NER. Most approaches build on the pioneering work of Collobert et al. (2011), which showed that word embeddings could be employed in a deep FFNN to achieve near state-of-the-art results on POS tagging, chunking, NER, and SRL. Santos et al. (2015) augmented the architecture of Collobert et al. (2011) with character-level CNNs, reporting improved performance on Spanish and Portuguese NER. Huang et al. (2015) employed BLSTMs in place of FFNNs for the POS-tagging, chunking, and NER tasks, but they employed heavy feature engineering instead of using a CNN to automatically extract character-level features. Lample et al. (2016) proposed LSTM-CRF and Stack-LSTM architectures for NER.

The earliest work on NER for Twitter, used a CRF model with global features from tweet clusters to conduct NER with the MUC-7 4 class task definition (Liu et al., 2011). Ritter et al. (2011) developed a suite of NLP tools explicitly for Twitter and expanded the task to the 10 class definition used in the WNUT shared tasks. A key difference between NER for Twitter and conventional NER is that the former also considers peripheral tasks such as named entity tokenization (Li et al., 2012), normalization (Liu et al., 2012), and linking (Guo et al., 2013; Yamada et al., 2015). The WNUT 2015 Shared Task included text normalization and named entity tokenization and detection tasks (Baldwin et al., 2015), with most systems using machine learning methods like CRF together with a variety of features including lexicons, orthographic features, and distributional information. In contrast with conventional NER, there was only one neural network entry (Godin et al., 2015), and most systems tended to prefer Brown clusters to word embeddings. The state of the art at WNUT 2015 used a cascaded model of entity tokenization, followed by linking to knowledge bases, and, finally, classification with random forests (Yamada et al., 2015).

Our system adopts the architecture of Chiu and Nichols (2016), which combined BLSTMs to maximize context over the tagged word sequence and word-level CNNs to automatically generate character-level features with a partial-matching lexicon to achieve the state-of-the-art for NER on both CoNLL 2003 and OntoNotes datasets. Our system can be viewed as an investigation into how well state-of-the-art neural approaches adapt to the challenges of NER on noisy Web data.

6   Conclusion

In this paper, we described the DeepNNNER entry to the WNUT 2016 Shared Task #2: Named Entity Recognition in Twitter, which adopted the BLSTM-CNN model of Chiu and Nichols (2016). Extensive evaluation showed that high word type coverage for word embeddings is crucial to NER performance, likely due to rare words in entities, and that both text normalization and partial matching on lexicons constructed from DBpedia (Auer et al., 2007) contribute significantly to performance. Our best-performing system uses text normalization, lexicon partial matching, and the GloVe word embeddings of Pennington et al. (2014) trained on 42B words of Common Crawl data, and it achieves a maximum F1-score of 47.24, performance surpassing that of the shared task's second-ranked system.

Acknowledgments

This research was supported by Honda Research Institute Japan Co., Ltd. We would like to thank Jason P.C. Chiu for the initial DeepNNNER implementation, the WNUT organizers for hosting this shared task, our anonymous reviewers for their useful feedback, the DBpedia contributors for the useful source of lexical knowledge, and Pennington et al. (2014) for releasing the GloVe word embeddings.

References

Sören Auer, Christian Bizer, Georgi Kobilarov, Jens Lehmann, Richard Cyganiak, and Zachary Ives. 2007. DBpedia: A nucleus for a web of open data. In *The semantic web*, pages 722–735. Springer.

Timothy Baldwin, Young-Bum Kim, Marie Catherine de Marneffe, Alan Ritter, Bo Han, and Wei Xu. 2015. Shared tasks of the 2015 workshop on noisy user-generated text: Twitter lexical normalization and named entity recognition. In *Proceedings of the Workshop on Noisy User-generated Text (WNUT 2015)*, Beijing, China, July. Association for Computational Linguistics.

Colin Cherry, Hongyu Guo, and Chengbi Dai. 2015. Nrc: Infused phrase vectors for named entity recognition in twitter. In *Proceedings of the Workshop on Noisy User-generated Text (WNUT 2015)*, pages 54–60. Association for Computational Linguistics.

Nancy Chinchor and Patricia Robinson. 1997. Muc-7 named entity task definition. In *Proceedings of the 7th Conference on Message Understanding*, page 29.

Jason Chiu and Eric Nichols. 2016. Named entity recognition with Bidirectional LSTM-CNNs. *Transactions of the Association for Computational Linguistics*, 4:357–370.

Marc Claesen, Jaak Simm, Dusan Popovic, Yves Moreau, and Bart De Moor. 2014. Easy hyperparameter search using Optunity. In *Proceedings of the International Workshop on Technical Computing for Machine Learning and Mathematical Engineering*.

Maurice Clerc and James Kennedy. 2002. The particle swarm-explosion, stability, and convergence in a multidimensional complex space. *Evolutionary Computation, IEEE Transactions on*, 6(1):58–73.

Ronan Collobert, Jason Weston, Léon Bottou, Michael Karlen, Koray Kavukcuoglu, and Pavel Kuksa. 2011. Natural language processing (almost) from scratch. *The Journal of Machine Learning Research*, 12:2493–2537.

Fréderic Godin, Baptist Vandersmissen, Wesley De Neve, and Rik Van de Walle. 2015. Multimedia lab @ acl wnut ner shared task: Named entity recognition for twitter microposts using distributed word representations. In *Proceedings of the Workshop on Noisy User-generated Text (WNUT 2015)*, pages 146–153, Beijing, China, July. Association for Computational Linguistics.

Stephen Guo, Ming-Wei Chang, and Emre Kiciman. 2013. To link or not to link? a study on end-to-end tweet entity linking. In *Proceedings of The 12th Annual Conference of the North American Chapter of the Association for Computational Linguistics*, pages 1020–1030.

Zhiheng Huang, Wei Xu, and Kai Yu. 2015. Bidirectional LSTM-CRF models for sequence tagging. *CoRR*, abs/1508.01991.

Guillaume Lample, Miguel Ballesteros, Sandeep Subramanian, Kazuya Kawakami, and Chris Dyer. 2016. Neural architectures for named entity recognition. In *Proceedings of the 2016 Conference of the North American Chapter of the Association for Computational Linguistics: Human Language Technologies*, pages 260–270, San Diego, California, June. Association for Computational Linguistics.

Chenliang Li, Jianshu Weng, Qi He, Yuxia Yao, Anwitaman Datta, Aixin Sun, and Bu-Sung Lee. 2012. Twiner: named entity recognition in targeted twitter stream. In *Proceedings of the 35th international ACM SIGIR conference on Research and development in information retrieval*, pages 721–730. ACM.

Dekang Lin and Xiaoyun Wu. 2009. Phrase clustering for discriminative learning. In *Proceedings of the Joint Conference of the 47th Annual Meeting of the ACL and the 4th International Joint Conference on Natural Language Processing of the AFNLP*, pages 1030–1038. Association for Computational Linguistics.

Xiaohua Liu, Shaodian Zhang, Furu Wei, and Ming Zhou. 2011. Recognizing named entities in tweets. In *Proceedings of the 49th Annual Meeting of the Association for Computational Linguistics: Human Language Technologies-Volume 1*, pages 359–367. Association for Computational Linguistics.

Xiaohua Liu, Ming Zhou, Furu Wei, Zhongyang Fu, and Xiangyang Zhou. 2012. Joint inference of named entity recognition and normalization for tweets. In *Proceedings of the 50th Annual Meeting of the Association for Computational Linguistics: Long Papers-Volume 1*, pages 526–535. Association for Computational Linguistics.

Tomas Mikolov, Ilya Sutskever, Kai Chen, Greg S Corrado, and Jeff Dean. 2013. Distributed representations of words and phrases and their compositionality. In *Proceedings of the Twenty-seventh Annual Conference on Advances in Neural Information Processing Systems*, pages 3111–3119.

Alexandre Passos, Vineet Kumar, and Andrew McCallum. 2014. Lexicon infused phrase embeddings for named entity resolution. In *Proceedings of the Eighteenth Conference on Computational Natural Language Learning*, pages 78–86. Association for Computational Linguistics.

Jeffrey Pennington, Richard Socher, and Christopher D Manning. 2014. GloVe: Global vectors for word representation. In *Proceedings of the 2014 Conference on Empirical Methods in Natural Language Processing*, pages 1532–1543.

Vu Pham, Théodore Bluche, Christopher Kermorvant, and Jérôme Louradour. 2014. Dropout improves recurrent neural networks for handwriting recognition. In *Proceedings of the 14th International Conference on Frontiers in Handwriting Recognition*, pages 285–290. IEEE.

Sameer Pradhan, Alessandro Moschitti, Nianwen Xue, Hwee Tou Ng, Anders Björkelund, Olga Uryupina, Yuchen Zhang, and Zhi Zhong. 2013. Towards robust linguistic analysis using OntoNotes. In *Proceedings of the Seventeenth Conference on Computational Natural Language Learning*, pages 143–152. Association for Computational Linguistics.

Lev Ratinov and Dan Roth. 2009. Design challenges and misconceptions in named entity recognition. In *Proceedings of the Thirteenth Conference on Computational Natural Language Learning*, pages 147–155. Association for Computational Linguistics.

Alan Ritter, Sam Clark, Oren Etzioni, et al. 2011. Named entity recognition in tweets: an experimental study. In *Proceedings of the Conference on Empirical Methods in Natural Language Processing*, pages 1524–1534. Association for Computational Linguistics.

Cicero Santos, Victor Guimaraes, RJ Niterói, and Rio de Janeiro. 2015. Boosting named entity recognition with neural character embeddings. In *Proceedings of the Fifth Named Entities Workshop*, pages 25–33.

Benjamin Strauss, Bethany E. Toma, Alan Ritter, Marie Catherine de Marneffe, and Wei Xu. 2016. Results of the wnut16 named entity recognition shared task. In *Proceedings of the Workshop on Noisy User-generated Text (WNUT 2016)*.

Jun Suzuki, Hideki Isozaki, and Masaaki Nagata. 2011. Learning condensed feature representations from large unsupervised data sets for supervised learning. In *Proceedings of the 49th Annual Meeting of the Association for Computational Linguistics: Human Language Technologies: Short Papers*, pages 636–641. Association for Computational Linguistics.

Erik F Tjong Kim Sang and Fien De Meulder. 2003. Introduction to the CoNLL-2003 shared task: Language-independent named entity recognition. In *Proceedings of the Seventh Conference on Natural Language Learning at HLT-NAACL 2003*, pages 142–147. Association for Computational Linguistics.

Joseph Turian, Lev Ratinov, and Yoshua Bengio. 2010. Word representations: a simple and general method for semi-supervised learning. In *Proceedings of the 48th Annual Meeting of the Association for Computational Linguistics*, pages 384–394. Association for Computational Linguistics.

Ikuya Yamada, Hideaki Takeda, and Yoshiyasu Takefuji. 2015. Enhancing named entity recognition in twitter messages using entity linking. In *Proceedings of the Workshop on Noisy User-generated Text (WNUT 2015)*, Beijing, China, July. Association for Computational Linguistics.

ASU: An Experimental Study on Applying Deep Learning in Twitter Named Entity Recognition

Michel Naim Gerguis, Cherif Salama, M. Watheq El-Kharashi
Computer & Systems Engineering Department, Ain Shams University, Cairo, 11517, Egypt
`michel.naim.naguib.gerguis@gmail.com,`
`cherif.salama@eng.asu.edu.eg,`
`watheq.elkharashi@eng.asu.edu.eg`

Abstract

This paper describes the ASU system submitted in the COLING W-NUT 2016 Twitter Named Entity Recognition (NER) task. We present an experimental study on applying deep learning to extracting named entities (NEs) from tweets. We built two Long Short-Term Memory (LSTM) models for the task. The first model was built to extract named entities without types while the second model was built to extract and then classify them into 10 fine-grained entity classes. In this effort, we show detailed experimentation results on the effectiveness of word embeddings, brown clusters, part-of-speech (POS) tags, shape features, gazetteers, and local context for the tweet input vector representation to the LSTM model. Also, we present a set of experiments, to better design the network parameters for the Twitter NER task. Our system was ranked the fifth out of ten participants with a final f1-score for the typed classes of 39% and 55% for the non typed ones.

1 Introduction

The social media dominance, especially Twitter, rapidly drives the text processing technologies for more automated understanding. Daily, there are billions of short, noisy, user-generated text fragments that represent and summarize the whole world. Although Natural Language Processing (NLP), in general, is a very challenging task, the importance of automatically processing those huge amounts of big data pushes the technology in dealing with more short and noisy data. The open world of social media, like Twitter, makes it easy for NLP researchers to grasp lots of information to present a holistic view of the world as represented by millions of users. Through NLP research on social media, one can analyze the political polarity of the crowds, identify trending events that attract parts of the world, key people, and hot areas instantaneously, detect emotion storylines and what can lead to or change people's attitudes, identify and collect data in disasters including natural ones to help in risk management, grasp the sentiment against new products or decisions, understand and predict actions based on opinion mining, and many more. Entity extraction is the basic unit in all these NLP tasks whether to be a singer, president, player, movie, song, or any entity of interest. The coarse-grained classes like person, location, and organization are not sufficient for a better representation and understanding of the vibrant world. That is why the fine-grained NERs are of utmost interest.

Our submission in COLING W-NUT 2016 Named Entity Recognition shared task in Twitter, in its second edition, (Strauss et al., 2016; Baldwin et al., 2015) relied on an experimental study on applying deep learning to the task. We experimented with many representations to define the network's input vector. The contribution of word embeddings (WEs), brown clusters (BCs), POS tags, a long list of shape features, vocabulary, and gazetteers was experimentally evaluated in details for the NER task. In addition, a series of experiments were directed to best tune our network design. Two different LSTM models were prepared: One for detecting entities regardless of entity type (non typed) and the other was trained for detecting and classifying the entities (typed).

Proceedings of the 2nd Workshop on Noisy User-generated Text,
pages 188–196, Osaka, Japan, December 11 2016.

The rest of the paper is organized as follows; In Section 2, we present the data sets available for the task and how we used them in ASU system. Section 3, illustrates an overview of our system and the process we followed. In Section 4, we present in details our experimental study in an incremental approach in which we experimented with lots of representations one-by-one and also, with the network parameters. Finally, we conclude in Section 5.

2   Data Sets

In this section, we discuss the distribution and the size of the four released data sets for the Twitter NER task. Also, we brief how those data sets were utilized in training our two models and then in submitting the final results.

Four data sets were released for the task. Table 1 indicates the four sets along with the total number of tweets per set, the total number of tokens, the total number of entity tokens, and the total number of entity tokens per entity class for the 10 classes. It is important to note that some of the entity classes are not well represented in the data sets like the TvShow, the Movie, and the SportsTeam classes. While the provided data set might represent the real world distribution of the entity classes, we believe that for some classes the data is not enough for deep learning.

ASU system relied on the training set plus the additional set for training purpose in the whole experimentation study while testing on the development set as discussed in Section 4. After the system was tuned, we re-trained the models using the whole available data, training, development, and the additional sets. These trained models were applied on the test set to submit our final results.

Data Set	Training Set	Dev. Set	Additional Set	Test Set
Num. Tweets	2394	1000	419	3850
Num. Tokens	46469	16261	6789	61908
Num. Entity Tokens	2462	1128	439	5955
Company Tokens	207	49	64	886
Facility Tokens	209	77	13	619
Geo-Loc Tokens	325	158	62	1101
Movie Tokens	80	30	5	82
MusicArtist Tokens	116	76	22	331
Other Tokens	545	229	91	1140
Person Tokens	664	266	113	782
Product Tokens	177	158	15	746
SportsTeam Tokens	74	83	46	195
TvShow Tokens	65	2	8	73

Table 1: W-NUT 2016 Twitter NER Data Sets Statistics.

3   Method

In this section, we brief the main methodology we followed to build our two models.

We relied on Microsoft's computational network toolkit (CNTK) [1] in building up our two models. We preferred to tackle the task using an LSTM network to benefit from sequence modeling. The network consists of an input layer, some hidden layers, and an output one. The input layer mainly represents the input tweet in a vector of nodes. The hidden layers of our network consist of an embedding layer and some LSTM layers. We initially set the embedding layer to be a 100-nodes layer and an only one hidden LSTM layer of 200-nodes. For the non typed model, the output layer of the network consists of only two nodes, one to detect entities and the other for non entities, while the typed model's output layer is represented by eleven nodes, one for each entity class and the last one for non entities.

For the experimentation procedures we conducted, first we pass the training data through an encoding component in order to convert the raw tweet into a vector which is the input representation of the network. Based on the experiment's feature representation, we produce a mapping function that maps the features into some identifiers. Using the same mapping function, we encode the development set. Then, we design the CNTK configuration file for the network by adjusting the input vector size, the output one,

---

[1] https://github.com/Microsoft/CNTK (October 2016)

and the whole network parameters. We then, train the two models and test over both the training set and the development one. Finally, we score our results and decide whether to include this feature in the main flow or discard it. We adopted an incremental approach in which we fix all the parameters and change only one to assess the value of adding/removing it.

4 Experiments and Results

In this section, all experiments we conducted are presented with details in how we built our LSTM models: Basically, we have two models. One for the non typed extractions and the other for the typed ones which work on ten entity classes. Figure 1 illustrates our experimentation efforts for the typed model while Figure 2 summarizes the history of the non typed model. We plot the f1-scores of the overall system on the training and the development sets for both models. Each experiment in the figures is given an integer identifier which will also be used in the following subsections. While we report the progress in the coming subsections, we preserved the best system as the first record in each table for reference. Also, we appended the index for the previous experiment on which we based the new experiment.

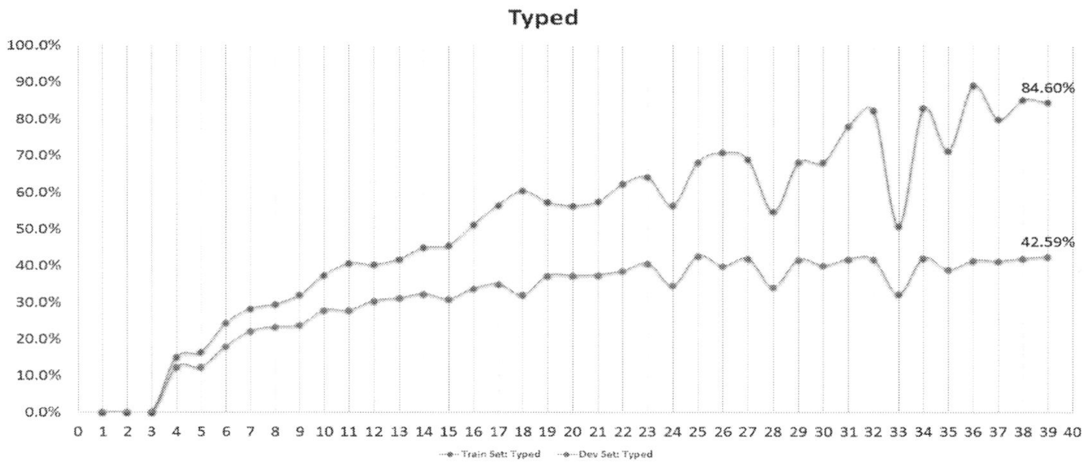

Figure 1: ASU incremental approach f1-scores for Typed LSTM model on Training/Dev. Set.

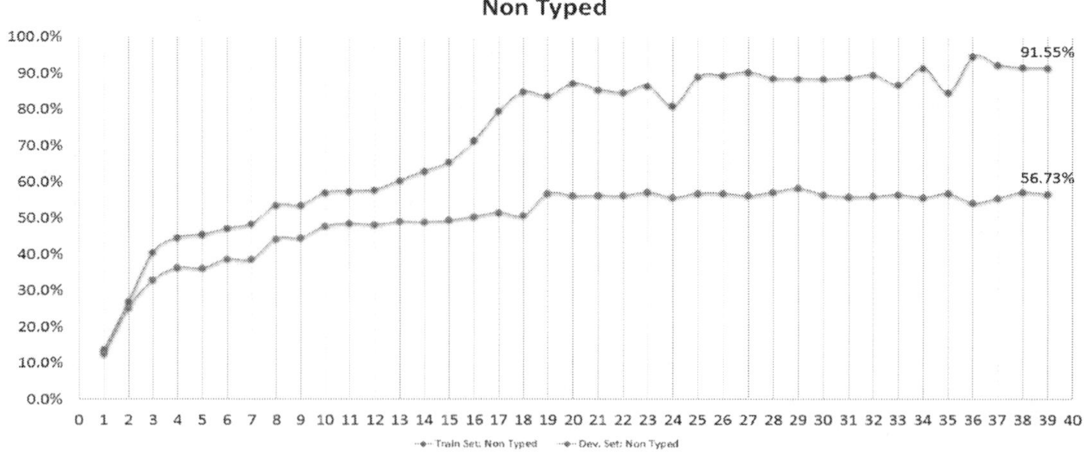

Figure 2: ASU incremental approach f1-scores for Non Typed LSTM model on Training/Dev. Set.

4.1 ASU Incremental Approach

In the coming subsections, we present the input vector evolution for our network and also our experiments in the network design. This study shows how our experimentation incrementally moved the overall f1-score in the typed model from 0% to about 43% in the last one on the development set (Figure 1).

4.1.1 POS Tags

Our experimentation started by deciding which POS tagger to use. We experimented with OpenNLP model (Morton et al., 2005), TweetNLP model (Owoputi et al., 2013; Gimpel et al., 2011), and Ritter's model (Ritter et al., 2011). While TweetNLP relied on a tagset of 25 tags, the two other taggers followed Penn Treebank tagset. We represented each token by its POS tag, just the current token. Table 2 reports the f1-scores for each tagger on the training and development sets for the typed model and the non typed one. We decided to use TweetNLP as it showed the best results. We then, experimented with the POS tags for some more context. In experiment 4, we added the POS tags for a window of only one token, the token before and the token after, while in experiment 5, we extended the representation for each token to a context window of two. Minor gains were introduced to claim the saturation so we finalized POS tags representation to be a windows of two.

ID	Experiment Description	Train. Set: Typed	Dev. Set: Typed	Train. Set: Non Typed	Dev. Set: Non Typed
1	POS Tags: OpenNLP	00.00%	00.00%	13.85%	12.80%
2	POS Tags: Ritter	00.0%	00.00%	27.05%	25.42%
3	POS Tags: TweetNLP	00.00%	00.00%	40.67%	33.12%
4	3 + POS Tags: Context (1)	15.11%	12.37%	44.69%	36.39%
5	4 + POS Tags: Context (2)	16.44%	12.42%	46.10%	37.27%

Table 2: POS Tags in ASU for Typed/Non Typed Models on the Training/Dev. Sets.

4.1.2 Brown Clusters

We experimented with the tweets brown clusters [2] (Owoputi et al., 2012) in various binary prefix lengths. We believe that BCs out of twitter data could be of more relevance (Derczynski et al., 2015; Cherry et al., 2015) than other sources like Wikipedia (Yang and Kim, 2015). Table 3 summarizes the f1-scores for each prefix length incrementally. Our experimental study indicates that brown clusters' prefixes of 4, 8, and 10 are the best. Contextual brown clusters for a window of one reported minimal gains.

ID	Experiment Description	Train. Set: Typed	Dev. Set: Typed	Train. Set: Non Typed	Dev. Set: Non Typed
5	4 + POS Tags: Context (2)	16.44%	12.42%	46.10%	37.27%
6	5 + BCs: Len. 4	24.33%	18.07%	47.19%	38.82%
7	6 + BCs: Len. 8	28.32%	22.15%	48.60%	38.73%
8	7 + BCs: Len. 12	29.55%	23.36%	53.71%	44.36%
9	8 + BCs: Len. 6	32.03%	23.88%	53.72%	44.70%
10	9 + BCs: Len. 10	37.44%	27.84%	57.16%	47.90%
11	10 + BCs: Context (1) Len. 4	40.76%	27.84%	57.56%	48.62%
12	11 + BCs: Context (1) Len. 6	40.41%	30.45%	58.96%	48.34%
13	12 + BCs: Context (1) Len. 8	41.90%	31.15%	60.51%	49.19%
14	13 + BCs: Context (1) Len. 10	45.05%	32.32%	63.09%	49.10%
15	14 + BCs: Context (1) Len. 12	45.67%	30.96%	65.59%	49.54%

Table 3: Brown Clusters in ASU for Typed/Non Typed Models on the Training/Dev. Sets.

---

[2]http://www.cs.cmu.edu/ ark/TweetNLP/ (October 2016)

4.1.3 Word Embeddings

ASU system utilizes Google's word embeddings models Word2Vec[3] which are based on 300 dimensional vectors (Mikolov et al., 2013). We believe that generating embeddings out of tweets would boost the results (Toh et al., 2015). In experiment 16, 300 nodes of WEs were added to the input representation. Context window of one and two were also tested in experiments 17 and 18 respectively. Enhancements in the results on the training set were noticed when we added the context window of two, while regressions on the development set which we classified as a sort of over-fitting so we discard it. Table 4 summarizes the three WEs experiments in ASU.

ID	Experiment Description	Train. Set: Typed	Dev. Set: Typed	Train. Set: Non Typed	Dev. Set: Non Typed
15	14 + BCs: Context (1) Len. 12	45.67%	30.96%	65.59%	49.54%
16	15 + WEs: 300 Dim	51.33%	33.78%	71.42%	50.61%
17	16 + WEs: Context (1)	56.65%	34.98%	79.55%	51.72%
18	17 + WEs: Context (2)	60.48%	32.02%	84.84%	50.86%

Table 4: Word Embeddings in ASU for Typed/Non Typed Models on the Training/Dev. Sets.

4.1.4 Shape Features

So far, the token itself is not represented in the input vector. A list of shape features was collected from previous efforts (Akhtar et al., 2015; Toh et al., 2015) and then extended to reach the following set of 11 features:

1. StartsWithUpper, whether the token starts with an upper letter.

2. StartOfTweet, whether the token is the first one in the tweet.

3. AllUpper, whether the token is all capitalized.

4. TweetAllUpper, whether the tweet is all capitalized.

5. ContainsUpper, whether the token contains a capital letter other than the first one.

6. IsAplhaNumeric, whether the token contains numbers and letters.

7. AllDigit, whether the token is a digit or a decimal number.

8. AllPunc, whether the token is a punctuation or a symbol.

9. ContainsPunc, whether the token contains a punctuation or a symbol letter.

10. IsHashTag, whether the token is a hashtag, starts with a # marker.

11. IsTag, whether the token is a twitter tag, starts with an @ marker.

Table 5 shows results obtained when the shape features were added. We got some enhancements when we applied the shape features to the token itself while when we appended the shape features for the token before and the token after, creating a context window of size one, regressions were noticed.

ID	Experiment Description	Train. Set: Typed	Dev. Set: Typed	Train. Set: Non Typed	Dev. Set: Non Typed
17	16 + WEs: Context (1)	56.65%	34.98%	79.55%	51.72%
19	17 + Shape	57.40%	37.28%	83.70%	56.89%
20	19 + Shape: Context (1)	56.47%	37.30%	87.24%	56.32%

Table 5: Shape Features in ASU for Typed/Non Typed Models on the Training/Dev. Sets.

---

[3]https://github.com/3Top/word2vec-api (October 2016)

4.1.5 Non Entity Features

We then, started to rely on some dictionaries. Two new nodes were added in the input representation. One to indicate whether the token is a stop word or not and the other to mark being a frequent lower word. We relied on the available dictionaries which lead to a slight regression in the non typed model results. We believe that the top 10K lowered words are not enough so it needs further additions. With simple error analysis, we found lots of tokens not in the lower list like Sunday and club for example. We also, experimented with those two features in a context window of one showing reasonable gain as summarized in Table 6.

ID	Experiment Description	Train. Set: Typed	Dev. Set: Typed	Train. Set: Non Typed	Dev. Set: Non Typed
19	17 + Shape	57.40%	37.28%	83.70%	56.89%
21	19 + IsStop IsLower	57.58%	37.47%	85.50%	56.39%
22	21 + IsStop IsLower: Context (1)	62.35%	38.61%	84.69%	56.36%

Table 6: Non Entity Features in ASU for Typed/Non Typed Models on the Training/Dev. Sets.

4.1.6 Vocabulary Features

To represent the vocabulary of the tokens, we collected a unique list of the tokens in the training data sorted descendingly by frequency of occurrences. A threshold of 3 was used to select the top 1.75K tokens to be represented in the input vector. As Table 7 shows, a good gain could be noticed due to adding the vocabulary information to the input vector representation.

ID	Experiment Description	Train. Set: Typed	Dev. Set: Typed	Train. Set: Non Typed	Dev. Set: Non Typed
22	21 + IsStop IsLower: Context (1)	62.35%	38.61%	84.69%	56.36%
23	22 + Tokens: Freq. GT 3	64.20%	40.68%	86.55%	57.27%

Table 7: Vocabulary in ASU for Typed/Non Typed Models on the Training/Dev. Sets.

4.1.7 Embedding Layer Size

Next, we focused on the network design itself. The defaults used in all previous experiments were a 100-nodes embedding layer followed by a single 200-nodes hidden layer. We tried out various sizes for our embedding layer to find out that a 150-nodes layer added two more f1-score points to our typed system as shown in Table 8.

ID	Experiment Description	Train. Set: Typed	Dev. Set: Typed	Train. Set: Non Typed	Dev. Set: Non Typed
23	22 + Tokens: Freq. GT 3	64.20%	40.68%	86.55%	57.27%
24	23 + EM: 50	56.59%	34.61%	80.92%	55.91%
25	23 + EM: 150	68.28%	42.76%	89.12%	57.02%
26	23 + EM: 200	70.95%	40.03%	89.54%	57.00%
27	23 + EM: 300	69.15%	41.97%	90.37%	56.36%

Table 8: Embedding Layer Size Tuning in ASU for Typed/Non Typed Models on the Training/Dev. Sets.

4.1.8 Hidden Layer Size

As Table 9 illustrates, the default size we used in previous experiments, denoted by id 25, showed the best f1-score for the typed model. The 400-nodes hidden layer increased the ability of our system to score in movie and tvshow classes. Only the scores of those two classes did not improve along with all previous experiments, so we preferred the 400-nodes hidden layer.

ID	Experiment Description	Train. Set: Typed	Dev. Set: Typed	Train. Set: Non Typed	Dev. Set: Non Typed
25	23 + EM: 150	68.28%	42.76%	89.12%	57.02%
28	25 + HL: 1 * 150	54.79%	34.20%	88.67%	57.40%
29	25 + HL: 1 * 250	68.16%	41.74%	88.60%	58.39%
30	25 + HL: 1 * 300	68.26%	40.16%	88.49%	56.66%
31	25 + HL: 1 * 400	78.18%	41.91%	88.81%	56.11%
32	25 + HL: 1 * 500	82.47%	41.78%	89.58%	56.18%

Table 9: Hidden Layer Size Tuning in ASU for Typed/Non Typed Models on the Training/Dev. Sets.

4.1.9   Number of Hidden Layers

Another dimension was subject to our experimentation, the number of the hidden layers. The default was just one layer but when we extended to two hidden layers, we experienced a huge loss on the results as Table 10 details. That is why, we stopped investing more time in this direction.

ID	Experiment Description	Train. Set: Typed	Dev. Set: Typed	Train. Set: Non Typed	Dev. Set: Non Typed
31	25 + HL: 1 * 400	78.18%	41.91%	88.81%	56.11%
33	31 + HL: 2 * 400	51.00%	32.18%	86.81%	56.67%

Table 10: Number of Hidden Layers Tuning in ASU for Typed/Non Typed Models on the Training/Dev. Sets.

4.1.10   Number of Epochs

The last parameter, we experimented with, in our network design was the number of epochs. The default was to pass by the data 7.5 times in the learning phase. We tried to study the change when our system doubles the times in passing by the whole data. We also, experimented with some more variants as Table 11 summarizes. We favored the SeeData rate of 10 times for the benefit of the typed system.

ID	Experiment Description	Train. Set: Typed	Dev. Set: Typed	Train. Set: Non Typed	Dev. Set: Non Typed
31	25 + HL: 1 * 400	78.18%	41.91%	88.81%	56.11%
34	31 + SeeData: 10	83.04%	42.16%	91.56%	55.93%
35	31 + SeeData: 5	71.35%	38.94%	84.64%	56.88%
36	31 + SeeData: 15	89.27%	41.55%	94.75%	54.36%

Table 11: Number of Epochs Tuning in ASU for Typed/Non Typed Models on the Training/Dev. Sets.

4.1.11   Gazetteers

Finally, we experimented with gazetteers. To include the gazetteers in our representation, 10 more nodes in the input vector were added, one per entity class. We mapped the 10 entity classes to the supported gazetteers to end up with two classes with no data which were movie and musicartist. Relying on Wikipedia and a fine-grained entity classification platform, we built, we have managed to get a long list of movies and music artists from Wikipedia. To make sure of precise matches, all single token entities were removed if they match one of the top 10K frequent lower tokens. We then, matched the data against the gazetteers starting from the lengthy entities first. Our experimental results, documented in

Table 12, showed that the gazetteers negatively affected the system when applied to the current tokens only, experiment 37. When we used them for the token before and after along with the current token, experiment 38, acceptable enhancements showed up. Our last experiment, experiment 39, preserved the gazetteers features for the context windows of one while bypassing the current tokens to show the best results.

ID	Experiment Description	Train. Set: Typed	Dev. Set: Typed	Train. Set: Non Typed	Dev. Set: Non Typed
34	31 + SeeData: 10	83.04%	42.16%	91.56%	55.93%
37	34 + GAZ: Current	80.06%	41.38%	92.35%	55.76%
38	37 + GAZ: Context (1)	85.41%	42.05%	91.63%	57.33%
39	34 + GAZ: Context (1) No Current	84.60%	42.59%	91.55%	56.73%

Table 12: Gazetteers in ASU for Typed/Non Typed Models on the Training/Dev. Sets..

4.2 Final System

Our final results are reported in details in Table 13. We report our final precision, recall, and f1-score on the training, development, and the testing sets. After we tuned the two models, we appended the training and development sets to act as a new training set for our final model which was used in the final submission as detailed in Section 2.

Type	Training Set			Development Set			Testing Set		
	P	R	F1	P	R	F1	P	R	F1
company	85.44%	86.27%	85.85%	19.75%	41.03%	26.67%	51.18%	31.40%	38.92%
facility	82.73%	81.98%	82.35%	32.50%	34.21%	33.33%	21.82%	18.97%	20.30%
geo-loc	86.51%	91.61%	88.99%	49.32%	62.07%	54.96%	60.60%	61.56%	61.08%
movie	63.16%	64.86%	64.00%	20.00%	20.00%	20.00%	02.78%	02.94%	02.86%
musicartist	64.06%	60.29%	62.12%	22.73%	12.20%	15.87%	12.28%	03.66%	05.65%
other	66.92%	65.44%	66.17%	32.86%	34.85%	33.82%	21.97%	20.21%	21.05%
person	96.56%	96.74%	96.65%	58.51%	64.33%	61.28%	43.45%	64.73%	52.00%
product	83.33%	75.47%	79.21%	09.68%	08.11%	08.82%	12.90%	08.13%	09.98%
sportsteam	88.24%	87.21%	87.72%	55.81%	34.29%	42.48%	30.41%	40.14%	34.60%
tvshow	82.86%	72.50%	77.33%	11.11%	50.00%	18.18%	09.09%	06.06%	07.27%
Overall	84.69%	84.50%	84.60%	40.98%	44.33%	42.59%	40.58%	37.58%	39.02%
No Types	92.45%	90.67%	91.55%	54.62%	59.00%	56.73%	57.55%	52.98%	55.17%

Table 13: Results of ASU System on Training, Development, and Testing Set.

5 Conclusion

We presented the ASU system in the COLING W-NUT 2016 Twitter NER task. Our system experimentally shows an incremental approach in designing two LSTM models: One for entity detection and the other for extracting and classifying a set of 10 fine-grained classes. This study presents experimentally the effect of adding/removing many features in the input representation along with an analysis on the network design. We report a 39% f1-score for the typed model on the test set and a 55% for the non typed one bringing ASU to the fifth place out of ten participants.

We believe that word embeddings, if generated out of a corpus of tweets, would greatly benefit our system. Also, the Wikipedia fine-grained entity classification platform showed a great potential in collecting lots of Wikipedia entities based on a small input set of ten examples. Although we did not invest a lot in gazetteers and we only use it for two classes, the Wikipedia platform showed a great potential that it can scale for any fine-grained entity class.

References

Md Shad Akhtar, Utpal Kumar Sikdar, and Asif Ekbal. 2015. *Iitp: Multiobjective differential evolution based twitter named entity recognition.* ACL-IJCNLP.

Timothy Baldwin, Young-Bum Kim, Marie Catherine de Marneffe, Alan Ritter, Bo Han, and Wei Xu. 2015. *Shared tasks of the 2015 workshop on noisy user-generated text: Twitter lexical normalization and named entity recognition.* ACL-IJCNLP.

Colin Cherry, Hongyu Guo, and Chengbi Dai. 2015. *NRC: Infused Phrase Vectors for Named Entity Recognition in Twitter.* ACL-IJCNLP.

Leon Derczynski, Isabelle Augenstein, and Kalina Bontcheva. 2015. *USFD: Twitter NER with Drift Compensation and Linked Data.* ACL-IJCNLP.

Kevin Gimpel, Nathan Schneider, Brendan O'Connor, Dipanjan Das, Daniel Mills, Jacob Eisenstein, Michael Heilman, Dani Yogatama, Jeffrey Flanigan, and Noah A. Smith. 2011. *Part-of-speech tagging for twitter: Annotation, features, and experiments.* Association for Computational Linguistics.

Thomas Morton, Joern Kottmann, Jason Baldridge, and Gann Bierner. 2005. *Opennlp: A java-based nlp toolkit.* https://opennlp.apache.org/.

Tomas Mikolov, Ilya Sutskever, Kai Chen, Greg S. Corrado, and Jeff Dean. 2013. *Distributed representations of words and phrases and their compositionality.* Advances in neural information processing systems.

Olutobi Owoputi, Brendan OConnor, Chris Dyer, Kevin Gimpel, and Nathan Schneider. 2012. *Part-of-speech tagging for Twitter: Word clusters and other advances.* School of Computer Science.

Olutobi Owoputi, Brendan O'Connor, Chris Dyer, Kevin Gimpel, Nathan Schneider, and Noah A. Smith 2013. *Improved part-of-speech tagging for online conversational text with word clusters.* Association for Computational Linguistics.

Alan Ritter, Sam Clark, and Oren Etzioni. 2011. *Named entity recognition in tweets: an experimental study.* Empirical Methods in Natural Language Processing.

Benjamin Strauss, Bethany E. Toma, Alan Ritter, Marie Catherine de Marneffe, and Wei Xu. 2016. *Results of the WNUT16 Named Entity Recognition Shared Task.* Workshop on Noisy User-generated Text (WNUT 2016).

Zhiqiang Toh, Bin Chen, and Jian Su. 2015. *Improving twitter named entity recognition using word representations.* ACL-IJCNLP.

Eun-Suk Yang and Yu-Seop Kim 2015. *Hallym: Named Entity Recognition on Twitter with Induced Word Representation.* ACL-IJCNLP.

UQAM-NTL: Named entity recognition in Twitter messages

Ngoc Tan Le

Computer Science Faculty
UQÀM, Montreal, Canada
`le.ngoc_tan@`
`courrier.uqam.ca`

Fatma Mallek

Computer Science Faculty
UQÀM, Montreal, Canada
`mallek.fatma@`
`courrier.uqam.ca`

Fatiha Sadat

Computer Science Faculty
UQÀM, Montreal, Canada
`sadat.fatiha@`
`uqam.ca`

Abstract

This paper describes our system used in the 2nd Workshop on Noisy User-generated Text (WNUT) shared task for Named Entity Recognition (NER) in Twitter, in conjunction with Coling 2016. Our system is based on supervised machine learning by applying Conditional Random Fields (CRF) to train two classifiers for two different evaluations. The first evaluation aims at predicting the 10 fine-grained types of named entities; while the second evaluation aims at predicting no type of named entities. The experimental results show that our method has significantly improved Twitter NER performance.

Keywords: *Twitter, named entity recognition, machine learning, CRF.*

1 Introduction

Named entity recognition is one of the key information extraction tasks. This concerns the identification of named entities and the classification of named entities such as person, organisation, location, time and event (Nadeau and Sekine, 2007). The existing standard NER systems are usually trained on formal texts, such as the newswire. However, these linguistic tools do not work well on the new and challenging noisy tweet messages because the style of Tweet messages is short (length upto 140 characters) and unstructured. The content is highly noisy, contains many ill-formed words and covers several topics. Sometimes even human annotators do not have enough context to disambiguate the entities reliably (Baldwin et al., 2015).

Our team at UQAM is interested by social media analysis research within the NLP context (Sadat et al, 2014a; Sadat et al, 2014b; Sadat, 2013). Thus, our participation at the 2nd Workshop on Noisy User-generated Text (WNUT) shared task for Named Entity Recognition in Twitter, in conjunction with Coling 2016, is very fruitful. This shared task consists of two separate evaluations aiming at: (1) predicting the 10 fine-grained types of named entities, and (2) predicting the no-type of named entities. For both evaluation, our system is based on supervised machine learning and trained with a sequential labeling algorithm, using Conditional Random Fields (CRF). Our contribution here consists of the proposal about the new features regarding the polysemy count based on an lexicalized semantic network and ontology, such as an encyclopedic dictionary, and the longest n-gram sequence length of each word in a tweet based on a language model about actualities, news and also syntactic features by parsing each tweet.

The present paper is organized as follows: In the section 2, we report the proposed system about the features extraction. The experimentations and the evaluations are presented in the sections 3 and 4 respectively. Finally, the section 5 summarizes our work and gives future perspective.

2 Features extraction

In this section, we describe a variety of features that are used during the modelling of our NER system for tweets. Our model is composed of the following features: *(1) orthographic, (2) lexical and (3)*

Proceedings of the 2nd Workshop on Noisy User-generated Text,
pages 197–202, Osaka, Japan, December 11 2016.

syntactic features as well as (4) POS (part-of-speech) tags, (5) polysemy count and (6) longest n-gram length.

(1) The **orthographic features** templates are as follows:

- **Affixes:** The suffixes of the current word are extracted with length upto 4 characters from its last character. The prefixes of the current word are extracted with length upto 4 characters from its firts character.
- **Capitalization:** There are three patterns for the current word and two other patterns for the previous word and the next word.
- **Punctuation** and **Digit:** There are six patterns in order to check whether the current word, the previous word and the next word contain punctuation marks and/or numbers.

(2) The **lexical features** consist of the number of occurrences of a word in the sentence, the number of occurrences of the lemma of a word in the sentence and the word in lowercase format.

(3) The **syntactic features** consist of the constituent labels and the distance of a word to root. The word's constituent label (*Constituent Label*) and its depth in the constituent tree (*Distance to Root*) are extracted using a syntactic parser. We used Berkerley parser (Petrov and Klein, 2007).

(4) The **POS tags features** in the task of NE recognition contain many useful information for classifying and predicting named entities. In this work, we use a POS tagger, named TwitIE (Bontcheva et al., 2013), providing the output in the same format given by the organizers. Predicted tags are used as features as follows:

- **POS tags:** The search space windows is 4. There are a combination of patterns with the current word, the two previous words and the two next words and their corresponding POS tags: (w_{-2}, p_{-2}), (w_{-1}, p_{-1}), (w_0, p_0), (w_{+1}, p_{+1}), (w_{+2}, p_{+2}).

(5) The **polysemy count**: We extract the polysemy count, which is the number of meanings of a word in a given language. The BabelNet (Navigli et al., 2012) API is used to extract this feature.

(6) The **longest n-gram length**: We seek to get the length $(n + 1)$ of the longest left sequence (w_{i-n}) concerned by the current word (w_i) and known by the language model (LM) concerned. For example, if the longest left sequence w_{i-2}, w_{i-1}, w_i appears in the longest n-gram value for w_i will be 3. This value ranges from 0 to the max order of the LM concerned (Servan et al., 2015). We used a language model from WMT-2016[1]:

n-gram	#tokens
1	167 333
2	3 330 169
3	5 129 254

Table 1. Statistics of the n-gram of the language model from WMT-2016

These features were chosen because of their relevance in several NLP tasks such as POS tagging, chunk tagging and NE recognition, following the WNUT 2015 workshop[2]. The features for the tokens, in the patterns, were based on uni-grams, bi-grams, tri-grams and within a context window of size 3 (previous token, current token, next token).

3 Experimental setup

3.1 Preparation of corpus

Our model is trained with the data provided by the 2nd shared task workshop organizers.

---

[1] Language model from WMT-2016: http://www.quest.dcs.shef.ac.uk/quest_files_16/lm.tok.en.tar.gz
[2] WNUT 2015 workshop: http://noisy-text.github.io/2015/

Dataset	#tweets	#tokens
train_2016 (= train_2015 + dev_2015)	2 394	37 619
dev_2016 (= test_2015)	1 000	16 429
new_dev_2016	420	14 400
test_2016	3 856	48 782

Table 2. Statistics of the corpora provided by the 2nd shared task at WNUT-2016

There are 2 datasets corresponding to two seperate evaluations: one where the task is to predict fine-grained types and the other in which no type information is to be predicted. The training data consists of the *train_2015* and *dev_2015* data. The first dataset is annotated with 10 fine-grained NER categories such as person, geo-location, company, facility, product, music artist, movie, sports team, tv show and other. The second dataset is annotated without any type information, just only with B, I, O tags.

The training corpus consists of 2 394 tweets while the development corpora consist of 420 tweets. The testing data consists of 3 856 tweets (see Table 2). A total of 3 590 NEs are manually annotated in the corpora with 1 128 NEs in the training data and 2 462 NEs in the development data respectively (see Table 3).

NE category	Training data	Development data
person	266	664
geo-location	158	325
company	49	207
facility	77	209
product	158	177
music artist	76	116
movie	30	80
sports team	83	74
tv show	2	65
other	229	545
Total	**1 128**	**2 462**

Table 3. Statistics of the 10 fine-grained types of named entities in the training data and the development data provided by the 2nd shared task at WNUT-2016

3.2 Experimentations

In the preprocessing phase, we apply Twitter tokenization, POS tagging on tokenized data with TwitIE[3] (Bontcheva et al., 2013).

Once the final feature extraction has been completed, in the training phase, we make use of Conditional Random Fields (CRF) (Lafferty et al., 2001) as machine learning technique. We use the CRF implementation Wapiti[4], version 1.5.0 toolkit to create our model. The optimization algorithm is *l-bfgs (Limited-memory Broyden-Fletcher-Goldfarb-Shanno)*. During decoding phase, our model classifies, from a test corpus, whether a word should be labelled as named entities. Our model was evaluated on two tasks: (1) to predict 10 fine-grained types of named entities and (2) to predict no type of named entities.

We propose three templates with different features as follows:

---

[3] TwitIE: https://gate.ac.uk/wiki/twitie.html
[4] Wapiti 1.5.0: https://wapiti.limsi.fr

Features	Template 1 (with unigrams)	Template 2 (with bigrams)	Template 3 (with trigrams)
(1) Orthographic features	x	x	x
(2) Lexical features	x	x	x
(3) Syntactic features		x	x
(4) POS tags	x	x	x
(5) Polysemy count			x
(6) Longest n-gram length			x

Table 4. Three CRF templates for the evaluations

The features for the tokens in the templates are in uni-grams (*Template 1*), bi-grams (*Template 2*), tri-grams (*Template 3*) and within a context window of size 3 (previous token, current token, next token) (see Table 4). We combine the *train* data, the *dev* data for training our model.

We use the metrics of precision, recall and weighted harmonic mean of precision and recall (F1) to evaluate the performance of the proposed system in two cases: (1) 10 types of named entities and (2) no-types of named entities.

4   Evaluations

The experiments are performed by training the model on all the features defined in section 2. We have trained, tested and evaluated iteratively the system in order to find out the best fitting feature sets. The results are presented in table 5 with models trained on the combination of training and development data with **2 814** tweets, then tested on the *dev_2015* with **1 000** tweets which are used in the baseline system (see README[5] file of WNUT-2016 workshop).

	10-types			No type		
	P	R	F1	P	R	F1
Baseline (provided by WNUT-2016)	40.34	32.22	**35.83**	54.21	49.62	51.82
Exp1 (template 1)	38.91	23.91	29.62	74.33	59.33	65.99
Exp2 (template 2)	40.36	23.82	29.96	74.33	60.00	66.40
Exp3 (template 3)	36.82	27.36	31.39	76.00	69.00	**72.33**

Table 5. Evaluations with model trained by applying tree templates
with (train, dev, test) = (2 814, 0, 1 000) tweets

We realised that the performance of NER system was improved by applying the second template and the third template versus the first template with **F1 of 65.99%, 66.40%, 72.33%** for no-type of NEs and with **F1 of 29.62%, 29.96%, 31.39%** for 10-types of NEs respectively (see Table 5). We observed that the combination of all features with trigrams (*Template 3*) provided the best performance of NER model with **F1 of 72.33%** for no-type of NEs and with **F1 of 31.39%** for 10-types of NEs. While the experiments 1, 2, 3 give a better performance than the baseline with a gain of **+14.17%, +14.58%, +20.51% of F1**, respectively, in the evaluation of no-type of NEs, the experiments 1, 2, 3 give a performance less than the performance of the baseline, with a loss of **-6.21%, -5.87%, -4.44% of F1,** respectively, in the evaluation of 10-types of NEs.

Table 6 illustrated the effect of each features on the classifier when added to the baseline system which contains only the orthographic features and the POS tags features. We observed that not all features are equally useful in the classification and identification tasks. Some features get more

---

[5] README file of WNUT-2016 workshop: https://www.dropbox.com/s/yaoy7zi9vz71nki/wnut_ner_evaluation.tgz?dl=0

improvement in one context than in another, i.e. the syntactic features (**+1.72%** of F1) versus the lexical features (**+0.45%** of F1) for 10-types of NEs but the syntactic features (**+0.33%** of F1) versus the lexical features (**+1.00%** of F1) for no-types of NEs. And features can vary in effacity depending on the classification paradigm in which they are used. We noticed that each feature had separately a little bit improvement versus the baseline. The overall features get the significant enhancement upto **+5.03%** of F1 for 10-types of NEs and **+8.66%** of F1 for no-types of NEs.

	10-types			No type		
	P	**R**	**F1**	**P**	**R**	**F1**
Baseline : **orthographic + POS tags features**	42.64	22.91	26.36	73.67	57.67	63.67
+ lexical features	40.73	23.73	26.82 *(+0.45)*	74.33	59.33	64.67 *(+1.00)*
+ syntactic features	43.00	24.18	27.64 *(+1.27)*	73.00	58.67	64.00 *(+0.33)*
+ the polysemy count	44.45	23.55	27.18 *(+0.82)*	74.33	58.67	64.33 *(+0.67)*
+ the longest n-gram length	42.18	23.55	26.91 *(+0.55)*	74.33	58.67	64.33 *(+0.67)*
All features	36.82	27.36	**31.39** *(+5.03)*	76.00	69.00	**72.33** *(+8.66)*

Table 6. Effect of each features on the classifier when added to the baseline system with (*train, dev, test*) = (*2 814, 0, 1 000*) tweets

Moreover, we observed that the language model of WMT-2016 was trained on newswire and actualities information. So the data are similar to the contents inside Twitter messages. Indeed, the new feature of polysemy count allows to disambiguate a word by checking the number of meanings of this word in a Twitter message in an encyclopedic dictionary.

This is one reason why we have submitted our model trained with the template 3 for the WNUT-2016 workshop. The results are showed in the table 7. We have performed two experiments with different datasets as follows:
- Experiment 1: *(train, dev, test)* = *(2 814, 0, 3 856)* tweets,
- Experiment 2: *(train, dev, test)* = *(3 534, 280, 3 856)* tweets, where *train* set is composed by *train_2016* (*2 394* tweets), *dev_2016* (*1 000* tweets) and some of *new_dev_2016* (*140* tweets).

We have purposely experimented with different size of the training set and the development set, but the same size of the testing set in order to examine the performance of our model. We observed that the variation of size in the training set and the development set gives an impact on our model performance. We noticed that the model trained in the experiment 2 performed globally better for the both evaluations than the model trained in the experiment 1. The experiment 2 gains **+5.49% of F1** more than the experiment 1 about the evaluation of 10-types of NEs, but slightly **+1.96% of F1** more than the experiment 1 about the evaluation of no-types of NEs. We realised that the larger the size of in the training set and the development set is, the better the performance of our model.

Official evaluation, with our model trained in the experiment 2 (submitted), have shown **F1 of 29.82%** for the 10-types fine grained named entities types and **F1 of 44.30%** for the no-type of named entities, as explained in Table 7.

	10-types			No type		
	P	**R**	**F1**	**P**	**R**	**F1**
Experiment 1	34.73	26.36	29.97	76.33	67.67	71.74
Experiment 2 (submitted)	40.73	23.52	29.82	53.21	37.95	44.30
Experiment 2	40.90	31.30	**35.46**	77.00	70.67	**73.70**

Table 7. Evaluations with model trained with template 3,
Experiment 1: (train, dev, test) = (2 814, 0, 3 856) tweets,
Experiment 2: (train, dev, test) = (3 534, 280, 3 856) tweets

5   Conclusion

In this paper, we have presented our work in WNUT-2016 – The 2nd shared task of named entities recognition in Twitter. We have proposed a set of features which improves the NER system performance. We have considered various combinations of features. Our system shows the official evaluation results of **29.82% (F1)** for the 10 fine-grained types of named entities and **44.30% (F1)** for the no-type of named entities.

Further work will focus on adding more domain-specific features and additional features such as word embeddings, to improve the accuracy of the system. In addition, we would like to investigate neural network architectures such as bidirectional LSTM, that have shown great promise in many NLP tasks, for named entities recognition and co-reference resolution.

Reference

David Nadeau And Satoshi Sekine. 2007. *A Survey of Named Entity Recognition and Classification.* Lingvisticae Investigationes 30 (1):3-26.

Timothy Baldwin, Marie-Catherine de Marneffe, Bo Han, Young-Bum Kim, Alan Ritter and Wei Xu. 2015. *Shared Tasks of the 2015 Workshop on Noisy User-generated Text: Twitter Lexical Normalization and Named Entity Recognition.* Proceedings of the ACL 2015 Workshop on Noisy User-generated Text, Beijing, China, July 31, 2015:126–135.

J. Lafferty, A. McCallum, and F. Pereira. 2001. *Conditional Random Fields: Probabilistic Models for Segmenting and Labeling Sequence Data.* In Proceedings of 18th International Conference on Machine Learning. Morgan Kaufmann, San Francisco, Californie, Etats-Unis d'Amerique, 2001: 282–289.

K. Bontcheva, L. Derczynski, A. Funk, M.A. Greenwood, D. Maynard and N. Aswani. 2013. *TwitIE: An Open-Source Information Extraction Pipeline for Microblog Text.* In Proceedings of the International Conference on Recent Advances in Natural Language Processing, ACL.

R. Navigli and S. P. Ponzetto. 2012. *BabelNet: The Automatic Construction, Evaluation and Application of a Wide-Coverage Multilingual Semantic Network.* Artificial Intelligence, 2012 (193):217–250.

S. Petrov and D. Klein. 2007. *Improved Inference for Unlexicalized Parsing.* in HLT-NAACL, 2007.

Christophe Servan, Ngoc-Tien Le, Ngoc Quang Luong, Benjamin Lecouteux, Laurent Besacier. 2015. *An Open Source Toolkit for Word-level Confidence Estimation in Machine Translation.* The 12th International Workshop on Spoken Language Translation (IWSLT'15), Dec 2015, Da Nang, Vietnam.

Sadat, F., Kazemi, F., Farzindar, A. 2014a. *Automatic identification of arabic language varieties and dialects in social media.* SocialNLP 2014, 22.

Sadat, F., Mallek, F., Sellami, R., Boudabous, M. M., Farzindar, A. 2014b. *Collaboratively constructed linguistic resources for language variants and their exploitation in nlp applications–the case of tunisian arabic and the social media.* In Proceedings of the Workshop on lexical and grammatical resources for language processing, The 25th International Conference on Computational Linguistics, COLING 2014, August 2014, Dublin, Ireland, 102-110.

Sadat Fatiha. 2013. *Arabic social media analysis for the construction and the enrichment of NLP tools.* In Corpus Linguistics 2013. Lancaster University, UK. Jul. 22-26, 2013.

Semi-supervised Named Entity Recognition in noisy-text

Shubhanshu Mishra
School of Information Sciences
University of Illinois at Urbana-Champaign
Champaign, IL – 61820, USA
smishra8@illinois.edu

Jana Diesner
School of Information Sciences
University of Illinois at Urbana-Champaign
Champaign, IL – 61820, USA
jdiesner@illinois.edu

Abstract

Many of the existing Named Entity Recognition (NER) solutions are built based on news corpus data with proper syntax. These solutions might not lead to highly accurate results when being applied to noisy, user generated data, e.g., tweets, which can feature sloppy spelling, concept drift, and limited contextualization of terms and concepts due to length constraints. The models described in this paper are based on linear chain conditional random fields (CRFs), use the BIEOU encoding scheme, and leverage random feature dropout for up-sampling the training data. The considered features include word clusters and pre-trained distributed word representations, updated gazetteer features, and global context predictions. The latter feature allows for ingesting the meaning of new or rare tokens into the system via unsupervised learning and for alleviating the need to learn lexicon based features, which usually tend to be high dimensional. In this paper, we report on the solution [ST] we submitted to the WNUT 2016 NER shared task. We also present an improvement over our original submission [SI], which we built by using semi-supervised learning on labelled training data and pre-trained resourced constructed from unlabelled tweet data. Our ST solution achieved an F1 score of 1.2% higher than the baseline (35.1% F1) for the task of extracting 10 entity types. The SI resulted in an increase of 8.2% in F1 score over the baseline (7.08% over ST). Finally, the SI model's evaluation on the test data achieved a F1 score of 47.3% (~1.15% increase over the 2nd best submitted solution). Our experimental setup and results are available as a standalone twitter NER tool at https://github.com/napsternxg/TwitterNER.

1   Introduction

A common task in information extraction is the identification of named entities from free text, also referred to as Named Entity Recognition (NER) (Sarawagi, 2008). In the machine learning and data mining literature, NER is typically formulated as a sequence prediction problem, where for a given sequence of tokens, an algorithm or model need to predict the correct sequence of labels. Additionally, most of the NER systems are designed or trained based on monolingual newswire corpora, which are written with proper linguistic syntax. However, noisy and user generated text data, which are common on social media, pose several challenges for generic NER systems, such as shorter and multilingual texts, ever evolving word forms and vocabulary, improper grammar, and shortened or incorrectly spelled words. Let us consider a fictional tweet: *"r u guyz goin to c da #coldplay show @madisonsqrgrdn☺?"*. This tweet contains two named entities, namely: "Coldplay", a music band, and "Madison Square Garden, NYC, USA", a geolocation, which references the place at which the band is playing. Many of the terms present in the exemplary tweet would be considered as out of vocabulary (OOV) terms by traditional NER systems. Furthermore, using a large set of such OOV tokens for training a classifier is likely to result in a sparse and high dimensional feature space, thereby increasing computing time. The phenomenon of concept-drift, i.e., the meaning of terms shifting over time, has also been found to affect the accuracy of NER systems over time, resulting in poor performance of a classifier trained on older data (Cherry & Guo, 2015; Derczynski, Maynard, et al., 2015; Fromreide et al., 2014; Hulten et al., 2001; Masud et al., 2010).

Proceedings of the 2nd Workshop on Noisy User-generated Text,
pages 203–212, Osaka, Japan, December 11 2016.

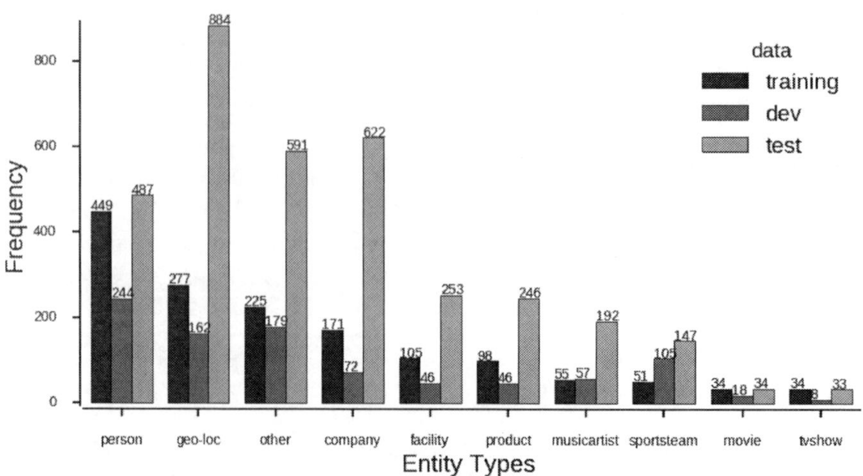

Figure 1: Frequency of named entity types in training, development, and test datasets.

The Workshop on "Noisy User-generated Text" (WNUT) continued its 2015 shared task on NER on tweets (Baldwin et al., 2015) in 2016. In 2016, the task was divided into two parts: (1) identification of named entities in tweets, and (2) NER on 10 types of entities, namely *person, geo-location, other, company, sports-team, facility, product, music-artist, movie, and tv-show.*

In this paper we introduce two solutions to perform NER on tweets. The first system, which we will refer to as the submitted solution [ST], was submitted as an entry to the WNUT 2016 NER shared task. It uses random feature [RF] dropout for up-sampling the dataset. This system was improved into a semi-supervised solution (our 2nd solution [SI]), which uses additional, unsupervised features. These features have been found to be useful in prior information extraction and NER tasks. The semi-supervised approach circumvents the need to include word n-gram features from any tweets, and builds upon the successful usage of word representations (Collobert et al., 2011), and word clusters (Lin & Wu, 2009; Miller et al., 2004; Ratinov & Roth, 2009; Turian et al., 2010) for NER by utilizing large amounts of unlabelled data or models pre-trained on a large vocabulary. The SI system was designed to mitigate the various issues mentioned above, and utilizes the unlabelled tokens from the all the available datasets (including unlabelled test data) to improve the prediction quality on the evaluation datasets, a form of transductive learning (Joachims, 2003). The SI system outperforms ST by ~7% (F1 score) when using the development set for evaluation, and by ~11% when using the test set (1% higher than the 2nd best team in the task). The SI model does not utilize any word n-gram lexical features. We believe that the approach taken for SI is useful for situations that require refinement or adaptation of an existing classifier to perform well on a new test set. We have released our experimental setup and code at https://github.com/napsternxg/TwitterNER.

2 Data

The training, development, and test dataset were provided by the task organizers. The training set consists of 2,394 tweets with a total of 1,499 named entities. The organizers provided two separate development datasets, which we merged to create a dataset of 1,420 tweets with 937 named entities. This merged dataset was used as the development dataset for all of our experiments. The test dataset comprises 3,856 tweets with 3,473 named entities. Most of the tweets in the provided data lack any entities mentions (42% in training, 59% in development, and 47% in test data), resulting in sparse training samples. Furthermore, certain types of entities, such as *movie* and *tvshow,* have only a few instances. The frequency distribution of the different types of named entities in the training, development, and test data are shown in Figure 1. Additionally, we found that the training, development, and test data have an average of 19.4 (±7.6), 16.2 (±6.8), and 16.1 (±6.6) tokens per sequence, respectively, and mostly contain less than 3 entities per tweet. This implies that the presence of certain entity types might be reflective of the category of the tweet, e.g. *movie* entities will be found in tweets about movies, and *sports-team* entities will be found in tweets about sports. Additionally, some types of entities are more likely to co-occur with each other than others. Using the provided data, we found that both *person* and *geo-location* entities were most likely to co-occur with entities of other 8 types, compared to the co-occurrence of the rest of the entities.

Although the original dataset was tagged using the **Begin-Inside-Outside** (BIO) encoding, we converted that into the **Begin-Inside-End-Outside-Unigram** (BIEOU) encoding, which has been found to be more efficient for sequence classification tasks (Ratinov & Roth, 2009). However, the predicted tags were converted back to the BIO encoding to make our submission compatible with the evaluation system.

3 Feature Engineering

We trained our system using multiple combinations of features. Features were chosen with the intent to increase the generalizability and scalability of our classifier. Some of the considered features can be updated with the availability of new unlabelled data, while other features capture the general token patterns in tweets. All features are described in detail in the following subsections.

3.1 Regex features [RF]

Regular expressions are rules describing regularities in data, and are typically empirically derived. For example, in regular English corpora, named entities usually being with capital letters. Although regex based approaches can be effective, they are likely to result in retrieving large amounts of false positives. Most NER systems use token level regex features (Baldwin et al., 2015; Ratinov & Roth, 2009). We extended these regex features by including features which detect syntax patterns of tokens commonly present in tweets. Our patterns return "true" if the regex pattern matches the token. A detailed list of our regex features is described in Table 1. These features were extracted per token, and every pair of the neighbouring tokens' regex features were multiplied to create pairwise features.

isHashtag - Identifies if token is a hashtag	**endsWithDot**- Identifies if token only consists of alphanumeric and ends with a `.`, e.g. *Dr*
isMention - Identifies if token is a user mention	**containsDashes** - Identifies if token only contains dashes
isMoney - Identifies if token represents monetary values	**containsDigits** - Identifies if token only contains digits
isNumber - Identifies if token is a number	**singlePunctuation** - Identifies if token is only single punctuation
isDigits - Identifies if token only consists of digits	**repeatedPunctuation** - Identifies if token only consists of repeated punctuations
isAllCapitalWord - Identifies if token only consists of capital alphabets	**singleDot** - Identifies if token only consists of a single dot
isAllSmallCase - Identifies if token only consists of small alphabets	**singleComma**- Identifies if token only consists of a single comma
isWord - Identifies if token only consists of letters	**fourDigits**- Identifies if token only consists of four digits
isAlphaNumeric - Identifies if token only consists of digits and letters	**singleQuote**- Identifies if token only consists of a single quotation mark
isSingleCapLetter - Identifies if token only consists of single capital letter	
isSpecialCharacter - Identifies if token only consists of special characters such as: #;:-/<>'"()&	

Table 1: List of regex features

3.2 Gazetteers [GZ]

The task organizers provided a set of gazetteer lists. Although being helpful, these lists include some irregularities, such as words composed of or containing non-ascii characters, garbled strings, and missing names of important named entities in many categories. Furthermore, the provided gazetteers did not include names of movies or music artists. We increased the given set of gazetteers by including an additional 41K person names, 63K music artist names, 8K TV show titles, 2K sports team names, and 110K movie titles from WikiData (https://www.wikidata.org), additional 8.3M locations from GeoNames (http://www.geonames.org/), and 4.5M music artist names and their 1.4M name variants from the Discogs' public data dump (http://data.discogs.com/). Improved gazetteer features were also used as features in last year's shared task (Derczynski, Augenstein, et al., 2015). The gazetteer features were implemented on a per token level, where we look up a gazetteer phrase in a range of window sizes W (min=1 and max=6) both left and right of the current token. Additionally, we encode the window size and the identified gazetteer name. Finally, we include interaction terms computed as the product of all pairs of gazetteer features for each token.

3.3   Word representations [WR]

Distributed word representations have been shown to improve the accuracy of NER systems (Collobert et al., 2011; Turian et al., 2010). We used 200 dimensional GloVe word representations [WR_G] (Pennington et al., 2014), which were pre-trained on 6 billion tweets. Furthermore, we built a set of word clusters by performing an agglomerative clustering of word representations [WR_{FTC}] and fine tuning them on the training plus development dataset by running the word2vec model (Mikolov, Chen, et al., 2013; Mikolov, Sutskever, et al., 2013).

3.4   Word clusters [WC]

Word clusters are word groupings that get generated in an unsupervised fashion, and they have been successfully used as features for NER tasks (Lin & Wu, 2009; Miller et al., 2004; Ratinov & Roth, 2009; Turian et al., 2010). One algorithm for creating such sets is Brown clustering (Brown et al., 1992), which produces a hierarchical cluster of words in the corpus while optimizing the likelihood of a language model based on a Hidden Markov Model (HMM). We used pre-trained 1000 brown clusters [WC_{BPT}] that were prepared by using a large corpus of tweets (Gimpel et al., 2011; Owoputi et al., 2013). Additionally, we built another set of brown clusters [WC_{BD}] with a cluster size of 100 based on all of the available data by using the code provided by Liang (2005)[1]. Furthermore, we also used an implementation[2] of the algorithm proposed by Clark (2003) to create 32 (default option) additional word clusters from our training plus development data based on the regex and sequential features of the words. We choose to call these Clark clusters [WC_{CC}]. Additionally, for each token, we also included all word cluster features for their immediate neighbours along with interactive terms; with the latter capturing the product of the token cluster with the neighbouring cluster.

3.5   Additional features

Even though the strength of our system lies in its semi-supervised nature and its non-reliance on data specific features such as lexical tokens [LT], we still included lexical tokens for comparison. Additionally, we used certain global features [GF] for helping with the prediction. Global features capture the overall composition of the sequence. We constructed the GF using the average values of the word representations and the binary presence of cluster and dictionary features. Additionally, another feature was constructed, which approximates the probability of the sequence being of a certain type. This feature adds an additional context to the token level prediction task, e.g. a tweet about sports is more likely to mention a sports team, and similarly, a tweet about a company is more likely to mention a product and vice-versa. To use this global feature, we first trained a Logistic regression classifier to predict if a tweet is about any of each of the 10 types of entities. The predicted probability per type is used as a feature for each of the tokens in the sequence.

3.6   Random up-sampling with feature dropout [RS_{FD}]

Since the training dataset is comparatively small and its features are sparse, we create synthetic examples by dropping interaction and lexical features with probability p. These features were chosen for random dropout because our earlier experiments had shown that the classifier identifies large weights for these features. We further scaled the training data size by a factor of k. This technique is inspired by the success of the dropout technique (Srivastava et al., 2014), which serves as a regularization function for deep neural networks. However, our technique is slightly different in that we use dropout to create a larger number of noisy samples from our data. Also, in contrast to the basic dropout technique, we did not re-weight the feature weights using the dropout probability (Srivastava et al., 2014) during evaluation.

---

[1] https://github.com/percyliang/brown-cluster
[2] https://github.com/ninjin/clark_pos_induction

4   NER classification algorithm

We used a linear chain CRF (Lafferty et al., 2001; McCallum & Li, 2003) as implemented in CRFSuite (Okazaki, 2007) package for training all our models. The models were trained using stochastic gradient decent (SGD) with an L2 norm (C=1e-3). We also tested some of the recently popular deep learning based approaches, such as word embedding based and character based recurrent neural networks, for our prediction task. However, these techniques did not yield competitive results and were too slow to converge on CPU. Furthermore, training the CRF model was faster (average training time of the CRF algorithms was ~3 mins on CPU, compared to >15 minutes for the character/word based 3-layer deep recurrent neural network solution), and gave interpretable results while beating the baseline model provided by the task organizers. In the following sections, we will first describe the model we used in our submission to the shared task, and then our improvement over the initial model and results.

4.1   Shared task submission solution [ST] based on random feature dropout up-sampling

Our original submission to the shared task [ST] was based on a system that uses the lexical, regex, and dictionary based features with random feature dropout based up-sampling. All the interaction terms were randomly dropped out with $p=0.5$, and the scaling factor k was chosen to be 5. The dictionary based features were created using a context window of size 2 to the left and right of the token. Additional interaction features were included by calculating the product of the dictionary features of the token and the neighbouring tokens. Finally, ST was based on a classifier trained only on the training dataset, and was corpus specific in that it used the vocabulary created from the training data.

4.2   Semi-supervised word clusters and representation based solution [SI]

The described lexicon based solution [ST] had one major drawback: The most highly weighted features were mainly tokens descriptive of entity types as occurring in the training data. For example, the highest weighted feature for the label *U-person* was *word_normed:pope*. Similarly, for many of the other entity types, the highest weighted features were the names or labels of popular entities. Although these features help to achieve a decent evaluation score on the development dataset, they can lead to overfitting of the classifier to the vocabulary of the training corpus. In order to circumvent this issue, a semi-supervised (Blum, 1998; Blum & Mitchell, 1998) solution builds on the general recent success of using word representations and word clusters in NER tasks, while disregarding lexical vocabulary based features. The intuition behind our approach to the 2nd solution [SI] was to ensure that the classifier learns higher level representations of the observed tokens. All the features used for our second solution augment the tokens present in the given tweets. This allows us to scale-up the underlying resources, such as gazetteers, and improve word representations and clusters using the new unlabelled test data, while still being able to update the classifier from the initially provided, limited training data. We replicate this behaviour in our classifiers by training our clusters on all of the unlabelled data generated by merging tweet texts from the training, development, and test data (only un-labelled) [TDT$_E$] (Blum & Mitchell, 1998), and comparing the resulting performance to that obtained with unsupervised training that does not consider the test data [TD]. Although it might appear that our classifier has access to the unlabelled test data sequences while learning, it rather is the case that we resemble an online setting where we continuously update our unsupervised features using the new batch of unlabelled test data, and then retrain our model on the original training data (Blum, 1998; Blum & Mitchell, 1998; Carlson et al., 2010; Chapelle et al., 2009; Liang, 2005; Turian et al., 2010; Zhu & Goldberg, 2009). In this case, the unlabelled data prevent the classifier from overfitting to the training data by acting as a regularization factor. An alternative approach would be to train these clusters on a large number of unlabelled tweets that match the time range and search domain of the test tweets.

5   Results

In the following sections, we describe the evaluation of the accuracy of both the ST and SI system in comparison to BL and against each other. All evaluations were done by using the evaluation script provided by the organizers. We use the classifier provided by the organizers as the baseline (BL) system. The baseline system uses lexical, gazetteer, and regex features.

5.1 Performance in WNUT NER shared task

Using BL as a point of comparison, ST scored 1.1% (F1 score) higher for the 10-types task (based on the development set), and 1.2% (F1) lower for the no-types task. Our ST is based on random feature dropout based sampling.

Among the 10 participating teams, our solution placed 7th for the 10-types category with an overall F1 score of 36.95%, and 6th in the no-type category with an overall F1 score of 51.38%. The top team on both tasks (same team in both cases) achieved F1 scores of 52.41% and 65.89%, respectively. Overall, we found that ST performed best on the geo-location type (F1 score of 64.72%), and behind the top two teams (score of 72.61% and 68.36%, respectively) for this category. We placed 3rd in terms of F1 (37%) in the facility category shown Table 2.

Rank	1	2	3	4	5	6	7	8	9	10	TD	TDT_E
10-types overall	52.4	46.2	44.8	40.1	39.0	37.2	**37.0**	36.2	29.8	19.3	**46.4**	**47.3**
No-types	65.9	63.2	60.2	59.1	55.2	51.4	**47.8**	46.7	44.3	40.7	57.3	59.0
company	57.2	46.9	43.8	31.3	38.9	34.5	**25.8**	42.6	24.3	10.2	42.1	46.2
facility	42.4	31.6	36.1	36.5	20.3	30.4	**37.0**	40.5	26.3	26.1	37.5	34.8
geo-loc	72.6	68.4	63.3	61.1	61.1	57.0	**64.7**	60.9	47.4	37.0	70.1	71.0
movie	10.9	5.1	4.6	15.8	2.9	0.0	**4.0**	5.0	0.0	5.4	0.0	0.0
musicartist	9.5	8.5	7.0	17.4	5.7	37.2	**1.8**	0.0	2.8	0.0	7.6	5.8
other	31.7	27.1	29.2	26.3	21.1	22.5	**16.2**	13.0	22.6	8.4	31.7	32.4
person	59.0	51.8	52.8	48.8	52.0	42.6	**40.5**	52.3	34.1	20.6	51.3	52.2
product	20.1	11.5	18.3	3.8	10.0	7.3	**5.7**	15.4	6.3	0.8	10.0	9.3
sportsteam	52.4	34.2	38.5	18.5	34.6	15.9	**9.1**	19.7	11.0	0.0	31.3	32.0
tvshow	5.9	0.0	4.7	5.4	7.3	9.8	**4.8**	0.0	5.1	0.0	5.7	5.7
Rank	1	2	3	4	5	6	**7**	8	9	10	~2	~2

Table 2: Results of the WNUT NER 2016 shared task. Rank denotes the rank of the winning team, which we use as an ID to identify the evaluation performance of each of the participating teams in the shared task. Our solution was ranked 7th (in bold) and (6th not shown) in the 10-types and no-types categories, respectively. Columns with TD and TDT_E show the performance of the improved model on the test data, and their ranks denote the best rank in the competition which they beat.

5.2 Improved model performance [SI]

In this section we describe the evaluation of our improved system SI, which was developed after the release of the shared task results. Since we received the gold standard labels for the test-set late in the process, we evaluated most of the improved models based on the development set. We present the additive effect of a series of features to the model in Table 3. Additionally, that table also shows the performance of ST and BL. We do not include any lexical features in SI, however, lexical features were part of the ST and BL models. We found that the addition of the gazetteer [GZ] features improved the classification accuracy considerably. The next two big jumps in accuracy increase in SI came from using brown clusters [WC_{BTP}] and fine-tuned word representations based clusters [WC_{FTC}]. From all of the improved models that we trained, we selected the 10-types category model with the highest overall F1 score, namely $RF+GZ+WR_G+WC_{BPT}+WC_{CC}+WR_{FTC}$ model, also referred to as SI herein. Only the SI model was also evaluated on the test data with [TDT_E] as well as without [TD], using the test data for enriching the unsupervised features. Although the model with the global features [See +GF in Table 3] is not the top one in terms of the F1 score, it achieved considerably high scores for *movie* and *tvshow* class, which have very few training instances. Similarly, the random dropout up-sampling based solution showed improvements by 15% and 6% F1 score in terms of predicting named entities of the types movie

Additive Features →	RF	+GZ	+WR$_G$	+WC$_{BPT}$	+WC$_{CC}$	+WR$_{FTC}$	+GF	+RS$_{FD}$	ST	BL	TD	TDT$_E$
10-types	5.3	34.8	36.7	41.6	41.0	43.3	40.9	40.0	36.2	35.1	46.4	**47.3**
company	0.0	30.0	34.5	33.3	35.2	33.3	32.0	33.3	27.7	26.2	42.1	**46.2**
facility	0.0	12.4	9.6	20.8	18.6	17.9	14.5	16.7	30.4	19.2	**37.5**	34.8
geo-loc	5.2	47.2	48.1	53.8	54.4	55.9	56.7	56.1	49.7	48.4	70.1	**71.0**
movie	8.0	7.4	6.5	8.3	7.7	9.5	23.5	**28.6**	8.3	0.0	0.0	0.0
musicartist	0.0	6.6	8.5	9.1	9.5	12.7	6.5	**14.7**	0.0	0.0	7.6	5.8
other	5.8	18.6	18.7	22.5	20.9	26.6	22.1	17.7	24.2	27.7	31.7	**32.4**
person	11.4	55.1	58.5	63.4	63.8	64.8	**65.0**	60.2	53.4	50.2	51.3	52.2
product	2.9	12.7	**20.0**	16.7	18.2	15.4	10.8	11.9	9.0	11.9	10.0	9.3
Sportsteam	0.0	12.9	27.9	30.5	29.0	28.1	27.7	25.4	12.8	13.1	31.3	**32.0**
tvshow	0.0	0.0	0.0	16.7	16.7	16.7	**18.2**	13.3	0.0	14.3	5.7	5.7
No-types	13.1	48.3	52.5	56.7	56.4	57.4	53.7	52.9	50.5	51.7	57.3	**59.0**

Table 3: Change in F1 score for the NER classifier on the development dataset on incremental addition of different types of features (from left to right). ST refers to submitted solution, BL refers to baseline solution provided by the organizers. Bolded values are the best scores across classifiers.

and music-artist, respectively. Finally, these models were trained in almost half the time as the ST models.

5.3   Features learned by the model

We extracted the learned features from the top performing model on the 10-types category (the RF+GZ+WR$_G$+WC$_{BPT}$+WC$_{CC}$+WR$_{FTC}$ model). The features with the highest positive and negative weights for each of the category labels are presented in Table 4. The table also shows that for *person*, *product*, *movie*, and *tvshow* the top features were specific dimensions of the pre-trained word embedding. Furthermore, the brown cluster ids of the token word are more informative for the named entities of *geo-location*, *other*, and *company* types, while the brown cluster id of neighbouring tokens is likely to indicate if a named entity is of type *musicartist*, *sportsteam*, or *facility*. Additionally, if the token belongs to a phrase in a gazetteer of music artist names, then it is less likely to be a *geo-loc*, *company*, or *product*.

Type	Most positive weight		Most negative weight	
Entity	feature	w	feature	w
person	WV_90→U	1.27	WV_46→U	-1.02
other	BC_2_:1001000→U	1.28	isAllSmallCase|isAlphaNumeric[+1] →U	-0.88
geo-loc	BC_0:11100110101->U	2.33	DICT=musicartist_names→U	-0.88
facility	BC_2[-1]:1001111110→B	1.63	WV_185->B	-0.68
company	BC_0:111001100001→U	1.30	DICT=musicartist_namevars->U	-0.77
product	WV_199→U	1.07	DICT=musicartist_namevars→U	-0.97
musicartist	BC_2[-1]:11110010→U	1.21	DICT=geonames→U	-0.80
movie	WV_75→B	0.76	isAlphaNumeric[+1] →E	-0.50
sportsteam	BC_0[+1]:1111011010→B	1.29	WV_30→U	-0.86
tvshow	WV_154→U	0.76	isInitCapitalWord|singlePunctuation[+1] →E	-0.40

Table 4: Feature weights (**w**) in the SI model for each of the 10 entity types. WV is word vector; BC is brown cluster. [-/+ num] denotes features for left or right neighbour, respectively. → BIEOU denotes which boundary type for the entity type the feature belongs to.

We also investigated the transition features of the linear chain CRF model. The transition matrix (based on transition weights) is presented in Figure 2, and coloured as red for negative weights and black for positive weights. Some trends become obvious from the transition matrix: For most entity types, the model is able to find high transition weights for going from *B* to *I* to *E*, while penalizing transitions between the other states. The choice of using *BIEOU* tagging is supported by the results shown in the transition matrix since for most entity types, there is a high negative weight for going from the B or I tag to the O tag. However, a transition from the U tag to O tag is usually supported. Our earliest experiments (not reported here) revealed that there was a considerable improvement from using the BIEOU tagging scheme. This finding aligns with the existing research which argues for the usage of this tagging scheme for NER tasks.

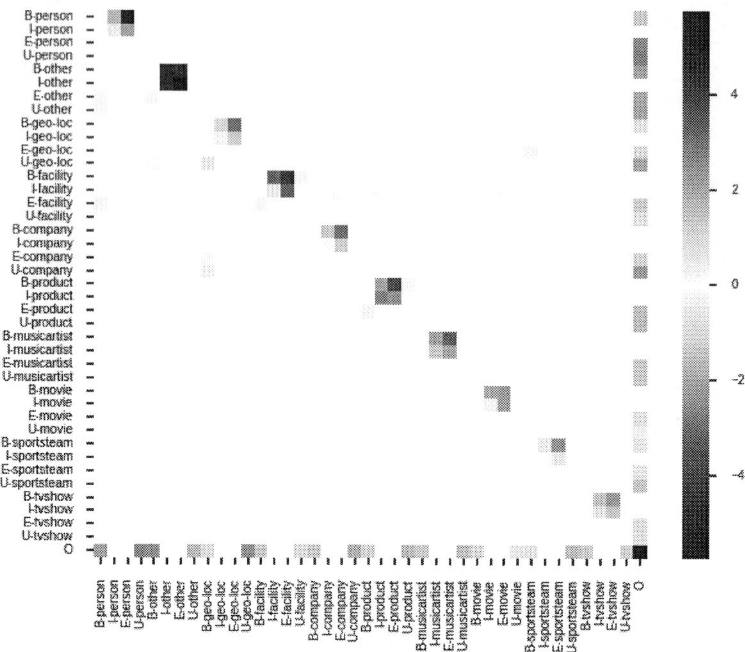

Figure 2: Transition weights learned by the SI model.

6   Discussion and conclusion

Prior work has shown that semi-supervised algorithms can perform decently for NER tasks with sparse labelled data (Blum, 1998; Carlson et al., 2010; Chapelle et al., 2009; Liang, 2005; Turian et al., 2010; Zhu & Goldberg, 2009). We leverage this fact in our SI model via the use of unsupervised word clusters, word representations, and refined gazetteers; all of which contributed to a cumulative increase in accuracy over our initial submission [ST] by ~11% when using the test data for evaluation. Furthermore, the transition features learned by our model are reflective of correct learning of NER sequences and demonstrate the strength of using the BIEUO encoding scheme. Additionally, the supervised training of our classifier on features extracted from the unlabelled data, as opposed to lexical token features, reduces the dimensionality of the training data for the classifier and results in increased performance in terms of both accuracy and training time. Furthermore, our model can be adjusted on the arrival of new unlabelled data by updating the underlying learned word clusters and representations, and retraining the model on the existing labelled data. As identified by Turian et al. (2010), the importance of word representations and word clusters increases as the availability of unlabelled data increases. We can add additional entity names to the gazetteers. Retraining the model on the same training data would then allow for accommodating to the new feature representations. Finally, the random feature dropout based up-sampling can help to increase the amount of training data available, and can also be improved by random swapping of entity types in the training data with their nearest neighbours in the word representations and clusters, or by choosing entities from the most correlated gazetteers. We believe that our described models can help in improving NER on noisy-text, and our open source implementation can be further extended.

7   Acknowledgements

We would like to acknowledge the three anonymous reviewers for their useful feedback.

Reference

Baldwin, Timothy, de Marneffe, Marie-Catherine, Han, Bo, Kim, Young-Bum, Ritter, Alan, & Xu, Wei. (2015). Shared tasks of the 2015 workshop on noisy user-generated text: Twitter lexical normalization and named entity recognition. In *First Workshop on Noisy User-generated Text at ACL '15*, (pp. 126-135), Association for Computational Linguistics, Beijing, China.

Blum, Avrim. (1998). On-line algorithms in machine learning. In A. Fiat & G. J. Woeginger (Eds.), *Online algorithms: The state of the art* (pp. 306-325): Springer Berlin Heidelberg.

Blum, Avrim, & Mitchell, Tom. (1998). Combining labeled and unlabeled data with co-training. In *Eleventh Annual Conference on Computational Learning Theory (CoLT '98)*, (pp. 92-100), ACM, Madison, Wisconsin, USA.

Brown, Peter F., deSouza, Peter V., Mercer, Robert L., Watson, T. J., Della Pietra, Vincent J., & Lai, Jenifer C. (1992). Class-based n-gram models of natural language. *Computational Linguistics, 18*(4).

Carlson, Andrew, Betteridge, Justin, Wang, Richard C., Estevam R. Hruschka, Jr., & Mitchell, Tom M. (2010). Coupled semi-supervised learning for information extraction. In *Third ACM International Conference on Web Search and Data Mining (WSDM '10)*, (pp. 101-110), ACM, New York, New York, USA.

Chapelle, O., Scholkopf, B., & Eds, A. Zien. (2009). Semi-supervised learning (Vol. 20). *The MIT Press*.

Cherry, Colin, & Guo, Hongyu. (2015). The unreasonable effectiveness of word representations for twitter named entity recognition. In *Conference of the North American Chapter of the Association for Computational Linguistics: Human Language Technologies (HLT-NAACL '15)*, (pp. 735-745), Association for Computational Linguistics, Denver, Colorado

Clark, Alexander. (2003). Combining distributional and morphological information for part of speech induction. In *Tenth Conference on European Chapter of the Association for Computational Linguistics (EACL '03)*, (pp. 59-66), (Vol. 1), Budapest, Hungary.

Collobert, Ronan, Weston, Jason, Bottou, Léon, Karlen, Michael, Kavukcuoglu, Koray, & Kuksa, Pavel. (2011). Natural language processing (almost) from scratch. *Journal of Machine Learning Research (JMLR), 12*, 2493-2537.

Derczynski, Leon, Augenstein, Isabelle, & Bontcheva, Kalina. (2015). Usfd: Twitter ner with drift compensation and linked data. In *First Workshop on Noisy User-generated Text at ACL '15*, Beijing, China.

Derczynski, Leon, Maynard, Diana, Rizzo, Giuseppe, van Erp, Marieke, Gorrell, Genevieve, Troncy, Raphaël, Petrak, Johann, & Bontcheva, Kalina. (2015). Analysis of named entity recognition and linking for tweets. *Information Processing & Management, 51*(2), 32-49.

Fromreide, Hege, Hovy, Dirk, & Søgaard, Anders. (2014). Crowdsourcing and annotating ner for twitter #drift. In *Ninth International Conference on Language Resources and Evaluation (LREC '14)*, European Language Resources Association (ELRA), Reykjavik, Iceland.

Gimpel, Kevin, Schneider, Nathan, O'Connor, Brendan, Das, Dipanjan, Mills, Daniel, Eisenstein, Jacob, Heilman, Michael, Yogatama, Dani, Flanigan, Jeffrey, & Smith, A. Noah. (2011). Part-of-speech tagging for twitter: Annotation, features, and experiments. In *49th Annual Meeting of the Association for Computational Linguistics: Human Language Technologies (HLT-ACL '11)*, (pp. 42-47), Association for Computational Linguistics, Stroudsburg, PA, USA.

Hulten, Geoff, Spencer, Laurie, & Domingos, Pedro. (2001). Mining time-changing data streams. In *Seventh ACM SIGKDD International Conference on Knowledge Discovery and Data Mining (KDD '01)*, (pp. 97-106), ACM, San Francisco, California, USA.

Joachims, Thorsten. (2003). Transductive learning via spectral graph partitioning. In *Twentieth International Conference on Machine Learning (ICML '03)*, (pp. 290-297), (Vol. 3), Washington, DC, USA.

Lafferty, John, McCallum, Andrew, & Pereira, Fernando. (2001). Conditional random fields: Probabilistic models for segmenting and labeling sequence data. In *Eighteenth International Conference on Machine Learning (ICML '01)*, (pp. 282--289), Morgan Kaufmann Publishers Inc., San Francisco, CA, USA.

Liang, Percy. (2005). *Semi-supervised learning for natural language.* (PhD Thesis), Massachusetts Institute of Technology.

Lin, Dekang, & Wu, Xiaoyun. (2009). Phrase clustering for discriminative learning. In *Joint Conference of the 47th Annual Meeting of the ACL and the 4th International Joint Conference on Natural Language Processing of the AFNLP (ACL '09)*, (pp. 1030-1038), Association for Computational Linguistics, Suntec, Singapore.

Masud, Mohammad M., Chen, Qing, Khan, Latifur, Aggarwal, Charu, Gao, Jing, Han, Jiawei, & Thuraisingham, Bhavani. (2010). Addressing concept-evolution in concept-drifting data streams. In *Tenth IEEE International Conference on Data Mining (ICDM '10)*, (pp. 929-934), IEEE Computer Society, Sydney, Australia.

McCallum, Andrew, & Li, Wei. (2003). Early results for named entity recognition with conditional random fields, feature induction and web-enhanced lexicons. In *Seventh Conference on Natural Language Learning at North American Chapter of the Association for Computational Linguistics: Human Language*

Technologies (HLT-NAACL '03), (pp. 188-191), (Vol. 4), Association for Computational Linguistics, Stroudsburg, PA, USA.

Mikolov, Tomas, Chen, Kai, Corrado, Greg, & Dean, Jeffrey. (2013). Efficient estimation of word representations in vector space. *Computing Research Repository (CoRR), abs/1301.3781*.

Mikolov, Tomas, Sutskever, Ilya, Chen, Kai, Corrado, Greg S, & Dean, Jeff. (2013). Distributed representations of words and phrases and their compositionality. In *Twenty Sixth Neural Information Processing Systems (NIPS '13)*, (pp. 3111-3119), (Vol. 26), Lake Tahoe, USA.

Miller, Scott, Guinness, Jethran, & Zamanian, Alex. (2004). Name tagging with word clusters and discriminative training. In *Human Language Technology Conference of the North American Chapter of the Association for Computational Linguistics (HLT-NAACL '04)*.

Okazaki, Naoaki. (2007). Crfsuite: A fast implementation of conditional random fields (crfs). Retrieved from http://www.chokkan.org/software/crfsuite/

Owoputi, Olutobi, O'Connor, Brendan, Dyer, Chris, Gimpel, Kevin, Schneider, Nathan, & Smith, A. Noah. (2013). Improved part-of-speech tagging for online conversational text with word clusters. In *Conference of the North American Chapter of the Association for Computational Linguistics: Human Language Technologies (HLT-NAACL '13)*, (pp. 380-390), Association for Computational Linguistics, Atlanta, GA, USA.

Pennington, Jeffrey, Socher, Richard, & Manning, Christopher D. (2014). Glove: Global vectors for word representation. In *Empirical Methods in Natural Language Processing (EMNLP '14)*, (pp. 1532-1543), (Vol. 14), Doha, Qatar.

Ratinov, Lev, & Roth, Dan. (2009). Design challenges and misconceptions in named entity recognition. In *Thirteenth Conference on Computational Natural Language Learning (CoNLL '09)*, (pp. 147-155), Association for Computational Linguistics, Boulder, Colorado.

Sarawagi, Sunita. (2008). Information extraction. *Foundations and Trends in Databases, 1*(3), 261-377.

Srivastava, Nitish, Hinton, Geoffrey E, Krizhevsky, Alex, Sutskever, Ilya, & Salakhutdinov, Ruslan. (2014). Dropout: A simple way to prevent neural networks from overfitting. *Journal of Machine Learning Research (JMLR), 15*(1), 1929-1958.

Turian, Joseph , Ratinov, Lev, & Bengio, Yoshua. (2010). Word representations: A simple and general method for semi-supervised learning. In *48th Annual Meeting of the Association for Computational Linguistics (ACL '10)*, (pp. 384-394), Association for Computational Linguistics, Uppsala, Sweden.

Zhu, Xiaojin, & Goldberg, Andrew B. (2009). Introduction to semi-supervised learning. *Synthesis Lectures on Artificial Intelligence and Machine Learning, 3*(1), 1-130.

Twitter Geolocation Prediction Shared Task of the 2016 Workshop on Noisy User-generated Text

Bo Han
Hugo AI
Sydney, Australia
bhan@hugo.ai

Afshin Rahimi
The University of Melbourne
Melbourne, Australia
arahimi@student.unimelb.edu.au

Leon Derczynski
The University of Sheffield
Sheffield, UK
leon.d@shef.ac.uk

Timothy Baldwin
The University of Melbourne
Melbourne, Australia
tb@ldwin.net

Abstract

This paper describes the shared task for the English Twitter geolocation prediction associated with WNUT 2016. We discuss details of the task settings, data preparation and participant systems. The derived dataset and performance figures from each system provide baselines for future research in this realm.

1 Introduction

With ever-increasing numbers of people interacting with social media, social data has become a gold mine of insights into the people, opinions and events of the world. Perhaps the greatest insights come when that data is partitioned into meaningful sub-populations, with one of the most obvious such partitioning dimensions being geographical. In many social platforms, however, geographical information is either missing, incomplete or not accessible. This greatly restricts the utility of social data for location-related applications such as regional sentiment analysis, local event detection, and geographically-bounded marketing and healthcare. This shared task focuses on predicting geographical location (i.e., geotagging) using English Twitter text data. The task provides a benchmark dataset for comparing different geotagging methods, and more generally sheds light on how to expand geotagging from social media to a more general domain.

In this shared task paper, we present the task scope and evaluation metrics; how training, development and test data were collected and filtered; and we also summarise and compare the key innovations of each participant system. Overall, we had five teams submit 21 results. Three of the five teams described their approach in peer-reviewed papers. We found that the system from FUJIXEROX achieved the best median distance error, using a neural net, and that the system from CSIRO using an ensemble had the highest accuracy and a competitive median distance error.

2 Geotagging Shared Task

In machine learning terms, the geotagging shared task can be expressed as two different problems. By assigning a latitude/longitude pair to a given input tweet and measuring the distance between the predicted point and the true GPS labelled point, it can be cast as a (multi-target) regression problem. If the aim is to predict one from a set of pre-defined mutually exclusive classes (e.g. metropolitan city centres), then geotagging becomes a multiclass classification problem. In this shared task, we adopt the later classification setting. Participants were given training and development data based on metropolitan

Proceedings of the 2nd Workshop on Noisy User-generated Text,
pages 213–217, Osaka, Japan, December 11 2016.

city representations derived from GeoNames.[1] The goal is to predict the class label (i.e. city) for each item in the test dataset.

The shared task was carried out on two levels: tweet-level and user-level. The tweet-level is more practical in real world applications, as a tweet is a basic text unit created by a Twitter user and often is associated with a unique location. However, because a single tweet text can be terse and will often not contain explicitly geolocating information, the more popular setting for geolocation research has been user-level prediction, aggregating a user's tweets. This assumes that each user has a primary location, and that the primary location can be inferred from the aggregated tweet data.

To comply with Twitter's terms of service, participants were given tweet IDs and a downloading script to obtain data and annotations. Participants then built geotagging systems using the released training and development data. When the test data was released, participants had three days to run their experiments and submit results.

The shared task has the following goals:

1. Provide a large-scale carefully-sampled dataset for the Twitter geotagging task, and as an enabler for future research on the topic;

2. Evaluate the effectiveness of different methods within a consolidated experimental setting, to better benchmark geotagging methods;

3   Datasets and Evaluation

As a compromise between the competing desires to provide a comprehensive, large-scale dataset, and to provide a manageably-sized dataset, we selected 1 million users for training, and 10K users for development and test, respectively. Each user has a unique class label to denote their primary location. The class labels are derived from metropolitan city centres in GeoNames, following Han et al. (2012). In total, the class set is made up of 3362 cities. The training data for the tweet-level task is based on a unique tweet from each of the same 1 million users. The development and test data sizes are both 10K messages in size, different from the user-level development and test data. We deliberately chose to keep strict separation between the data for the user- and tweet-level tasks to prevent the use of user-level predictions for the tweet-level task. A team could have up to 5 members, and submit up to 3 three runs for each of the two tasks.

We filter geotagged tweets from 2013 to 2016 via archived data from the 10% Twitter Streaming API. All the training and development data is from 2013 to 2015. For the test data, 50% is from 2013 to 2015, and the other half is from 2016. This is reserved for analysis of the impact of temporal differentiation on model generalisation (Han et al., 2014; Dredze et al., 2016). All tweets are filtered by Twitter's language ID code, retaining only those which are labelled as English. We run the filter in two passes: in the first round, we take all users with geotagged tweets; and in the second pass, we only keep users with at least 10 geotagged tweets. The requirement of 10 geotagged tweets was determined empirically, to get a reliable estimation of a user's primary location, while avoiding incorporating bot-generated messages. To be eligible as a data record in the geotagging dataset, a user must have 50% of their tweets coming from the same metropolitan area.[2] The number of unfiltered geotagged tweets was initially 419M, from which 172M English tweets were extracted. After filtering out users with less than 10 geotagged tweets and those who didn't have at least 50% of tweets from a single city, we randomly chose 1M users for training and 10k each for the development and test sets. The training set consists of 12.8M tweets, the user-level development and test sets consist of 128k and 99k tweets, respectively, and the tweet-level development and test sets each contain 10k tweets.

Candidate geotagging systems were evaluated using three metrics. "Accuracy" indicates how well a given system performs in a "hard" classification task setting, in terms of whether they correctly predict the city or not. In comparison, distance-based metrics (relative to the centre of the city the user is assigned to) provide a "soft" evaluation, in the sense that they reward near-miss predictions, and penalise

---

[1] http://www.geonames.org/
[2] Defined as a circle of radius 50km around the centre of a given city.

SUBMISSION	ACCURACY	MEDIAN	MEAN
FUJIXEROX.2	0.409	69.5	1792.5
CSIRO.1	0.436	74.7	2538.2
FUJIXEROX.1	0.381	92.0	1895.4
CSIRO.2	0.422	183.7	2976.7
CSIRO.3	0.420	226.3	3051.3
DREXEL.3	0.298	445.8	3428.2
AIST.1	0.078	3092.7	4702.4
IBM.1	0.146	3424.6	5338.9
DREXEL.2	0.082	4911.2	6144.3
DREXEL.1	0.085	5848.3	6175.3

Table 1: Tweet-level results ranked by median error distance

SUBMISSION	ACCURACY	MEDIAN	MEAN
FUJIXEROX.2	0.476	16.1	1122.3
FUJIXEROX.1	0.464	21.0	963.8
CSIRO.1	0.526	21.7	1928.8
CSIRO.2	0.520	23.1	2071.5
FUJIXEROX.3	0.451	28.2	1084.3
CSIRO.3	0.501	30.6	2242.4
DREXEL.3	0.352	262.7	3124.4
IBM.1	0.225	630.2	2860.2
AIST.1	0.098	1711.1	4002.4
DREXEL.2	0.079	4000.2	6161.4
DREXEL.1	0.080	5714.9	6053.3

Table 2: User-level results ranked by median error distance

wildly-wrong predictions. Specifically, as our distance-based metrics, we measure (in kilometres): (a) the median error distance; and (b) the mean error distance. Although distance-based metrics are more intuitive, class-based predictions such as city labels are often easier to use in downstream applications.

4   Systems and Results

In total, 5 teams uploaded 21 runs, among which 3 teams submitted system description papers.

Miura et al. (2016) ("FUJIXEROX") applied vectorised inputs in linear models for both tweet-level and user-level geotagging tasks. They used tweet text, user self-declared locations, timezone values, and user self-descriptions as input sources. Each source of input is transformed from a one-hot bag-of-word representation into a vector. Vectors from the same source are averaged, and vectors from different sources then are concatenated and used as the input to linear models. A softmax function is used to select the most probable class.

Jayasinghe et al. (2016) ("CSIRO") adopted ensemble learning methods with carefully extracted features from various available sources in both text and metadata. Namely, the authors implemented label propagation methods among tweet posts, location name mappings, text retrieval methods that assume similar text comes from the same region, and language-based classifiers. Having obtained outputs from each of the individual methods, the authors combined the resultant features in different ways. The best accuracy is achieved by using accuracy-ordered predictions, i.e. taking the prediction from the best

SUBMISSION	ACCURACY	MEDIAN	MEAN	ACCURACY	MEDIAN	MEAN
FUJIXEROX.2	0.377	77.7	1205.4	0.441	60.9	2379.6
CSIRO.1	0.344	230.4	2242.7	0.529	10.1	2833.7
FUJIXEROX.1	0.345	105.9	1594.1	0.417	79.7	2196.7
CSIRO.2	0.319	649.3	2811.6	0.525	10.1	3141.8
CSIRO.3	0.315	689.8	2773.6	0.524	10.2	3329.0
DREXEL.3	0.270	605.8	3531.5	0.327	340.7	3324.8
AIST.1	0.063	2259.1	3886.4	0.093	4164.1	5518.5
IBM.1	0.121	3105.8	4867.5	0.170	3852.7	5810.3
DREXEL.2	0.074	3800.3	5461.5	0.089	6897.3	6827.1
DREXEL.1	0.078	5498.6	5616.0	0.091	6986.7	6734.5

Table 3: Tweet-level results comparison for pre 2016 (left) and 2016 (right) test sets

SUBMISSION	ACCURACY	MEDIAN	MEAN	ACCURACY	MEDIAN	MEAN
FUJIXEROX.2	0.417	50.6	919.0	0.534	0.0	1325.6
FUJIXEROX.1	0.404	48.0	818.8	0.524	0.0	1108.9
CSIRO.1	0.413	66.6	1996.3	0.640	12.9	1861.2
CSIRO.2	0.402	111.3	2121.6	0.638	13.0	2021.3
FUJIXEROX.3	0.401	55.0	849.8	0.502	0.0	1318.8
CSIRO.3	0.370	267.8	2075.7	0.631	13.7	2409.0
DREXEL.3	0.287	617.9	3413.3	0.417	85.7	2835.6
IBM.1	0.196	611.7	2232.8	0.254	689.2	3487.6
AIST.1	0.089	1450.7	3333.9	0.106	2289.3	4670.9
DREXEL.2	0.069	3659.8	5503.0	0.088	6229.9	6819.8
DREXEL.1	0.071	5268.0	5586.8	0.090	6514.4	6519.8

Table 4: User-level results comparison for pre 2016 (left) and 2016 (right) test sets

method in the validation stage, and if no results are found, backing off to the next classifier. As highly accurate methods rely on location-based services or reliable social network information, this ensemble approach is primarily precision-oriented.

Chi et al. (2016) ("IBM") applied multinomial naive Bayes methods over different sets of features. Unlike other teams, they only used tweet text data in their system. The system used an existing set of location-indicative words, gazetted location names from GeoNames, hashtags, users mentions, and a combination of all of these features. In addition, a frequency-based method was used to filter the combined feature set. Experimental results show feature selection over the methods combined achieved the best results across all metrics.

Tweet-level and user-level results are shown in Table 1 and Table 2, respectively. FUJIXEROX achieved the best median error distance. The best accuracy was achieved by CSIRO; this system also achieved very competitive median error distance. Both teams systematically used metadata embedded in tweets, which supports the hypothesis that metadata contains abundant high-quality location information (Han et al., 2014). Nonetheless, the system from IBM provides insights into how well pure text-based methods can perform. Unfortunately the other two teams did not submit description papers, and we do not have insights into the methods they experimented with.

Interestingly, the gap between user-level and tweet-level results was fairly modest for those systems which made use of metadata. This is partly due to the fact that everything is mapped to a city-level representation, but provides further evidence that metadata plays a major role in geotagging.

Our test data consists of 5K 2016 data and 5K 2013-2015 data. We also show results for those two subsets in Figure 3 and Figure 4 to analyse the temporal impact. Interestingly, we found that 2016 test cases are more likely to predict compared with pre 2016 data in terms of accuracy and median distance error. As the 2016 test data is from new users created in 2016, this suggests people are more open to sharing their location information either in their profiles or in the tweet text data.

5 Conclusion and Future work

This paper presents an overview of the English Twitter geolocation prediction shared task. It detailed the two tasks, data preparation process, and evaluation metrics used in the shared task. It also outlined the approaches adopted by the participant systems, and reported results across multiple metrics. We found that tweet metadata offers abundant high-quality location information, which contributes to the geotagging tasks at both the tweet- and user-level. In the future, we plan to make the data replication procedure easier, allowing a wider audience to evaluate systems and compare with others.

Acknowledgements

Leon Derczynski acknowledges partial support from the EC under the 7th Framework Programme in the form of grant No. 611223, PHEME.

References

Lianhua Chi, Kwan Hui Lim, Nebula Alam, and Christopher J. Butler. 2016. Geolocation prediction in Twitter using location indicative words and textual features. In *Proceedings of the 2nd Workshop on Noisy User-generated Text (WNUT)*, Osaka, Japan.

Mark Dredze, Miles Osborne, and Prabhanjan Kambadur. 2016. Geolocation for twitter: Timing matters. In *Proceedings of the 2016 Conference of the North American Chapter of the Association for Computational Linguistics: Human Language Technologies*, pages 1064–1069.

Bo Han, Paul Cook, and Timothy Baldwin. 2012. Geolocation prediction in social media data by finding location indicative words. In *Proceedings of the 24th International Conference on Computational Linguistics (COLING 2012)*, pages 1045–1062, Mumbai, India.

Bo Han, Paul Cook, and Timothy Baldwin. 2014. Text-based Twitter user geolocation prediction. *Journal Artificial Intelligence Research (JAIR)*, 49:451–500.

Gaya Jayasinghe, Brian Jin, James Mchugh, Bella Robinson, and Stephen Wan. 2016. CSIRO Data61 at the WNUT geo shared task. In *Proceedings of the 2nd Workshop on Noisy User-generated Text (WNUT)*, Osaka, Japan.

Yasuhide Miura, Motoki Taniguchi, Tomoki Taniguchi, and Tomoko Ohkuma. 2016. A simple scalable neural networks based model for geolocation prediction in Twitter. In *Proceedings of the 2nd Workshop on Noisy User-generated Text (WNUT)*, Osaka, Japan.

CSIRO Data61 at the WNUT Geo Shared Task

Gaya Jayasinghe, Brian Jin, James McHugh, Bella Robinson, Stephen Wan
CSIRO Data61
Australia
`firstname.lastname@data61.csiro.au`

Abstract

In this paper, we describe CSIRO Data61's participation in the Geolocation shared task at the Workshop for Noisy User-generated Text. Our approach was to use ensemble methods to capitalise on four component methods: heuristics based on metadata, a label propagation method, timezone text classifiers, and an information retrieval approach. The ensembles we explored focused on examining the role of language technologies in geolocation prediction and also in examining the use of hard voting and cascading ensemble methods. Based on the accuracy of city-level predictions, our systems were the best performing submissions at this year's shared task. Furthermore, when estimating the latitude and longitude of a user, our median error distance was accurate to within 30 kilometers.

1 Introduction

Social media platforms present an attractive source of real-time and large volume data for analysts. Publicly available data from these platforms can provide insights that shape our understanding of a number of different topics, such as early signals on the outbreaks of diseases (for example, see Robinson et al. (2015)), natural disasters such as earthquakes and fires (Yin et al., 2012), or the mental health of populations as represented by online data (Larsen et al., 2015).

For analytics where aggregated data is used to provide insights, geographical information is important. For example, responses to early signals of disease outbreaks or natural disasters are more effective with geolocation metadata. Geographical information could be used at different granularities, such as comparing rural and city mental health. However, most social media platforms do not provide geographical metadata. For example, it is reported that less than 3% of Twitter data has geo-coordinates provided (Jurgens et al., 2015), even though the platform supports geolocation metadata. Other platforms, such as public discussion forums and blogs often do not have geolocation capabilities. There is thus a need to develop approaches to automatically determine location information for social media content.

As part of the 2016 Workshop on Noisy User-generated Text, a shared task to infer geolocation for Twitter posts and users was organised (Han et al., 2016).[1] The goal was twofold: (i) for an English Twitter post, infer the city location; and (2) for a Twitter user (authoring mainly English Tweets), infer the user's base city.

In this paper, we describe the approach of the CSIRO Data61 team to this shared task. We adopted an ensemble approach combining four complementary methods for predicting geolocation.

The shared task results revealed that our system was placed first for accuracy for city location. As we optimised for city location, we narrowly missed out on first place for the median accuracy when predicting latitude and longitude coordinates.

2 Preparing Data

In this section, we describe the collection and preparation of the shared task data and addition geospatial resources used by some of the component methods.

---

[1] `http://noisy-text.github.io/2016/geo-shared-task.html`

Proceedings of the 2nd Workshop on Noisy User-generated Text,
pages 218–226, Osaka, Japan, December 11 2016.

2.1 Shared Task Data

Starting with the data release from the shared task organisers, our first task was to download the training and validation sets as JSON[2] objects from the Twitter Application Programming Interface (API). The JSON data includes the text of the Twitter post and the profile information for the Twitter users, as well as associated metadata. At the time of collection, not all the data was available as some users had elected to remove or change the privacy settings of accounts and/or content. We were able to collect 9,472,450 training tweets (73.84% of the data set) and 783,492 distinct users (78.35% of the data set).

The data was then loaded into a database so that queries could be used, as needed by each of the different approaches. The primary table of the database was designed with each Twitter post as a record. Queries could then retrieve the different JSON metadata fields for a given post. As this also contains identifiers for the Twitter user who authored the post, we could retrieve the posts for given Twitter user.

2.2 A GeoNames Mirror

Some of our approaches require a service to map from locations to the corresponding latitude and longitude coordinates. Such translations are provided by web services such as GeoNames[3]. We created a local version of the GeoNames service and indexed it with Apache Solr, which allows spatial indexing allowing queries such as "find places within X km", as well as place name searches. We refer to this resource as the *GeoNames Solr Mirror*. We also loaded GeoNames data into a PostgreSQL database with the PostGIS extension in order to map city labels to time zones using the "point within polygon" function.

2.3 A Mapping from Shared Task City Labels to Geonames

We created mappings between the 3363 shared task labels found in the training and validation data sets and their corresponding GeoNames cities. In most cases, this was done automatically by using the first section of the label as the query to our GeoNames Solr Mirror. With this approach, we mapped most shared task labels to a GeoNames location within 100km of the gold label coordinates. Only 11 shared task labels could not be mapped automatically, which we created manually.

2.4 A Mapping from Twitter Time zones to the "TZ" resource

Twitter uses a non-standard string format for time zone, making it difficult to link to other geospatial resources such as the publicly available time zone resource, *TZ*, which provides time zone boundaries.[4] To utilize this resource, we obtained mappings from Twitter time zones to the TZ resource. As the Twitter format is very similar to those the Ruby on Rails (RoR) tool, we started with existing RoR to TZ resources.[5] Missing mappings were then added manually. The mappings and the TZ resource were stored in a Postgres/PostGIS database.

3 Our Approaches to Geolocation

Our approach to the shared task was to use ensemble approaches, as the strengths of each component approach can offset the weakness of any individual approach. This was inspired by arguments about the strengths of combining social network methods with natural language processing methods (Jurgens et al. (2015), Rahimi et al. (2015)), and by work by Han and Cook (2013), who combined text classifiers and metadata approaches. Here, we explore a larger set of component methods: (i) use of heuristics based on metadata, (ii) a social network inference method, (iii) an information retrieval method, and (iv) a text classification method. We will now briefly describe these in more detail.

3.1 Metadata Methods

We used five methods based on Twitter metadata inspired by approaches described in Schulz et al. (2013). For all approaches, a list of candidate shared task labels was produced. We ranked shared task labels

---

[2]JavaScript Object Notation
[3]http://www.geonames.org/
[4]http://efele.net/maps/tz/world/
[5]http://api.rubyonrails.org/classes/ActiveSupport/TimeZone.html

based on the prior probability of observing them in the training data. The most probable shared task label was then chosen as the city prediction, with GeoNames Solr Mirror providing the relevant latitude and longitude coordinates.

3.1.1   Metadata Text-to-Gazetteer

This method looks at the Twitter post text for mentions of place names. The text was tokenised and stopwords, punctuation sequences and URLs were removed. All remaining tokens were used as search input to our GeoNames Solr Mirror. Potential matching GeoNames places were then mapped to candidate shared task labels.

3.1.2   Metadata Location-to-Gazetteer

This method uses the location text field found in the user profile section of the Twitter post. This is a free-text field that may be left blank. We first checked if the location is a set of coordinates, for example "-6.156277, 106.57207". For these, we mapped the coordinates to a candidate city using the GeoNames Solr Mirror, which provides the closest city location within 50km of the coordinates. For all other cases, the location text was treated similarly to text in the Metadata Text-to-Gazetteer method.

3.1.3   Metadata Time Zone

In this approach, we utilised the time zone information in the user's profile, which takes a value from a finite set specified by Twitter. We mapped any time zone information to the equivalent TZ time zones (there may be more than one). For each TZ time zone, we issued a database query to find cities within the time zone boundaries. This provided a list of candidate cities.

For example, if the user has "Sydney" as their Twitter time zone setting, this was mapped to the "Australia/Sydney" TZ time zone, which contains a number of candidate shared task labels: e.g., *north shore-02-au, canberra-01-au, sydney-02-au*.

3.1.4   Metadata UTC (Coordinated Universal Time)

This method utilises the UTC offset setting that is automatically generated by Twitter based on user's time zone setting; it is not set directly by the user. This method defines a geographical area from which candidate cities are generated. For example, the UTC offset value 32400 (GMT+09:00) mapped to the Twitter time zones: Seoul, Osaka, Sapporo, Tokyo and Yakutsk. These were then converted into TZ time zones which are used to produce a list of candidate cities.

3.1.5   Metadata Application

Metadata for each Twitter post indicates the application used to create the content, for example "Twitter for iPhone" and "Twitter for Android". We note that some apps are more popular in some countries than others. We thus used the training data to create probability distributions of countries for each possible application value, allowing country-level predictions to be made. Given a prediction for the country, we then generated list of candidate cities. As this metadata is always present, this method always provides a location prediction.

3.1.6   Metadata URL IP-Lookup

This method uses the Uniform Resource Locators (URLs) found in either the Twitter post text itself or in the user profile. We assumed that people are likely to include URLs hosted in their home country. After excluding URLs that refer to worldwide services with no specific host country (such as Facebook, Instagram and YouTube)[6], we then converted URLs to Internet Protocol (IP) addresses. These can be used to look up the host country using the public domain resource, the IP2Location LITE database[7]. This allowed a list of host countries to be predicted, from which we generated a list of candidate cities.

---

[6]We exclude these URLs with the following regular expression patterns: *.com, *.net, *.ly, *.fm, *.be, *.me, *.gl, and *.co.
[7]http://lite.ip2location.com

3.1.7 Metadata Location-Based Service (LBS) Links

We implemented a second URL-based approach (unrelated to the prior method) to capitalise on links geolocation-centric web applications, or a *Location-Based Service* (LBS). LBSs have been shown to provide high precision estimates of location (Schulz et al., 2013). Using the training set, we identified the LBSs which commonly occurred: FourSquare[8], Swarm[9], Path[10], Facebook[11] and Instagram[12].

We first extracted the URL from metadata. If no tweet URLs were found in the post text, then URLs found in the user's profile data were also considered. For Facebook and Instagram URLs, we mined the links to create queries for the respective platform Application Programming Interfaces (APIs). For the others, we scraped metadata from the target page of the link for geographic coordinates, using code specific to each LBS platform. We then used the GeoNames SOLR Mirror to retrieve a city which could then be mapped to a shared task label.

For Facebook links, we are interested in Pages, representing public entities, or Events. These are often publicly accessible and may have geolocation information attached. We can identify if a node is a Facebook Event or Page by checking whether it conforms to the following Facebook URL templates.[13] For those templates that resulted in public (HTML) content, we extracted the relevant location latitude and longitude metadata.

For Instagram links, we mined the target webpage JSON for an Instagram-specific location identifier. This identifier could then be mapped to the web page for a location (using a prescribed URL pattern), providing latitude and longitude metadata.[14]

3.1.8 Metadata Combination

We also defined an ensemble using just metadata approaches. All techniques were executed individually with each producing a list of candidate cities. Each city was given a manual weighting depending on the method that produced it, using the following manual weighting scheme based on experiments with the validation set: (i) Metadata Location-based Service Links: 10; (ii) Metadata Text-to-Gazetteer: 6; (iii) Metadata Location-to-Gazetteer : 5; (iv) Metadata Time Zone: 3; (v) others: 1. The weighted candidate lists from each method were then combined, and weightings for cities appearing in more than one list were added together. The city with the maximum final weighting was selected.

3.2 Label Propagation Approaches

We implemented a label propagation-like method based on the work of Jurgens et al. (2015) and inspired by Jurgens' publicly available code[15]. In this work, social media networks are defined using Twitter post interactions, specifically *mentions* within the Twitter post to other Twitter users (often with the pattern @screen name). A relationship between two Twitter users was only included in the network if both users mentioned each other (edges were bidirectional).

In this shared task, however, one constraint was to only use the network information induced from the shared task data, which led to small networks when using bidirectional edges. Following (Rahimi et al., 2015), we thus used unidirectional edges. Furthermore, we also included interaction edges based on replies, again adding unidirectional edges (User X replies to User Y). Once the network was constructed, edge direction was then ignored.

Using these definitions, we transformed the Twitter post data into a network, which we stored in a database as a series of relationships between a *source* and *target* Twitter user. Each Twitter post contains

---

[8]`https://foursquare.com`

[9]`https://www.swarmapp.com`

[10]`https://path.com`

[11]`https://www.facebook.com`

[12]`https://www.instagram.com`

[13]URLs for Events typically take the form, `https://www.facebook.com/Events/Event_ID`, whereas Pages are either of the form, `https://www.facebook.com/Page_UNIQUE_IDENTIFIER` or `https://www.facebook.com/Page-NAME-Page_ID`. The latter is used when the Page has not been designated a unique identifier (only the most popular pages are given these).

[14]`https://www.instagram.com/explore/locations/LOCATION_ID`

[15]`https://github.com/networkdynamics/geoinference`

an author screen name as metadata. For links based on mentions, we extracted mentioned authors screen name in metadata. For reply links, we found the metadata about the post that triggered the reply and extracted the author screen name. For predictions on the test set, although the Twitter user identifiers were hashed, the metadata still existed to create a mention and reply network which could be linked to the networks derived from the training and validation sets.

Our label propagation method used a single iteration, and inferred the location of a Twitter user based on the neighbours in the graph. Issuing the appropriate database queries provided the neighbours for a user using the network. For all neighbours, we computed the majority city. For the users sharing the majority city, we calculated the average latitude and longitude. In situations where there was a tie for the majority city, we randomly selected a city.

We applied two variants of this approach that differed in the depth of the neighbourhood. For a single "hop" (which we refer to as the *1-hop label propagation* method), we looked at the immediate neighbours of a user. For hop depth of 2, (which we refer to as the *2-hop label propagation* method), we recursively retrieved the neighbours of the neighbours and treated these as if they were 1-hop neighbours. We then applied the 1-hop method to the Twitter user in question.

We evaluated these approaches on a network based on the training data and using the validation set as our gold standard. The *1-hop* method performed well, with an accuracy of 62%. The accuracy of the *2-hop* method was approximately 31%. However, the *1-hop* network only covered 16% of validation set while *2-hop* covered 66%. We note that increasing the hop depth beyond 2 hops did not increase coverage substantially. The two variants thus introduce a trade-off between coverage and accuracy, which we exploit in the ensemble methods.

3.3 Information Retrieval Approaches

We employed an information retrieval approach based on the premise that a Twitter post is likely to originate from the same location as the majority of similar tweets in the training dataset. This hinges, of course, on the definition of similarity. For example, consider content in the form *I'm at place_X in city_Y* and also *I am in place_X, city_Y*: that is, Twitter posts with similar mentions. For such posts, we assume that they occur in the same location. We now describe method to capture such similarity efficiently.

To retrieve Twitter posts with similar text, we index the training data using the Apache Solr search engine. Twitter post text is indexed using hash signatures that can capture similarity. Such approaches have been used in information retrieval to detect near duplicates (Broder, 1997). One benefit of using hash signatures in the index is that we avoid pairwise comparisons of documents.

Specifically, we used the following procedure. We first preprocessed the text of the Twitter post to normalise for case and then tokenised the text. We then generated a MinHash signature of 100 integers for each token in the normalised Twitter post, as described in Broder (1997). Finally, we divided the MinHash signature into 25 bands to produce locality sensitive hashes (LSHs) (Leskovec et al., 2014). The locality sensitive hashes were indexed. For a given Twitter post, we transformed it into an LSH, and retrieved the top 10 search results in our Solr search engine.

Any @mentions were also specifically indexed, again using an Apache Solr search engine. For a given Twitter post, we retrieved the top 10 search results having similar mentions.

For each set of search results, we then retrieved the associated shared task labels for these results and obtained a probability estimated for each label, computed as the frequency normalised by the number of retrieved search results. The label with the highest probability from either method was then selected as the prediction. We refer to this approach as the *Information Retrieval* method.

3.4 Text Classification Approach

Our final approach was one based on text classification. We created a time zone variant of the *Pigeo System* described in Rahimi et al. (2016), akin to the classification approach of Mahmud et al. (2012). The Pigeo system first clusters content geographically, using the cluster labels for supervised machine learning with a logistic regression classifier. Automatically labelled Twitter posts are then assigned the centroid latitude and longitude for the cluster.[16]

At training time, we iterated through the list of unique time zones found in the training set. For each subset of data sharing a time zone, we trained a classifier, using a modified version of the Pigeo. We first preprocessed and tokenised the Twitter post text in the training set using the CMU Twokenizer tool[17] (Gimpel et al., 2011).

The system then performs k-means clustering on the Twitter posts for a given time zone. We used $k = 200$ for this work. This provides a cluster identifier that can be used as a label for each Twitter post. This label is associated to the median latitude and longitude for the cluster.

We use the cluster labels to train a logistic regression classifier, using the default feature set (unigrams with TFIDF weights) and parameters of the Pigeo system, with minor changes (i) to handle time zone models, and (ii) to use our own geospatial resources.

After training, this resulted in approximately 300 classifiers. To apply the time zone text classifiers, our approach identifies the timezone of the Twitter post to be classified and then uses the relevant classification model to predict latitude and longitude. We use our geospatial resources to then map the latitude and longitude to a shared task label.

4 Producing Twitter Post and User Predictions

The approaches described in the preceding section are generally oriented toward producing a prediction for the Twitter post. The exceptions are the label propagation methods, which predict user locations.

We applied heuristics to allow each component method to work for either scenario. For the label progation methods, to predictions for a Twitter post, we simply applied the predicted location of the user. For all other methods, to produce predictions for a user, we retrieved the Twitter posts authored by that user in the test set and computed a shared task label for the post.[18] Then, for all posts, the majority label was found and chosen as the label prediction for the user. We calculated the mean latitude and longitude from those posts sharing the majority label to compute the coordinates for the user.

5 Submitted Ensembles

We submitted three ensemble approaches for each of the two variants of the shared task (the first focusing on Twitter posts, the second on Twitter users). These are listed in Table 1. We now describe each of these.

5.1 Ensembles for Twitter Post Geolocation

The *Full Cascade*[19] system was a cascade of components. Components were ordered based on their accuracy at predicting the city location in the validation set, with the best performing systems occurering earlier. We note that earlier components also have the benefit of providing only high-quality predictions or none at all. That is, they err on the side of precision.

The *Heuristic Cascade*[20] system only includes methods based on the Metadata of the Twitter post, and also the label propagation (which only propagates location metadata). These were again ordered based on their accuracy on the validation set.

The *Voting Variant*[21] system used a mixture of cascades and voting methods to combine the component methods. We started with a cascade of the high precision heuristic and label propagation methods. We then used a voting mechanism for the other methods. Finally, for any Twitter posts that were left unlabelled, we used the Combined Metadata approach to provide a prediction. The voting mechanism was such that there had to be more than one vote for a city prediction, and there could be no ties.

---

[16]The full Pigeo system also combines the text classification approach with a label propagation approach, however this functionality was not available in the version that was downloaded.

[17]https://github.com/brendano/ark-tweet-nlp/blob/master/src/cmu/arktweetnlp/
Twokenize.java

[18]For the text classification approach, there was a slight variation which was to use a label generated from the latitude and longitude coordinates, accurate to 1 decimal place.

[19]This is csiro.1.tweet in the shared task results.

[20]This is csiro.2.tweet in the shared task results.

[21]This is csiro.3.tweet in the shared task results.

Ensemble: Full Cascade	Ensemble: Heuristic Cascade

Task: User, Post
  1 Metadata LBS Links
  2 1-hop Label Propagation
  3 Metadata Location-to-Gazetteer
  4 2-hop Label Propagation
  5 Time zone Text Classifier
  6 Information Retrieval
  7 Metadata Combination
	Task: User, Post
	  1 Metadata LBS Links
	  2 1-hop Label Propagation
	  3 Metadata Location-to-Gazetteer
	  4 2-hop Label Propagation
	  5 Metadata Combination

Ensemble: Voting Variant	**Ensemble: Ablation Variant**

Task: Post
  1 Metadata LBS Links
  2 1-hop Label Propagation
  3 Metadata Location-to-Gazetteer
  4 Voting:
    • 2-hop Label Propagation
    • Time zone Text Classifier
    • Information retrieval
    • Metadata Time Zone
    • Metadata Application
    • Metadata Text-to-Gazetter
    • Metadata UTC
    • Metadata URL IP-Loopup
  5 Metadata Combination
	Task: User
	  1 Metadata LBS Links
	  2 1-hop Label Propagation
	  3 Metadata Location-to-Gazetteer
	  4 2-hop Label Propagation
	  5 Information Retrieval
	  6 Metadata Combination

Table 1: Ensembles submitted.

5.2 Ensembles for Twitter User Geolocation

We submitted 3 systems to the Twitter user variant of the shared task. The Full Cascade and Voting Variant systems were as described above, except that, for each component, the version that produced user-level predictions was used.[22] The *Ablation Variant*[23] system uses all (user prediction) approaches in the Full Cascade except the time zone text classification approach.

6 Results

In Table 2, we report the official evaluation results for the Twitter post variant of the shared task.[24] The two metrics reported are the classification accuracy (for a city-level label), and the median error distance. For accuracy, the higher the score, the better. For the median error distance, the aim is to minimise this score. We also list the maximum, mean and minimum scores.

Based on the accuracy, our Full Cascade submission was the best performing system submitted. In fact, our three systems come in the top 3 ranks. In terms of median error distance, our Full Cascade submission is the second best system. Our other two submissions come in 3rd and 4th place. All three submissions do better than the mean.

In Table 2, we report the official evaluation results for the Twitter user variant of the shared task in the same format as above. In terms of the accuracy metric, our Full Cascade submission was the best performing system and our three systems again come in the top 3 ranks. The systems come in 3rd, 4th and 6th place when examining median error distance. All three submissions do better than the mean.

---

[22]These were csiro.1.user and csiro.3.user respectively in the shared task results.

[23]This is csiro.2.user in the shared task results.

[24]http://noisy-text.github.io/2016/geo-shared-task.html

System	Accuracy	Median
Full Cascade	**0.4362**	74.6866
Heuristic Cascade	0.4217	183.7280
Voting Variant	0.4195	226.3125
Eval. Best	0.4362	69.4985
Eval. Mean	0.2755	1836.8786
Eval. Worst	0.0778	5848.3488

Table 2: Evaluation results for Twitter posts.

System	Accuracy	Median
Full Cascade	**0.5265**	21.6853
Ablation Cascade	0.5202	23.1475
Voting Variant	0.5006	30.5772
Eval. Best	0.5265	16.1326
Eval. Mean	0.3428	1132.7192
Eval. Worst	0.0787	5714.9461

Table 3: Evaluation results for Twitter users.

7 Discussion

Our variants were chosen to explore two questions: (i) what is the contribution of language technology approaches; (ii) can voting approaches help when no clear cascade ordering is apparent. We describe some early insights from the published evaluation results.

We find that language technologies, at least in their current implementations here, had a small effect on accuracy. This is evidenced by the small drop in performance between the Full Cascade and the Heuristic Cascade, where, in the latter, the two language technology approaches, the time zone text classifier and the information retrieval approach, have been removed.

We note, however, that the time zone text classifier had the ability, where it was applicable, to minimise the median error distance. Indeed, omitting this classifier worsens the median error distance, as can be seen in Table 2, where the Heuristic Cascade (without language technology) has a higher mean error distance than the Full Cascade (with language technology).

Our implementation of the voting mechanism could not out-perform our cascades with manual orderings of components. We note that our components do not always expose a ranked list of candidate locations, and so only a hard voting is possible.

In future work, we will explore alternative ways to harness language technologies. This might include an exploration of ambiguous cases where a Twitter post is about events that do not coincide with the Twitter user's location.

We would also like to examine approaches that utilise the probability of predictions in producing the final location estimate. We note that our systems did well when measuring performance with accuracy, which may be because we optimised our cascade for this metric. We may have obtained a different ordering had we use the median error distance. In future work, we will explore this interaction further.

8 Conclusion

We described the submitted CSIRO Data61 systems in the Geolocation shared task at the Workshop for Noisy User-generated Text. Based on the accuracy at the predicting the city of a Twitter post or user, our systems were the best performing submissions. For estimating the latitude and longitude of a user, our median error distance was accurate to within 30 kilometers. Our approach was to use ensemble methods to capitalise on four component methods: heuristics based on metadata, a label propagation method, time zone text classifiers, and an information retrieval approaches.

Acknowledgements

We would like to thank the shared task organisers for their efforts in running this event. The preparation of the code for the submissions was the work of the five authors. However, we would like to thank the CSIRO Data61 Language and Social Computing Team for their advice and support, particularly Sarvnaz Karimi, Mac Kim, and Cecile Paris. We would also like to thank the anonymous reviewers for their feedback.

References

Andrei Z. Broder. 1997. On the resemblance and containment of documents. In *Proceedings of the Compression and Complexity of Sequences 1997*, pages 21–29. IEEE.

Kevin Gimpel, Nathan Schneider, Brendan O'Connor, Dipanjan Das, Daniel Mills, Jacob Eisenstein, Michael Heilman, Dani Yogatama, Jeffrey Flanigan, and Noah A. Smith. 2011. Part-of-speech tagging for twitter: Annotation, features, and experiments. In *Proceedings of the 49th Annual Meeting of the Association for Computational Linguistics: Human Language Technologies: Short Papers - Volume 2*, HLT '11, pages 42–47, Stroudsburg, PA, USA. Association for Computational Linguistics.

Bo Han and Paul Cook. 2013. A stacking-based approach to twitter user geolocation prediction. In *In Proceedings of the 51st Annual Meeting of the Association for Computational Linguistics (ACL 2013): System Demonstrations*, pages 7–12.

Bo Han, Afshin Rahimi, Leon Derczynski, and Timothy Baldwin. 2016. Twitter geolocation prediction shared task of the 2016 workshop on noisy user-generated text. In *Proceedings of the 2nd Workshop on Noisy User-generated Text (W-NUT 2016), Osaka Japan*.

David Jurgens, Tyler Finethy, James McCorriston, Yi Tian Xu, and Derek Ruths. 2015. Geolocation prediction in twitter using social networks: A critical analysis and review of current practice. In *Proceedings of the Ninth International Conference on Web and Social Media, ICWSM 2015, University of Oxford, Oxford, UK, May 26-29, 2015*, pages 188–197.

Mark E. Larsen, Tjeerd W. Boonstra, Philip J. Batterham, Bridianne O'Dea, Cecile Paris, and Helen Christensen. 2015. We Feel: Mapping Emotion on Twitter. *IEEE Journal of Biomedical and Health Informatics*, 19(4):1246–1252.

Jure Leskovec, Anand Rajaraman, and Jeffrey David Ullman. 2014. *Mining of massive datasets*. Cambridge University Press.

Jalal Mahmud, Jeffrey Nichols, and Clemens Drews. 2012. Where is this tweet from? inferring home locations of twitter users. In John G. Breslin, Nicole B. Ellison, James G. Shanahan, and Zeynep Tufekci, editors, *ICWSM*. The AAAI Press.

Afshin Rahimi, Trevor Cohn, and Timothy Baldwin. 2015. Twitter user geolocation using a unified text and network prediction model. In *Proceedings of the 53rd Annual Meeting of the Association for Computational Linguistics and the 7th International Joint Conference on Natural Language Processing (Volume 2: Short Papers)*, pages 630–636, Beijing, China, July. Association for Computational Linguistics.

Afshin Rahimi, Trevor Cohn, and Timothy Baldwin. 2016. pigeo: A python geotagging tool. In *Proceedings of ACL-2016 System Demonstrations*, pages 127–132, Berlin, Germany, August. Association for Computational Linguistics.

Bella Robinson, Ross Sparks, Robert Power, and Mark@Article10.1109/MIS.2012.6, Title = Using Social Media to Enhance Emergency Situation Awareness, Author = Jie Yin and Andrew Lampert and Mark Cameron and Bella Robinson and Robert Power, Journal = IEEE Intelligent Systems, Year = 2012, Number = 6, Pages = 52-59, Volume = 27, Address = Los Alamitos, CA, USA, Doi = http://doi.ieeecomputersociety.org/10.1109/MIS.2012.6, ISSN = 1541-1672, Owner = wan049, Publisher = IEEE Computer Society, Timestamp = 2016.08.22 Cameron. 2015. Social Media Monitoring for Health Indicators. pages 1862–1868.

Axel Schulz, Aristotelis Hadjakos, Heiko Paulheim, Johannes Nachtwey, and Max Mhlhuser. 2013. A multi-indicator approach for geolocalization of tweets. In *International AAAI Conference on Web and Social Media*.

Jie Yin, Andrew Lampert, Mark Cameron, Bella Robinson, and Robert Power. 2012. Using social media to enhance emergency situation awareness. *IEEE Intelligent Systems*, 27(6):52–59.

Geolocation Prediction in Twitter Using Location Indicative Words and Textual Features

Lianhua Chi[†], **Kwan Hui Lim**[‡†], **Nebula Alam**[†] and **Christopher J. Butler**[†]

[†]IBM Research - Australia
[‡]The University of Melbourne, Australia
`lianhuac@au1.ibm.com, limk2@student.unimelb.edu.au,`
`anebula@au1.ibm.com, chris.butler@au1.ibm.com`

Abstract

Knowing the location of a social media user and their posts is important for various purposes, such as the recommendation of location-based items/services, and locality detection of crisis/disasters. This paper describes our submission to the shared task "Geolocation Prediction in Twitter" of the 2nd Workshop on Noisy User-generated Text. In this shared task, we propose an algorithm to predict the location of Twitter users and tweets using a multinomial Naive Bayes classifier trained on Location Indicative Words and various textual features (such as city/country names, #hashtags and @mentions). We compared our approach against various baselines based on Location Indicative Words, city/country names, #hashtags and @mentions as individual feature sets, and experimental results show that our approach outperforms these baselines in terms of classification accuracy, mean and median error distance.

1 Introduction

Determining the location of a social media user and where a message is posted from is important for location-based recommendation (Ye et al., 2010), crisis detection and management (Sakaki et al., 2010), detecting location-centric communities (Lim et al., 2015), demographics analysis (Sloan et al., 2013) and targeted advertising (Tuten, 2008). This work aims to assign a geographical location (most probable location from a list of pre-defined locations, such as cities or countries) to a piece of text. For this textual content, we focus on the Twitter social networking site, which boosts more than 500 million tweets posted on a daily basis (Internet Live Statistics, 2016). In Twitter, tweets are short messages of 140 characters or less, and can also include #hashtags to indicate the topic of the tweet and @mentions to refer to another user. Fig. 1 shows an example of a tweet that contains a text message with a mention of @westernbulldogs, two hashtags of #7NewsMelb and #bemorebulldog, along with an embedded image.

Figure 1: Example of a tweet message containing a mention (@westernbulldogs), two hashtags (#7News-Melb and #bemorebulldog) and an attached picture.

Proceedings of the 2nd Workshop on Noisy User-generated Text,
pages 227–234, Osaka, Japan, December 11 2016.

Despite the popularity of Twitter and a large volume of tweets, only a small amount of tweets (les than 1%) are geotagged with the location that they were posted from (Sloan et al., 2013), thus restricting the usability of many tweets for location-based services and studies. Due to this motivating factor, the geolocation prediction of tweets and Twitter users have garnered immense interest in recent years. In this paper, we describe our submitted geolocation prediction algorithm for the shared task "Geolocation Prediction in Twitter" in the 2nd Workshop on Noisy User-generated Text (Han et al., 2016). Our algorithm utilizes a multinomial Naive Bayes classifier, using a textual feature set that includes a combination of location indicative words, city/country names, #hashtags and @mentions, which are automatically learnt from a large collection of Twitter data.

Here, we use two examples respectively from tweet level and user level to describe the basic application of our method. From tweet level, for instance, "I plan to take a tram to the federation square this arvo to watch the cricket..." is assigned to Melbourne, Victoria, Australia. The text doesn't contain gazetted terms such as "Melbourne", but our geotagger is able to geolocate this text on basis of location indicative words like "tram", "federation square" and "arvo" and other textual features. From the user level, we can see an example from Figure 2. In Figure 2, the input is the twitter ID of Barack Obama (the president of United States), and the predicted location is Washington.

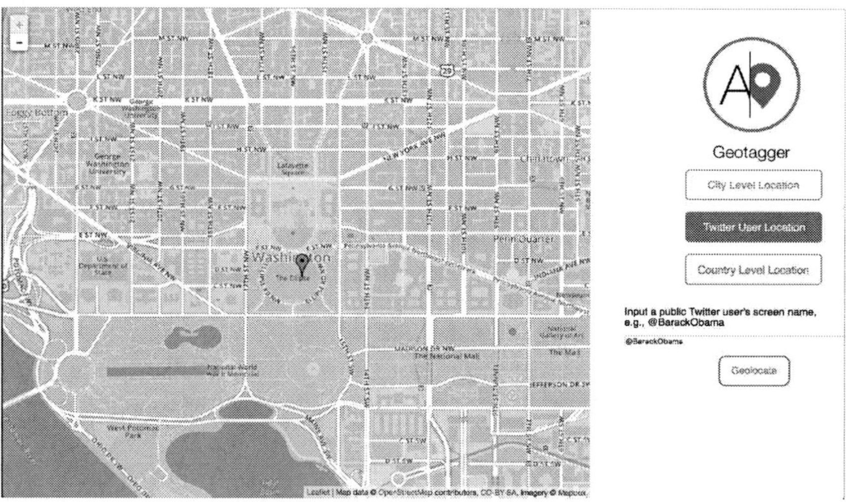

Figure 2: A simple demo from the Twitter user level prediction task.

1.1 Main Contributions

Our main contributions include:

1. We present a geolocation prediction algorithm for Twitter based on a multinomial Naive Bayes classifier, using text-based features that are automatically learnt from tweets.

2. We study the effects of using various feature sets including location indicative words, city/country names, #hashtags, @mentions and a combination of all of the above.

3. We experiment on a Twitter dataset comprising 9.05 million tweets generated by 778K users and show that our approach out-performs a state-of-the-art text-based classifier that solely uses location indicative words.

1.2 Structure and Organization

The rest of the paper is structured as follows. Section 2 describes our proposed approach, including data pre-processing, feature set selection, model training, and evaluation. Section 3 presents the experimental results of our proposed approach and various baselines. Section 4 summarizes our paper and highlights some future directions for geolocation prediction.

2 Proposed Approach

In this section, we describe our proposed approach to the geolocation prediction of Twitter users and tweets. Our proposed approach comprises three main phases, namely: (i) data pre-processing to identify the set of textual features; (ii) model training to train our prediction algorithm based on multinomial Naive Bayes classifier; and (iii) evaluating our prediction algorithm on the development and testing sets.

2.1 Data Preprocessing and Feature Set Selection

Our pre-processing of tweets in the training set comprises the following: (i) converting all text in the tweets to lowercase; (ii) removing all punctuation characters; (iii) tokenizing tweets into individual words based on whitespaces. These processed tweets are then used as input to our multinomial Naive Bayes classifier, where the usage frequency count of a set of feature words is derived from these processed tweets. We now describe the various feature sets used in our experiments, which are:

1. **Location Indicative Words (LIW)**. The set of words that are indicative of a specific city, as generated in (Han et al., 2014; Han et al., 2012). These LIWs are uni-grams that are used in only one or a small subset of all cities in the world and are selected from the set of all unigrams based on their information gain ratio.

2. **City/Country Names (CC)**. The set of city names and country names as listed in the GeoNames database (GeoNames, 2016) and U.S. Department of State list of countries (U.S. DoS, 2016). The basic intuition is that a Twitter user is more likely to mention a city or country that this user is residing in, compared to a city or country that is not.

3. **#Hashtags (HASH)**. The set of #hashtags used in our training set of tweets, we select the top 10,000 #hashtags based on their usage frequency. Twitter #hashtags are typically used to indicate the topic associated with the tweet and this choice of feature set allows us to capture any location-based topics that are indicative of a specific city or country, e.g., #bemorebulldog is used to support the Western Bulldogs, an Australian Football League team that is based in Victoria, Australia.

4. **@Mentions (MENT)**. The set of @mentions used in our training set of tweets, we select the top 10,000 @mentions based on their usage frequency. Twitter @mentions are used as a reference to another user and appears on the wall/notification page of that user. Similar to our use of the HASH feature set, the MENT feature set allows us to infer the location of a user based on who he/she is mentioning, e.g., @7NewsMelbourne is the twitter username of a Melbourne-based news broadcaster.

5. **Combination of all the above (ALL)**. A combination of the LIW, CC, HASH and MENT feature sets as a single feature set.

Using these feature sets, we then proceed to train our multinomial Naive Bayes classifier, which we describe in more details in the next section.

2.2 Training of multinomial Naive Bayes classifier

The multinomial Naive Bayes classifier has been frequently used for various text classification tasks such as sentiment analysis (Melville et al., 2009), news categorization (Kibriya et al., 2004), among others. Using the feature sets described in Section 2.1, we apply a multinomial Naive Bayes classifier to our five different set of features using a bag-of-features approach, which we now describe in greater detail.

Given that C is the set of all cities (i.e., our labels) and T is the set of all tweets in our training set, our aim is to geotag each tweet $t \in T$ with a city $c \in C$ such that the probability $P(c|t)$ is maximized. We utilize a bag-of-features approach and represent each tweet t as a set of features $f_i \in t$ (out of N total features), where each feature f_i indicates the number of times (frequency count) that a feature word f_i is used in a tweet t. Thus, we have:

$$\arg\max_{c \in C} P(c|t) = \arg\max_{c \in C} P(c) \prod_{1 < i < N} P(f_i|c) \tag{1}$$

Given that t_c is the set of all tweets that are posted in a specific city c and T is the set of all tweets, we can calculate the prior probability based on:

$$P(c) = \frac{|t_c|}{|T|} \tag{2}$$

To cater for feature words that may not appear in our training set, we apply Laplace smoothing by adding 1 to the frequency count of each feature word. Let $Freq_f, c$ be the frequency count of a feature word f in tweets from a specific city c, we have the conditional probability:

$$P(f_i|c) = \frac{Freq_f, c + 1}{\sum_{f_x=1}^{N} Freq_{f_x,c} + N} \tag{3}$$

Our geolocation prediction task is targetted at two levels, namely: (i) at tweet-level for individual tweets; and (ii) at user-level for an individual user based on his/her collection of posted tweets. For the tweet-level prediction task, Equation 1 is defined based on individual tweets and can be utilized for this task. For the user-level prediction task, there are two possible approaches to apply Equation 1 for a single user, namely:

1. **Tweet Aggregation As One**. In this approach, we aggregate all tweets posted by a user as a single document and apply Equation 1 on this combined document. As our multinomial Naive Bayes classifier accounts for the frequency of feature word usage, this approach is suitable for the users who are likely to mention words associated with his/her home city multiple times in their tweets, compared to cities that they do not reside in.

2. **Most Frequent Tweet City**. Alternatively, we can apply Equation 1 to the collection of tweets posted by a user, then perform a frequency count of each city that is labelled to each tweet. Thereafter, the home location of a user is assigned based on the city that has the highest frequency count.

We performed some preliminary experiments to evaluate both approaches and found that "Tweet Aggregation As One" (Approach 1) out-performs "Most Frequent Tweet City" (Approach 2). As such, we selected Approach 1 for the user-level geolocation task and use it in for the remaining of this paper.

2.3 Algorithms and Baselines

There are different variants of our geolocation prediction algorithms, with each algorithm differing based on the different set of features (described in Section 2.1) that it was trained with. The five algorithms used in our paper are:

1. **MNB-LIW**: A multinomial Naive Bayes classifier trained using the LIW feature set, i.e., the set of location indicative words. This algorithm also serves as the baseline for the current state-of-the-art on text-based geolocation prediction on Twitter (Han et al., 2012).

2. **MNB-CC**: A multinomial Naive Bayes classifier trained using the CC feature set, i.e., the list of city and country names.

3. **MNB-HASH**: A multinomial Naive Bayes classifier trained using the HASH feature set, i.e., the top 10,000 #hashtags used in our training set.

4. **MNB-MENT**: A multinomial Naive Bayes classifier trained using the MENT feature set, i.e., the top 10,000 @mentions used in our training set.

5. **MNB-ALL**: A multinomial Naive Bayes classifier trained using a combination of location indicative words, city/country names, #hashtags and @mentions as a single feature set.

6. **MNB-PART**: Same as MNB-ALL, except that we select a subset of features from the combined feature set, using a collection frequency-based feature selection strategy (Manning et al., 2008).

2.4 Evaluation Metrics

To evaluate these six algorithms, we use the following evaluation metrics:

- **Accuracy**. The proportion of tweets (and users) that is correctly classified to their home location (city), out of all tweets (and users). This metric allows us to measure the correctness of our prediction algorithm in terms of percentage of correct labelled cities.

- **Mean Error Distance**. The average error, in terms of distance, between the predicted cities and the ground truth cities of the tweets (and users). Even for mislabelled cities, a mislabelled city that is nearer to the ground truth city is deemed better, e.g., New York mislabelled as Chicago, is considered better than New York mislabelled as London. This metric aims to measure this aspect.

- **Median Error Distance**. The median error, in terms of distance, between the predicted cities and the ground truth cities of the tweets (and users). Similar to the Mean Error Distance, except that we are measuring the error distance in terms of median values

3 Experiments and Results

In this section, we describe the dataset used in our experiment, highlight our experimental setup and discuss the key results of our proposed algorithm and various baselines.

3.1 Dataset Description

As part of the shared task, a total of 12 million tweets were made available, which the participants have to retrieve via the Twitter API. However, due to inactive Twitter accounts, deleted tweets and time constraint, we were only able to crawl a total of 9.05 million tweets. Similarly, for the validation dataset, we were only able to crawl 7,215 users and 7,789 tweets out of the 10,000 users and 10,000 tweets. As the testing dataset was directly provided by the organizers, we were able to experiment on all 10,000 users and tweets. Table 1 shows the summary statistics of our training, validation, and testing dataset.

Table 1: Dataset description

Set	Prediction Task	No. of Users	No. of Tweets
Training	N.A.	778,383	9,053,573
Validation	User-level	7,215	-
Validation	Tweet-level	-	7,789
Testing	User-level	10,000	-
Testing	Tweet-level	-	10,000

3.2 Experimental Setup

Our experimental setup is aligned to the setup of the shared task and comprises three main phrases. In the first phrase, we use the training dataset to extract our various feature sets and train our geolocation predictors (MNB-LIW, MNB-CC, MNB-HASH, MNB-MENT, MNB-ALL, MNB-PART). In the second

Table 2: Results for Tweet-level Geolocation Prediction. The bolded results indicate the best performing statistics (highest value for accuracy and lowest value for mean/median error) for the validation and testing set.

Algorithm	Set	Accuracy	Mean Error	Median Error
MNB-LIW	Validation	0.1013	8751.9379	8153.5067
MNB-CC	Validation	0.0608	12438.9015	10790.024
MNB-HASH	Validation	0.0815	5293.6749	6216.3957
MNB-MENT	Validation	0.0449	11576.5707	9552.6721
MNB-ALL	Validation	0.1163	3314.5639	4993.7693
MNB-PART	Validation	**0.1221**	**3129.8084**	**4933.3203**
MNB-LIW	Testing	0.125	7778.6698	7453.0552
MNB-CC	Testing	0.0862	11395.3637	9439.0232
MNB-HASH	Testing	0.0991	5532.4149	6379.0754
MNB-MENT	Testing	0.0461	9458.3402	9016.1264
MNB-ALL	Testing	0.1376	3582.5483	5457.1922
MNB-PART	Testing	**0.1455**	**3424.6398**	**5338.8984**

phase, we evaluate our trained predictors (models) on the validation dataset. For the final phrase, we re-run our various predictors on the testing dataset. As the ground truth labels for the testing dataset was made available only after the shared task, we selected the best performing predictor (MNB-PART) from the second phrase and submitted it to the shared task for the third phrase.

3.3 Results

Table 2 shows the geolocation prediction results for the tweet-level, in terms of accuracy, mean and median error distances. The results show that our proposed MNB-PART algorithm outperforms all baselines for the validation and testing datasets, in terms of all three evaluation metrics. In particular, MNB-PART shows a relative improvement of more than 16% compared to MNB-LIW in terms of accuracy, and offers predictions with less than half the mean error distances than that of MNB-LIW.

Similarly, Table 3 shows the user-level geolocation prediction results, in terms of the same three evaluation metrics. In terms of accuracy, MNB-PART shows a relative improvement of 7.1% over MNB-LIW for the testing dataset, while MNB-LIW out-performs MNB-PART by 4.5% for the validation dataset. In terms of mean and median error distances, MNB-PART incurs less than half the mean error distances and less than two-thirds of the median error distances for the testing dataset.

4   Conclusion and Future Work

In this paper, we proposed an approach for geolocation prediction on Twitter based on a multinomial Naive Bayes classifier using a feature set derived from the textual features of tweets. Specifically, our feature set is based on a combination of location indicative words, city/country names, #hashtags and @mentions as a combined feature set. Instead of using the entire feature set, our approach uses a subset of the features, which are selected based on a frequency-based feature selection strategy. We compared our proposed approach MNB-PART against various baselines that uses location indicative words, city/country names, #hashtags and @mentions separately as independent feature sets, i.e., MNB-LIW, MNB-CC, MNB-HASH and MNB-MENT, respectively. The experimental results show that MNB-PART outperforms all baselines in most cases, including against its counterpart MNB-ALL that utilizes all features. These results show the effectiveness of using a combined feature set of location indicative words, city/country names, #hashtags and @mentions, then employing a feature selection strategy to use a sub-

Table 3: Results for User-level Geolocation Prediction. The bolded results indicate the best performing statistics (highest value for accuracy and lowest value for mean/median error) for the validation and testing set.

Algorithm	Set	Accuracy	Mean Error	Median Error
MNB-LIW	Validation	**0.2046**	662.3987	2970.8039
MNB-CC	Validation	0.1476	8605.2476	7994.2556
MNB-HASH	Validation	0.1609	872.7039	2706.0175
MNB-MENT	Validation	0.0973	3377.6792	5292.4654
MNB-ALL	Validation	0.1767	928.2935	2599.0432
MNB-PART	Validation	0.1953	**629.8692**	**2290.3172**
MNB-LIW	Testing	0.21	1373.1077	4533.2978
MNB-CC	Testing	0.1976	5207.3125	7037.8555
MNB-HASH	Testing	0.1812	961.3378	3352.8145
MNB-MENT	Testing	0.0944	4650.7975	5933.8057
MNB-ALL	Testing	0.1996	962.144	3234.4641
MNB-PART	Testing	**0.225**	**630.2436**	**2860.1745**

set of these features for training and testing on a multinomial Naive Bayes classifier.

Our work focuses on the use of textual features in tweets for geolocation prediction. Apart from textual features, there are interesting future directions for utilizing non-textual features of a user for this geolocation prediction task, such as:

1. Using friendship (bi-directional) and following (uni-directional) links to infer the location of a user based on his/her friends and followings.

2. Using demographics information listed in a user's profile, such as the user description, selected timezone, user-entered location field.

3. Using the temporal information in posted tweets, use the time distribution of a user's tweeting activities to determine possible time zones and thus cities that a user is in.

References

GeoNames. 2016. Geonames database. Internet. http://www.geonames.org/.

Bo Han, Paul Cook, and Timothy Baldwin. 2012. Geolocation prediction in social media data by finding location indicative words. In *Proceedings of COLING 2012*, pages 1045–1062.

Bo Han, Paul Cook, and Timothy Baldwin. 2014. Text-based twitter user geolocation prediction. *Journal of Artificial Intelligence Research*, 49:451–500.

Bo Han, Afshin Rahimi, Leon Derczynski, and Timothy Baldwin. 2016. Twitter Geolocation Prediction Shared Task of the 2016 Workshop on Noisy User-generated Text. In *Proceedings of the 2nd Workshop on Noisy User-generated Text (W-NUT)*. ACL.

Internet Live Statistics. 2016. Twitter usage statistics. Internet. http://www.internetlivestats.com/twitter-statistics/.

Ashraf M. Kibriya, Bernhard Pfahringer Eibe Frank, and Geoffrey Holmes. 2004. Sentiment analysis of blogs by combining lexical knowledge with text classification. In *Proceedings of the 17th Australasian Joint Conference on Artificial Intelligence (AI'04)*, pages 488–499.

Kwan Hui Lim, Jeffrey Chan, Christopher Leckie, and Shanika Karunasekera. 2015. Detecting location-centric communities using social-spatial links with temporal constraints. In *Proceedings of the 37th European Conference on Information Retrieval (ECIR'15)*, pages 489–494.

Christopher D. Manning, Prabhakar Raghavan, and Hinrich Schütze. 2008. Introduction to information retrieval. Cambridge University Press.

Prem Melville, Wojciech Gryc, and Richard D. Lawrence. 2009. Sentiment analysis of blogs by combining lexical knowledge with text classification. In *Proceedings of the 15th ACM SIGKDD international conference on Knowledge discovery and data mining (KDD'09)*, pages 1275–1284.

Takeshi Sakaki, Makoto Okazaki, and Yutaka Matsuo. 2010. Earthquake shakes twitter users: real-time event detection by social sensors. In *Proceedings of the 19th international conference on World wide web (WWW'10)*, pages 851–860.

Luke Sloan, Jeffrey Morgan, William Housley, Matthew Williams, Adam Edwards, Pete Burnap, and Omer Rana. 2013. Knowing the tweeters: Deriving sociologically relevant demographics from twitter. *Sociological Research Online*, 18(3):7.

Tracy L Tuten. 2008. *Advertising 2.0: Social Media Marketing in a Web 2.0 World: Social Media Marketing in a Web 2.0 World*. ABC-CLIO.

U.S. DoS. 2016. A-z list of country. Internet. http://www.state.gov/misc/list/.

Mao Ye, Peifeng Yin, and Wang-Chien Lee. 2010. Location recommendation for location-based social networks. In *Proceedings of the 18th SIGSPATIAL international conference on advances in geographic information systems (SIGSPATIAL'10)*, pages 458–461.

A Simple Scalable Neural Networks based Model for Geolocation Prediction in Twitter

Yasuhide Miura
Fuji Xerox Co., Ltd. / Japan
`yasuhide.miura@fujixerox.co.jp`

Motoki Taniguchi
Fuji Xerox Co., Ltd. / Japan
`motoki.taniguchi@fujixerox.co.jp`

Tomoki Taniguchi
Fuji Xerox Co., Ltd. / Japan
`taniguchi.tomoki@fujixerox.co.jp`

Tomoko Ohkuma
Fuji Xerox Co., Ltd. / Japan
`ohkuma.tomoko@fujixerox.co.jp`

Abstract

This paper describes a model that we submitted to W-NUT 2016 Shared task #1: Geolocation Prediction in Twitter. Our model classifies a tweet or a user to a city using a simple neural networks structure with fully-connected layers and average pooling processes. From the findings of previous geolocation prediction approaches, we integrated various user metadata along with message texts and trained the model with them. In the test run of the task, the model achieved the accuracy of 40.91% and the median distance error of 69.50 km in message-level prediction and the accuracy of 47.55% and the median distance error of 16.13 km in user-level prediction. These results are moderate performances in terms of accuracy and best performances in terms of distance. The results show a promising extension of neural networks based models for geolocation prediction where recent advances in neural networks can be added to enhance our current simple model.

1 Introduction

The growth of social media has brought demands to develop techniques to automatically extract a variety of information from it. A geolocation predictor is one such technique that has been widely studied to strengthen business activities such as advertisement and marketing. This paper describes a model that we developed to tackle this geolocation prediction task. The model is a neural networks based model that uses various user metadata along with message texts. We participated W-NUT 2016 Shared task #1: Geolocation Prediction in Twitter (Rahimi et al., 2016) with this model.

The architecture of our model is designed by following previous researches that have targeted geolocation prediction in Twitter. Cheng et al. (2010) proposed a probabilistic model based on local (location indicative) words to estimate city-level geolocation prediction of Twitter users. Han et al. (2014) implemented a city-level geolocation prediction system for Twitter users, and constructed a Naive Bayes learner using location indicative words and user metadata. We decided to use both message texts and user metadata which have shown effectiveness in these past studies.

Another characteristic of our model is that we decided to use neural networks as a machine learning method to train a geolocation predictor. Neural networks are being extensively applied to tasks of image processing, speech processing, or text processing and have shown the state of the performances (Goodfellow et al., 2016). In a context of geolocation prediction, Liu and Inkpen (2015) have showed that a model based on stacked denoising auto-encoders achieves a comparable performance to the state of the arts models. Although neural networks with deep complex layers have recently received attention as achieving high performance, we designed our model to be a simple scalable neural networks based model considering the following two reasons:

1. A city-level geolocation prediction of Twitter is a large scale task that requires a scalable machine learning method which can handle millions of tweet with thousands of classes (Han et al., 2014).
2. A model based on shallow simple neural networks has recently marked close performance to deep models with high scalability on several tasks (Joulin et al., 2016).

In the following sections of this paper, we first describe the specification of datasets to train and to test our model in Section 2. The detail of our neural networks based model is explained in Section 3,

Proceedings of the 2nd Workshop on Noisy User-generated Text,
pages 235–239, Osaka, Japan, December 11 2016.

Name	#tweet	#user
Training (tweet/user)	9026924	781889
Validation (tweet)	7260	4725
Validation (user)	94872	7826
Training10 (user)	7809590	622133
Validation10 (user)	87084	6807

Table 1: The number of tweet and the number of user we collected for each dataset.

Name	#tweet	#user
Experimental Training (tweet)	8846145	766251
Pseudo Test (tweet)	7819	7819
Experimental Training10 (user)	7653295	609691
Pseudo Test10 (user)	78173	6221

Table 2: A summary of the experimental training datasets and the pseudo test datasets.

accompanying Section 4 that explains experiments and the test run which were performed to evaluate the model. Finally, Section 5 summarizes and concludes the paper with some future directions.

2 Data

2.1 Tweets and Users

We collected the training dataset and the validation dataset using the official download script. Table 1 shows the statistics of tweets and users that we successfully downloaded with the script. For the user geolocation prediction task, we only used users that have 10 or more tweets in the datasets. Training10 (user) and Validation10 (user) in Table 1 are the subsets of Training (tweet/user) and Validation (user) that fulfill this condition. We used Training10 (user) and Validation10 (user) in the experiments of user-level prediction systems which will be described in Section 4.

The training datasets are further split to experimental training datasets and pseudo test datasets since the test datasets were not available at the development period of the task. For each training dataset, 98% and 1% of the users were randomly sampled as an experimental training dataset and a pseudo test dataset respectively[1]. Furthermore, one tweet per user were selected to form Pseudo Test (tweet) so that the number of tweets in the dataset becomes close to Validation (tweet). Table 2 summarizes these experimental training datasets and pseudo test datasets.

2.2 Geo Coordinates of Tweet Cities

We realized that the tweet-level geo coordinates of the training data and the validation data are not the geo coordinates of the corresponding tweet cities. To obtain the geo coordinates of the tweet cities, we replaced the geo coordinates of the tweets with user city geo coordinates. For tweet cities that are not apparent in the user cities, we referred to GeoNames[2] to obtain geo coordinates of them.

3 Model

The training datasets consists of 8–9M tweets and the number of class is over 3K in the geolocation prediction task. Because of the large dataset size and the number of class, we decided to construct a simple and efficient model. Our model is a variant of Joulin et al. (2016), that is called fastText. Although the fastText model is simple, the accuracy of fastText is on par with deep complex models on several tasks. Moreover the fastText model trains much faster compared to typical deep complex models. The original fast text model is targeted for text classification that deals with one sentence. The Twitter

---

[1]The remaining 1% of the users were kept for an alternative pseudo test dataset but were not used in the experiments of our submission systems.

[2]http://www.geonames.org/

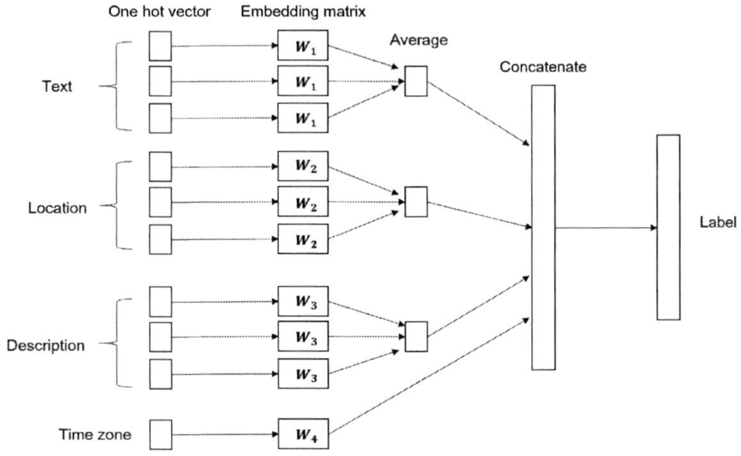

Figure 1: Model architecture.

Parameter	Message-level	User-level
Text word embedding dimension	300	300
Location word embedding dimension	300	300
Description word embedding dimension	300	300
Time zone embedding dimension	50	100
n-gram	2	2
Batch size	1500	160

Table 3: The parameters of the best performing models.

data in this shared task includes not only message text but also user metadata. Therefore we extend fast text model to deal with message text and user metadata.

Our model for message-level prediction is shown in Figure 1. We use the text field of tweet and three metadata fields of user: location, description, and time zone. In the text, the location, and the description fields, the word embeddings of words in a field are averaged to form a representation of the field. The weights of word embeddings are not shared across the fields because the unique weights resulted to better performance than the shared weights. Similar to fastText, we also use bag of n-gram features to capture word orders. According to Guo and Berkhahn (2016), the embeddings of categorial variables can reduce the network size and capture the intrinsic properties of the categorical variables. Therefore, we decided to embed the value of the time zone field into a fixed size vector as a time zone representation. All representations are then concatenated as a tweet representation. Finally the tweet representation is fed into a linear classification layer. The objective function of our model is defined as cross-entropy loss. We minimize the objective function through stochastic gradient descent over shuffled mini-batches with Adam (Kingma and Ba, 2014).

We basically used the same model for user-level prediction except that the text fields of tweets in a user instance are concatenated into one long text. The three metadata fields are also used in the user level predictor.

4   Experiments

4.1   Model Configurations

Text Processors

We used Twokenizer (Owoputi et al., 2013) to segment words from texts. Prior to word segmentations, all upper case characters in texts were converted to lower case correspondants and Unicode Normalization

	Validation	Pseudo Test	Test		
	Acc. (%)	Acc. (%)	Acc. (%)	Median Dist. Err.	Mean Dist. Err.
Message-level	39.1	39.6	40.91	69.50	1792.53
User-level	45.0	45.2	47.55	16.13	1122.26

Table 4: Evaluation results of the test run with the accuracies of the validation datasets and the pseudo test datasets.

in form NFKC[3] is applied to texts. We also normalized Twitter user names to "USER" and URLs to "URL" using regular expressions.

Pre-training of Word Embeddings

In our model, words are input to the model as n-dimensional word embeddings. We pre-trained word embeddings using the text, the location, and the description fields of the full training data (Training (tweet/user) in Section 2) and the method of Bojanowski et al. (2016)[4] with skip gram algorithm to speed up a training process of the user-level prediction task. For the parameters of skip gram, we used learning rate=0.025, window size=5, negative sample size=5, and epoch=5.

Model Parameters

We prepared three user-level systems and two message-level systems for the submission. These systems are all variants of the model explained in Section 3 with different parameters. Table 3 lists the parameters that are used in the user-level prediction system 2 and the message-level prediction system 2 which were our best systems in the test run. These parameters were decided prior to the submission with grid search using the validation datasets and the pseudo test datasets.

4.2 Evaluations

The message-level prediction system 2 and the user-level prediction system 2 were evaluated on the test run with classification accuracy, median distance error, and mean distance error. Table 4 shows the result of the test run along with the accuracies of the validation datasets and the pseudo test datasets. The performances of our model was moderate in terms of accuracies compared to the best systems (tweet-level-best=43.62% and user-level-best=52.65%) and best in terms of median distance errors.

5 Conclusion

We developed a simple neural networks based model for geolocation prediction in Twitter. In the test run, the model performed the accuracy of 40.91% and the median distance error of 69.50 km in message-level prediction and the accuracy of 47.55% and the median distance error of 16.13 km in user-level prediction. These results indicate that a neural networks based model has high scalability and is a competitive approach in geolocation prediction.

As future work, we plan to expand our model to have a deeper complex structure which has shown effectiveness in other tasks. We found out that the current model is quite simple only taking several hours of training time with a use of a single modern GPU. Some expansions using current advances in neural networks can possibly boost the performances of the model without losing the scalability of the model.

Acknowledgments

We would like to thank the anonymous reviewers for their valuable comments to improve this paper.

References

Piotr Bojanowski, Edouard Grave, Armand Joulin, and Tomas Mikolov. 2016. Enriching word vectors with subword information. *arXiv preprint arXiv:1607.04606*.

---

[3] http://unicode.org/reports/tr15/
[4] https://github.com/facebookresearch/fastText

Zhiyuan Cheng, James Caverlee, and Kyumin Lee. 2010. You are where you tweet: A content-based approach to geo-locating Twitter users. In *Proceedings of the 19th ACM International Conference on Information and Knowledge Management*, CIKM '10, pages 759–768.

Ian Goodfellow, Yoshua Bengio, and Aaron Courville. 2016. Deep learning. Book in preparation for MIT Press (http://www.deeplearningbook.org).

Cheng Guo and Felix Berkhahn. 2016. Entity embeddings of categorical variables. *arXiv preprint arXiv:1604.06737*.

Bo Han, Paul Cook, and Timothy Baldwin. 2014. Text-based Twitter user geolocation prediction. *Journal of Artificial Intelligence Research*, 49(1):451–500.

Armand Joulin, Edouard Grave, Piotr Bojanowski, and Tomas Mikolov. 2016. Bag of tricks for efficient text classification. *arXiv preprint arXiv:1607.01759*.

Diederik P. Kingma and Jimmy Ba. 2014. Adam: A method for stochastic optimization. *arXiv preprint arXiv:1412.6980*.

Ji Liu and Diana Inkpen. 2015. Estimating user location in social media with stacked denoising auto-encoders. In *Proceedings of the 1st Workshop on Vector Space Modeling for Natural Language Processing*, pages 201–210.

Olutobi Owoputi, Brendan O'Connor, Chris Dyer, Kevin Gimpel, Nathan Schneider, and Noah A. Smith. 2013. Improved part-of-speech tagging for online conversational text with word clusters. In *Proceedings of the 2013 Conference of the North American Chapter of the Association for Computational Linguistics: Human Language Technologies*, pages 380–390.

Afshin Rahimi, Bo Han, Leon Derczynski, and Timothy Baldwin. 2016. Twitter geolocation prediction shared task of the 2016 workshop on noisy user-generated text. In *Proceedings of the 2nd Workshop on Noisy User-generated Text (W-NUT)*. ACL.

Author Index